Homo Economics

Homo Economics
Capitalism, Community, and Lesbian and Gay Life

Edited by
Amy Gluckman
and
Betsy Reed

ROUTLEDGE

New York and London

Published in 1997

Routledge
29 West 35th Street
New York, NY 10001

Published in Great Britain by

Routledge
11 New Fetter Lane
London EC4P 4EE

The following material was previously published, and the editors wish to thank all who granted permission for it to appear here.

"The Gay Marketing Moment" by Amy Gluckman and Betsy Reed, in *Dollars and Sense* (November/December 1993), reprinted by permission of the Economic Affairs Bureau, Somerville, MA; "High Anxiety: I Was a Stepford Queer at the Inaugural Ball" by Donna Minkowitz, reprinted by permission of the author and *The Village Voice*; "Sexuality, Class, and Conflict in a Lesbian Workplace" by Kath Weston and Lisa B. Rofel, in *SIGNS* 9:4 (1984), pp. 623–646, reprinted by permission of The University of Chicago Press; originally titled, "Some Theoretical Implications of Gay Involvement in an Urban Land Market" "Gentrification and Gay Neighborhood Formation in New Orleans: A Case Study" by Lawrence Knopp, in *Political Geography Quarterly* 9:4 (1990), reprinted by permission of Elsevier Science Ltd., Butterworth Heinemann Imprint, Oxford, England; "Beyond Biased Samples: Challenging the Myths on the Economic Status of Lesbians and Gay Men" by M.V. Lee Badgett, reprinted by permission of the National Organization of Gay and Lesbian Scientists and Technical Professionals Inc., Pasadena, CA and the Institute for Gay and Lesbian Strategic Studies; "The Sexual Division of Labor, Sexuality, and Lesbian/Gay Liberation: Toward a Marxist-Feminist Analysis of Sexuality in U.S. Capitalism" by Julie Matthaei, *Review of Radical Political Economics* 27:2 (1995), reprinted by permission of Blackwell Publishers, Cambridge, MA; "Homosexual Liberation: A Socialism of the Skin" by Tony Kushner, *The Nation*, July 4, 1994, reprinted by permission of *The Nation* magazine, (c) The Nation Company, L.P.; "AIDS and the Moral Economy of Insurance" by Deborah A. Stone, *The American Prospect*, Fall 1990, reprinted by permission of *The American Prospect*, (c) New Prospect Inc.

Library of Congress Cataloging-in-Publication Data

Homo economics : capitalism, community, and lesbian and gay life /
    edited by Amy Gluckman and Betsy Reed.
        p.   cm.
    Includes bibliographical references and index.
    ISBN 0-415-91378-0 (alk. paper). — ISBN 0-415-91379-9 (pbk. :
    alk. paper)
    1. Gays—United States—Economic conditions.   2. Gays—Employment—
United States.   3. Gays—United States—Social conditions.   4. Gay
consumers—United States.   5. Lesbian consumers—United States.
I. Gluckman, Amy, 1961–   .   II. Reed, Betsy, 1968–   .
HQ76.3.U5H63   1986
305.9'0664—dc20   96-16035
                                                                             CIP

To the memory of
Elaine Louise Gluckman-Popowitz
and for our parents

Contents

Acknowledgments

It was during a weekly meeting of the *Dollars and Sense* collective in Somerville, Massachusetts, that we first discussed the issues explored in this volume. For the last twenty years and through many different incarnations, that collective has put out the progressive economics magazine *Dollars and Sense*, in which we initially published the piece on gay marketing that appears here. In countless ways, the unique environment fostered by the *D&S* staff and volunteers nurtured and shaped our ideas. In particular, *Dollars and Sense* granted Betsy, who was an editor there, the flexibility necessary to complete this project.

Throughout the editing process, we benefitted from the insights of several thoughtful advisors. Lee Badgett and Beth Stroud provided critical guidance early on. Provocative questions, criticism, and support came from Randy Albelda, Liberty Aldrich, Katherine Zoe Andrews, Ros Baxandall, Phineas Baxandall, Nina Davenport, Alison Demos, Janice Fine, Nancy Folbre, Alison Humes, Susannah Hunnewell, John Plotz, John Stamm, and Alexander Star. Martha Nadell, Brian Burgoon, and Kevin Leppman lent us their extensive libraries. In addition, several close friends provided invaluable moral support.

Jeffrey Escoffier coined the phrase "Homo Economics" for a conference on the subject in the spring of 1994, sponsored by the Center for Lesbian and Gay Studies of the City University of New York. It was there that we met many of this book's contributors, to whom we owe the greatest debt. We are also very grateful to Cecelia Cancellaro, our editor at Routledge, for her receptiveness, enthusiasm, and enduring patience, and Kathleen Silloway, our copyeditor, for attending to substance as well as detail in the essays.

Finally, thanks to our families for their faith and encouragement, and to our partners, Susan Cayouette and John Stamm, who saw us through it from start to finish.

Introduction

Amy Gluckman and Betsy Reed

More than ever before in U.S. history, lesbians and gay men are living open lives.
Some are even celebrities, admired rather than despised for their sexual orientation.
With the recent debate on gays[1] in the military, the new ad campaigns winking
knowingly at a gay audience, and the fresh-scrubbed gay faces now familiar on TV,
it is suddenly difficult to imagine a mainstream social world that flatly refuses to embrace any lesbian or gay members.

Yet it was just a century ago that medical textbooks, rather than glossy magazines,
detailed the nature of gay life. Sexual interest in a member of one's own gender was
seen as a disorder, an inversion of all that was healthy and morally sound. While doctors huddled in mental hospitals scrutinizing the so-called sexual inverts, conduct
books and Sunday sermons celebrated the upstanding, middle-class nuclear family—
with male breadwinner, virtuous homemaking wife, and children schooled in rigid
gender roles and heterosexual mores. Throughout the nineteenth century and into
the twentieth, the U.S. economy rested on this ingeniously self-reproducing institution.

Since then, the nuclear family has hardly disappeared as a basic social structure, but
its edges have softened. By most accounts, families are still supposed to have a mother
and a father; judges frequently refuse to recognize same-sex parents, and lesbian and
gay marriages are not legally recognized in any state. Yet for the first time, issues of
gay marriage and parenting are widely considered worthy of debate. At this writing a
Hawaiian court is in the midst of deliberating whether to legalize same-sex unions.
And the fight for gay rights floods city streets each spring, as millions raise banners for
gay pride. Today the psychiatric notion of the homosexual as sexual invert is less a
source of shame for lesbians and gay men than for the medical profession, because it
is such a graphic reminder of the subjectivity of science.

In some arenas, social and economic policies are following cultural shifts and beginning to accommodate lesbian and gay life as well. Antidiscrimination laws are now on the books in nine states and almost one hundred cities and counties.[2] Albeit at a glacial pace, domestic partners of gay employees are winning health benefits. While some corporations have hired consultants to promote more gay-tolerant work atmospheres, others have devised marketing plans to court a lesbian and gay customer base. In fact, from one angle it appears that society has rotated 180 degrees: the image of the gay community as a prosperous elite is now so prevalent as to be politically dangerous. To bolster antigay campaigns in Colorado, Oregon, and Maine, right-wing groups have seized on the legal advances that lesbians and gay men have won, arguing that homosexuals are now a privileged minority and that antidiscrimination statutes are unnecessary "special rights."

Many of the social and political forces that have fueled recent advances for lesbians and gay men are well known. The Sexual Revolution has been studied so much that it has entered common parlance. A new generation of gay historians has begun to document the valiant efforts of early gay political organizers and community leaders, while issues of cultural representation and gay identity have ignited hot debate in academia. Though the gay-studies field is still young, scholars in philosophy, anthropology, African American studies, politics, film, literature, and history have opened new lines of inquiry into many dimensions of homosexual life.

The same cannot be said of economists. While cultural and political shifts contributing to the rise of a gay movement have been scrutinized, the ways in which the U.S. economy has shaped modern gay life remain virtually unexplored. Economic theory remains largely oblivious to sexuality, and on an empirical level, standard economic surveys have omitted sexual orientation as a category. It's even possible that the political right wing has offered more in the way of economic misinformation on lesbians and gay men than economists have offered in the way of information.

One of the aims of this collection is to address the empirical deficiency by sketching the gay community's economic profile. How much do gay people actually earn? Are they privileged as the Right asserts, or are they disadvantaged? Do gay men work disproportionately in the service sector, as hairdressers, waiters, and the like? Do lesbians avoid sexist and homophobic occupations? Until now, only anecdotal answers have been available to many such questions, and those have often been wrong. For a small segment of the gay population has been taken to be representative of the community as a whole—leading, among other things, to the belief that gays are exceptionally wealthy. Several essays in this book provide new research that helps distinguish myth from reality, to combat popular stereotypes as well as the propaganda of the Right.

Once the illusion of widespread gay economic privilege is stripped away, the gay community comes into view in all of its variety. As the Queer Nation slogan proclaims, "We are everywhere"; economically speaking, gay people are in every occupation, in every income bracket, in every tax break, and in every poverty program. Lesbians and gay men have experienced neither seamless prosperity nor uniform suffering in the U.S. economy.

But this diversity of economic experience doesn't mean that homosexuality is somehow independent of the economy, or that the lives of gay people aren't touched in similar ways by certain economic trends and configurations. In fact, as the essays in this volume show, gay men and lesbians as a group have long been entangled in a contradictory relationship with capitalism. Open homosexuals face occupational segregation and discrimination, but they also owe much of their newfound freedom to economic trends.

These trends do not simply represent a development of the last twenty-five years, during which we have witnessed the most conspicuous progress toward gay liberation. The shift toward modern gender roles and sexual mores began when wage labor became the predominant method of producing society's goods in the nineteenth century, at which time it became possible to build a life outside of the nuclear family, where most economic activity had previously taken place.[3] Along with various cultural developments of the time, this transformation permitted the first few self-conscious homosexuals to leave traditional family structures.

More recently, the force of the economy has helped to break down the rigid sexual division of labor that had confined women to heterosexual marriage and the mothering role. As more well-paying jobs have opened up to women, it has become easier for them to survive without a husband's salary, which in turn has encouraged the proliferation of lesbian households. And since various services previously performed by wives have become available in the marketplace, marriage has become less of an economic necessity for men as well.

While industrial capitalism and its recent adaptations have made modern gay and lesbian life possible, being lesbian or gay today does exact various economic costs—lost jobs, fewer promotions, discrimination in housing and health care. Citing recent civil-rights "advances" is rather like viewing the glass as one-fifth full, when it's really four-fifths empty: in forty-one states, it's still legal to fire an employee solely because he or she is homosexual. In surveys, gay men and lesbians report high levels of job discrimination.[4] (Ironically, little is known about the overall extent of antigay job discrimination, because without legal protection against discrimination, gay people have no reason to report such incidents.) Even now, few gay people have access to benefits such as health insurance through their partners. And the economic oppression that women still experience as a group hits lesbian households with particular force, since they do not have access to male incomes.

At almost every turn, the impact of the economy on gay life has had two sides, offering an escape route from heterosexual family life, but one riddled with hazards and insecurities. Today's market has a new twist in the way it benefits some gay people more than others. Some lesbians and gay men own their own houses in suburban communities, have high-powered jobs, mutual funds, and Jeeps to drive on the weekends. Others, sometimes by fate and sometimes by choice, hang out in urban ghettoes, drifting from job to job in an unstable service economy, while still others count themselves among the rural poor. The explosion of marketing to lesbians and gay men has only made such contrasts more visible. As advertisers vie for the loyalty of wealthy, professional gay shoppers, clean-cut models appealing to that demographic group have suddenly appeared in magazines, on television, and on billboards. Because other segments of the gay community do not enjoy such attention, this phenomenon has highlighted deep fissures in a group that has used its unity to push for political advances. By privileging some gay people (and some visions of what it means to be gay) over others, recent economic advances have called into question the very premise of a gay community that is united more powerfully by sexual orientation than it is divided along economic, racial, and gender lines.

This is but one example of how a fact of economics—e.g. class stratification—can achieve political and cultural expression. The essays here look at various ways in which the economy has shaped—and been shaped by—gay culture and politics, a complex and even delicate task given the varied, ambiguous, and rapidly evolving relationship of gay people to the economy. Because gay interests and experiences are so diverse, the gay movement has never had a clear-cut stance on economic issues—on whether, for instance, economic inequality is a problem in the United States, or whether the liberal welfare state is worth defending.

Still, some broad shifts in the tide of gay politics can be discerned, as the movement's zeitgeist has moved alternately toward and away from the constellation of other conventionally "left" or "liberal" causes. Indeed, the gay movement's critique of U.S. social and economic arrangements has evolved quite a bit since its watershed during the period of social protest around the Vietnam War. At that point, the "establishment" was clearly hostile to the interests of all lesbians and gay men, and gay communities were severely marginalized, both culturally and economically. At the same time, radical challenges to authority characterized the broader political climate. The Stonewall uprising of 1969, in which gay men and lesbians spontaneously swarmed the streets of New York City decrying police repression, inaugurated a decade of pathbreaking gay political action in the 1970s. Under the leadership of such active and visible groups as the Gay Liberation Front, a kind of utopian spirit briefly prevailed, as many took "gay liberation" to mean overturning gender hierarchies as well as lifting constraints on same-sex relationships and eliminating oppression based on race and class as well. But before long, the Gay Activists Alliance, a more reform-oriented, middle-class organization, split off from the Front to focus exclusively on narrowly defined gay issues, eschewing links with controversial groups like the Black Panthers, which the Front supported.[5]

As early gay activism began to pay off and it became easier to come out of the closet, "gay ghettos" flourished in various urban areas. Before then, carefully coded bars and shops had catered mostly to closeted gays, but in the seventies more and more businesses were explicit about their mission to serve the gay community. Many of their customers (mostly men) began to display a penchant for conspicuous consumption, and some activists complained that the gay male "clone"—sculpted, moustached, and studiously dressed—cared more for clothes than for politics.[6] This decline of political consciousness was accompanied by a subtle but distinct shift in the demands of gay organizations. In her recent book *Virtual Equality*, former National Gay and Lesbian Task Force director Urvashi Vaid dated the "mainstreaming" of gay politics—the pursuit of "legitimation . . . rather than social change"—from the late 1970s.[7]

In the 1980s, the advent of AIDS forced many gay men (and some lesbians) to fix their gaze once again on the ugliness of social injustice. The AIDS crisis inspired a tremendous surge of confrontational activism, frequently informed by the conviction that the motives and goals of business and government were selfish, callous, and even murderous. Some AIDS activist groups, such as local chapters of ACT-UP, still struggle in this vein, and many radical gay organizers continue to work against class, race, and gender-based oppression as well as against homophobia.

But few would say this is the prevailing spirit of today's gay political movement. Just as, in the view of some observers, broad-reaching political consciousness faded away in those thriving gay commercial districts of the late 1970s, the social and economic successes of the nineties appear to have had a powerful effect on the political thinking of some gay men and lesbians, especially those who have most enjoyed the fruits of expanding economic opportunities. After all, inside a cozy brownstone, curled up next to a health-insured domestic partner in front of a Melissa Etheridge video on MTV, flipping through *Out* magazine and sipping an Absolut and tonic, capitalism can feel pretty good.

Unlike the atmosphere surrounding Stonewall, today there is a gay-friendliness in the air that is worth savoring. How many lesbians can honestly say they didn't run out to buy a copy of *Vanity Fair* with k. d. lang on the cover, or *Essence* with Linda Villarosa and her mom—or at least bury their noses in a friend's copy? The hunger for visibility and acknowledgement—not to mention for a long list of specific products and services—is a strong one for gay men and lesbians, and it's a hunger that market forces are finally poised to satisfy.

Twenty-six years after Stonewall, many lesbians and gay men have also undergone turning points in their personal lives. Some have settled in the gay ghettoes of San Francisco and New York; but others have left them, deciding to live in any number of small- and medium-sized towns for reasons other than sexual identity—often to reconnect with their families. Some are having babies. Many are developing the kind of stake in the status quo that homeowners and parents have, with a direct interest in matters such as real estate values and property taxes.

So the protests of those who still denounce an entity called the establishment, shunning polite lobbying in Washington in favor of community organizing and the painstaking process of building coalitions with other disenfranchised groups, are falling on increasingly deaf ears. This is ironic, because—at least in part—the perks consumed by the gay middle class represent the gains of what was originally a radical movement.[8] And again, a fading interest in politics among some is accompanied by a shift to the right among others. Today, a small but outspoken group of gay conservatives wants to separate the issue of homophobia from what they consider an inconvenient laundry list of other oppressions, to exclude from "gay issues" those that are not "theirs": that is, if they are white, issues that are specifically black (such as racism among gays, or tension between the straight and gay black communities); if they are rich, those that are more working-class (class conflict within the gay community, issues of health care and discrimination in blue-collar occupations); or if they are male, those that are specifically lesbian (lesbians' economic disadvantages, misogyny directed at lesbian life). There is also a great wariness of coalition-talk in such quarters, which Tony Kushner captures well in his essay here. Roughly speaking, among gay conservatives, the goal is often assimilation, and so if the issue or strategy smacks of radicalism, they don't want any part. Calling ACT-UP meetings "a cacophony of rival oppressions," Andrew Sullivan, former editor of *The New Republic* and an eloquent proponent of such a tinker-with-the-status-quo, reformist gay agenda, writes in his book *Virtually Normal,* "queer politics in the 1990s found itself almost immediately fractured into a whole plethora of other related and sometimes utterly unrelated grievances."[9]

The charge that multi-issue agendas are sometimes hard to practice does have some basis in experience; like ACT-UP in the nineties, the Gay Liberation Front frequently found consensus elusive in the seventies. Rather than belittling "rival oppressions," this collection aims to air a discussion of the relationship between gay politics and issues of class, gender and race. Michael P. Jacobs, looking at the tensions between gay men and feminists on economic issues, finds that their interests are in fact in conflict, and argues that therefore a gay/feminist alliance may not be the most fruitful political strategy for the gay movement. Other writers here urge gay leaders to adopt a broadly progressive political platform, emphasizing the needs and views of lesbians, working-class gays, and gays of color, as well as the desirability of greater social and economic justice in its own right.

Whatever their differences on matters of strategy, however, contributors to this volume share a sensitivity to the economic dimensions of all forms of oppression. From this perspective, it appears that at least in some ways, the gay movement has reached the limits of narrowly defined identity politics. Yet the way to a fuller, fairer political program might nonetheless be *through* the politics of identity: retaining the spirit that has animated the best identity-based activism, we might arrive at an inclusive vision of justice capable of uniting a broader social movement. In other words, if some gay men and lesbians (like some blacks and women) have broken down barriers in corporate settings, perhaps it's time for progressives, gay and straight alike, to think more about class. Then the experience of lesbian and gay suffering, and the lessons learned in the struggle to alleviate it, can both illuminate and intensify the fight against other social inequalities. In any case, if profound change, not gradual assimilation, is the goal of a movement for gay liberation, such a broadly galvanizing approach seems the only one with any hope of success.

Hence the importance of understanding the connection between gay life and the economy—in particular, the ways in which it interweaves the lives of gays and straights, blacks and whites, men and women. Since so little is known about the economics of any gay life—white, black, rich, poor, immigrant, Jewish, WASP, Latino/a—this book is both broad-ranging and sketchy, suggesting many areas for further inquiry. One day, we'd love to see a database search for library materials relating to "homosexuality" and "economics" produce something other than the phrase, "Your search retrieved no items." Including essays by writers, academics, and activists, the volume has three parts. The first section looks at gay and lesbian communities from an economic perspective, exploring their relationships to the worlds of marketing and advertising, their forays into commercial enterprise, and their economic compositions. The second section considers the contradictions of capitalism for lesbians and gay men, delving into history, politics, and economic theory to question common assumptions. The concluding section addresses contemporary gay political activism, covering its connections to other political efforts, the implications of diversity, and recent trends in gay politics.

I. A Community Divided

In 1992 and 1993, when k. d. lang was suddenly a celebrity lesbian, glossy gay magazines were sprouting and flourishing, and a gay political elite was whispering into the ear of an affable new president, it looked like the previously padlocked pop-cultural closet had swung wide open. The suddenness of the blitz suggested that, most likely, it was not the result of a wrenching process of soul-searching on the part of individual media decision makers and political leaders, who all happened to see the lavender light at once. Rather, it seems that—emboldened by the example of those who floated the first few gay-friendly signals into the mass media—members of the country's business and political establishment were finally gambling on certain powerful claims being made by gay groups.

These claims weren't just that sexual orientation was an illegitimate basis of discrimination, or that gay men and lesbians needed certain protections and services. Gay marketing organizations were churning out compelling self-promotional materials boasting of a community with impressive demographics, profligate spending habits, and high levels of discretionary income. Once this image caught on, it stuck. Gay men were dubbed a velvet mafia (and lesbians a "muffia," by one sarcastic Brit). While some segments of the gay community enjoyed increased visibility and power because of this marketing fad, others, such as lower-income gays and gays and lesbians of color, haven't been so fortunate. At the same time, the political right wing seized on the statistics depicting gay men and lesbians as a prosperous minority and used those numbers in attempts to repeal civil rights legislation in various cities, counties, and states. In a stark illustration of the discrepancy between image and reality, in 1993, at the height of the "gay moment," nineteen initiatives around the nation to repeal progay legislation or to institute antigay policies passed, while not one local or statewide legislative effort on behalf of gays prevailed.[10] "The Gay Marketing Moment," an exploration of this phenomenon which we originally wrote for *Dollars & Sense* in 1993, is the first essay presented here.

Sudden as it seemed—and whatever its implications for the gay community as a whole—the recognition of gay men and lesbians as an important economic constituency in the early nineties was a long time in the making. A large share of the responsibility for the change lies with gay business and marketing pioneers. Dan Baker's piece in this book, "A History in Ads," narrates the story behind the corporate change of heart. It was Michel Roux, marketer of Absolut vodka, who first thought of the gay community as a profitable consumer niche, which he exploited adeptly by hiring high-profile gay artists such as Keith Haring to design his ads. His foresight was rewarded first with brand loyalty among gay men and lesbians, and then with imitation by a slew of corporate rivals. First in subtle, closeted ways, and then in overt appeals to gay consumers, company after company has warily approached the gay community, casting sidelong glances at competitors each step of the way. The furniture chain Ikea, for instance, recently cracked the closet on television, airing a spot featuring a male couple shopping for their mutual home, engaging in some painfully self-conscious body contact. Such exposure, however coy and awkward, has had its advantages. For without the support of mainstream advertisers, several national gay magazines would not exist. And, perhaps, if it weren't for advertiser support and the growing awareness of a gay market, the meaningful same-sex handshakes and hugs gay TV characters are now allowed to share might be written out altogether.

Yet some observers contend that gay men and lesbians have been so eager for this long-awaited attention that they are settling for too little. This has occurred in the political realm as in the media, described in this volume by Donna Minkowitz in "High Anxiety: I Was a Stepford Queer at the Inaugural Ball." As gay celebrants of Clinton's 1992 election lined up to shake hands with David Mixner, friend-of-Bill of the hour, "the partygoers could have been nerds doing high fives with the gofer for the football star," she writes. She catches gay leaders seeking recognition but not much else, serving themselves up as "cheap dates" rather than demanding rewards more substantive than champagne and cocktails.

Minkowitz captures a scene of gay privilege, a scene inaccessible to many lesbians and gay men who have not won admission to the corridors of power. Perhaps such instances have surfaced more frequently lately, but the gay movement has a history of alienating those gay people who, for lack of economic resources, education, or inclination, do not fit into a middle-class mold—a phenomenon that has been eloquently described elsewhere by writers such as Dorothy Allison.[11]

Kath Weston and Lisa Rofel look closely at class conflict in one lesbian community in their essay, "Sexuality, Class, and Conflict in a Lesbian Workplace." This is the story of Amazon Auto Repair (not its real name), a lesbian shop torn apart by a strike. After an initial period of camaraderie and lesbian solidarity at the shop, Amazon's workers and managers found themselves on opposite sides of a bitter struggle. For Weston and Rofel, it is not someone's background but her economic role—that is, her position as either a waged worker or an owner—that defines her class identity. The article employs techniques of anthropological analysis to illuminate many dimensions of each event leading up to the workers' decision to strike. Initially published in the lesbian issue of the feminist journal *Signs* in 1984, this was one of the first critical attempts to comprehend the relationship between sexual identity and economics.

It's important to dissect the interplay between class and sexual identity because gay entrepreneurial efforts have been so vital to the development of the gay community, and they have been plagued by class tensions. Similarly, class troubles have surfaced in lesbian and gay residential enclaves, which have also played a significant role in shaping the gay community. On this subject, this volume also includes a case study, "Gentrification and Gay Neighborhood Formation in New Orleans" by Lawrence Knopp. Knopp, a geographer, describes the dual processes of gentrification and building a gay neighborhood in an urban area. Based on numerous personal interviews as well as secondary sources, Knopp pieces together the complex story of a neighborhood in transition where gay men were the prime movers, highlighting many of the contradictions that surface along the way. For example, some gay men presented themselves as a "responsible middle class" rather than as gay in order to facilitate their pursuit of gentri-fication, but they thereby limited the specifically gay political gains they could have made even after their neighborhood had acquired some political clout.

Gentrified urban enclaves like the one Knopp studied have stimulated much cre-ative gay and lesbian cultural and political activity. However, they have been wrongly interpreted to represent the whole gay community as generally wealthy, free spend-ing, and insular. This stereotype, pushed by gay magazines, marketing firms, and the right wing, needs a reality check.

Enter the economist M. V. Lee Badgett. Until recently, representative data on any parameter of lesbians' and gay men's lives have been nonexistent. While the psychi-atric gaze has long focused on homosexuality, looking hard for dysfunction in the family lives of a very nonrandom sample of gay people, lesbians and gay men have been invisible in large sets of data dealing with more mundane matters such as in-come. In "Beyond Biased Samples," Badgett reports the results of her research on gay men's and lesbians' incomes, based on large-scale social survey data. The survey she uses has only very recently included questions that permit the identification of gay subjects. Although, as she explains, this set of data has some limitations, her results suggest that gay men's average income is *lower* than straight men's, and that lesbians' incomes are comparable to straight women's. She also provides a primer on the vari-ous abuses of statistics that have contributed to inflated notions of gay wealth.

Information on the occupations that lesbians and gay men hold is similarly scant. In a separate article, "Lesbian and Gay Occupational Strategies," Badgett and Mary King begin to piece together what they can, comparing gay and lesbian patterns of employment to those of straight women and men. In order to assess these data and establish some directions for future research, they develop an analysis of the likely fac-tors—both workplace and household-related—that influence gay people's occupa-tional choices. Their investigation yields some perplexing results, particularly for lesbians, who appear to be disproportionately represented in occupations that do not pay well *and* where the climate is likely to be hostile for an out lesbian. Thus, Badgett and King's discovery of clusters of lesbians and gay men in certain areas sheds light on a previously obscure economic dimension of the gay community.

II. The Contradictions of Capitalism for Lesbians and Gay Men: Some Theoretical Perspectives

Just as economic surveys have omitted questions on gay life, economic theorists have rarely considered the relevance of sexual orientation to the study of economics. For the most part, theorists have pondered such questions as how the free market serves people's needs, or how companies profit from the value their employees add to their products. Lesbians and gay men have been invisible, as subjects *and* as economists; as University of Iowa economist Deirdre (formerly Donald) McClosky observed in an article in *Eastern Economic Review*, the heterosexual assumption seems always to lurk just beneath the surface, whether in statistical samples, theorems, or in casual conver-sation at conferences.[12]

As mainstream, neoclassical economists see it, rational individuals navigate the free market, which propels society efficiently forward and produces the ideal allocation of society's resources. The preferences consumers express in markets are assumed to represent their "true" tastes. But as Richard Cornwall shows in "Queer Political Economy: The Social Articulation of Desire," people's tastes are in fact subject to intricate and imperfect sculpting by society. The choices they make do not necessarily reflect their genuine tastes. There is a complex network of social codes embedded in language, he argues, and this determines how we articulate desire, including sexual desire.

Given the conservative to barely liberal politics implicit in most neoclassical work, its blindness to the formation of lesbian and gay desire is hardly surprising. It is more disturbing that Marxists and neo-Marxists have been nearsighted in this regard, since it is their mission to understand social inequalities. Those few Marxist economists who have focused on sexuality have tended to treat it as a mere ideological "reflex" of the more fundamental economic "base"; in this view, sexual relations have little autonomy from economic relations, and the shape of sexuality can be explained largely by economic forces.[13] Following political philosopher Louis Althusser, Cornwall points out that if Marxists are to begin to account more fully for sexuality, they will have to alter and elaborate their theory of ideology: "The roles of 'ideology' are much more central to cognition, and hence to political economy, than even Marx imagined. This is not mere 'superstructure,' frosting on the basic productive/technological relations of labor inputs to other inputs which ultimately determine the 'social relations of production,' but rather 'ideology' describes the deepest patterning of human mental software."

In recent years, feminist and queer theorists have challenged programmatic Marxist models, developing analytical frameworks that are sufficiently nuanced and complex to comprehend the tangled web of sexual, social, and economic relations from which sexual identities emerge. Gayle Rubin broke new ground in this direction in 1975, arguing that a "sex-gender system" with some autonomy from economic structures helps organize culture and society. Since then, various theorists have expanded and refined this analysis, often employing Marxist concepts and insights in innovative ways. Yet few of these scholars have been economists; there hasn't been much of a response to the barrage of criticism of reductive economic analyses of sexuality from within the ranks of the economics profession. The sharpest and most subtle economic insights into sexual identity have instead come from cultural critics, historians, anthropologists, and sociologists.

In this volume, sociologist Jeffrey Escoffier looks at history to discover how the cultural stigma against homosexuality has produced economic effects. In his examination of economic life in U.S. gay communities between World War II and Stonewall, Escoffier analyzes the economics of the closet, including the costs it has imposed on gay men and lesbians and the limitations it has placed on the development of an institutionalized gay community. While the debilitating effects of the closet on the personal lives of gay men and lesbians have been well explored, the closet's impact on gay social and economic life has not. His analysis takes as its starting point Erving Goffman's notion of an "invisible stigma," whose bearers must constantly manage information about themselves. Escoffier argues that this restriction of information has prevented the earlier development of a gay market, since markets depend on the availability of information to both producers and consumers.

As Escoffier demonstrates, sexuality is not an easily separable object of study, since various other forces (such as economics) are constantly coming into play. This makes historical inquiry into homosexuality extremely difficult, even delicate. The work of Jeffrey Weeks and the British social constructionists, who published many pioneering articles in the short-lived 1970s journal *The Gay Left*, has been crucial in showing how it can be done efficiently yet with subtlety. Among other questions, these writers asked if there was a connection between capitalism and gay oppression, a link less straightforward and more historically credible than Marxists had imagined. These British constructionists followed Mary McIntosh, who wrote a 1968 article entitled "The Homosexual Role," which provided a new way of thinking historically about homophobia and homosexuality: rather than assuming that homosexuality is an essence that one either has or doesn't have, McIntosh argued that society creates the identities that people inhabit. "The homosexual should be seen as playing a social role rather than as having a condition,"[14] she wrote.

Why did this role emerge in western society? As Michel Foucault described in *The History of Sexuality: Part 1*, the category of the homosexual that arose in the late 19th century was an integral part of a new set of sexual ideas, a "deployment of sexuality" fueled by the nascent bourgeoisie's desire for self-affirmation:

> The primary concern was not repression of the sex of the classes to be exploited, but rather the body, vigor, longevity, progeniture, and descent of the classes that "ruled." This was the purpose for which the deployment of sexuality was first established, as a distribution of pleasures, discourses, truths and powers; it has to be seen as the self-affirmation of one class rather than the enslavement of another."[15]

In this context, the homosexual "became a personage, a past, a case history, and a childhood, in addition to being a type of life, a life form, and a morphology, with an indiscreet anatomy and possibly a mysterious physiology. . . . The sodomite had been a temporary aberration; the homosexual was now a species."[16] In other words, an understanding of homosexuality emerged—along with Victorian icons of chaste femininity and lustful, predatory male sexuality—as part of the process of elaborating class identity.

That change was the result of a complex interplay of culture and economics, both in the sense that the idea of "the homosexual" was a bourgeois (and therefore a class) invention, and in the sense that the economic transformations of the nineteenth century created the structural preconditions for long-term lesbian and gay relationships. The latter point was the primary subject of John D'Emilio's pathbreaking 1983 essay, "Capitalism and Gay Identity." As D'Emilio explained, the movement away from the household family-based economy toward the creation of a formal labor force allowed women and men to sustain themselves by working for wages in the labor market instead of by participating in a nuclear family that was an independent unit of production. "As wage labor spread and production became socialized," he wrote, "it became possible to release sexuality from the 'imperative' to procreate. . . . In divesting the household of economic independence and fostering the separation of sexuality from procreation, capitalism has created conditions that allow some men and women to organize a personal life around their erotic/emotional attraction to their own sex."[17]

This analysis is perhaps more powerful for gay men than for lesbians, since only very recently have women been able to build economically viable households together. Throughout the nineteenth century and well into the twentieth, men worked in the public sphere, while women often toiled in private, raising children and providing the unpaid domestic labor on which the economy rested. When women did work in the formal labor market, they were paid substantially less than men, never receiving a "family wage," since they were supposed to rely on male breadwinners to support themselves and their children. As Julie Matthaei argues in "The Sexual Division of Labor, Sexuality, and Lesbian/Gay Liberation," it was not the rise of wage labor per se but the breakdown of the sexual division of labor in the twentieth century, and the resulting increase in women's economic independence, that paved the way for modern lesbian life.

A careful look at the history of the sexual division of labor reveals a relationship between sexuality and economics that is, again, more ambiguous than first meets the eye. As Matthaei points out, the sexual division of labor simultaneously helped to construct both heterosexuality and homosexuality. Assigning distinct roles to the genders in the economy provided an incentive to enter into heterosexual marriage, particularly for women, many of whom had little choice but to rely on men for financial support (Adrienne Rich made this observation in "Compulsory Heterosexuality and Lesbian Existence"). Yet this division of labor also created a space for homoerotic feelings to flourish. Rigid gender roles opened a chasm between the sexes, fostering close relationships among women drawn together in a circumscribed world. "Boston marriages"—lesbianlike unions of respectable, cohabitating ladies that were socially tolerated in Victorian America—emerged out of a cult of domesticity that celebrated women's separate sphere.

As women have won more access to economic resources, it has become easier for them to eschew heterosexual marriage, building their own households, communities, and institutions. Indeed, as droves of women have entered the work force, marriage rates have declined; the share of women who are married dropped from 71 percent in 1970 to 60 percent in 1993. While women's economic advancement has not been the sole propulsion behind lesbian liberation, the two trends appear to be closely linked.

Unfortunately, continuing discrimination against women in the labor force—the legacy of the sexual division of labor—hits lesbians particularly hard because they lack access to men's incomes. Although the confinement of women to domestic roles (and of both sexes to marriage) impeded both lesbian and gay male life styles, sexism in the labor market hurts just lesbians. This provokes an uncomfortable question for the gay movement: are there growing discrepancies between the interests of gay men and lesbians? In his essay "Do Gay Men Have a Stake in Male Privilege?" Michael P. Jacobs concludes that there are. Socialist feminists have occasionally explored lesbian and gay issues, but, as Jacobs demonstrates, few have rigorously examined the relative positions of lesbians and gay men in the economy and polity. As a result, some misconceptions about gay interests persist, including the notion that gay men have a logical affinity with all feminist goals.

Feminist critics have noted that in recent years, as women have moved into the work force, the nuclear family has receded as a site of women's oppression. "Public patriarchy," in the form of occupational segregation and a gender gap in wages, has become a relatively more important source of gender inequality. While gay men's interests are united with women's in resisting the dominance of the patriarchal nuclear family, gay men actually benefit from these newly prevalent public forms of sexism. Like all men, they benefit from gender discrimination in hiring and promotion, and from the fact that, on average, even now women earn only about 70 cents for every dollar men earn. Moreover, since gay men are often estranged from their families of origin both emotionally and financially, they often see their wage-earning power as intimately linked to their ability to lead a gay life. Between these trends, Jacobs sees the potential for rising friction between gay men and feminists.

Jacobs believes in the possibility of "political pluralism"—in which the gay and feminist movements work separately but harmoniously toward their different ends. Achieving gay goals, he argues, means mobilizing gay men to fight against homophobia, a feat that can best be accomplished by telling the truth about their interests. But his analysis not only enlightens the pursuit of such a segmented political strategy; it also provides a road map to possible pitfalls for those interested in a more concerted gay/feminist alliance.

The case for cooperation among progressive movements is eloquently expressed by Tony Kushner, in "Homosexual Liberation: A Socialism of the Skin"—his response to the mounting push for gay marriage and acceptance in the military. Homophobia might fade, he speculates, and gays might be granted those coveted rights to wed, to pillage, and to protect, yet this could still leave both gays and straights in a dismal place. "Are officially sanctioned homosexual marriages and identifiably homosexual soldiers the ultimate aims of homosexual liberation?" he asks, and answers: "Clearly not, if by homosexual liberation we mean the liberation of homosexuals, who, like most everyone else, are and will continue to be oppressed by the depredations of capital until some better way of living together can be arrived at." His vision of gay liberation, inspired in part by the iconoclastic socialism of Oscar Wilde, goes beyond marriage and military rights to encompass desire, and those connections among the "skin and heart and mind and soul" that animate the people who call themselves gay.

For many reasons, a generous definition of gay liberation such as Kushner's is unfashionable. Most conspicuously, such a vision has not taken hold among the masses of apolitical gays, and the popular gay pundits Kushner criticizes eschew connections with other efforts to reform or undermine aspects of capitalist society. But objections to the idea that one's sexual orientation should be the starting point for a larger politics have even been raised within the academic Left, among those who consider gay identity an effect of exploitative social and economic forces, a limiting, "essentializing" role etched in the margins of a heterosexist society. If the category itself is an oppressive construct, one might ask, how can it serve as the basis for resisting sexual oppression or, for that matter, any other form of oppression? Foucault inspired many such questions, as he warned that attempts at resistance are frequently caught within the paradigms produced by the powers being resisted. But on the other hand, if it follows from his meticulous description of this overdetermined world that all we have are social effects, perhaps they are as good a basis for resistance as any. This does not necessarily entail embracing the concept of gayness as a perpetually stable identity perfectly inhabited by those it naturally suits; rather, essays here such as Cornwall's and Matthaei's examine the social processes of producing gay identities, allowing us to glimpse the historical contours of sexuality, both its variability and its relative constancy in specific milieus and periods.

Each of the pieces in this section contends with deep and difficult assumptions, which arise out of neoclassical blindness, Marxist reductionism, sexism, and political expediency. The ideological frameworks discussed here can help inform political practice, but a host of questions remain about how they might be implemented. For instance, if we are convinced of the value of political coalitions, how can we make them function? How well do they work, after all? We turn to these issues now.

III. Arguments and Activism

Often, the struggle for gay liberation has been viewed—by both sides—as a cultural struggle (or, as Pat Buchanan puts it, a *Kulturkampf*): a struggle of sexual freedom vs. sexual repression, or of free expression vs. censorship, or of authenticity vs. hypocrisy. But it is also a struggle with a complex political-economic dimension that needs to be brought to the fore in the gay movement's debates on agenda, strategy and tactics.

For example, Boston, our hometown, as well as many other cities, has seen annual debates over the gay pride parade. One side wants to "clean it up" by pushing out the drag queens, the dykes on bikes, the bar floats, and any angry political rhetoric. The other side fights back by reminding people about the butches and queens at the Stonewall Inn, and debates whether to keep fighting for an inclusive parade or start a new one.

On its face, this debate appears to have everything to do with cultural representation and nothing to do with economics. Yet partisans on both sides of the debate could benefit by attending more to the kinds of economic and class issues discussed by several of the authors in this volume. For example, those who want to clean up and tone down the parade might want to consider whether eliminating all "nonconformist" lesbians and gay men—i.e., those who do not look middle-class and assimilated—from the family portrait is really the way to build an effective gay movement. Pat Hussain, Barbara Smith, and Susan Moir all contend that it is not. "Middle-class" and "assimilated," after all, may not be wholly discrete categories; Moir suggests that the more visibly queer, gender-bending side of the gay community is disproportionately working class. In addition, the strategic value of such an act of cultural cleansing is questionable. If, as Jean Hardisty and Amy Gluckman posit in "The Hoax of 'Special Rights,'" the impetus behind the Right's current antigay campaign has as much to do with right-wing organizations' desire for new funds and new members as it does with their sexually-conservative ideology, then we should not expect this campaign to end if only the gay community stops shocking the public with images of queer sexual pleasure and gender nonconformity.

As for those who want to keep the parade on the cultural edge, they might consider that periodic moments of shock theater are not a substitute for a well-thought-out progressive politics that addresses the factors underlying the honest anxieties on which the Right so effectively capitalizes. Such a politics needs to recognize the importance of building progressive alliances and to be prepared for the negotiation and compromise that are required to do so. In a particular local setting, such a compromise might validly ask that gay activists *not* put on their queerest face, or at any rate that they listen to the insights of longtime local organizers about how best to "act up" in their communities. In our interview with Barbara Smith, she discusses a situation of this kind that arose in Albany, New York, where she has been an organizer for many years.

The annual debate over the makeup of gay pride parades mirrors the more fundamental split between the conservative and progressive arms of the gay movement. Perhaps the central argument between the two is over whether gay rights ought to be advanced as a single issue or as part of a broader progressive agenda. (With one or two exceptions, no one appears interested in advancing gay rights as part of a broader *conservative* agenda.) Like the rest of the volume, Part III does not offer an evenhanded approach to the debate. Most of the authors here address the links between gay rights and a progressive politics grounded in an understanding of the centrality of our economic system, making a case for how and why such links should be built.

The view that gay rights should be isolated from any progressive social-change agenda is in some ways typified by Marshall Kirk and Hunter Madsen's *After the Ball: How America Will Conquer Its Fear and Hatred of Gays in the '90s*,[18] which lays out a battle plan for a progay public relations campaign. *After the Ball* should not be taken to represent the entire range of conservative gay politics. However, the book does highlight some of the common patterns of analysis on this side of the debate.

After the Ball analyzes homophobia only as prejudice, not as discrimination. In other words, the authors look at it only on an individual, psychological level, not on a systemic social, political, or economic level. One need only consider a figure like Ronald Reagan, who may personally harbor little antigay prejudice yet who for political reasons provided great succor to antigay forces, to recognize that these two kinds of homophobia are independently significant. A strategy that aims to change the psychological sources of homophobic feelings in individuals may be one part of gay-rights organizing, but as an overall program, it fails to come to grips with either the social-structural dimension of gay oppression or with the political-economic uses to which homophobia is often put by politicians and right-wing organizations alike.

Absent from Kirk and Madsen's book are gay people of color and of the working class. Thus, the authors end up presenting precisely that portrait of the gay community—comfortable, white collar, and white—that the Right is using as it argues that legal protections for gay men and lesbians are unnecessary; how, it is argued, can such a well-positioned, affluent group seriously claim to be suffering from the effects of discrimination? Lesbians, too, are largely absent from the analysis, and the authors never address the deep link between homophobia and sexism. Homophobia—especially men's fear and hatred of women who are strong and independent and women's fear of being perceived as one of *those* women—is an important weapon in the antifeminists' arsenal,[19] and antifeminism in turn is a strong force perpetuating homophobic attitudes and policies. In *After the Ball*, the aspect of gay liberation that had to do not only with being able to love someone of the same sex but also with getting free of the constraints of gender is completely gone, and so are the butches and queens, who are asked to avoid letting their queerness show in public. What good does liberation do a queen if his rights depend on no longer being a queen?

These are the patterns of analysis that several of the authors in Part III dissect.[20] In their view, to design political strategies for the gay movement with only a narrow segment of the gay community in mind is to risk fundamentally misunderstanding what lesbians and gay men are up against and how they can move forward. At the same time, to see the gay movement as part of a larger progressive movement does not in itself determine a specific agenda or establish particular strategies. If anything, it can make these choices more complex.

The difficulties in settling on a progressive gay agenda have their roots in real tensions between the divergent goals that different segments of the gay community consider most critical, between short-term and long-term goals, and between specifically gay and other progressive goals. There is a parallel here to the history of feminism, in particular to socialist-feminism. According to Judith Van Allen, the first wave of socialist-feminists in the 1960s viewed capitalist patriarchy as a seamless system that had the heterosexual nuclear family as its keystone. Thus, altering and in some ways weakening the traditional family structure was understood as a strategy for undermining both capitalism and patriarchy. But that strategy found its limits as it became clear that capitalism itself was weakening the family: it demanded mobility and separated families, offered a panorama of consumer goods and services as substitutes for traditional family-centered pasttimes, encouraged women to enter the labor force, and placed enormous stress on the child-rearing and domestic functions of families. The recognition that capitalism was already undermining family life has made the selection of goals and strategies for socialist-feminism far more complicated.[21]

Likewise progressive gay activism. The fact that some business sectors have begun embracing the gay market, supporting gay employee organizations and so forth, makes it clear that heterosexism and the U.S. economic system are not a seamless web, either. In fact, some would argue that the two systems are discrete; in other words, that the free market could provide full rights and benefits to, and generally assimilate, gay men and lesbians without otherwise altering its course. Others would argue that there *are* ties that bind homophobia to our economic system and to class, race, and gender oppression. However, few have analyzed precisely what these ties are, with the crucial exception of Suzanne Pharr and others who have examined the links between sexism and homophobia.

With such connections in mind, activist and publisher Barbara Smith, in an interview, provides insights about the direction she sees gay politics taking today and the direction it needs to take. She believes that a capitalist economic system is capable of absorbing gay men and lesbians to some degree and offering the gay community certain things that it wants; however, she thinks that there are limits both to how far capitalism will go in extending gay rights, and to how far the liberatory potential of those rights and benefits will extend. She argues for a progressive, multi-issue gay politics primarily on the grounds that the lives of that majority of lesbians and gay men who are not well-off, white, and male will not be significantly improved unless social change occurs on many fronts. She also stresses the fact that the many groups whose interests form the core of progressive politics are frequently targets of the same patterns of oppression—she mentions police harassment as an example—and share some common enemies. "The enemy of my enemy is my friend" may sound like a simplistic guideline for political decision-making; on the other hand, as Smith points out, the gay movement cannot afford to ignore the useful alliances the adage recommends.

Smith voices a deep concern about the growing right wing in U.S. politics; she sees the current antigay campaign that the Right is waging across the United States as part of a larger movement against civil rights and economic justice. Jean Hardisty's essay "The Hoax of 'Special Rights'," co-written for this volume by one of the editors, gives a detailed portrait of this campaign and the organizations behind it. Hardisty, who directs the watchdog group Political Research Associates, argues that age-old homophobic attitudes on the Right stem from religious doctrine. However, she stresses that the prominent place the antigay campaign now holds in the Right's agenda has more to do with the tactics and opportunism of established right-wing organizations. For example, some of these groups are currently taking great pains to reach out to low-income communities and communities of color; painting the gay community as wealthy, highly educated, and free spending is one way they believe they can expand the appeal of right-wing politics in these communities.

Hardisty and Gluckman's portrait of the Right suggests that homophobia has become an easy-to-use wedge issue, and that antigay movements may have their origins in political dynamics that have little to do with gay men and lesbians. The sort of rapid reversal of fortune that lesbians and gay men experienced in Germany, for example, from the 1920s to the 1930s,[22] can only be understood in the context of broader political forces. While many political and economic issues may not seem on their face very related to gay life, they may actually turn out to be quite, and unfortunately, relevant.

The right-wing groups Hardisty and Gluckman depict are hoping to play upon the stereotypical social conservatism of working-class communities. Whether or not this accurately describes certain pockets, as an overall label it is as inappropriate as is the notion that all gays are wealthy, according to Duncan Osborne and Susan Moir. Osborne's article "Lavender Labor" and the interview with Moir focus on gay activism among union workers.

Osborne, a journalist, narrates a partial history of the gay movement within unions. It's a surprising story to many who tend to see unions as socially backward institutions—for it's a story of early acceptance and principled progay solidarity. In fact, in many instances, unions have stood up for gay men and lesbians, only to have gay organizations fail to hold up their end of the bargain with organized labor.

Moir, a long-time union member and an activist in the Boston-area Gay and Lesbian Labor Activists Network (GALLAN), analyzes the importance of unions to the gay-rights struggle. Although she does not claim that every homophobic union member has been reborn a homophile, Moir is convinced that unions provide a set of institutions and procedures within which positive change can occur as well as an ideology of solidarity that can motivate change. She says, "We're not just talking diversity; we're doing it. We're sitting down, dinosaurs and queers, in the same room and hashing it out." And at the moment, she contends, organized labor is the only place in the progressive sector with the resources and organizational stability to support social-change movements, including the gay-rights movement.

Like Moir, Pat Hussain, an organizer with Southerners on New Ground and a member of the steering committee for the 1993 March on Washington, is concerned with how resources are amassed and used by political organizations. In "Class Action," Hussain discusses the ways in which the assumptions made about class by gay organizations shape the work they do. Focusing on the nitty-gritty side of political work, she demonstrates how groups that function in a casual way around apparently mundane matters such as reimbursing expenses can effectively prevent the participation of low-income and working-class lesbians and gay men. She argues that this dynamic shapes organizational decision making and limits political effectiveness. Hussain also gives a personal, behind-the-scenes account of planning for the March on Washington in 1993, including some very painful moments: "Another man insisted we 'be honest with each other,' that women and people of color were lazy and just didn't do the work. Some of the men sitting around him were nodding in agreement."

Hussain's discussion highlights tensions among different strains of progressive gay thought. In her interview, Barbara Smith bemoans what she refers to as the 501(c)(3)'ing of the gay movement—the disappearance of small-scale, low-budget activist groups and their replacement by an infrastructure of staffed organizations operating on a service-provider/client model. Yet if we're to take Hussain's complaint seriously, then it is important for the gay movement to build up adequately funded institutions that can cover the expenses of political work and pay organizers a living wage. Smith, in turn, worries that such organizations sometimes lose their edge.

There is no way around this dilemma, only through it. The same is true for some of the other dilemmas examined in these pages. Both Smith and Moir, for example, object to domestic partnership and gay marriage; Smith does not want to see gay men and lesbians parroting long-oppressive straight institutions, and Moir stresses the need to make social benefits such as health care available to all regardless of employment or family ties. Hussain, however, sees domestic partnership and gay marriage as critical goals; gay working people need health coverage today, she points out, not sometime in the future, and domestic partnership is the surest road to it.

Hussain's view is probably more in line with the majority of lesbian and gay political organizations, which are working actively to obtain domestic partnership rights. Yet, to view the health insurance needs of gay men and lesbians through a narrow, gay-specific lens may mean missing out on critical opportunities for coalition-building and gay political advancement. This is the story Deborah Stone tells in her essay "AIDS and the Moral Economy of Insurance"; her piece and Robert M. Anderson's essay "Domestic Partner Benefits," taken together, offer a primer for anyone working on these issues.

Anderson, an economist, explains how the insurance industry functions, laying out a body of information useful for dissecting and countering the arguments that insurers and employers have made against the feasibility of providing domestic-partner benefits. In his view, there are valid reasons for insurance companies to object to an arrangement in which an employee could choose absolutely anyone to include under his or her health coverage; however, he argues, it is *not* reasonable for them to refuse to offer domestic-partner coverage as long as domestic partners are defined in a specific way.

Anderson's analysis deals with the current system of health care financing. Both the AIDS epidemic and the widespread lack of access to health coverage, though, have led many in and outside of the gay community to question the structure of the U.S. health care system at a more fundamental level. Deborah Stone, a political scientist, looks at how AIDS has both revealed and deepened the cracks in that system. She describes how insurers have attempted to exclude people they view as being at high risk for AIDS, first by the use of crude selection criteria (single men over twenty-five living in certain urban areas or in certain occupations) and then by the use of the HIV antibody test. The experience of these men in the insurance market foreshadows what may happen to many of us as predictive tests become available for more and more diseases. Because of this, she suggests that a political strategy that reads the insurance industry's treatment of gay men solely as a matter of antigay discrimination misses the mark. The issue, she believes, is a much bigger one, or at least one that potentially has a much larger and more diverse constituency: "Because opponents of testing framed the issue as discrimination against gays, they lost the opportunity for alliances with other groups whose members stand to lose from increased medical underwriting but do not see themselves as victims of discrimination." Her conclusion: "If ever there were an issue that ought to have propelled us to national health insurance, the AIDS epidemic should have been it. No recent experience so graphically demonstrates the limits of private health insurance as a method of paying for sickness."

Stone's analysis calls for exactly the kind of coalition-building that many of the authors in this volume favor. As we write, in 1996, discussion of the health care crisis has all but disappeared from the national radar screen. But two or three years ago, lesbian and gay political organizations had the opportunity to throw their growing resources behind the hotly contested proposals for health care reform. That such an opportunity for coalition-building passed nearly unnoticed should be a wake-up call to gay activists, both those who are interested in working only in all-queer settings and those who wish to keep gay politics safe from "other people's" issues.

In this vision, gay politics is not about seeing the gay community as one among many interest-groups, each trying to tinker with the present system in small ways that enhance its own position. Rather, it is about viewing lesbians and gay men as integral members of the human species, using the particular gay experience to illuminate injustice and highlight the shape of economic, social, and political changes that will improve the lives of lesbians and gay men—and everyone else, too.

Notes

1. When not specified otherwise, "Gay" refers to both men and women. While the book does not systematically address issues relevant to bisexuals and transgenders, to the extent that they share experiences with lesbians and gay men, some of the analysis will shed light on their economic lives as well.

2. "Lesbian, Gay and Bisexual Civil Rights Protections in the U.S.," National Gay and Lesbian Task Force Policy Institute, June 1995.

3. See John D'Emilio, "Capitalism and Gay Identity," in *Powers of Desire: The Politics of Sexuality*, ed. Ann Snitow, Christine Stansell, and Sharon Thompson (New York: Monthly Review Press, 1983).

4. Urvashi Vaid, *Virtual Equality: The Mainstreaming of Gay & Lesbian Liberation* (New York: Doubleday, 1995), p. 10.

5. Martin Duberman, *About Time: Exploring the Gay Past* (New York: Meridian, 1991), p. 228.

6. See Gregg Blachford, "Male Dominance and the Gay World," in *The Making of the Modern Homosexual*, ed. Kenneth Plummer (London, 1981), p. 208.

7. Vaid, p. 36.

8. Feminists have had a similarly bittersweet experience of success. As those bred in the sixties and seventies took stock in the eighties, they faced the disturbing reality that many women identified with the label "postfeminist" purveyed by the press. At the same time that women were enjoying the fruits of feminism and defending their rights as women to enjoy them, they were distancing themselves from politics and the movement. Among women, this phenomenon has taken the form of reducing feminist social goals to matters of individual lifestyle, which parallels the trend toward a consumption-oriented individualism in today's gay community. See Judith Stacey, "Sexism by a Subtler Name?" and Rayna Rapp, "Is the Legacy of Second-Wave Feminism Post-Feminism?" in *Women, Class, and the Feminist Imagination*, ed. Karen V. Hansen and Ilene J. Philipson (Philadelphia: Temple University Press, 1990).

9. Andrew Sullivan, *Virtually Normal: An Argument About Homosexuality* (New York: Alfred A. Knopf, 1995), p. 89.

10. "The Record on Gay-Related Referenda Questions," National Gay and Lesbian Task Force, March 7, 1995.

11. See her anthology *Skin* (Firebrand Books, 1994), specifically the essay "A Question of Class."

12. "Some News That Will At Least Not Bore You," *Eastern Economic Review*, Fall 1995.

13. Robert Padgug provides a thorough discussion of theoretical quandaries facing historians of sexuality in "Sexual Matters: Rethinking Sexuality in History," *Radical History Review* 20 (Spring/Summer 1979), pp.3–23.

14. Mary McIntosh, "The Homosexual Role," in *The Making of the Modern Homosexual*, ed. Kenneth Plummer (London: Hutchinson: 1981), p. 33.

15. Michel Foucault, *The History of Sexuality, Volume I, An Introduction* (New York: Random House, 1978), p. 123.

16. Ibid.

17. D'Emilio, p. 107.

18. Marshall Kirk and Hunter Madsen, *After the Ball: How America Will Conquer Its Fear and Hatred of Gays in the '90s* (New York: Doubleday, 1989).

19. For a thorough analysis of this point, see Suzanne Pharr, *Homophobia: A Weapon of Sexism* (New York: Chardon Press, 1988).

20. In *Virtually Normal*, Andrew Sullivan offers a far more scholarly conservative analysis of gay politics. But his description of that portion of the gay movement that *does* want to address racism, sexism, and class oppression is nearly unrecognizable. His view is that progressive gay activists are beholden to Foucault, and that their mercilessly deconstructionist assumptions lead them toward a political dead end where only nihilism and campus speech codes can be found. In this critique, Sullivan seems to be addressing himself to a small coterie of queer academics, conflating them with the larger corps of progressive, not

necessarily queer, gay activists; he unfairly interprets the call for a multi-issue agenda as an inability to make rational choices or to envision "social goods or common ends."

21. Judith Van Allen, "Capitalism without Patriarchy," *Socialist Review* 77 (September–October 1984), p. 81.

22. See James D. Steakley, *The Homosexual Emancipation Movement in Germany* (New York: Arno Press, 1975) and Lillian Faderman and Brigitte Eriksson, eds., *Lesbians in Germany: 1890s–1920s* (Tallahassee: Naiad Press, 1990).

Part I

A Community Divided

1

The Gay Marketing Moment

Amy Gluckman and Betsy Reed

This piece examines the recent surge in mainstream media attention to the gay community, looking at the origins and implications of corporate interest in the gay market.

Since a cocky k. d. lang reveled in Cindy Crawford's feminine attentions on the cover of *Vanity Fair* in the summer of 1993, other icons of "lesbian chic" have been showing off their buzzcuts in androgynous ads, while gay men flex their pecs in mainstream magazines and, more figuratively, in the upper echelons of the business world. *Newsweek,* having declared cuddly, cohabitating "Lesbians" all the rage the previous year, observed a sudden bisexual moment sweeping the nation in 1995. Fashionably late, following centuries of invisibility punctuated by hostile caricatures, a conspicuous kind of gay liberation announced its own important arrival in the 1990s.

Gay and lesbian political activists, who have toiled for decades at the grassroots level to promote a welcoming climate for gay men and lesbians, certainly deserve a large share of the credit for the proliferation of gay-positive images, both in ads and in other media. But it is not as if liberation has suddenly become the bottom line for many of those peddling glamorous pictures of lesbians, bisexuals, and gay men. Marketers, who make it a rule to tolerate their markets, have had a revelation. The profits to be reaped from treating gay men and lesbians as a trend-setting consumer group finally outweigh the financial risks of inflaming right-wing hate. As George Slowik, Jr., publisher of the prosperous, glossy *Out* magazine, said in a 1993 interview, "Our demographics are more appealing than those of 80-year-old Christian ladies."

"Untold millions,"[1] or so the title of one recent business book proclaims, lie in the deep pockets of gay consumers, a demographic group that can best be tapped by placing ads in outlets like *Out,* as well as in predominantly straight venues that allow tantalizing glimpses of gay life. Advertisers are steering toward gay publications that promote a stylish, widely palatable vision of gay life—primarily glossy mags like *Out* and *The Advocate* that have been cleansed of the objectionable: phone sex ads, radical politics, and hard core leather culture. This foray into even sanitized gay media is big news in the advertising business. Marketing and business publications exhibit a wary excitement, with headlines like "The Gay Market: Nothing to Fear But Fear Itself," "Untapped Niche Offers Marketers Brand Loyalty," and "Mainstream's Domino Effect: Liquor, Fragrance, Clothing Advertisers Ease into Gay Magazines." Along with Absolut, Calvin Klein, and Benetton, corporations that have taken the lead in advertising in mainstream gay publications include Philip Morris, Columbia Records, Miller beer, Seagram's, and Hiram Walker.

These newfound suitors of gay consumers have not come calling without any encouragement. Rather, their interest has been piqued by organizations—usually run by gays—that conduct surveys and employ selected information about gay consumers to persuade advertisers that a viable gay and lesbian market exists. For instance, Strub Media Group, led by openly-gay *Poz* publisher Sean Strub, distributes a flyer claiming that readers of gay publications have an average household income of $63,100, compared to $36,500 for all households. Gay marketing groups also point out that since gay men and lesbians have no children (more and more a false assumption), their disposable income is even higher than their average income would suggest. According to well-publicized data from another gay marketing organization, Overlooked Opinions, 80 percent of gay men eat out more than five times a month. And a promotional package used by a network of local gay newspapers asserts that gay men and lesbians travel more, buy more CDs, use their AmEx card more, and generally spend more money on the good life than do their straight counterparts. The most valuable target market—the one that is most conspicuous in the marketing literature—is white, urban, white-collar, and predominantly male.

Prime conditions exist for these notions to color popular views of gay men and lesbians. Unlike other subgroups that could never "pass," the clearest characteristic of gay men and lesbians has been, until recently, their invisibility. To be sure, there have been some stereotypes out there, focusing mostly on sexual promiscuity and mental instability. But most straight Americans have harbored few ideas about whether gay men and lesbians were rich or poor, spendthrift or frugal. Past gay invisibility has provided a blank slate of sorts, a slate that is rapidly filling up with notions that have more to do with marketing than with reality.

And the fault lies partly with overzealous gay marketing groups. While anecdotes about free-spending, double-income gay households do accurately represent one segment of the gay community, they have unfortunately been presented as descriptive of all gay men and lesbians. Eager to persuade reluctant corporations of a lucrative yet dormant gay market, Overlooked Opinions circulated misleading statistics depicting gay people as disproportionately rich. As M. V. Lee Badgett contends in her essay "Beyond Biased Samples" in this volume, such assertions of high gay incomes are common but inaccurate, as marketers have confused survey data referring to the readers of gay publications with the demographics of the community as a whole. Badgett's findings reveal that gay men earn substantially less than their straight counterparts, while lesbians are roughly even with heterosexual women in earning power.

Still, the bottom line for advertisers is that targeting the group of gays that is most prosperous can be quite lucrative. It might not be as large as it appears in the literature, but there is certainly a stack of gay money to be had. Moreover, lesbians and gay men have proven to be vulnerable to the advances of corporate marketers because they have been ignored as a consumer group for so long. The makers of Absolut vodka were the first to discover and exploit the gay community's brand loyalty, which is now a veritable legend among advertisers. Tracking consumption patterns after local ads appeared in gay media, Absolut charted dramatic jumps in specific requests for its brand name in gay bars.

Ads don't feature glamorous gays just to connect with gay consumers, either. Firms placing gay-themed ads are also counting on the ability of attractive gay idols to set trends for straight shoppers—a bet that has already paid off for some. Resplendent in red, RuPaul, the queen of drag and Mac cosmetics model, has inspired hordes of genetic girls to buy the company's lipstick through ads placed primarily in mainstream straight media. And there is the demonstrated power of ordinary gay people to establish trends followed by straights; it has become common lore, for instance, that gay men popularized Levi's button-fly jeans.

Before such money-making fads take hold in any community, media images usually introduce the novel idea. Sometimes ads alone will do it (such as vodka bottles by Keith Haring), but marketers uniformly believe that to take optimum effect, advertising has to be placed in a complementary environment. This suggests that a sort of mercenary collusion between advertising and editorial forces might have provided much of the impetus for the recent gay media moment. Circumstantial evidence abounds; flip over k. d. and Cindy and you will find Absolut. Ads for Benetton, Calvin Klein, and other companies known for their keen interest in the gay market lurk in the shadows of many of the recent gay-moment stories.

Some of the supposed attributes of the new gay target consumer group are probably harmless. *Out* magazine's media kit, for example, says that lesbians and gay men are "homemakers" and "aesthetes." And the new gay visibility has distinct advantages. The very presence of gay men and lesbians in the media—as celebrities, authors, and social actors—is a long-sought triumph, while being respected as a market often translates into political clout. In Hawaii, for instance, the argument for gay marriage has been bolstered by the prospect of a windfall from gay tourism. One economist has even estimated that the first state to recognize gay marriage could reap a $4.3 billion boon.[2] And, of course, money itself can buy a good degree of political influence. As the work of the Human Rights Campaign has shown, carefully targeted donations to political campaigns can cement the loyalty of key politicians (though the Log Cabin Republicans discovered the limits of this approach when Bob Dole returned their carefully rendered gift in the fall of 1995). Certainly, the gay and lesbian community can wield its newly recognized market power wisely by rewarding social responsibility and by punishing capitulation to the Right.

To the extent that gay advances hinge on financial interests, however, they are precarious. What if a future backlash depletes gay incomes, or the right wing proves the greater economic force? Far-right boycotts have hurt progressive causes before and the right wing remains a formidable force in some areas of the marketplace. In

1995, for instance, when PFLAG—Parents, Families and Friends of Lesbians and Gays—tried to buy $1 million worth of TV air time for antihate public service spots, protests from Pat Robertson's Christian Broadcasting Network caused most TV stations to refuse to run the ads. In general, companies that don't serve a substantial conservative, fundamentalist constituency—such as liquor firms—are the ones that have avidly been cultivating gay consumption. In the case of alcohol, this has made for some unpleasant bedfellows, with ads for Dewar's, Miller beer, and the like sustaining mainstream gay magazines, while radical gay media like *Gay Community News* struggle to survive.

In addition, there are concrete political risks in projecting a rich, powerful image to get wide attention. The religious right has appropriated gay marketing statistics to portray gay men and lesbians as a rich special interest undeserving of civil rights protection. Overlooked Opinions received a request for evidence of the gay community's financial power from the Colorado Attorney General's office, charged with defending antigay ballot initiative Amendment 2. And the antigay group Colorado for Family Values has argued that "homosexuals are anything but disadvantaged," citing statistics that gay male households earn an average of $55,400 annually—in the same range estimated by Overlooked Opinions. This campaign, directed at lower-income communities, has succeeded in fanning antigay hate as a response to real economic despair. In the fall of 1995, a similar attempt to convince Maine voters that gay men and lesbians were an advantaged group seeking preferential treatment was defeated by a margin of just 6 percentage points (ironically, this victory occurred only after progay forces outspent their opponents 10 to 1).

And in May 1996, when the U.S. Supreme Court overturned Colorado's Amendment 2, Justice Antonin Scalia's dissenting opinion made specific reference to the "high disposable income" that gay people have allegedly used to build up "disproportionate political power."[3]

Stereotypes of gay wealth play not only into the hands of the far Right; more moderate opponents of a broad-reaching lesbian and gay agenda have seized on them as well. In the May 1993 issue of *The New Republic*, gay social critic Jonathan Rauch invoked popular stereotypes about gay wealth to argue that gay men and lesbians should not consider themselves oppressed. His piece opened with chilling scenes of gay bashing, but then proceeded to claim that gay men and lesbians are not oppressed because they meet only one of his criteria of oppression—they face direct legal discrimination. They can vote, have a right to education, and are entitled to basic human rights, but the point he returned to most is that they are also free of "impoverishment relative to the remainder of the population."[4] After citing Overlooked Opinions' income data, Rauch offered one anecdotal example after another of the wealthy gay man: a college professor friend who owns a split-level condo and a Mazda Miata; gay acquaintances with $50,000 incomes and European vacations who whine about being victims.

Rauch's analysis was not only built on a faulty empirical foundation. It was also blind to the link between the legal discrimination that he acknowledged and economic oppression. In his discussion of whether gay people are economically oppressed, Rauch never mentioned the occupational segregation faced by openly gay men until literally the last few years. Like Jews throughout European history, openly gay men have been shunted into a severely limited number of occupational fields. And just as the success of the Rothschilds should never have been used to belittle the wide-ranging effects of the systematic discrimination that Jews faced over many centuries in Europe, so the success of some gay figures in the arts and entertainment business (or in Rauch's circle of acquaintance) should not obscure the real effects of having to choose between being openly gay and access to a wide range of jobs. Moreover, although discrimination against lesbians is less conspicuous because all women have faced economic oppression, it is clear that women's lower incomes place lesbian households at a unique disadvantage.

This is not to say that, as a group, gay men and lesbians experience seamless economic exploitation; indeed, the case of gay marketing reveals the very complex relationship between gay people and the economy. We are witnessing a new stage in this relationship, and perhaps some signs of improvement in it, but gay people have always both prospered and suffered at the hands of the market. As the historian John D'Emilio has argued, gay people have enjoyed the economic freedom to build same-sex households in capitalist societies, but culturally they have served as scapegoats for the expression of various anxieties—family pressures but also class frustration, which might threaten the economic status quo were it to find its proper target. "Materially," he wrote, "capitalism weakens the bonds that once kept families together so that their members experience a growing instability in the place they have come to expect happiness and emotional security. . . . [L]esbians, gay men, and heterosexual feminists have become the scapegoats for the social instability of the system."[5]

Now, suddenly, it has become useful to business interests to cultivate a narrow (and widely acceptable) definition of gay identity as a marketing tool, and to integrate gay people as gay people into a new consumer niche. The speed with which the needs of the market can steamroll the strongest of social traditions and taboos is awe-inspiring. Yet in keeping with history, the outcome for gay men and lesbians is double-edged.

Today, the sword of the market is slicing off every segment of the gay community that is not upper-middle class, (mostly) white, and (mostly) male. Lesbians and gay men who do not see themselves in Ikea TV spots or Dewar's ads feel alienated. Perhaps more importantly, gay politics now reflects this divide, and a growing chorus of conservative gay writers is calling for gay activism to separate itself from any broader progressive vision that might address the needs and interests of the less visible, less privileged members of the gay community.

Just a few years ago, the AIDS crisis helped give an edge to gay politics by encouraging just those sorts of connections to develop. AIDS politicized a large group of white, middle-class gay men, who suddenly discovered what it was like to live in fear of losing housing or medical coverage, and who had to fight the medical, insurance, and real estate establishments to survive. The crisis moved many gay men to come out, and it also prompted some of them to link the fight against homophobia to other progressive political efforts.

After fifteen minutes in the glow of the gay moment, however, this militant stance became distinctly less fashionable. Queer Nation's slogan, "We're here, we're queer, get used to it," says to straight people, "We will stretch your concept of morality, of family, of politics." But many who have reaped the benefits of corporate acceptance seem to be saying, "We're here, we're just like you, don't worry about it." When asked about Philip Morris's gay marketing campaign for Special Kings cigarettes, the publisher of L.A.'s gay magazine *Genre* responded: "*Esquire* takes tobacco ads and that is the kind of publication we want to be."

It is too early to tell whether concrete, day-to-day political action in the gay community will change as well, coming more into line with the typical politics of groups led by individuals who feel they are faring well under capitalism. But it is already clear that in some important ways, the gay moment is more of a hurdle for gay politics than a source of strength. The delicate bonds between the gay and African American communities, for example, are only being stretched closer to the breaking point. The current blitz contains hardly any images of gay African Americans or references to black gay culture or organizations. As Eric Washington pointed out in *The Village Voice*, a recent Overlooked Opinions survey asked gay New Yorkers which publications they read, listing several dailies and weeklies but omitting Harlem's *Amsterdam News*. And a question about hospital services to gays and lesbians left Harlem Hospital off the list. Such omissions only reinforce the alienation of black lesbians and gay men from the rest of the gay community. The images of a seamlessly white, middle-class gay community tap into "an undercurrent of resentment [in the African American community] . . . fed by the perception that gays are affluent and indifferent to racism."[6]

It's tempting to embrace today's recognition ecstatically and unconditionally; as Andrew Schneider (who wrote *Northern Exposure*'s lesbian episode) told *Vogue*, the network was inundated with letters from lesbians after the show aired. "They were very grateful, like starving people getting a crust of bread," he said. But seizing the gay moment even as it reinforces racial and class hierarchies will allow for only limited gains. As the best feminism is sensitive to more than questions of gender, the fight against homophobia will take on its most liberating forms only if it is conceived as part of a broader vision of social and economic justice.

Notes

This article originally appeared in the November/December 1993 issue of *Dollars & Sense* magazine. It has been revised for this volume.

1. Grant Lukenbill, *Untold Millions: The Gay and Lesbian Market in America* (New York: HarperCollins, 1995).
2. "Bet on a Gay Tourism Boost in Hawaii," *Detroit News*, 1995. Reprinted in *Liberal Opinion*, Sept. 18, 1995, p. 6.
3. "Excerpts from Court's Decision on Colorado's Provision for Homosexuals," *New York Times*, May 23, 1996, p. A21.
4. Jonathan Rauch, "Beyond Oppression," *The New Republic*, May 10, 1993, p. 18.
5. John D'Emilio, "Capitalism and Gay Identity," in *Powers of Desire*, ed. Ann Snitow,

Christine Stansell, and Sharon Thompson (New York: Monthly Review Press, 1983), pp. 100–117.

6. Eric Washington, "Freedom Rings? The Alliance Between Blacks and Gays is Threatened by Mutual Inscrutability," *Village Voice*, June 29, 1993, pp. 25–33.

2

A History in Ads
The Growth of the Gay and Lesbian Market

Dan Baker

A nationally recognized gay market was a long time in the making. After much lobbying and cajoling on the part of gay-marketing advocates, corporations have slowly come around to their message, as evidenced by new TV spots featuring gay characters, and the proliferation of glossy, homoerotic print ads. Dan Baker, publisher of *Quotient: The Newsletter of Marketing to Gay Men and Lesbians,* gives a behind-the-scenes account of this process. This piece is based on the book *Cracking the Corporate Closet* by Dan Baker and Sean Strub with Bill Henning.

Lesbians and gay men have always been consumers, but the idea that there is a "gay market" is relatively new. Even today, there are people who deny it. In the September 1994 issue of the direct-mail industry magazine *Who's Mailing What,* an editorialist responding to an AT&T ad targeted at gay men and lesbians wrote, "What in the world does being gay have to do with long distance telephone service? Is the next step a mailing to redheads? Or thin people? Or people with freckles?"

In fact, the proof that the market exists is that marketers like AT&T *believe* that it exists; commercial interest is, after all, what defines a market. Such interest in the gay market has come about gradually over the last twenty-five years.

The 1969 Stonewall uprising in New York City heralded the emergence of a self-conscious gay community, and various small businesses responded by starting up to serve gay men and lesbians. While their founders certainly had commercial motives, they also saw themselves as gay pioneers, and they were all involved in the gay liberation movement of the day. Some of these businesses are still alive today, often having undergone several metamorphoses: Liberation Publications (publishers of *The Advocate*); Lambda Rising bookstore chain and mail order service (founded by Deacon Macubbin as a 1970s "head" shop); other bookstores, such as A Different Light in

San Francisco (now also in New York and Los Angeles) and the Oscar Wilde Memorial Bookshop in New York; community newspapers like *The New York Native* and *The Washington Blade* (originally the *Gay Blade*); Bob Damron's guide to gay bars and baths; Olivia Records, directed at a lesbian audience; and the first direct-mail fundraising operation for gay organizations founded by Sean Strub in 1980.

In the early '70s, every major city in the United States could boast a gay bookstore and at least one gay publication. These publications were crucial to the development of the sense of the gay market, in part because they were largely supported by advertisements—both business advertising and personal classifieds. The business advertising was largely for local bars and for small gay-owned businesses. A high proportion of the advertising was sexually oriented (toward men)—for pornographic magazines and, later, videos and phone sex services. What the early gay publications did not contain was the kind of advertising that financed other newspapers or magazines—the local department store, for example, or mass-market national advertisers.

This began to change in 1979, when the first Absolut vodka ads ran in *The Advocate*. Absolut was imported from Sweden by Carillon Importers of New Jersey, which was headed by Michel Roux, a straight man. Faced with the prospect of finding a market for an unknown alcohol, Roux looked around for a niche that had not yet been exploited, and he found the gay community. He took a gamble that we would respond to a product that took us seriously enough to advertise in our publications and that we were a trendy, fashion-setting segment of society. (Of course, it helped that he hired Keith Haring to create his clever ads.) The gamble paid off royally. Very soon, gay men (at least) started asking for "Absolut and tonic" in bars, and the brand took off. Since then, Absolut's full-color back-page ads have kept several of our publications alive.

During the 1980s, aspiring national gay publications began to realize that they needed large advertisers such as Absolut in order to survive and expand. At the same time, large corporations became more aware (or rather were *made* more aware) of the size and potential of the gay market. Simmons Market Research Bureau was the first to try to raise this awareness in 1988, conducting a readers' survey of eight gay and lesbian newspapers that belonged to the National Gay Newspaper Guild. Their data were the original source of the idea that gay men and lesbians are unusually affluent and well-educated. Simmons reported an average per capita income of $36,800, versus $12,287 for the population as a whole. A much greater proportion had college degrees (59.6 percent vs. 18 percent) and managerial or professional positions (49 percent vs. 15.9 percent). This survey painted the first picture of the readership of those gay and lesbian newspapers surveyed, and gave them much-needed ammunition to convince "mainstream" advertisers to buy space. In spite of the numerous misuses to which the information has since been put, this survey never purported to say anything about the gay community as a whole.

Impressed with these remarkable demographics, another company set out to profile the gay community overall and to sell the data to mainstream companies. In November 1990, Overlooked Opinions, a Chicago-based marketing company, mailed out a questionnaire that was answered by 1,357 gay men and lesbians. Once again, the gay and lesbian market was shown to be disproportionately wealthy and well-educated: 34

percent had household incomes over $50,000 (compared to 25 percent for the population as a whole), and about 26 percent had graduate degrees, compared to 5 percent of the total population.

The problem was that the Overlooked Opinions survey was a "convenience survey" made up of people who read gay publications or who signed up to be interviewed at Gay Pride parades. It therefore disproportionately represented the politically active and the affluent. Yet the company took the numbers to be representative of the whole gay and lesbian population. Using the one-in-ten Kinsey gay/straight ratio, Overlooked Opinions calculated the community's total annual income to be $514 billion—an unrealistically high estimate.

In 1993, a more scientific survey by the Yankelovich Partners found that gay men and lesbians have incomes that are, in fact, very comparable to the population as a whole. Yankelovich found that gay men had average annual household incomes slightly lower than the total of all men ($37,400 vs. $39,300), while lesbians were slightly higher than other women ($34,800 vs. $34,400). (For a detailed analysis of demographic studies of the gay population, see M. V. Lee Badgett's paper in this volume.) One of the most important findings of the 1993 survey was that, while average individual gay incomes were comparable to the national average, white gay men were two to three times more likely than the average white male to have household incomes of over $100,000 a year. This may be the source of the notion that there is a high-income, high-consuming class of gays that should appeal to marketers with trendy products to sell.

The 1993 Yankelovich survey did not address the issue of whether gay households had higher averages of "discretionary" income because, for example, they have fewer children or are more likely to rent rather than own a home. So it did not test the common theory that the consciously gay market is mostly an urban one, made up of either single people or two working partners, few of whom have children. Marketers who subscribe to this theory think of many gay people as "guppies" (gay, urban professionals) and/or "dincs" (double income, no children). These issues were addressed in a 1995 Yankelovich survey.

The Domino Effect

Despite their limitations, the Simmons Market Research study and the Overlooked Opinions survey got an enormous amount of publicity. The perceptions that they fostered are partially accurate. For even if their real incomes are lower than the popularized figures, a segment of the gay population is well off and tends to have more discretionary income than does the general population. Moreover, it does not take a lot of research to recognize that, however diverse it might be, the gay community is a community, and as such it is subject to trends. Once a trend catches on within a community—especially a hip urban one—there is a good chance it will spread elsewhere.

In recent years, consciousness of these aspects of the gay market has spread from company to company within industries. While some, like Carillon under Roux, have been pioneers, most companies look for some outside assurance that their marketing choices are financially sound, so they watch and follow their competitors, resulting in a "domino effect." Capitalizing on Absolut and Roux's success, the alcohol industry was the first to perceive a clear interest in cultivating the gay market. It is unlikely that Coors, Philip Morris, or Anheuser-Busch would currently be advertising in lesbian and gay media if Absolut had not jumped in first. Other alcohol marketers, such as Hiram Walker, Schieffelin and Somerset Company, and William Grant have followed.

Just as interest in the gay market has spread within industries, it is likely to make its way throughout different divisions of big corporations, as they test the waters with one product and learn that it pays off. In early 1994, Absolut moved its business from Carillon to New York's Joseph E. Seagram and Sons, while Carillon was signed to market and distribute Stolichnaya vodka, which is owned by the beverage and fast food giant PepsiCo, whose products and franchises include Pepsi-Cola, Mountain Dew, Frito-Lay snack foods, KFC, Pizza Hut, and Taco Bell. When asked by *The Advocate* about the advertising plans for his new vodka client, Roux (still the head of Carillon) declared, "We are planning on staying very close to the gay community. The investment will be in the same style and backed by the same dollars as before. You can count on it."

It's possible that PepsiCo's approach to the gay market for Stoli might eventually spread to some of the company's other products. Leaving Stoli's marketing to Carillon allows PepsiCo the luxury of approaching the gay market indirectly. If Roux can bring the same kind of success to Stoli that he brought to Absolut by advertising to lesbians and gay men, wouldn't PepsiCo be tempted to approach gays and lesbians with some of its other products?

With its Miller Brewing Company already there, it was logical for Philip Morris to begin advertising its cigarettes in the gay media. In 1992, Philip Morris became the first tobacco company to advertise in a national gay magazine when it included ads in *Genre* as part of its new ad campaign for Benson & Hedges Special Kings. Philip Morris also took the unusual and laudable step of moving into the political arena for lesbians and gays, when Miller joined several other large businesses (including Levi-Strauss) in supporting California's proposed gay-rights law in 1992. (Governor Pete Wilson had cited corporate opposition as a factor in his veto of a similar bill in 1991.) In late 1993, Philip Morris made its highest-profile lesbian and gay marketing commitment to date when the Miller Brewing Company signed on (with Continental Airlines) as one of the first major, mainstream companies to sponsor June 1994's Gay Games IV and Cultural Festival in New York City, the year's premiere lesbian and gay event.

Seagram, the only Fortune 1000 liquor distributor to advertise in the lesbian and gay media, has made a point of cultivating a similarly broad relationship with the gay community. Seagram has sponsored events in the lesbian and gay community, including Labor Day L.A., events during Palm Springs' annual White Party weekend, and events for the Gay and Lesbian Alliance Against Defamation. Seagram has also been involved with New York's Hetrick Martin Institute, which supports and educates lesbian, gay, and bisexual youth.

Of course, a company's mere presence in the pages of gay magazines doesn't mean that it is gay-positive in its internal practices, such as hiring gay employees or promoting a gay-friendly work atmosphere. Some advertisers with an apparent interest in gay consumers are even reluctant to be identified as marketing to the gay community. The Gap, for example, refuses to discuss its marketing strategies, even though it appears to target some of its ads to gays.

Whatever the political practices of companies that market to the gay community, their ads have fueled a boom in upscale national gay and lesbian magazines, dating from the 1992 launches of *Out* and *Genre*, both of which set strict guidelines limiting sexual content in order to attract mainstream national advertisers. Shortly thereafter, *The Advocate* spun off its sexually explicit classifieds section and repositioned itself with an overall redesign. These three publications were soon followed by *On Our Backs, Deneuve*, and *Girlfriend*, and the glossies *Ten Percent, POZ*, and, most recently, *Urban Fitness*. At least three new magazines were launched in 1995: *Men's Style, Wilde*, and *50/50*.

Ad Watching

The timidity of companies like The Gap seems to be receding, as a more honest and direct approach proves more effective in winning over the gay community. This evolution of marketing strategies manifests itself in the direct-mail campaigns that MCI and AT&T have conducted, which utilized the large databases that have been developed by direct-mail marketers as a result of years of appeals for AIDS and civil-rights causes.

MCI was first. Of the big three long-distance telephone companies, it was the first one to come out with a direct-mail piece that targeted lesbians and gay men. Mailed in November 1993, the advertising flyer promoted MCI's "Friends and Family" service with the slogan, "When your friends are family." The mailer was sent to gay and lesbian direct-mail lists, but the piece itself was terribly closeted, never once mentioning the "g" word or the "l" word: the "Marketing that Dare Not Speak Its Name."

Still, this mailing was groundbreaking in many ways. Without using the words "gay" or "lesbian," it nevertheless contains a cornucopia of queer codes and images. Its envelope features a photograph of almost a dozen vibrant, multiracial, twenty- and thirty-somethings running up a beach holding hands. Eschewing gender parity—and the possibility of perfect heterosexual pairing-off—the group consists of four women and seven men. Despite the disparity in numbers, however, the photo almost manages to avoid same-sex touching. With men on both ends of the line—and one man mysteriously lurking behind it (and behind a woman)—the models are arranged boy-girl-boy-girl, except for two men next to each other in the center.

What do these projections of the target audience look like? Three of the women have a glamorous appearance, wearing fashionable skirts or dresses with serious hair and make-up, while the fourth woman, in baggy jeans and a t-shirt, has a shaved head (stereotypical lesbian, anyone?). The men are all gym-bodied and well-coiffed and they, too, look as if they are dressed not for the beach but for nightclubbing. One wears a button-down shirt with the sleeves cut off and one is shirtless. Most wear boots—even combat boots or workboots on the ones wearing shorts. The suggestive but restrained photograph is captioned "When your friends are family."

Inside, the message continues this "nontraditional family values" tack, but gets slightly more obtuse: "Long-distance lovers, friends who are important to you but live far away. Some of the closest families today don't necessarily share the same house, same area code, or even the same state." It goes on: "MCI is the best way for you, your friends, family, and lover to stay close." And then there is another picture of the models on the beach. The rigidity of the pose on the envelope has dissolved. The eleven are piled on top of each other, grinning for the camera, and the restraints on same-sex touching are relaxed. Three of the four women are lumped together, lying on top of each other's backs, with arms out of sight. The men are also piled on top of each other's backs, but their hands are everywhere—touching each other's arms and shoulders and chests. The homoeroticism hinted at by physique and dress on the cover of the mailer is explosively realized inside MCI's appeal. At the end of the letter there is one last blatant queer reference. Below the post-script, MCI's satisfaction guarantee appears—in a large triangular box. Even if we didn't know that the piece had been sent out to rented "lesbian and gay" mailing lists, the mailer itself was obviously designed to appeal not just to a young, hip, urban market but to a young, hip, urban, lesbian and gay market. Ultimately, though, despite all the tense suggestion of MCI's mailer, it is still closeted. Even the most blatant sign is still just a sign.

For tens of thousands of lesbians and gay men across the country who had received MCI's closeted mailer, it felt like *déja vu* in May 1994 when they pulled from their mailboxes a letter from AT&T in a lavender envelope with a rainbow-colored phone cord snaking across its front. But this package was different. Not only did it use the "g" and "l" words absent in MCI's piece, but it also included a letter signed by Jody Geiger, manager of AT&T's Long Distance Service, saying that AT&T "respects the diversity that all people represent." AT&T's mailer went out to 70,000 potential customers who were on gay and lesbian mailing lists maintained by Strubco, the community's largest direct mail list broker (coauthor Sean Strub is the company's founder).

Developed with Howard Buford, president of PrimeAccess, a New York City–based agency that specializes in the gay and lesbian market, the mailer's slogan was "It's time for a change." In contrast to MCI's ambiguous imagery, the AT&T mailer depicted several same-sex couples. The glossy image inside was a slightly more professionally oriented version of MCI's mailer: assorted, attractive twenty-somethings (now in suits and dressy casual clothes, instead of beach- or club-wear) were clumped together in various groups, touching each other to suggest lesbian or gay relationships.

AT&T made these suggested relationships unmistakable through its use of captions. A polo-clad man rests his arm on the shoulder of another man in a suit who remarks, "When David's away on business we like to stay close. I love to know what he's doing and what's on his mind." Elsewhere, a lone short-haired woman is pictured saying, "Saving money on long distance is important to me. I don't know who talks to my grandmother longer, me or Claire." The crafty long-distance giant also uses at least one model who has appeared on the cover of a gay magazine—New York City's *Homo Xtra*, a guide to gay nightlife that every week reaches 30,000 of the kind of prospects AT&T is no doubt hoping to attract.

AT&T polished and perfected the suggestive language and symbolism that MCI was experimenting with. And like the MCI letter, AT&T's glossy brochure manages to address its targeted lesbian and gay audience without ever calling them by name. But then AT&T takes the approach one step further—and out into the open. A separate letter is enclosed that begins: "At AT&T, we believe it's important for you to feel good about the company you do business with." It continues: "In fact, AT&T has an environment in which gay, lesbian, and bisexual people feel comfortable in the workplace—and has a longstanding nondiscrimination guideline regarding sexual orientation." That sentence is not only good politics; it's good marketing, enabling lesbians and gay men to feel comfortable about doing business with AT&T in a way that the carefully closeted MCI mailer never could.

The letter is signed not only by AT&T's Long Distance Service Manager but also by the two national co-chairs of LEAGUE, AT&T's very large and powerful gay and lesbian employees' group, and another insert in the envelope details LEAGUE's mission and history. The company is trading on its support of its lesbian and gay employee group—and the group is fully cooperating. By actively helping the company to reach lesbian and gay customers, LEAGUE raised its cooperation with management to an unprecedented level among gay and lesbian employee groups.

AT&T spokesperson Matthew Benner, a marketing manager for domestic consumer services, says that the company was surprised and pleased at the number of people who complimented them on the campaign, including a large number of people who had not gotten a copy in the mail (because they were already AT&T customers) but wanted one.

The mailer was one of a series of campaigns that AT&T sent to various "niche" markets: Asian Americans, seniors, the deaf, and so on; but it was AT&T's first foray into our market. AT&T has been unwilling to reveal the campaign's results, but an indication of its success is that four AT&T divisions have since signed on to work with PrimeAccess: long-distance, corporate, business communications, and consumer products.

"The big thing in this market is being first," says Howard Buford. "People who come in second are seen as cowards by this market." In this case, the important thing was to be first into the market with an *openly* gay campaign.

The trend toward marketing to the gay community intensified in 1993 and 1994. In March 1994, the Swedish furniture and housewares chain Ikea began an advertising campaign in the United States that featured a gay male couple shopping for a dining room table together and discussing how they met and about possibly adding a leaf to the table if the relationship flourishes.

Ikea said that this was the first advertisement featuring a gay couple to appear on mainstream television, whereas many mainstream advertisements had appeared in the gay press or other gay media outlets. The Ikea ad was run on local television in four major markets where Ikea has stores—New York, Los Angeles, Philadelphia, and Washington.

Joining the home furnishings advertisers who are targeting the gay market is Dial-a-Mattress, the well-known telemarketing company with the slogan, "Take off the last 's' for savings." The company had a full-page ad in the December/January 1994/1995 issue of *Out* magazine. Unlike some other advertisers (such as Saab, also in *Out*), Dial-a-Mattress created two special ads for its gay-themed campaign: both show two men together on a mattress. One is titled "A King for Every Queen," and the other reads "We Support More Than Your Back." The copy in each piece says the company can "help you choose the right mattress for your lifestyle." The mattress is delivered by a delivery woman.

"We wanted to show gays and lesbians that Dial-a-Mattress knows them as people and as customers," said Daniel Flamberg, the company's director of marketing. "It's taken some time, but we've recognized this as a niche market which requires a separate creative approach and media strategy, the same way we have recognized the Hispanic market and the deaf market." The ads were created by Mulryan/Nash, a New York ad agency specializing in the gay and lesbian market.

There are now two "affinity" credit cards being marketed specifically to gay men and lesbians issued by People's Bank of Bridgeport, Connecticut. People's is among the top thirty national credit card issuers. In June 1994, People's launched a nationwide Visa affinity credit card, Uncommon Clout, marketed specifically to the gay and lesbian community. Since then, the bank has established a second card, PointOne, also directed to the gay and lesbian market. The company spent more than a half a million dollars on event sponsorships and other marketing in conjunction with the launching of the cards, much of which featured same-sex couples.

The high-tech companies of Silicon Valley and elsewhere have been extraordinarily open to their gay and lesbian employees, offering domestic partnership benefits before firms in any other industry. Some of these companies, such as Apple Computer, have also specifically targeted the gay market with their products. Apple advertised its laptop "Powerbook" computer in the October/November 1993 issue of *Out* magazine, representing the first time a large high-tech company had advertised in a gay and lesbian publication. The ad showed a young male pre-law student and an older established lawyer. On the student's list of files on his PowerBook was a sexually ambiguous phrase: "love letter to Kelly." Gay staffers at Apple campaigned successfully with the advertising department to use the name "Kelly" rather than "Kimberly" (of course, it could have said "Keith," but by such small steps is progress made).

Beyond Backlash

One of the major deterrents to firms thinking about marketing to the gay community is the fear of a backlash from the homophobic elements of our society, especially the organized religious right. But the threat of a right-wing backlash is often overestimated. Probably the most concerted campaign was the boycott of Levi Strauss and Co., conducted by the Rev. Donald Wildmon's American Family Association after the company withdrew funding for the Boy Scouts of America in response to its homophobic policies. The campaign inundated the Levi Strauss headquarters in San

Francisco with 100,000 preprinted postcards. But a company spokesperson said that the campaign had no measurable effect. In fact, in the year it was conducted, 1993, the company experienced record sales and profits. Similarly, Miller Brewing reports that its sponsorship of the Gay Games elicited a small and easily containable negative reaction.

In any case, the benefits of marketing to gay men and lesbians outweigh the risks. As the experience of Absolut vodka shows, those companies that are willing to become identified with the gay community are often able to develop a devoted following. Similarly, Naya Water, a sponsor of the Gay Games as well as many other gay events, has created a name for itself by becoming "our" water. We have even heard gay men in our neighborhood chiding their friends for buying another brand.

Noting such success stories, company after company is following suit, and many are finding that nontraditional means are often the best way to reach the gay community. A Naya competitor, Calistoga Water, handed out flyers at the most recent Gay Pride Parade in San Francisco that said, "We don't label people, just bottles." Perrier passed out a circular to all the houses at the gay resort Fire Island Pines, reminding the residents of the dates for all of the summer's upcoming benefits and prominently displaying its familiar green bottle.

In some cases, there is no threat of a backlash at all, because the products, such as alcoholic beverages, do not appeal to a conservative religious constituency. Michel Roux did not have to worry about a negative effect on sales of Absolut in the Bible Belt by advertising in the gay media, because those sales were negligible. And as the CEO of the ad agency that created the Ikea television spot told the *New York Times*, the company had little concern about right-wing backlash because "the Donald Wildmon fans probably aren't Ikea shoppers in the first place."

On the other hand, marketers of products with mass appeal do take these threats very seriously. Some suspect that one of the reasons MCI and AT&T decided to conduct a targeted direct-mail campaign rather than a print-ad campaign was because they would be less visible. Nonetheless, it didn't take long for the religious right to find out about AT&T's campaign and respond. In the July 1994 issue of the official publication of Pat Robertson's Christian Coalition, readers were alerted to AT&T's direct-mail piece and were encouraged to send letters of protest. The *Philadelphia Inquirer* published a front-page story about an evangelical Christian in Mississippi who canceled his AT&T service in protest.

What the Christian Coalition's exhortations failed to mention, however, was that the religious right is actively trying to line up subscribers for its own affinity long-distance provider: LifeLine. LifeLine declares itself "built on biblical values and centered around the Lord Jesus Christ." It donates 10 percent of its billings to "organizations that oppose abortion, homosexual rights and pornography and that espouse the traditional-family, pro-prayer, home-schooling agenda of the religious right." The organizations funded by LifeLine include the Christian Coalition and Wildmon's American Family Association. LifeLine is currently donating $1 million to these organizations and plans a breathtaking expansion campaign—from 80,000 subscribers at present to 3.5 million in the next five years.

So while the threat of backlash should not be exaggerated, neither should it be dismissed. It makes financial sense for companies to treat the gay community with respect, which means not only supporting our publications with ads but also backing our causes and fighting the antigay work of the right. Things have changed in the last two decades; more and more companies are leaving homophobia behind in their marketing practices and their internal policies. But much more progress remains to be made. Like the first gay business pioneers who saw their new enterprises as a way of serving and helping to create a newly conscious gay community, today's marketers are still fighting the battle to gain acceptance for gay men and lesbians in our society.

3

High Anxiety
I Was a Stepford Queer
at the Inaugural Ball

Donna Minkowitz

This piece, first published in *The Village Voice* during the heady days following Clinton's election in 1992, offers a sobering glimpse of what is now a blurry memory for many—the buoyant mood among gay politicos at glitzy gay and lesbian inaugural events. Reflecting on political shifts since then, Donna Minkowitz wrote the foreword to this volume.

It's strange to reflect that when I wrote this piece, mainstream success and commercialism had not yet become the dominant themes in gay culture. Clinton's victory and our response to it betokened a new era in gay and lesbian politics—an era in which the ideas of gay "power" and "success" have increasingly been interpreted in the most crassly conventional ways.

As part of this shift, gay and lesbian media have become increasingly conservative—especially in economic matters. To lure major advertisers, glossy magazines like *Out*, *The Advocate,* and *Genre* have increasingly focused on so-called lifestyle features—articles about homosexuals who take expensive vacations, cook elaborate meals, go shopping for fun, and never worry about how to pay the rent. Other articles unequivocally celebrate gays and lesbians who've acquired money and power. Gay publications that took more of an interest in working-class gays, like *Gay Community News* and much of the older lesbian press, have largely gone by the wayside (*Gay Community News* has recently been revived by a dedicated collective, but there are no plans for it to resume on a weekly basis).

And for the first time, there are glossy lesbian magazines, in whose pages a new figure, the glossy lesbian, gladly pursues consumerism, mainstream success, and conventional beauty. In these mags, lesbians are much more interested in attending the right parties than in protesting Newt, Clinton, or anybody else.

As I hope to show in the article that follows, assimilation is terribly seductive, and all of us are drawn to it to some degree. Every time we give in to the impulse to be thought *important enough, beautiful enough, powerful enough, real enough, rich enough,* we have spurred the transition from queer to certified.

*   *   *

Could anyone have predicted that the 1993 presidential inauguration would feature no fewer than six homosexual events (not including what went on in houses and bushes throughout the District)? After years of donning straight disguises to cover Republican events, I never thought I'd be brushing up my tux for a salute to a homosexual Friend of Bill.

This was the tribute to L.A. politico David Mixner, sponsored by the Gay and Lesbian Victory Fund. In a video modeled on the Bill films shown at the Democratic convention, the pudgy political consultant was eulogized as the man who made the gay and lesbian community great. "When I am talking to David Mixner," activist Tanya Domi intoned, "I know that whatever I am telling this man, he is taking directly to the president-elect." I kept watching for testimonials from Mixner's tricks, but in this brave new gay world, it is social, not sexual, power that matters. Both sides of the Capitol Hilton's stage were bedecked with the presidential seal. Above, in gold script, was this credo: " 'I have a vision, and you are part of it'—Bill Clinton."

Clinton had uttered this fateful sentence at a campaign fundraiser sponsored by a gay group in Los Angeles. It was quoted endlessly by speakers at the various gay inaugural events, who seemed to feel that it carried the weight of a signature on a check. Activists who had been devalued their entire lives suddenly felt *authorized,* whether it was from seeing David Wilhelm, the new Democratic National Committee chair, hug a gay man onstage, or from the tickets some had snagged to elite parade-viewing bleachers or balls for *machers* only.

People kept whispering that they felt like they were back at their high school graduations. Lining up to shake hands with Mixner, the partygoers could have been nerds doing high fives with the gofer for the football star. Finally, to know someone who knows someone who knows power! In the intoxicating glow of straight approval, no one thought to examine the price of transition from queer to certified.

I felt trippy and lightheaded myself when, to a roomful of professional activists and conscientious scions attending the National Gay and Lesbian Task Force's inaugural eve dinner, Janis Ian proclaimed herself a lesbian. "To someone like me, growing up a homosexual in America, it's exciting to go to P-town now and to see these 14 year-old girls in crew cuts who think nothing of asking each other for a date." Then she sang, "At Seventeen," and the song revealed its hidden meaning: "We all play the game, and when we dare/Cheat ourselves at solitaire/Inventing lovers on the phone/Repenting other lives unknown. . . . It isn't all it seems at 17."

The following evening, Melissa Etheridge followed her out. "I'm proud to be a lesbian," the singer told revelers at the Triangle Ball. The parade of female stars willing to consider tribadism got nearly as long as Emily's List. No less a personage than Elvira said she wasn't gay but could easily be convinced. Then a soused k. d. lang draped herself over a balcony to declare, "The best thing I ever did in my life was to come out."

By the time I saw Peri Jude Radecic, acting executive director of NGLTF, hoisting a toast to Bill's "health and long life" in her black leather skirt, I knew I wasn't a friend of Dorothy's anymore. I was a friend of Bill. I anxiously waited for word of whether he would bestow the ultimate validation by attending any of the gay events. Despite the buzz, he didn't show. "We wanted the money we raised to go to gay and lesbian candidates," explains William Waybourn, executive director of the Gay and Lesbian Victory Fund, which sponsored the Mixner tribute. "The president's people told us he would only appear at events where the proceeds went to pay for the inaugural."

Meanwhile on the Capitol steps, Clinton said "AIDS" and Maya Angelou said "gay." We watched the swearing-in on three TV screens, downing mimosa after mimosa at a Human Rights Campaign Fund brunch for major donors. Breakfasting on salmon mousse and asparagus, hobnobbing with homos of wealth, it occurred to me that my working-class girl's elation at fine dining and scoping was the same as the gay and lesbian revelers' awe at the Mixner event. Access, even sixth-removed, is intoxicating to anyone who's been shut out—but I kept wishing we hadn't been such cheap dates.

At the Triangle Ball, kicked-out Midshipman Joe Steffan sang the national anthem while an honor guard of homosexuals purged from the military carried in the flag. I had to keep reminding myself that the military was at the moment bombing hotels in Iraq. Earlier, gay and lesbian activists had proclaimed a "gay corner" on Pennsylvania Avenue, from which to view the inaugural parade. It was filled with sodomites waving American flags. As I watched queer couples waving to the crowd from their perch on the American Family float, I wondered what was next—a Harvey Milk balloon in the Thanksgiving Day parade?

What had become of our war with traditional values? Where were sexual freedom, the critique of the family, and the memory of a group called the Gay Liberation Front as we swayed to the Sousa played by a gay marching band? Even women in tuxes had become just another signifier of power. And why were there only two men in drag at the ball, and hundreds of women in tails? Because the festivities were about power, not transgression. Even the frisson of genderbending was lost in the glow of privilege, and I was glad to shed my tux. I'd begun to feel as crimped and molded as any straight man in a suit and tie.

At the Triangle Ball, we got a gay version of the Fleetwood Mac-with-multicolored-balloons moment that had given the Democratic convention its buzz. As "Don't Stop" played, homoerotic images from the election flashed on a giant video screen; delegates with "Gay and Lesbian Rights" signs, Tipper and Hillary close-dancing, Bill and Al holding hands aloft. Red, white, and blue balloons, some of them enormous, fell from the ceiling, and we started to play volleyball with them. I flashed back to the moment at the Republican convention when a similar flood of balloons had fallen from the top of the Astrodome. Forgetting the hatred I had heard minutes earlier, I started to play with the balloons, caught up in the ebullience of the crowd. Politicians of all stripes manipulate by fostering the feeling of inclusion; under balloons that are always dispensed at such events, regardless of their meaning, I caught the feeling, gay liberation as Pepsi commercial.

Note

Reprinted with permission from *The Village Voice*, February 2, 1993, p. 30.

4

Sexuality, Class, and Conflict in a Lesbian Workplace

Kath Weston and Lisa B. Rofel

On its publication in 1984, this study of strife at a lesbian auto repair shop was one of the first critical attempts to comprehend the relationship between economics and gay life in the United States. The authors employ techniques of anthropological analysis to paint a rich, complex portrait of a lesbian community, narrating a tale of commitment and betrayal and revealing the roots of the conflict in dynamics of class and sexuality.

Lesbian-feminist discussions of class and conflict have defined class almost exclusively in liberal terms by reducing it to a matter of individual background.[1] "Liberal" in this sense describes not a position on the political spectrum from left to right but a conception of society as a collection of individual actors who make independent choices based on free will alone. These liberal assumptions are not unique to lesbian feminism; indeed, they underlie the dominant world view in American society, with intellectual antecedents far back in the western tradition.[2] As lesbians concerned about recent conflicts in lesbian institutions, we have found that liberal interpretations leave too many questions unanswered about how class affects the way power and privilege are structured in those institutions. Socialist-feminist and Marxist analyses offer valuable criticisms of individualistic approaches to class theory, but are of limited use insofar as they ignore debates about sexuality and sexual identity or assume that sexuality and class constitute discrete levels of oppression.[3]

Our intention in this article is to move toward an integrated theory of class and sexuality that views class as the ongoing production of social relations structured through the division of labor, rather than simply as class background, and that also comprehends the significance of lesbian identity as a historical construct affecting social relations in lesbian institutions.

In order to examine these issues in a specific context, we undertook a case study of a recent strike at a lesbian auto-repair shop in a metropolitan area with a sizable lesbian community. The study was based on in-depth interviews with eight of the ten women who worked in the shop at the time of the strike, including the two owners.[4] Although this is just one example of the conflicts that have emerged in lesbian institutions in recent years, its dynamics clarify cultural constructs and material relations that operate in larger social processes.

The women we interviewed constitute a fairly diverse group of self-identified lesbians. The different conceptions they have of their lesbian identity are reflected in the labels they choose to describe themselves—"queer," "gay," "dyke," or "lesbian." Some consider themselves feminists; others do not. Some are in long-term relationships with lovers; some are not. Two coparent children. They range in age from mid-twenties to late thirties. They locate their class backgrounds along a continuum from working class to upper-middle class, with both workers and owners at each end of the spectrum. Everyone is white; two of the women are Jewish. For reasons of space, we are unable in this analysis to explore the interconnections among race, ethnicity, class, and sexuality, a topic we believe is crucial for any comprehensive theory of conflict in lesbian institutions.

Although all the women interviewed were willing to be quoted by name, we have chosen to alter their names as well as the name of the business. This strike has generated a certain amount of controversy, and we want to be able to explore the theoretical issues it raises without reducing those issues to the sum of the personalities involved.

History of the Conflict

Amazon Auto Repair was founded in 1978 by two lesbian auto mechanics, Carol and Lauren, with $1,400 in capital from personal savings. Within the first two years, their financial success led them to hire several more mechanics, who were paid on a commission basis of 50 percent. In the summer of 1981, the owners embarked on a major expansion, raising the total number of employees to eleven. When their clerical worker left in August of that year, both owners went into the office, discontinuing the practice of one owner supervising on the shop floor at all times.

The first overt incident in the conflict occurred about this time when Mary, the parts runner at the bottom of the job hierarchy, refused to stop working on a car in order to get lunch for everyone, as had been her custom. The owners not only insisted that this task was one of her job responsibilities but also added office filing to her duties, a change she resisted. In Mary's view, they also reneged on their earlier promise to make her an apprentice.

When the owners responded to new problems and pressures associated with expansion by tightening shop discipline, conflicts with other employees seemed to escalate as well. Tensions erupted at Christmas when the owners gave each employee a small gift that included a nail brush and chocolate-covered almonds. The workers, insulted by what they regarded as insignificant gifts in place of bonuses, presented the owners with a list of issues and demands calling for continued commissions with a guaranteed base pay of $200 per week, paid sick leave, and a paid vacation, and a salaried shop manager. On February 2, 1982, the owners distributed statements rejecting the employees' demands, accompanied by nonnegotiable job descriptions that put everyone on an hourly wage effective the following week. That Friday, the workers asked the owners to postpone implementation of the descriptions and to meet with them in order to discuss salaries, the apprenticeship promised Mary, and other issues.

At this meeting the owners informed their employees they could no longer work at Amazon if they did not sign the job descriptions by 8 A.M. that day. Employees refused and, claiming they felt sick, left the shop. While the owners insist the employees walked out on their jobs, the workers say they were essentially locked out. The workers promptly filed charges of unfair labor practices with the National Labor Relations Board and set up a picket line, successfully turning away much of Amazon's business.

On February 24, the owners offered immediate and unconditional reinstatement under the old working conditions if the workers would drop all charges. But contrary to their stated intentions, the owners instituted speedups, set up procedures for signing in and out, and fired Mary for refusing to do filing. Two days later the workers went on strike. After picketing for several weeks with no sign of negotiations resuming, the workers reluctantly decided to join the Machinists Union and sought other employment. The owners continue to operate the business with a reduced staff of new employees. Technically the Amazon conflict still has not been resolved, but a year after the strike workers have given up hope of reaching a settlement.

Bridging the Public and Private

The establishment of Amazon as a lesbian workplace challenged one of the deepest cultural divisions in American society: the split between private and public life. The very categories "lesbian" and "work" mirror this dichotomy, since lesbian identity has historically been defined in terms of the sexual and the personal,[5] whereas wage work in a capitalist context constitutes the public activity par excellence. In a homophobic society, any attempt to establish an institution that links lesbian identity and productive activity entails—not as a matter of ideological principle but by definition—a renegotiation of the culturally constructed boundary that differentiates public and private spheres. To the degree that Amazon integrated these spheres by hiring lesbians and bringing them into an environment that encouraged them to be "out" on the job, it not only provided a space sheltered from the heterosexism of the wider society but also undermined the compartmentalization of lives and self characteristic of most workplaces. Out of this radical potential to create a nonalienating work environment emerged an atmosphere of involvement, excitement, and commitment at Amazon during its early years. An analysis of the reconciliation of private and public inherent in the project of a lesbian workplace cannot explain Amazon's ultimate failure to realize this radical potential. But because sexual and class politics meet at the boundary between personal and public life,[6] such an analysis is crucial for understanding aspects of the Amazon case that resemble conflicts in other lesbian institutions and that distinguish it from more traditional labor disputes.

The measure of what made Amazon a specifically lesbian workplace was not the sexuality of individual employees or the women's music played on the shop floor but the extent to which sexual identity received public affirmation in a place where being a lesbian was the rule rather than the exception.[7] Being out at Amazon was different from "coming out" at a straight workplace because, as one mechanic put it, workers "didn't *have* to talk about being dykes. It was pretty obvious!" Yet, as another woman said, "You could go in and when you're sitting around having lunch you could talk about your family, you could talk about your lover, you could talk about what you did last night. It's real nice to get that out and share that." Conversations at work led to friendships that carried over into the evenings and weekends. Women went to flea markets together, carpooled to work, cooked dinner for one another, and attended each other's sporting events. Lovers were treated as members of the extended Amazon "family" and welcomed into the shop during business hours. One woman's lover acknowledged: "There's nothing like walking into a women's[8] business and being able to walk right up to my lover and kiss her and have lunch with her and have my kids behind me, our kids. But you can't do that in the straight world, you know? It was a real valuable place to be." Friendship spanned all levels of the job hierarchy, weaving together employees' lives inside and outside work.

In a sense, Amazon resembled other small and alternative businesses that foster the development of multiplex ties among employees. Although such businesses often promote an integration of personal and work relationships, the size of an enterprise does not necessarily contribute to a breakdown of the private/public split within the self. The compartmentalization of life in western industrial societies often leads individuals in public situations to withhold full expression of their feelings, sexuality, and other central aspects of identity regarded as private.[9] One decisive difference between Amazon and the "straight" businesses that employees mentioned in contrast was the way public and private aspects of the self were united once lesbian identity became linked to productive activity. In attempting to elucidate how lesbian identity shaped social relations at Amazon, we are not asserting that the reconciliation of the cultural dichotomy between public and private is characteristic of lesbian institutions alone. A similar integration may occur in any organization of an oppressed group that explicitly invokes racial, ethnic, gender, or sexual identity to set the institution and its members apart from the dominant society. At the same time, we believe there are factors unique to lesbian institutions that affect the way conflicts are generated and negotiated but that cannot be explored here. These include the effect of same-sex romantic and sexual involvements on work relationships; the possibility that lesbian institutions foster what Audre Lorde calls "the power of the erotic," which may contribute to the transformation of alienated labor;[10] and the ways in which lesbian-feminist ideology, the organization of production, and systems of meaning originating in the wider lesbian community interact in the formation of lesbian workplace culture.

A principal effect of structuring Amazon so that lesbians could "be themselves" at work was the integration of emotions into workplace dynamics. "There was far more feeling than there ever is when it's just a cold business situation with men," remembered one owner. The reason was not simply, as she surmised, that women are socialized to express their feelings more freely than are men. Most former Amazon employees emphasized that their present work situations in straight businesses are not as emotional for them. But as a lesbian-identified workplace, Amazon encouraged the women who worked there to bring with them onto the shop floor the entire range of emotions and personal attributes associated with identity in American culture.[11]

Despite the lesbian-feminist principles of Amazon's owners, it is important to remember that this integration of public and private was not the product of a shared ideology. The commitment workers felt to Amazon was developed on the job, not brought to the workplace from other contexts. Some started their jobs with a nine-to-five attitude, only to find themselves becoming increasingly involved in what happened during business hours. It would therefore be a mistake to portray the Amazon conflict as a case in which women's unrealistically high expectations for an alternative institution led to disappointment when those expectations could not be met.

When she first came to Amazon from her job in a straight repair shop, one woman said, "I didn't *have* different expectations." But within a month, she was "like a kid in a candy store." It was precisely because working at Amazon had been such a positive, fulfilling experience, said another, that the rift between the owners and workers came as such a shock and a loss: "That's why [leaving Amazon] feels like death. It was a part of my life—it was a part of our [family's] life—that would have gone on and on." By December 1981 the excitement of earlier years had given way to feelings of anger and betrayal, feelings so intense that the women involved in the dispute still dream about Amazon a year after the strike. "It hurts more with lesbians," concluded one mechanic, recalling that it had felt as though her whole being were under attack. The hurt was as much a product of the integration of private and public as the fulfillment that preceded it. In most work situations, the compartmentalization of life and self that accompanies alienation also protects individuals from the destructive effects of fixed power inequities.[12] Without that protection, the women at Amazon found themselves particularly vulnerable as tensions began to explode.

When Mary refused to get the mechanics' lunches, her intention was to defend herself against what she regarded as the owners' arbitrary exercise of power. Because she refused on the grounds that this task was a personal favor rather than a job duty, she tacitly reinvoked the private/public split. As the conflict deepened, attempts to reaffirm this distinction assumed a key position in the strategies of both parties. Workers called for a "businesslike" handling of affairs and tried to put their emotions aside. The owners took steps to distance themselves from workers by curtailing friendships and adopting written rules. By the time women were called back to work, the employee phone had been disconnected, giving symbolic emphasis to the new segregation of work from personal life.

Even as Amazon's radical potential to provide a nonalienating work environment was being undermined, its distinctive characteristics as a lesbian workplace continued to shape the course of the conflict by focusing the struggle on the division between the private and the public. But with the reaffirmation of the private/public split, many of the special qualities that distinguished Amazon from straight repair shops seemed to disappear. "I'm not in business to be a machine, to be a man, to be something I don't want to be," protested one owner. "This wasn't what we wanted to create," insisted the other. Both sides were left wondering how the conflict could have escalated so quickly, destroying relationships of trust and cooperation built up over three and one-half years.

The Politics of Trust

In the eyes of everyone who worked there, Amazon was built on trust. The owners trace this to their political commitment to lesbian feminism, which fostered a sense that a common lesbian identity would override other differences.[13] Before the February 8 walkout/lockout, neither owner seriously believed a strike could occur at Amazon. They displayed a similar degree of confidence in each other when they elected to go into business without a partnership agreement. For the workers, trust was not so much an outgrowth of ideology as a consequence of the multiplex ties that developed in the workplace. Not all employees identified strongly as feminists or saw themselves engaged in the project of creating a feminist business. But for workers and owners alike, trust was underpinned by friendships and the support Amazon provided for being openly and proudly lesbian.

From the beginning Lauren and Carol stressed that they were the owners, that Amazon was not a collective, and that they reserved the right to make all business decisions. Beyond these ground rules, however, they assumed a basic compatibility between their needs and those of their employees. In accordance with a feminist ideology that valued being "nurturing" and "supportive," the owners installed a separate phone for employees' use and agreed to flexible scheduling around women's extrawork commitments. The lack of set policy and formalized rules, combined with the owners' efforts not to "act like bosses," made it easy to believe that everyone was equal at Amazon and that trust grounded in the integration of public and private life would constitute a sufficiently radical solution to the problems of oppression women face in other workplaces. But in the absence of a clearly defined business structure, this trust became politicized when owners and workers had to rely on interpersonal relationships to negotiate labor relations from day to day. The emergence of a politics of trust at Amazon points to a conclusion the owners never reached and the workers only gradually realized: the personal can be political, even among lesbians, whenever the personalization of work relations obscures power differentials structured through property relations and the division of labor.

As managers, the owners had the authority to define and evaluate others' needs, transforming what would otherwise have been examples of mutual agreement into instances of benevolence. Even if they had been able to satisfy every request or concede every point raised by employees, control of the business altered the meaning of their actions. What the owners perceived as gifts or favors the workers often saw as customs or rights. It is not surprising, then, that the owners began to get angry when workers stopped asking permission for routine procedures such as leaving early when work was finished for the day. Conversely, the workers' mistrust for the owners developed when Lauren and Carol chose to assert their covert power—for example, when they tried to force Mary to get lunches or do filing. For some workers the strike came to be seen as a fight to create a work environment in which the owners "would not have the power to say one thing and do another thing and change things around" when their decisions could have a major impact on employees' livelihoods.

It was not coincidental that the politics of trust fragmented along class lines, pitting owners/managers against workers. But because such a politics was grounded in interpersonal relationships, it tended to personalize the issues for the women involved, leading them away from a relationally defined class analysis. The politics of trust, rooted in the liberal conception of autonomous selves interacting on a basis of equality, supported interpretations that reduced the conflict to a matter of individual actions, intentions, and capabilities.

The analysis of the conflict favored by the owners was built on a personality/provocateur theory, which held that the strike was instigated either by chronically dissatisfied workers or by someone in league with outside forces interested in destroying a "growing, thriving lesbian business." The owners alternately portrayed the workers as lazy, irresponsible, resentful because of unrequited love, or consciously determined to undermine their business. Power enters into this analysis only in the owners' focus on the individual psychology of certain employees who allegedly were not comfortable accepting authority and so created a strike situation in order to feel some measure of control.[14]

Explanations that ascribe the conflict to static personality traits fail to account for the workers' movement from enthusiasm to anger over time. The provocateur theory provides no better explanation, since it discounts the solidarity maintained by the workers throughout the struggle.[15] To speak of the "mob mentality" that held workers together, or the weakness of character that prevented individuals from standing apart from the group, implies that the workers followed one another like sheep, without legitimate grievances and a clear understanding of their own actions. The owners' preoccupation with the personality/provocateur theory also draws attention away from the possibility that they too might be implicated in the conflict.

The workers were less inclined to reduce the conflict to personalities, insisting instead that "nobody [at Amazon] was a good guy or a bad guy." They learned to distinguish between an individual's particular attitudes or competencies and her standing in the job hierarchy. Rather than defending Mary's actions, they identified broader problems with training and apprenticeship. Rather than attacking Carol's decision to side with Lauren about the lunches, they criticized the division of labor that induced the owners to take the same position. However, this growing awareness of structural factors underlying the conflict existed alongside, and in contradiction with, a set of liberal presuppositions evident in the workers' two most popular explanations for the dispute: the miscommunication theory and the mismanagement theory.

The miscommunication theory represents the women of Amazon as equal, rational, independent individuals who came into conflict only because they misunderstood one another. Individual interviews clearly show, however, that both sides in the dispute could accurately reproduce the other's point of view. In addition, the premises of this theory are invalidated by the power differential that allowed the owners to set the terms for communication and to refuse to negotiate with their employees.

The mismanagement theory depicts the owners as incompetent managers; presumably, if Lauren and Carol had taken a few business courses or had acquired more experience running a shop, the conflict could have been avoided. Although this analysis recognizes the power differential at Amazon, it does not call for a redistribution or redefinition of power, because it shares the owners' basic assumption that the needs of employers and employees can always be reconciled. But if we consider needs as historical products tied to a changing division of labor,[16] it becomes apparent that merely substituting more competent actors or rectifying individual "mistakes" would not have been sufficient to prevent these needs from coming into conflict.

We believe that a class analysis is essential for comprehending the social, historical, and structural factors shaping the conflict that these theories ignore. By class we mean the relations of property and production mediated by the division of labor that separated the women of Amazon into owners/managers and workers, adding a dimension of power to personal relationships that politicized bonds of mutual trust. In our view, material factors like ownership, the division of labor, and the organization of production are dynamically interrelated with the production of needs, culture, perceptions, and feelings. Obviously, then, we disagree with those who interpret class in a narrowly economistic or deterministic sense. The way in which the public/private split is bridged by linking lesbian identity to productive activity demonstrates that class relations alone cannot explain events at Amazon. But without an understanding of class relations, lesbian feminism remains grounded in the same liberal, individualistic assumptions that originally led the women of Amazon to expect the bonds of trust to prevail over any dissension that could arise.

Class Relations and the Organization of Production

Class relations at Amazon, based on a hierarchical division of labor that enabled two individuals to own the business and maintain the power to define the conditions under which the others would work, shaped the tensions that eventually led to the strike. From the beginning, these tensions were inherent in the organization of production at Amazon, particularly in four key areas: the commission system, job allocations, apprenticeships, and informal job definitions.[17] They surfaced and became the focus of overt conflict only after the owners decided to expand the business and work in the office, creating a dichotomy between mental and manual labor that sharply distinguished owners from workers. In the face of these changes, Lauren and Carol found themselves struggling to defend their prerogatives as owners as their needs increasingly came into contradiction with the needs of their employees.

Carol and Lauren certainly never aspired to be bosses. In establishing Amazon they were motivated not by the desire for profit or the will to exercise power for power's sake but by the vision of working independently and determining the conditions of their own labor. Like many entrepreneurs who open small businesses, they initially hoped to escape the alienation[18] they had experienced in other work situations: "Do we want to work for those creepy lawyers and doctors for the rest of our lives? Or do we want to try to set up something that's ours? It may be a lot of things, but it will at least be ours." The connection Lauren and Carol drew between ownership and self-determination lay behind their insistence on maintaining control as tensions heightened during the months prior to the strike.

When Carol and Lauren first began to hire mechanics to work under them, they decided to pay them by commission rather than by salary to ensure that the fledgling business would not go in the red. The commission system allowed mechanics a degree of control over their work, an arrangement that neither owner initially regarded as problematic but that later became a key issue in the struggle. Because mechanics were paid not by the hour but for jobs actually completed, they came to feel, as one mechanic phrased it, that "the time we worked there was our time." Some saw themselves more as subcontractors than employees, insisting, "All we were doing, really, is using [the owners'] space and giving them half the money we made." Workers felt not so much a time obligation to Amazon as an obligation to get the work done.

The commission system also tended to give employees a clearer picture of how Amazon made its profit and how much of that profit came from their labor: "We could see how much money they made off of our labor. . . . You doubled everybody's wages and they got it, plus the money they made on parts." This perception of the relation between their work and the business's prosperity fed the workers' sense of outrage when the owners refused to negotiate the terms of the February job descriptions.

The owners' control of job allocations constituted another potential source of conflict. A mechanic's commission-based income was contingent on the availability of work and on whether or not she received time-efficient jobs that matched her skill level. Several workers recalled being the "star" or the "fave" when they first arrived at Amazon only to become the recipients of time-consuming "shit jobs" as newer employees were given preferred assignments. Although not all the mechanics at Amazon experienced favoritism, concentration of the power to allocate jobs in the hands of the owners made the workers equally dependent on Carol and Lauren's continued good will.

Training and apprenticeship were vital under commission, since specialization in only a few tasks left an apprentice-level mechanic particularly vulnerable to job-allocation decisions. Without adequate supervision and opportunities to learn new skills, a novice assigned an unfamiliar task lost time and money, as did the more experienced mechanics she turned to for help. At Amazon, apprenticeship was not a formal program but a loosely structured arrangement in which employees were told an owner would be available to assist them when necessary. After the owners moved into the office, however, apprentices were largely left to fend for themselves in what became an increasingly untenable position.

Finally, the informality of job definitions under the politics of trust highlighted the inconsistencies between the owners' feminist ideals and Amazon's actual business structure. The owners promised their parts runner, Mary, that she could become an apprentice as part of their commitment to helping women enter the auto-repair trade. At the same time, however, the owners expected her to continue to make herself generally available to meet their needs because she was the only salaried worker below them in the job hierarchy. Without reorganizing the division of labor, the owners never provided the conditions that would have made it possible for Mary to become a mechanic. Nor were the owners willing to relinquish their control over defining the content of workers' jobs, as Mary discovered when she confronted them on this issue.

Because capitalist culture values conceptual work over the "mere" execution of ideas,[19] the mental/manual division between owners and employees that arose in the late summer of 1981 reinforced the owners' power to set the terms for the other women's labor. In practice, this separation meant that the two owners' needs and perceptions became more congruent and more opposed to those of their employees. One owner noted, "There's always been a kind of an 'us' and a 'them' between the office and the shop," a division that separated even the two owners when they worked in different spheres. "You're in the shop and you see everything from the mechanics' side. You're in the office and you see everything from the customers' side." For Carol, "the one thing that was a big pull for me about both of us being in [the office] was that we were going to be on the same side."

The way the owners chose to expand the shop and the creation of a mental/manual split deepened class divisions at Amazon and brought underlying tensions to the fore. A heavier work load, tighter scheduling, and a greater number of mechanics meant an increase in work pressures and a decrease in the time available to resolve conflicts as they emerged. As the owners perceived a need to cut overhead and raise productivity, they began to contest accustomed areas of worker self-determination in a general move to tighten up the shop.

Control over mechanics' hours became a matter of controversy once the owners decided to adhere to a strict 8:30-to-5:30 rule. When workers resisted rigid scheduling by arguing that their time was their own under commission, the owners interpreted their defiance as laziness and a lack of commitment to Amazon's success. In the proposed job descriptions, the owners finally decided to replace the commission system with salaries "because that was the only way . . . we could know we were going to get eight hours of work from people." Many mechanics opposed the change because their new salaries were based on individual averages of their previous year's wages, which meant that they would receive the same amount of money annually for working longer hours.

Meanwhile, the owners' preoccupation with office work meant a decline in income for apprentice-level mechanics, who lacked regular supervision. Although the more experienced mechanics were willing to offer their assistance, they nonetheless resented these costly intrusions on their time. The owners rebuffed the workers' suggestion to pay a mechanic to be a lead worker or supervisor, even though the owners previously had compensated themselves for the same responsibility. Problems involving novice mechanics' limited training and narrow specialization were compounded when the owners allocated simple but money-making jobs to a new employee hired in the fall of 1981, who turned out to be on an apprentice level. The other less-experienced mechanic in the shop promptly witnessed a sharp drop in her weekly paycheck as she lost most of the jobs she knew how to do well. Such actions incensed many workers, ultimately leading to their demand for a steady base pay.

Carol and Lauren found themselves in the middle of yet another struggle when what they saw as a need for greater efficiency with expansion led them to oppose Mary's efforts to renegotiate the definition of her job to meet her need for an apprenticeship. By insisting that Mary get the lunches and do the filing, the owners invoked tasks especially symbolic of female subordination. The other workers, disturbed by the way the owners were "jerking Mary around," made her right to an apprenticeship a major issue as the strike developed.

With tensions mounting, workers saw their Christmas presents as the "last straw." The owners still find it incomprehensible that the workers organized over such a seemingly trivial issue, largely because the owners fail to recognize the symbolic meaning of those presents. Since Christmas bonuses traditionally serve as a statement of evaluation from employers, these token gifts were taken as a "slap in the face" of the workers' commitment to Amazon. The gifts had economic as well as ideological significance, since they were associated with the owners' decision to close the shop for a week, leaving the workers with no income, no Christmas bonus, and, according to employees, no respect. Because the owners were now so clearly treating the other women not as friends and equals but as employees, the Christmas presents symbolized the demise of the politics of trust by marking the class division that later would separate the two sides in the dispute.

Paradigm Shifting:
From the Politics of Trust to the Politics of Contract

As the politics of trust began to disintegrate, the women of Amazon adopted an opposing symbolic paradigm, what we term the politics of contract. It represented an alternative mode of negotiating labor relations in which owners and workers ideally would bargain to agree on a business structure made explicit through written job descriptions and set policies. Although this formulation appears neutral from the standpoint of gender and sexual identity, the women at Amazon came to favor it precisely because the two paradigms of contract and trust were relationally defined by incorporating popular—and opposed—notions of male and female.[20] Although the women at Amazon did not consciously define themselves in relation to men, their understanding of a lesbian business as an "all-giving, all-nurturing, endlessly supportive" institution carried an implicit contrast with the "cold, unfeeling" world of heterosexual male business, where decisions were held to be determined legalistically without regard for workers' needs.[21] Because the categories of "female" and "male" exhaust the range of possible gender attributes in American society, the link between these categories and the two contrasting paradigms made those paradigms appear to be the only conceivable options for conducting labor relations. When the politics of trust proved inadequate, the politics of contract provided a readily available model sanctioned by the dominant society for attempting to settle the growing differences between workers and owners.

Both paradigms obscured class relations within Amazon. Under the politics of trust, the owners had asserted that Amazon was a non-oppressive environment by definition because it provided a haven from the "real world" where women have to "put up with crap from men." This belief allowed them to argue that any woman dissatisfied with working conditions should "go be with the boys," which had the double effect of augmenting their power and suppressing worker initiatives for change. At the same time, industry standards implicit in the contrast between Amazon and the straight male business world could be selectively invoked to justify practices such as paying the parts runner a minimal salary.

The owners' shift toward a politics of contract came in the wake of expansion. In light of their new concern with raising productivity and decreasing overhead, the owners began to perceive their employees as taking advantage of Amazon's loose structure. The institution of a written policy in October marked the owners' first attempt to establish a more structured work environment. To the owners, this deliberate decision to "act like bosses" meant abandoning the ideals of nurturance and sensitivity they associated with lesbian-feminist entrepreneurs to assume the straight male-identified role of a "wrist-slapping disciplinarian." By the time they handed out job descriptions in the form of ultimatums, they had come to see themselves as "behaving maybe the way the boys do when . . . they say, 'This is it. Either you do it or you're not here.' "

The workers also came to accept the framework of the politics of contract in their interactions with the owners, but for very different reasons. Workers began to press for job descriptions, monthly shop meetings, and more specific policies in order to protect themselves against what they regarded as arbitrary assertions of managerial power. The formal presentation of a list of issues and demands represented their attempt to "depersonalize [the situation at Amazon] and make it a business thing."

Because the politics of contract was identified with a combination of formality and male gender attributes, the women of Amazon began to belittle emotional reactions to the growing conflict as responses typical of women but inappropriate to businesslike conduct. In the process, they unknowingly rejected one of the most positive aspects of lesbian workplace culture: the integration of public and private that encourages bringing the whole self, including feelings, into work. Workers criticized the owners for responding "on this real emotional level to our demands, about how we were insulting their intelligence and honor." Meanwhile, the owners dismissed the strike as lacking substantive issues by referring to the emotional weight behind workers' actions. Maintaining the bridge between the private and public would have allowed both sides to acknowledge the intensity of feeling surrounding the dispute without separating emotions from more tangible bread-and-butter issues. Instead, the women at Amazon redrew the private/public boundary by shifting to a paradigm identified solely with the public sphere.

No one at Amazon was satisfied with the character of labor relations under the politics of contract, but the dualistic definition of the two paradigms made contractual relations seem to be the only possible substitute for relations based on friendship and trust. Since both sides viewed the loose structure and informal managerial style associated with the politics of trust as the source of the conflicts at Amazon, both initially expected a shift to a more formalized business structure to solve their differences. While some workers continued to hope for a consensual settlement, others began to understand the conflict as a power struggle rooted in the division of labor that would not be resolved by the establishment of a set policy. Implicit in the struggle over job descriptions was the recognition that measures intended to protect workers could also be used by the owners to maintain control. Workers who once had argued against the commission system opposed conversion to salary on the grounds that an hourly wage would "give [the owners] too much power" by allowing them to regulate employees' hours and subject workers to arbitrary requests.

Despite their growing awareness of the implications of the power differential at Amazon, workers believed the dispute could be resolved within the existing class structure. Yet the issues they raised posed a tacit challenge to relations of production that concentrated decision-making power in the owners' hands. This seeming paradox rests on the fact that, to the degree the workers' stand encompassed a claim to self-determination, their concerns could not have been adequately addressed while class relations at Amazon remained unaltered. Ownership never became an articulated issue, largely because the workers were tactically and philosophically committed to a politics of contract that limited their proposals to discrete, point-by-point demands.

Frustration with the restrictions of a bargaining procedure derived from male trade unionism led the workers to search for a "different way" to approach the owners, but their efforts to break through the paradigms that framed their struggle were unsuccessful. They failed in part because the shift from a politics of trust to a politics of contract focused discussions on questions of work discipline and managerial style. The deeper questions concerning ownership and the division of labor at Amazon, which were mediated by notions of gender and sexual identity, could not be addressed within the terms of either paradigm. The final irony was that the configuration of class relations at the heart of the Amazon conflict was never questioned as being incongruous in a lesbian institution but was instead uncritically adopted from the straight male world.

Lesbian Identity in the Formation of a Workers' Alliance

The radical potential created with the bridging of the private and public was not completely destroyed by the elaboration of class relations and the emergence of open conflict at Amazon. The commitment that accompanied the integration of personal and work life had the radicalizing effect of motivating workers to struggle against what they perceived to be unfair labor practices. The unusually high degree of solidarity maintained by the workers throughout this struggle also had its roots in the kind of workplace Amazon was before the strike. Solidarity among workers was not a deterministic consequence of their being lesbians per se, but an outgrowth of a social context that allowed them to be out on the job in a lesbian-identified institution. Any analysis that reduced events at Amazon to a class conflict without taking these distinguishing features into consideration would miss the dynamics that turned a situation of contention and contradiction into a full-blown labor dispute.

The workers' radicalization was gradual. In the beginning, one mechanic commented, "We weren't a political force; we were just a bunch of women working."

Concern about working conditions led them to meet as a group, but class and politics were not explicit topics at these initial meetings. At first women simply compared their reactions to incidents at work, breaking through the silence surrounding grievances that had kept individuals believing they were the only ones angered and confused by the owners' actions. As workers found their personal experiences confirmed by the experiences of others, they began to discuss the possibility of collective action.

Paradoxically, the same bonds of trust and friendship that made it difficult for many workers to break with the owners also stimulated their willingness to challenge the owners' position. Because the politics of trust masked power inequalities at Amazon, it had encouraged workers to consider all points negotiable and to believe they could ask for whatever seemed "fair" and "reasonable" according to their own needs. When the owners met their list of issues with a set of nonnegotiable job descriptions, the workers' fundamental point of unity became an agreement not to accept the job descriptions in the form of ultimatums.

The workers' ability to achieve and maintain such solidarity is all the more remarkable given the diversity of the group and the differences in their politics. But the foundation for the collective structure that enabled them to mediate their disagreements had already been laid by the patterns of cooperation and strong emotional ties the women had developed by working together in the shop. Workers referred to this sense of camaraderie and closeness to explain what differentiated Amazon from a shop employing straight women, suggesting that these patterns were a product of lesbian workplace culture rather than a composite of individuated ties: "Everybody was a tight group at Amazon. . . . You've got all these dykes! [The owners] used to be a part of that when we were smaller, but then we started getting bigger and everybody had different needs, and so it was 'us' and 'them.' Unfortunately it had to come to that. But we were all pretty grouped emotionally before this stuff came up, so that we were all grouped in battle."

The workers' alliance was based on the synthesis of lesbian identity and a growing awareness of class divisions tied to the division of labor. On the one hand, the women clearly interpreted the conflict as a labor dispute and took a stand based on their needs as workers. On the other hand, they directed their appeals primarily to other lesbians and selected their tactics with the aim of keeping the struggle within the lesbian community.

Sensitivity to stereotypes about lesbians' pugnacity and women's alleged incompetence in business affairs made the workers deliberately protective of Amazon at the gay/straight boundary. Workers consistently refused to address the general public or what they considered the "straight media." They turned to the National Labor Relations Board as a last resort in order to keep the owners' job proposals from taking effect as contracts. Workers reluctantly agreed to bring in the "big boys" from the union only after they felt they had exhausted alternatives within the lesbian community and faced the possibility of having to abandon the strike effort altogether. Today, the union's failure to make progress toward a settlement seems to confirm the workers' original skepticism about the union's commitment to the Amazon struggle and its ability to comprehend the concerns of a lesbian shop.

Stanley Aronowitz has argued that the most significant innovations in recent social theory have come from movements like feminism that have grown up outside the traditional boundaries of Marxist and trade unionist politics. Because strictly economic disputes appear to have lost their subversive potential under advanced capitalist conditions, Aronowitz predicts that questions raised by what he calls "cultural movements" will become the new focus of historical change.[22] Events at Amazon seem to corroborate both hypotheses. However, Aronowitz's thesis is qualified by the fact that lesbian workplaces represent a historically unprecedented form of organizing productive relations that cannot be adequately comprehended by a notion of culture set apart from economic factors. The culture that has emerged in institutions like Amazon is not a simple reflection of lesbian-feminist principles but results in part from the bridge between the public and private spheres created by bringing together in practice the hitherto ideologically opposed categories of labor and sexuality. In the Amazon case, the development of a lesbian workplace culture united workers in a struggle that encompassed both economic and cultural concerns. In this sense, the Amazon conflict challenges socialist-feminist theory to grapple with issues of sexuality, and urges lesbian-feminist theory to move beyond it to focus on sexuality and its legacy of liberal assumptions, in order to develop an analysis of class relations in lesbian contexts.

Conclusion: Class and Sexuality

Why has an ongoing dialogue about class comparable to the current discussion of race and racism failed to emerge within lesbian feminism? The Amazon case draws attention to several contributing factors: (1) the limited interpretation of class as class background favored by lesbian feminists; (2) liberal strains in lesbian-feminist theory that discourage a relational analysis of class focusing on social structure; (3) the institutional hegemony of an entrepreneurial and professional stratum within the lesbian community; and (4) the heterosexual bias of socialist and socialist-feminist approaches to class theory, which limits their applicability to lesbians.

Information on individuals' class backgrounds clearly cannot explain events at Amazon, for women from both middle-class and working-class backgrounds allied on opposite sides of the dispute. "It would be so much easier, in a way," observed the owner who grew up in a working-class household, "if Lauren and I were both upper class and my father gave me $50,000 and her father gave her $60,000, and we plunked it into the bank and started the business . . . but it's not that simple." To claim that class background does not determine present behavior does not mean it did not influence decisions made and strategies adopted during the conflict. For example, the limited resources available to workers from certain class backgrounds made it more difficult for them to remain out on strike. In general, however, Amazon's employees had a clear sense that their current position in the relations of production outweighed their varied class backgrounds: "We all knew where we came from, but we all were working, and we knew how hard we worked, and we knew how we were getting treated. When you're a worker, you're a worker."

A background interpretation of class has led most lesbian feminists to define class according to individualized criteria like occupation, income level, education, values, attitudes, and other indicators of socioeconomic status. While these attributes may be linked to class, they do not define class, unless one accepts the liberal view of society as an amalgam of autonomous actors fixed in absolute class positions. On the basis of occupation, all the women at Amazon could be labeled working class because of their blue-collar trade. If a combination of income and educational attainment were used as a gauge, some workers might be assigned a higher class position than the owners. Aside from the mutual inconsistency of these evaluations, neither offers any insight into the relations of class and power that actively shaped the Amazon conflict.[23] In contrast, placing the owners within the context of the job hierarchy at Amazon and the division of labor that structures ownership in society at large allowed us to explore the power differential that put Lauren and Carol in a position of dominance over other women working in the shop.

A relational analysis of events at Amazon supports the conclusion that, since property relations and the division of labor continuously generate class divisions, tactics of consciousness raising and moral exhortations to eliminate classism will be insufficient to keep conflicts from emerging in lesbian and feminist institutions. The expectation that "feminist morality" or a principled politics can mitigate class differences rests on a notion of politics as an individualized, ideological stance adopted at will, independent of material circumstances and capable of transcending them. But at Amazon, differences in the values and political commitments of the owners did not prevent them from taking the same side in the dispute once lines were drawn. Lauren felt "morally justified" in presenting the workers with nonnegotiable job descriptions, never realizing the extent to which she defined morality and "responsible action" with regard to the needs of the business. Carol, on the other hand, found it "bizarre to be on the side of the owner. It's so much easier for me to think of it from the workers' standpoint." Yet she held to her position.

The owners both supported the principle of solving Amazon's problems through dialogue rather than by firing dissenting employees, yet in the end their power as owners and managers allowed them to abandon this ideal. In Carol's words, "Somebody reached the point where they put their foot down and said, 'That's it.' And you can only do that when you are in the powered position, which we were." Both owners admitted having discussed strategy about the possibility of an employee walkout in response to their job descriptions: "We did discuss it. We said, 'If that happens, the two of us built this from nothing. Now we have the books, we have the diagnostic equipment, we have the customers, we got the building, we're way ahead.' "

In the workers' eyes, control of the property associated with the business gave the owners a decisive advantage during the struggle. When economic necessity forced the workers to drop the picket line to look for other jobs, the prospect of negotiation receded as the owners continued production in the building all ten women had shared before the strike. Since the owners established Amazon with minimal capital investment and took out few loans in the succeeding years, the property and equipment that helped them win the struggle actually came from surplus value created by the combined efforts of Amazon's employees and nonpartisan support from the women's community. The owners' exclusive claim to this property was based solely on a legal concept of ownership backed by a patriarchal state. The same principle of ownership underpinned the dominant class position that structured the owners' moral stance, neutralized their well-meaning intentions, and superseded their lesbian-feminist politics at the point of conflict.

It is true that Amazon is "not Bechtel" (a major multinational corporation), as the owners were quick to point out, but this fact obviously did not prevent class relations and a class-linked conflict from emerging in the shop. Although the lesbian community lies well outside the mainstream of American capitalism, it does include a stratum of entrepreneurs, professionals, and small capitalists like Carol and Lauren who own or control many of the institutions serving and symbolizing that community. We suggest that in practice such control allowed this group of women to maintain an institutional hegemony[24] that mediates the relation of lesbian identity to community in ways that alternately support and oppress lesbians who stand in different relations to the social division of labor.[25]

The concern with self-reliance and independence that originally led Carol and Lauren to become entrepreneurs also informed their argument that dissatisfied workers should open their own enterprises rather than challenge the owners' right to make unilateral decisions in matters affecting employees.[26] Yet what might otherwise be dismissed as regressive, petty-bourgeois values in the tradition of nineteenth-century entrepreneurial capitalism has different meaning, origin, and political significance in this lesbian context. For Lauren and Carol, self-sufficiency represented a liberating ideology that signified autonomy from men in the area of skills, training, and the ability to earn an equitable income. The same ideology became oppressive only when, as owners and employers, they confused self-determination with the need to control the labor of the women they hired.

The coincidence of entrepreneurial values with aspects of lesbian identity in the ideology of self-sufficiency is one more example of the recurrent theme in this study: there is no justification at the level of concrete analysis for abstracting class from sexuality or for treating heterosexism and class hegemony as two distinct types of oppression operating along separate axes. The strike at Amazon cannot be analyzed as a textbook labor conflict precisely because the male and heterosexist bias of most scholarly texts renders them incapable of grasping this integration. While a critique of the bias in class theory is beyond the scope of this paper, the Amazon case indicates why such an integration is necessary.

Lesbians are not simply exceptions to the rule who defy categorization as "nonattached" or "single" (but presumably self-supporting) women or as women residing in households with men.[27] Since most self-identified lesbians in American society expect to support themselves financially, the question of derived class becomes largely irrelevant in speaking of lesbian relationships.[28] None of the women in the Amazon study even suggested the possibility of defining her class position through her lover, though several were in relationships of long standing. Lesbians also fall outside the theoretical focus of most debates in socialist feminism, which tend to center on the sexual division of labor.[29] Although the sexual division of labor and job segregation by sex influence all women's experience, for most lesbians gender distinctions do not coincide with the split between home and work life or with the allocation of tasks within the home. When the split between personal and work life is linked to sexuality with the bridging of the private/public split in lesbian workplaces, socialist feminism proffers no theory capable of grasping the significance of what happens once lesbian identity is joined to productive activity.

At Amazon we saw how the reconciliation of the public and private created the potential for a nonalienating work environment where women were able to develop close ties with coworkers as well as to bring into the shop emotions and other ostensibly personal aspects of the self. After the walkout/lockout, this integration shaped the dispute by placing emotions at the center of the struggle so that at various points the struggle itself involved drawing and redrawing the boundary between elements of public and private life. While the bridging of the private/public split could not defuse class relations at Amazon, it generated the conditions for overcoming class divisions by fostering a lesbian workplace culture that promoted solidarity among the workers and motivated them to defend their needs in a situation where the owners held the balance of power.

One of Amazon's owners ended her interview with a plea that lesbians learn to "put aside personal feelings and vested interests" or risk the destruction of community institutions. A careful analysis of the Amazon dispute points to the importance of taking personal feelings into account rather than putting them aside and remaining within the limitations of the contrasting paradigms of trust and contract. The effect of suppressing or ignoring the personal will be to reinvoke the division between the private and public, when the ability to bridge that gap constitutes one of the greatest strengths of lesbian institutions. In this sense, the experience of the women of Amazon Auto Repair challenges both lesbian feminism and socialist feminism to break through old paradigms, to recognize that separating sexuality and class in theory merely replicates the segregation of the private from the public, and the personal from the political, in the realm of everyday life.

As for vested interests, they cannot simply be discarded at will, since they have material roots in socially constructed needs mediated by property relations and the division of labor. Yet there exist options for restructuring lesbian workplaces that reject ownership while providing leadership roles, job rotation, procedures for delegating responsibility, shared decision-making processes, and a division of labor that does not rest on a fixed power differential. The radical potential for nonalienated labor created in lesbian workplaces invites us to explore these alternatives as a means of redefining power as energy, skill, and capacity rather than as domination.[30] By drawing attention to the ongoing reproduction of class relations within the lesbian community, the struggle at Amazon advances the possibility of self-determination inside and outside the labor process for all lesbians, not just for the few who formally or informally control lesbian institutions.

Notes

This article originally appeared in 1984 in *Signs: Journal of Women in Culture and Society*, Vol. 9, No. 4, pp. 623–646.

Our thanks to the women of Amazon for their willingness to relive their experiences of the conflict with us; and to Jane Atkinson, Akhil Gupta, Nancy Hartsock, Rebecca Mark, Sabina Mayo-Smith, Kathy Phillips, Renato Rosaldo, the San Francisco Lesbian and Gay History Project, and Anna Tsing for their insights and support.

1. For examples of the interpretation of class as class background within the lesbian-feminist movement, see Charlotte Bunch and Nancy Myron, eds., *Class and Feminism* (Baltimore: Diana Press, 1974); Joan Gibbs and Sara Bennett, eds., *Top Ranking: A Collection of Articles on Racism and Classism in the Lesbian Community* (New York: Come!Unity Press, 1980).

2. See Zillah R. Eisenstein, *The Radical Future of Liberal Feminism* (New York: Longman, 1981).

3. Christine Riddiough, "Socialism, Feminism, and Gay/Lesbian Liberation," in *Women and Revolution*, ed. Lydia Sargent (Boston: South End Press, 1981).

4. One woman had moved out of the area, and we were unable to contact the remaining mechanic.

5. Regardless of where one stands in the definitional debate on lesbian identity (see Ann Ferguson, et al., "On 'Compulsory Heterosexuality and Lesbian Existence': Defining the Issues," *Signs: Journal of Women in Culture and Society* 7, no. 1 [Autumn 1981]: 158–99), it is clear that competing usages of the term "lesbian" all rest on criteria such as friendship, sexuality, and feeling, which historically have been assigned to the realm of the personal.

6. See Annette Kuhn and AnnMarie Wolpe, eds., *Feminism and Materialism: Women and Modes of Production* (London: Routledge & Kegan Paul, 1978); Iris Young, "Beyond the Unhappy Marriage: A Critique of Dual Systems Theory," in *Women and Revolution*, ed. Sargent, pp. 43–69.

7. Lesbian identity then becomes a defining element of a distinctive type of workplace culture, making Amazon something more than an aggregation of isolated employees who "happened" to be lesbians or a repository for the piecemeal importation of artifacts from lesbian feminism.

8. In our heterosexist society, "woman" and "feminist" often function as code words among lesbians for "lesbian" and "lesbian feminist," in much the same way as sexism encourages the substitution of "people" or "men" as generic terms for "women."

9. Nancy Hartsock, "Political Change: Two Perspectives on Power," in *Building Feminist Theory*, ed. Quest Staff (New York: Longman, 1981), pp. 3–19.

10. Audre Lorde, *Uses of the Erotic: The Erotic as Power* (New York: Out & Out Books, 1978).

11. The bridging of the private/public split provides a mechanism to explain the high levels of commitment often noted as characteristic of lesbian institutions. See Barbara Ponse, *Identities in the Lesbian World: The Social Construction of Self* (Westport: Greenwood, 1978). Contrary to Ponse's findings, no significant association between commitment and conformity appeared in the Amazon case.

12. See Hartsock.

13. An assumption widely criticized in recent years in the discussion on race and difference within the women's community. See Cherríe Moraga and Gloria Anzaldúa, eds., *This Bridge Called My Back: Writings by Radical Women of Color* (Watertown, MA: Persephone Press, 1981).

14. Compare Sherry McCoy and Maureen Hicks, "A Phological Retrospective on Power in the Contemporary Lesbian-Feminist Community," *Frontiers: A Journal of Women Studies* 4, no. 3 (1979): 65–69. Their exclusively personal conception of power ignores the possibility that both power and needs may be shaped by social relations like class that divide the lesbian community.

15. We do not mean to imply that the owners' fears for the survival of lesbian businesses are

groundless; we do question the allegation that the workers acted as agents of reactionary forces.

16. Agnes Heller, *The Theory of Need in Marx* (London: Allison & Busby, 1976), p. 25.

17. On the links between the changing organization of production and class relations under industrial capitalism, see Harry Braverman, *Labor and Monopoly Capital* (New York: Monthly Review Press, 1974); Richard Edwards, *Contested Terrain: The Transformation of the Workplace in the Twentieth Century* (New York: Basic Books, 1979).

18. Bertell Ollman, *Alienation* (London: Cambridge University Press, 1971), pp. 133-34. Following Ollman, we take alienation to mean a separation of the individual from her life activity, the products of her labor, and other human beings within the labor process.

19. Karl Marx and Fredrick Engels, *The German Ideology* (New York: International Publishers, 1978), pp. 51–52.

20. For cross-cultural discussions of relationally defined gender constructs, see Carol MacCormack and Marilyn Strathern, eds., *Nature, Culture and Gender* (London: Cambridge University Press, 1980); Sherry B. Ortner and Harriet Whitehead, eds., *Sexual Meanings: The Cultural Construction of Gender and Sexuality* (New York: Cambridge University Press, 1981).

21. On the owners' side, this understanding reflected lesbian-feminist ideology, but for most workers it developed through an appeal to notions of gender and sexuality to explain differences in their work experiences at Amazon and at other businesses.

22. Stanley Aronowitz, *The Crisis in Historical Materialism* (New York: Praeger Publishers, 1981), pp. 105–106, 133.

23. Anthony Giddens, "Class Structuration and Class Consciousness," in *Classes, Power, and Conflict*, ed. Anthony Giddens and David Held (Berkeley and Los Angeles: University of California Press, 1982), p. 158.

24. On the concept of hegemony, see Antonio Gramsci, *Selections from the Prison Notebooks* (New York: International Publishers, 1980), p. 12; Raymond Williams, *Marxism and Literature* (Oxford: Oxford University Press, 1977), pp. 108–14.

25. Introducing power as a variable challenges Susan Krieger's static view of lesbian communities as either supportive or coercive to individuals ("Lesbian Identity and Community: Recent Social Science Literature," *Signs* 9:4, 1984).

26. Clearly it would be impractical for every lesbian auto mechanic to open her own repair shop. This admonition also avoids dealing with the source of the divisions in the lesbian community by deprecating worker struggles and initiatives.

27. Elizabeth Garnsey advances these categories in an attempt to correct the androcentrism of such theories ("Women's Work and Theories of Class and Stratification," *Sociology* 12 no. 2 [1978]: 223–43).

28. Jackie West, "Women, Sex, and Class," in *Feminism and Materialism*, ed. Kuhn and Wolpe, pp. 220–53.

29. The isolated attempts to apply socialist-feminist analysis to lesbians ignore class relations within the lesbian community, directing their attention instead to the origins of women's oppression or to relations at the gay/straight boundary. In addition to Riddiough (see n. 3 above), see Susan Williams, "Lesbianism: A Socialist Feminist Perspective," in *Pink Triangles: Radical Perspectives on Gay Liberation*, ed. Pam Mitchell (Boston: Alyson Publications, 1980), pp. 107–16.

30. Hartsock (see n. 9 above) draws a useful distinction between power understood as domination and power understood as energy, capacity, and initiative.

5

Gentrification and Gay Neighborhood Formation in New Orleans
A Case Study

Lawrence Knopp

Surely the gay neighborhoods that now exist in many large cities represent one of the most significant ways in which gay men—far less so lesbians—have had an impact on the economic landscape. Here, geographer Lawrence Knopp describes the results of one of a handful of detailed case studies of the dual processes of gentrification and gay neighborhood building in an urban area.

Introduction

In the 1970s and 1980s, a political and social movement based on the development of gay and lesbian identities emerged in various countries around the world. In the United States, this movement has often been centered in neighborhoods. Openly gay and lesbian communities have achieved more of their social, cultural, and political goals in the inner cities of large urban areas than elsewhere.[1] This neighborhood-based gay and lesbian movement has in turn had an impact on land markets in these areas (usually through the vehicle of gentrification). . . . This paper analyzes the impact of a particular gay community's development on the land market in which it was situated during the 1970s. It then interprets this experience in terms of its implications for urban land market theory and certain broader debates in social theory concerning the connections between class, gender, and sexual relations.

Urban Land Markets and
Neighborhood-based Gay Community Development

. . . Castells's (1983:138–170) study of San Francisco's gay community in the 1970s is one of the few published empirical attempts to consider the connections between a gay community's social and political activity and an urban land market.[2] He does this primarily in the context of a discussion of gay involvement in gentrification.[3] Castells concludes that, in San Francisco, gay gentrifiers were "moral refugees" who "paid for their identity" by making enormous financial and personal sacrifices in order to survive. In the process, he argues, they contributed to an urban renovation that "reached proportions far above those of any other American city" and "helped to make the city beautiful and alive" (Castells 1983:161). Interestingly, there is little in the way of economic or class analysis in the study. He does not discuss displacement of the previous residents of the neighborhood at all, emphasizing instead how the most heavily gay community developed in a neighborhood that "was being abandoned by its Irish working class" (Castro Valley). Similarly, Castells asserts a connection between young, single gay males and "a relatively prosperous service economy" (1983:160), but fails to develop this. He does identify three categories of gay gentrifiers, but he appears to suggest strongly that gentrification as a survival strategy and form of cultural expression was more important for each of these than their class interests. Clearly, the material and class interests involved in gay community development (including, perhaps, links to the restructuring of occupational mixes in urban areas) need to be more carefully examined.

Lauria and Knopp (1985) provide the beginnings of a theoretical analysis along these lines, again in the context of a discussion of gentrification. They argue that during the 1970s, economic and social opportunities for gays (especially men) expanded in inner cities. Inner cities were affordable, they were the locus of gay cultural and institutional life, and they were also experiencing growth in white-collar and service employment (where, it is alleged, disproportionate numbers of gay men tend to be employed). Lauria and Knopp further argue that gay identity in the United States is skewed in terms of class, race, and gender, i.e., that while homosexual desire and behaviors are multiclass and multiracial phenomena involving both women and men, the self-identification of individuals as gay is more of a white, male, and middle-class phenomenon. This is because it is easier, economically and otherwise, for middle-class white males to identify and live as openly gay people than it is for women, non-whites, and non-middle-class people. They cite demographic studies of gay populations reported by sociologists to support this contention. The significance of this, they argue, is that gay people constitute a potentially large market for renovated housing in terms of discretionary income. They are not the only such market (single heterosexuals and childless couples are others), but they are perhaps the largest, the fastest-growing, and the one with the largest discretionary income (Foltz, et al. 1984).

Lauria and Knopp do not, however, provide a way of interpreting gay involvement on the production side of urban land market processes. And Castells (1983:158) merely sees such involvement in San Francisco as a means of "surviv[ing] the tough . . . housing market." Thus, a more general understanding of this aspect of gay involvement in land markets is still needed.

This paper contributes to the further elaboration of theory involving urban land markets and neighborhood-based gay community development through the presentation and interpretation of a narrative. . . . The purpose here is to explore the theoretical significance of the particular series of events and configuration of interests that were found in the larger study, not to summarize the entire project. Thus, economic and demographic data describing the neighborhood's transformation quantitatively are omitted, and interested readers are referred to the larger study (Knopp 1989).

The neighborhood in question is in New Orleans, Louisiana, and experienced a substantial degree of gentrification between the late 1960s and early 1980s. Personal interviews with key actors in the inner-city real estate market and the gay community during this period were a primary source of data from which the sequence of events and mapping of interests and alliances was produced. . . . Secondary sources (e.g., local histories and media accounts) were similarly collected. . . . The resulting narrative is presented below, followed by a discussion of its theoretical significance.

The Transformation of Marigny

New Orleans' Marigny neighborhood is a small but densely populated area located adjacent to New Orleans' famous French Quarter (also known as the Vieux Carre— see Figure 1). The upriver (western) half, immediately adjacent to the French Quarter, is known as the "triangle" and is the more heavily gentrified part of the neighborhood. The downriver half, known as the "rectangle," is more of a patchwork of renovated and unrenovated houses and blocks (see Figure 2).

Three sets of events, associated with distinct sets of actors, can be identified that were crucial in this neighborhood's transformation from a working class area experiencing disinvestment (in the 1950s and 1960s) to a more solidly middle-class and substantially renovated one (in the 1970s). These events were:

1. the movement of a small number of predominantly gay middle-class professionals to Marigny during the 1960s;
2. a movement for historic preservation in the neighborhood, organized primarily by gay men; and
3. the arrival of speculators and developers, who again were mostly gay, in the mid-to-late 1970s.

The Early In-movers

The first signs of gentrification in Marigny came in the 1960s, when the neighborhood overall was still experiencing disinvestment, increasing amounts of slum landlordism, so-called "white flight," and in-migration by poor blacks. A small-scale counter-trend of middle-class in-migration came with the founding in 1958 of the Louisiana State University at New Orleans (later the University of New Orleans, UNO) at a site on the New Orleans lakefront.

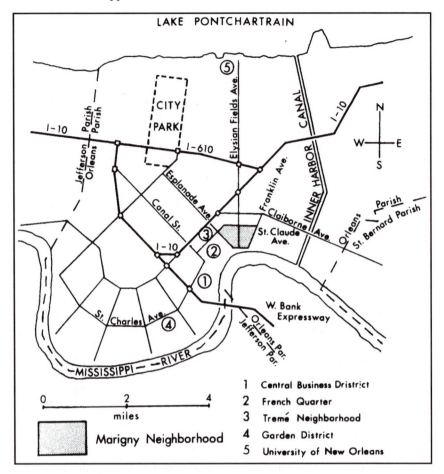

Figure 1   The location of the Marigny neighborhood in New Orleans

The early in-movers to Marigny consisted most notably of several faculty and other professionals employed by the university. Many of these were gay men from outside the New Orleans area who had chosen, upon arrival in New Orleans, to rent in the French Quarter rather than in the new, homogeneous, family-oriented neighborhoods near UNO. Later, when they had established themselves financially and sought to own property, they chose to locate in Marigny:

> The pioneers . . . were UNO people who also happened to be homosexuals. . . . [T]hey wanted the milieu [of the French Quarter] but they couldn't afford the property so they were attracted to places like the Marigny. (Personal interview.)[4]

The extreme family orientation of suburban neighborhoods was a disincentive rather than a draw for these people, and the adversity associated with living in

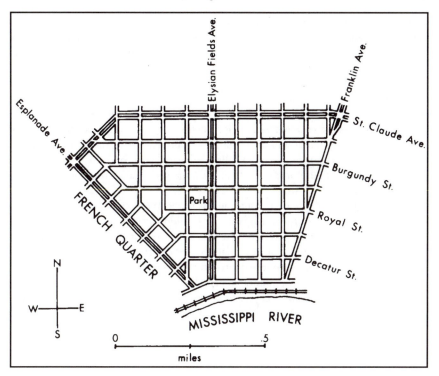

Figure 2   The Marigny neighborhood

Marigny appeared acceptable by comparison. House prices were quite low, and the French Quarter (the center of gay social and cultural life in New Orleans) was easily accessible by foot. Furthermore, the university was easily accessible by both car (ten minutes) and bus (twenty minutes).[5]

Racial tensions were also instrumental in encouraging middle-class whites to settle in Marigny. A predominantly black neighborhood, Treme, was very comparable to Marigny architecturally and in terms of its affordability and location (it is adjacent to the French Quarter on the northwest side.) It was also adjacent to one of New Orleans' ten large (and predominantly black) public housing projects, and very near another. Many whites feared the proximity to large numbers of poor blacks, and many blacks feared the effects of gentrification:

> They fought, they fought, they fought, they fought! The blacks. . . . [in Treme] resisted change because of the race situation. (Personal interview.)

Marigny, by contrast, was a predominantly white neighborhood and was much more removed from the housing projects. A vivid biracial and multicultural social history made it easy for liberal whites to settle there without feeling that they were applying racist standards in their decisions.

This predominantly gay middle-class settlement in the face of adversity had two significant outcomes. For most of the nineteenth and early twentieth centuries the neighborhood was a stable working class area. Except for the Creole[6] aristocrats who founded it in the early 1800s (including a substantial number of so-called "free persons of color" who lost their social standing after Reconstruction), it was never home to anyone but lower-middle-class laborers and shopkeepers—until the 1960s, when the in-migration of a few middle-class gay university employees established a stable nonworking-class presence in Marigny for the first time ever. The second significant outcome was the association of this middle-class presence with the French Quarter, New Orleans' gay community, and a college-educated population. All three of these associations would figure prominently in the large-scale transformation of Marigny that took place in the 1970s.

The in-migration of a few gay professionals in the 1960s can be interpreted as the laying of a foundation for the much larger-scale middle-class in-migration and neighborhood-based community development that followed. This laying of a foundation was a completely unorganized process, planned and directed by no one. Rather, it was a consequence of social and economic forces that defined both Marigny, in spite of its locational advantages, as an undesirable neighborhood and gay people, regardless of class standing, as undesirable people. In so doing, these forces produced a physical space that could be appropriated and commodified by enterprising members of the gay middle class.[7]

Historic Preservation and Neighborhood-based Political Action

The second significant set of events in Marigny's transformation was the political organization of the neighborhood, which began in the early 1970s. The issue around which residents mobilized was not gay community development or politics but, rather, historic preservation—in spite of the fact that most of the leaders of the movement were openly gay, and specifically encouraged gay in-migration to Marigny.

The most prominent leader of the historic preservation movement was an architect who moved to Marigny in 1971. His strategy consisted of making an inventory of properties that "needed saving," determining who their owners were, and then making "marriages of buildings and people" (personal interview). It also included taking advantage of his connections to the gay community:

He spoke to his gay friends and proposed to them that they move to Marigny. . . . Gay men were a part of his strategy. (Personal interview.)

He viewed the gay connection as part of what was happening . . . He saw that gay men would be a very good way to make the project work. (Personal interview.)

And, indeed, large numbers of middle-class gay men did begin moving to the neighborhood:

We were the only heteros on the block and we're still pretty close to that. There's a couple others on the block, but it's basically mostly gay men . . . [A]ll of them are professional people, at least white collar jobs. (Personal interview.)

After . . . enough people had moved to Marigny who were gay and who were, what, middle-class gay, if you like . . . then I felt it was safe to bring a wife and have a child here. (Personal interview.)

I really don't think it would have happened without the gay connection. (Personal interview.)

Concomitantly, the architect and his friends developed a formal organizational presence in the neighborhood. They founded the Faubourg Marigny Improvement Association (FMIA), a largely (but not exclusively) homeowners' group, during the architect's first year in Marigny. The organization of this group depended to a considerable extent on the forging of close personal ties among neighborhood residents. The architect became known for throwing large and very successful parties that were frequently indistinguishable from Improvement Association meetings. Attendance was predominantly (but never exclusively) gay and male:

The architect and his gay friends started the whole thing . . . And the fact that at his parties three-fourths of the men . . . were gay, was known. (Personal interview.)

Wives will stay home, because they just don't find enough women there to enjoy it. That has not changed. (Personal interview.)

FMIA cultivated contacts in various city departments (most notably the City Planning Commission), successfully lobbied the Mayor and City Council for land use regulations (a comprehensive rezoning plan for the neighborhood), and held candidate forums at election time. The organization was officially nonpartisan and concerned itself with historic preservation and closely related quality-of-life issues only. This enabled it to enlist the support of such conservative institutions as the local Catholic Archdiocese on certain issues (personal interviews).

This neighborhood-based political action, predicated on historic preservation, had three significant outcomes. First, it resulted in Marigny developing a new and strong sense of community and identity:

There were constantly meetings or potluck suppers or gatherings at the park, and we were constantly seeing each other and enjoying each other. (Personal interview.)

This kind of community cohesion had been disintegrating during the previous two decades, as many of the indigenous working-class residents moved out to cheap housing in new suburbs.

Second, Marigny's new organization and identity increased its clout in the New Orleans government and business communities. Financing and insurance became easier to get and local politicians made historic preservation a priority. The decision of mostly gay neighborhood activists to emphasize historic preservation, rather than gay issues, was crucial in this outcome.[8]

In spite of the strategy of downplaying specifically gay issues, however, a third significant outcome was the social and political development of the local gay community. Since the leaders of the neighborhood's preservation-based boosterism were mostly gay men, and their strategy for the neighborhood included recruiting others like themselves to settle in Marigny, a huge proportion of middle-class in-movers during this period were gay:

> I'd say by '74 it became kind of known as the gay ghetto or something like that. (Personal interview.)

Gay institutions also proliferated in Marigny. A number of gay bars opened in the neighborhood, as did gay-owned and/or gay-oriented bookstores, restaurants, and some organizational offices. An annual Gayfest, held in June to commemorate the 1969 Stonewall rebellion in New York City,[9] found a home in Washington Square Park in the heart of Marigny.

Eventually, the gay presence in Marigny expressed itself politically. The area's city council member introduced a citywide measure to ban discrimination in housing and employment on the basis of sexual orientation in the early 1980s (DuBos 1984). After considerable public outcry (including an intense campaign against the ordinance by Catholic Archbishop Phillip Hannon), this effort failed narrowly before the City Council (in 1984).[10]

Marigny's development as an organized middle-class community in the 1970s, with a preservation-based and substantial (but deemphasized) gay identity, was carefully planned. Specific individuals with specific agendas (and college educations) aggressively set out to build alliances with various interests in the city. They accomplished this by demonstrating the political and economic value of the Marigny neighborhood and community to politicians and business interests. This is in contrast to the largely unplanned and unorganized in-migration of a few middle-class gays in the 1960s.

The mostly gay actors in this campaign saw the involvement of other gay people as essential. They did not, however, see it as sufficient to ensure success. Rather, gay in-migration was packaged and presented as simply responsible middle-class in-migration. In this way fragile alliances with basically conservative interests, such as the Catholic Church, could be maintained:

> How do we want our city to see us?...[As] responsible businesspeople who have money, or fags coming out of the streets with makeup? (Personal interview.)

As a consequence, while most major historic preservation battles were won, the local gay community won very little. It was not until the early 1980s that a specifically gay-related issue (the nondiscrimination ordinance) reached the City Council, and the antigay forces ultimately prevailed in that battle. Neighborhood activists in Marigny, while supportive of the proposed ordinance, risked very little political capital to promote it. Rather, most of the lobbying was done by city and statewide gay political organizations (principally, the Louisiana Gay Political Action Committee [LAGPAC]) and the area's city council member.

The development of the local gay community that did occur in Marigny must therefore be seen as more of a consequence (rather than a central goal) of the strategies devised by Marigny's gay leaders to promote historic preservation. These strategies happened to involve exploiting personal ties in the gay community.

The Arrival of Speculators and Developers

Gay community development was a much more intentional consequence of the strategies of local speculators and developers who entered the scene in the mid-1970s. This was by far the most complex, if not most important, of the three significant sets of events in Marigny's transformation. Again, most of the key actors were gay men, of whom two groups in particular were important.

One group, centered on the firm of a Marigny-based real estate broker, focused on developing a market for all kinds of housing in the neighborhood among gays. The socioeconomic status and class interests of these consumers of housing were considered relatively unimportant (indeed, an aggressive effort was made to make housing available to young, low-waged, gay service-sector workers from the French Quarter who would otherwise not have had access to the housing market), and so-called creative financing (including illegal bribes to appraisers employed by financial institutions) was involved (see Knopp 1990 for a detailed discussion). A second group, consisting of a more capital-intensive development corporation, focused its efforts on using more conventional methods to develop a specifically upper-middle-class gay market for already renovated housing in the Marigny rectangle. Neither group focused *exclusively* on gays, but in both cases gay people (especially gay men) were considered the core of the market being developed.

The real estate broker's strategy was to encourage as much gay in-migration, home-ownership, and renovation in Marigny as was humanly possible, regardless of the in-migrants' class status:

All the waiters and all the gay people and all the people that were his friends in the Quarter that always wanted houses. . . . [J]ust nobody was ever going to look for that type of person. It was a natural! . . . [He] was the first person to go after that market. (Personal interview.)

This entailed developing the social and economic potential of the gay community. His real-estate firm became a significant community institution in its own right, and through a complex series of maneuvers (many of which were illegal), it helped members of the local gay community to secure financing for virtually the entire purchase price of homes (Berry 1979; Murphy 1979; Gsell 1979a through 1979l). This, and the fact that values in the area were severely depressed, made housing accessible to many first-time home-buyers who would otherwise not have been able to muster large enough down payments. Thus, the firm engaged in a conscious and deliberate project of gay community development—albeit for the purposes of enhancing property values and, ultimately, the material well-being of its members (who happened also to be predominantly gay).

This strategy pitted the firm against a number of entrenched interests in New Orleans. The providers of home mortgages (known locally as homesteads) were duped into assuming higher levels of risk than they would otherwise have accepted. They also had their control over the extremely political and value-laden process of property appraisal challenged. Traditional brokerages saw profits created and appropriated by an unorthodox competitor. Eventually, legal proceedings brought an end to the firm and its unusual practices. The traditional distribution of power and profits among the homesteads, traditional brokerages, and developers was restored, but not before the profit-producing potential of the Marigny neighborhood was revitalized.

Shortly after this real-estate firm came on the scene, a more conventional development corporation began developing luxury housing in the Marigny rectangle. Like the first group, this one concentrated its efforts on developing a gay male market for housing. The example of San Francisco's Castro district very much influenced its gay male owner. He owned a house in San Francisco at the time and spent ten days every month there:

> Castro was so wonderful and so alive, really great. It was so dynamic that if you could export that technology some place else, what a wonderful thing it would be. And Marigny was . . . where we were going to bring it. (Personal interview.)

His development strategy was much more conservative than that of the first group, however. First, he minimized risk by investing initially with cash:

> What we would do is we would buy for cash, driving the price down to the seller, renovate using my own crews, using my own cash, get the rental stream up, and then finance the buildings so that we'd only take out of the financing what the rental stream could sustain. So there was never any negative cash flow. (Personal interview.)

Second, he sold the properties once they had "reached their economic potential in terms of rental":

> I had already taken out of the property what I needed. I had high ordinary income as a result of oil revenues, I needed tax deductions 'cause the taxes, the way the tax code is written encouraged gentrification, and the rental stream paid for the units. So essentially it was a free ride for me. And the neighborhood got almost four million dollars of investment in a very short period of time. (Personal interview.)

Finally, he maintained close ties to New Orleans' conservative business community (from whence he came) and the local and state Republican party establishments.

Also unlike the first group, this more traditional corporation tried to develop a distinctly affluent gay community in the Marigny rectangle:

> The idea was to create an enclave of . . . upwardly mobile gay people. . . . [W]e could create an environment with pools and jacuzzis and . . . free love . . . essentially a gay enclave of fairly wealthy people. (Personal interview.)

This group's efforts were less financially successful, however, than those of the less traditional firm. A portion of the Marigny rectangle did experience heavy investment in housing as a result of the corporation's actions. This eventually resulted in significant increases in owner-occupancy rates in the area. Many gay people (particularly affluent couples) did move into properties developed by the corporation, which made a considerable amount of money. But the Marigny rectangle never underwent the wholesale transformation that the group had envisaged, and fortunes like those amassed by some in the less traditional firm were never made. The local economy declined precipitously with the collapse of the international oil market in 1983–84, and the corporation took a substantial loss on its last condominium development. It was eventually dissolved in 1986, and the corporation's owner went to work as the director of a local nonprofit spinoff of James Rouse's Enterprise Foundation. On the other hand, no one associated with this firm was ever indicted by a grand jury or forced out of the real-estate business.

Conclusion: Class, Sexuality and Urban Land Markets

The gentrification that took place during the 1970s and early 1980s in Marigny featured a complex configuration of interests and events. It took place within the context of a very unevenly developing and conservatively guided metropolitan economy. Many of the key actors in the neighborhood's development were gay, but these were people who represented a wide variety of social positions and class interests (e.g., young waiters from the French Quarter and affluent developers). Each set of actors allied with different factions of both capital and labor and pursued a different strategy for the neighborhood's development.

The result was an unusual form of gentrification. Renovation and middle-class immigration were selective, block-by-block, and even house-by-house phenomena (although there was enough change to alter the aggregate character of the neighborhood substantially).[11] Displacement effects appear to have been modest, and indigenous residents who remained in the neighborhood apparently maintained good relations with newcomers. Marigny homeowners developed substantial political clout, and the local gay community saw its resource base expanded.

At the same time, the local gay community became increasingly stratified along lines of class interest. Gay homeowners mobilized around homeowners' issues, not gay issues, and certain gay developers embarked on a conscious strategy of promoting specifically upper-middle-class gay in-migration to the Marigny rectangle. Other gays, by contrast, focused on promoting middle- and lower-middle-class gay in-migration (albeit as part of historic preservation and market-development strategies, respectively).

The most surprising of these results was the fact that the prime movers behind neighborhood-based gay community development were speculators and developers, while neighborhood-based political activists emphasized historic preservation and were resistant to specifically gay politics. Exactly the opposite result was expected. This expectation was due to the emphasis on conflicts between producers and consumers of housing in the urban land market literature, and on neighborhood-based gay politics in the small literature on gay communities (Castells 1983).

This result implies a revised interpretation of the role of gay community development and gay politics in gentrification. Rather than constituting an oppressed community's collective strategy for coping with discrimination or a "tough" housing market, as Castells's study suggests, this type of gay involvement in a land market can be seen primarily as an alternative strategy for accumulation. It is a strategy that happens to include the development of gay community resources. Gay people, like other minorities in major United States metropolitan areas in the 1970s, experienced discrimination and found decent, affordable housing quite difficult to obtain in central cities. Unlike other minorities, however, openly gay people often possess adequate economic resources to enter a middle-class housing market. Unlike more visible minorities, they are able to maintain a measure of control over the disclosure of their minority status, i.e., their sexual orientation. The issue is therefore not so much one of overcoming discrimination as it is one of overcoming institutional obstacles to investment in certain parts of the city. Gay speculators and developers in Marigny saw an opportunity first for themselves and only secondarily for the gay community as a whole, by making housing in these areas available to gay people. As one gay speculator put it,

In this country, in America, there's plenty of pie for everybody to make it. . . . The fact that we [gay people] have money, the fact that we spend it—that's a[n] economic contribution. (Personal interview.)

In terms of theories of how urban land markets work, this suggests that the class interests of certain actors (e.g., speculators) can be facilitated and legitimated by forming cross-cultural and cross-class *alliances* with certain groups of consumers (in this case, a diverse community of gay men, including relatively poorly paid service-sector workers from New Orleans' French Quarter). The stigmatization and segregation of these groups can thus be turned to the short-term advantage of both producers and consumers of housing. This is accomplished as part and parcel of the process of creating demand for housing. Certain social benefits can and do accrue from such strategies, which is why they can work. But the ultimate purpose is always to make money for the providers of housing. As one interviewee explained (with reference to a slightly different social investment),

It was in my interest here to promote Marigny. It was going to line my pockets and make the investment pan out for me. . . . [T]he symphony was in trouble.

There was no better way for me to help advertise my product . . . than to hire the symphony . . . to play a free concert in [a neighborhood park] and hold a huge party for the neighborhood. . . . [T]hat wasn't altruistic. It was purely economic. (Personal interview.)

Conversely, the lack of a commitment to the gay community evidenced by Marigny's neighborhood activists suggests that even in cases where the catalyst for residential location decisions may be to a considerable extent nonclass based (in this case, the particular attraction of Marigny for gay people), the power of class interests to prevail over other interests among consumers of housing is very strong. This is well illustrated by one lower-middle-class lesbian homeowner's attitude toward the Faubourg Marigny Improvement Association:

A friend of mine that lives around the corner got a citation for too many garbage cans! I mean, I don't know where they want to go. You know, do they want an Uptown [an affluent, consumption-oriented neighborhood] here? I think that's real possible. And that's not what it is. (Personal interview.)

Those who behaved most as expected were the property developers associated with the more conservative development corporation. Their goal was quite explicitly to gentrify a portion of the Marigny rectangle by emulating San Francisco's experience of neighborhood-based gay community development. Yet of all the actors involved in Marigny's transformation in the 1970s, it was this group who had the least ambitious plan (in terms of both geographical extent and short-term profit or benefit maximization) and who were, arguably, the least successful. The rectangle remained less gentrified and less gay than the triangle, and the small-scale San Francisco–style upper-middle-class gay enclave that was envisioned never materialized.

This is important because it indicates the limits to gay involvement in the land market in Marigny. The gay community clearly had the capacity to gentrify, but this turned out to be a relatively modest project. This may or may not have been due to a lack of money in the local gay community. Clearly it was *not* due to a lack of sufficient numbers, as the FMIA's and the "insurgent" real-estate firm's sizable gay constituencies demonstrate. More likely this simply reflects the relative power of the various interests involved in Marigny (and more exogenous forces influencing the level of demand for inner-city housing overall).

So while gay involvement in the urban land market in Marigny was very much structured by class interests, this was an extremely complex process, entailing cross-cultural and even cross-class alliances (e.g., between the "insurgent" real-estate firm and young, low-waged, gay service-sector workers from the French Quarter). Overall, the negative effects of gentrification were fewer than in many other cases (cf., N. Smith 1979). But this was not due to any conscious forms of resistance on the part of consumers of housing. Nor was it due to the benevolence of producers of housing or even the actions of people organizing around gay issues.[12] Rather, it was a consequence of the historically and geographically specific workings of the local land and labor markets.

A Note on Connections Between Gay Oppression and the Oppression of Women

The fact that gay involvement in gentrification is a predominantly male practice raises important questions about the connections between gender relations, gender roles, and the place of each within a society driven by accumulation. Lesbians' ability to cope with oppression through entry into the housing market (and hence the middle class) is generally more limited than that of gay men. Residential concentrations of lesbians in urban spaces therefore tend to resemble the patterns and processes of segregation that characterize other marginalized groups more than they do those that characterize gay men (Ettore 1978:514–518; Winchester and White 1988:48–49). Indeed, there is evidence that, in the United States, lesbian communities are in general less urban based, more spatially dispersed, and more dependent upon informal rather than formal institutions (e.g., personal networks) than are gay male communities (cf. Wolfe 1978; Castells 1983:140; Beyer 1985). These differences are usually attributed to women's economically disadvantaged position vis-a-vis men and to differences in the social structure and practices of the gay male and lesbian communities (see Winchester and White 1988:49, for such an analysis in the context of Paris, France).

These differences appear to hold in the case of New Orleans' Marigny neighborhood. All of the key gay actors in Marigny's gentrification (on both the production and consumption sides of the process) were male, as were most (but not all) of the participants in and institutions of the French Quarter–based gay community. The lesbian community was simply weaker economically, less spatially concentrated, and more dependent upon an informal institutional network than was the gay male community.

Gay gentrification thus had the effect in Marigny, and has the likely effect elsewhere, of further stratifying gay communities along gender lines, by extending men's economic advantage over women. This suggests a subtle new interpretation of the relationship between gay oppression and the economic and social oppression of women. Existing literature on the subject links the oppression of gays to efforts to enforce rigid gender roles characterized by male dominance (Weinberger and Millham 1979; Ponse 1978; Gagnon and Simon 1973). Sexual dominance in particular is viewed as crucial to the reproduction of both the ideology and the reality of male social dominance. Forms of sexual expression that do not entail male dominance (especially homosexual behavior, which does not entail women and men relating sexually at all) are therefore viewed as threatening to the survival of male social dominance. Yet in Marigny and other gentrified gay neighborhoods, we have examples of a form of social dominance (economic privilege) being facilitated, rather than undermined, by efforts to develop, not oppress, a gay community (albeit for purposes, primarily, of private accumulation). The perpetuation of male economic privilege within the context of a gay community's influence on a land market is thus a testament to the resilience of male social dominance generally in the face of what the literature suggests should be one of the most powerful threats to it.[13] The relationship between gay oppression and the oppression of women must therefore be seen as considerably more contingent than the existing literature suggests.

Acknowledgments

I am indebted to Amy Gluckman for her work in excerpting this paper from the longer original version and to Bob Reppe for his graphics work.

Notes

This article first appeared under the title "Some theoretical implications of gay involvement in an urban land market" in *Political Geography Quarterly*, Vol. 9, No. 4, October 1990, pp. 337–352. It is reprinted here with minor changes.

1. There are some exceptions to this, as in small enclaves such as Provincetown, Massachusetts, Key West, Florida, and certain coastal communities in California. But gay community successes are much more numerous in large cities.
2. He relies heavily, however, on the unpublished papers of Don Lee, a graduate student, in the study.
3. The study is more directly concerned, however, with the development of gay territory and gay political power than with the local land market.
4. This 1960s in-migration took place largely before the onset of the modern identity-based gay rights movement, which is usually considered to have begun in 1969. The French Quarter's long tradition as a relatively open center of gay culture afforded New Orleans gays a much greater opportunity to create integrated gay identities and life styles than was available in most other U.S. cities. The possibility of a middle-class residence and life style near the institutions of gay cultural life is one example of this.
5. It is located at the opposite end of Elysian Fields Avenue from Marigny (see Figure 1).
6. "Creole" is a term referring to Louisianans descended from French and Spanish settlers. The term originated in the West Indies, however, and was brought to Louisiana by West Indies immigrants. These immigrants were often of mixed African and European descent, while Louisiana Creoles are often alleged to be of exclusively European descent. Hence there is much controversy over what constitutes a "true" Louisiana Creole.
7. Gays were not the only out-of-the-mainstream group to settle in Marigny. Substantial numbers of "hippies, prostitutes, Cuban refugees and members of the local intelligentsia" also called Marigny home (Rushton 1970:56). But it is likely that gays were the only group that included in its ranks persons with substantial economic resources.
8. Historic preservation has a long history in New Orleans that is very much associated with local elites. The Vieux Carre Commission, which regulates development in the French Quarter, was established by local élites in 1936.
9. This is generally regarded as marking the beginning of the modern gay rights movement and is commemorated one weekend in June by gay communities in most U.S. cities.
10. Two years later, after the collapse of the city's oil-based economy and the plunge that the local real estate market took (including in Marigny), the measure was reintroduced by another City Council member. This time Marigny's representative changed his position (citing public fears about AIDS) and the measure failed by an even larger margin.
11. This can be contrasted with "classic" cases of gentrification (e.g., Philadelphia's Society Hill and Vancouver's Kitsilano) that have been characterized by wholesale transformations of large tracts of inner-city land (N. Smith 1979; Ley 1984).
12. There were, in fact, precious few of the latter in New Orleans at the time.
13. What is remarkable here is not that individual gay men participate in the oppression of

women. Rather, it is the fact that a successful collective struggle against gay oppression (through the development of a gay community) can have the effect of furthering the material oppression of women. This is not a result that most existing theory would appear to anticipate.

References

Beauregard, R.A. (1986). The chaos and complexity of gentrification. In *Gentrification of the City* (N. Smith and P. Williams, eds.), pp. 35-55. Boston: Allen & Unwin.

Berry, J. (1979). What price appraisal? *Figaro* (New Orleans), March 5, pp. 12–14.

Beyer, J. (1985). Geography of women's spaces: a progress report. Paper presented to a special session on women in the city: struggle for space, Annual Meeting of the Association of American Geographers, Detroit, MI, April 22.

Castells, M. (1983). *The City and the Grassroots.* Berkeley, CA: University of California Press.

———— and Murphy, K.A. (1982). Cultural identity and urban structure: the spatial organization of San Francisco's gay community. In *Urban Policy under Capitalism* (N. Fainstein and S. Fainstein, eds.), Beverly Hills: Sage Publications.

Chouinard, V. and Fincher, R. (1985). Local terrains of conflict within the Canadian state. Paper presented to a special session on the local state, Annual Meeting of the Association of American Geographers, April 24.

Cooke, P. (1985). Class practices as regional markers: a contribution to labour geography. In *Social Relations and Spatial Structures* (D. Gregory and J. Urry, eds.), pp. 213–241. New York: St. Martin's Press.

Cox, K. R. (1981). Capitalism and conflict around the communal living space. In *Urbanization and Urban Planning in Capitalist Society* (M. Dear and A. Scott, eds.), pp. 431–455.

———— and Mair, A. (1988). Locality and community in the politics of local economic development. *Annals of the Association of American Geographers* 78, 307–325.

DuBos, C. (1984). Gay politics emerges. *Gambit,* March 10.

Escoffier, J. (1985). Sexual revolution and the politics of gay identity. *Socialist Review* 15, 119–153.

Ettore, E.M. (1978). Women, urban social movement and the lesbian ghetto. *International Journal of Urban and Regional Research* 2, 499–520.

Foltz, K., Raine, G., Gonzalez, D., and Wright, L. (1984). The profit of being gay. *Newsweek* 1, 84, 89.

Gagnon, J. and Simon, W. (1973). *Sexual Conduct: The Social Sources of Human Sexuality.* Chicago: Aldine.

Gsell, G. (1979a). Four appraisers charged in overvaluation bribery. *The Times–Picayune* (New Orleans), February 23, pp. I–1;I–14.

———— (1979b). Appraisers charged with overvaluation. *The Times-Picayune* (New Orleans), March 28, p. I–16.

———— (1979c). Took payoffs, says appraiser. *The Times-Picayune* (New Orleans), May 15, p. I–5B.

———— (1979d). Appraiser denies taking pay for overvaluations. *The Times-Picayune* (New Orleans), May 16, p. I–10.

———— (1979e). Witness says appraiser took money for property overvalues. *The Times-Picayune* (New Orleans), June 12, p. I–4.

———— (1979f). Appraiser trial goes to jury. *The Times-Picayune* (New Orleans), June 13, p. I–16.

———— (1979g). Jurors acquit N.O. appraiser. *The Times-Picayune* (New Orleans), June 14, p. I–12.

———— (1979h). Appraiser's conviction on mail fraud overturned. *The Times-Picayune* (New Orleans), July 25, p. I–2.

———— (1979j). Former appraiser paid, 4 witnesses tell court. *The Times-Picayune* (New Orleans), September 11, p. I–5.

———— (1979k). Former appraiser denies taking cash kickbacks. *The Times-Picayune* (New Orleans), September 12, p. I–5.

———— (1979l). Ex-appraiser is guilty in lying case. *The Times-Picayune* (New Orleans), September 13, p. I–5.

Hartman, C. (1984). *The Transformation of San Francisco.* Totowa, NJ: Rowman and Allanheld.

Harvey, D. (1981). The spatial fix: Hegel, von Thunen, and Marx. *Antipode* 13(3), 1–12.

———— (1985). *The Urbanization of Capital.* Baltimore: Johns Hopkins University Press.

Knopp, L. (1989). Gentrification and Gay Community Development in a New Orleans Neighborhood. Ph.D. dissertation, Department of Geography, The University of Iowa, Iowa City, Iowa.

———— (1990). Exploiting the rent-gap: the theoretical implications of using illegal appraisal schemes to encourage gentrification in New Orleans. *Urban Geography* 11, 48–64.

Lauria, M. (1984). The implications of marxian rent theory for community-controlled redevelopment strategies. *Journal of Planning Education and Research* 4, 16–24.

———— and Knopp, L. (1985). Toward an analysis of the role of gay communities in the urban renaissance. *Urban Geography* 6, 152–169.

Lee, D.A. (1980). The Gay Community and Improvements in the Quality of Life in San Francisco. MCP Thesis, University of California.

Logan, J.R. and Molotch, H.L. (1987). *Urban Fortunes: The Political Economy of Place.* Berkeley, CA: University of California Press.

Massey, D. (1984). *Spatial Divisions of Labour: Social Structures and the Geography of Production.* London: Macmillan.

Mollenkopf, J. (1981). Community and accumulation. In *Urbanization and Urban*

Planning in Capitalist Society (M. Dear and A. Scott, eds.), pp. 319–337. New York: Methuen.

Molotch, H.L. (1976). The city as a growth machine. *American Journal of Sociology* 82, 309–332.

Murphy, J. D. (1979). Loan institutions also bilked. *The Times-Picayune* (New Orleans), May 5, pp. I–1;I–11.

Murphy, K.A. (1980). Urban Transformations: A Case Study of the Gay Community in San Francisco. MCP Thesis, University of California.

Personal Interview, September 1987.

———, September 1987.

———, October 1987.

———, November 1987.

———, October 22, 1987.

———, February 20, 1988.

———, June 27, 1988.

———, June 27, 1988.

———, June 27, 1988.

———, June 28, 1988.

———, June 28, 1988.

———, June 28, 1988.

———, June 29, 1988.

———, June 29, 1988.

———, June 30, 1988.

———, June 30, 1988.

Ponse, B. (1978). *Identities in the Lesbian World: The Social Construction of Self.* Westport, CT: Greenwood Press.

Rose, D. (1984). Rethinking gentrification: beyond the uneven development of marxist urban theory. *Environment and Planning D: Society and Space* 1, 47–74.

Roweis, S. (1981). Urban planning in early and late capitalist societies: outline of a theoretical perspective. In *Urbanization and Urban Planning in Capitalist Society* (M. Dear and A. Scott, eds.), pp. 159–177. New York: Methuen.

Rubin, G. (1975). The traffic in women: notes on the "political economy" of sex. In *Toward an Anthropology of Women* (R. Reiter, ed.). New York: Monthly Review Press.

Rushton, B. (1970). The faubourg Marigny: straddling the centuries. *New Orleans Magazine*, March, pp. 48–51;56.

Scott, A. and Roweis, S. (1977). Urban planning in theory and practice: a reappraisal. *Environment and Planning A* 9, 1097–1119.

Smith, M.P. (1979). *The City and Social Theory.* New York: St. Martin's Press.

Smith, N. (1979). Gentrification and capital: theory, practice and ideology in Society Hill. *Antipode* 11(3), 24–35.

——— and LeFaivre, M. (1984). A class analysis of gentrification. In *Gentrification, Displacement and Neighborhood Revitalization* (J. Palen and B. London, eds.), pp. 43–63. Albany: State University of New York Press.

Weinberger, L.E. and Millham, J. (1979). Attitudinal homophobia and support for traditional sex roles. *Journal of Homosexuality* 4, 237–246.

Wilson, D. (1987a). Institutions and urban revitalization: the case of Chelsea in New York City. *Urban Geography* 8, 129–145.

———— (1987b). Urban revitalization on the upper west side of Manhattan: an urban managerialist assessment. *Economic Geography* 63, 35–47.

Winchester, H.P.M. and White, P.E. (1988). The location of marginalised groups in the inner city. *Environment and Planning D: Society and Space* 6, 37–54.

Winters, C. (1979). The social identity of evolving neighborhoods. *Landscape* 23, 8–14.

Wolfe, D.G. (1978). *The Lesbian Community*. Berkeley, CA: University of California Press.

6

Beyond Biased Samples
Challenging the Myths on the Economic Status of Lesbians and Gay Men

M. V. Lee Badgett

A misleading myth of gay wealth and power has suddenly become a prominent part of anti-gay discourse. Economist M. V. Lee Badgett has made use of the available social survey data to begin to pin down gay men's and lesbians' actual incomes. Here, she summarizes her results and explains how inaccurate data on gay incomes has been produced.

The Myths

"'A Dream Market' . . . Gay households have characteristics sought by many advertisers. Average annual [gay] household income [is] $55,430."
—Wall Street Journal, July 18, 1991.

"Are homosexuals a 'disadvantaged' minority? You decide! Records show that even now, not only are gays not economically disadvantaged, they're actually one of the most affluent groups in America!"
—Literature published in 1992 by *Colorado for Family Values* in support of Amendment 2.

"Homosexual households had an average income of $55,400 compared with a national average of $36,500. . . . This is not the profile of a group in need of special civil rights legislation in order to participate in the economy or to have an opportunity to hold a decent job. It is the profile of an elite."
—Joseph E. Broadus, Testimony against the Employment Nondiscrimination Act of 1994, July 29, 1994.

". . . Research showed that the gay and lesbian population . . . has an average income of $36,800, compared with the average single American's income of $19,082."
—*Advertising Age*, August 9, 1993, quoted in brochure for "Targeting Gay & Lesbian Consumers," a conference sponsored by The Marketing Institute.

From right-wing opponents of lesbian and gay civil rights to businesses trying to find new groups of affluent consumers, everybody seems to be talking about how well-off and well-educated lesbians and gay men are. Many gay people themselves point to the same numbers to illustrate our ability to function in society and as evidence of our economic clout.

But before accepting these numbers as "facts," step back and consider whether they make sense. After all, why should gay people earn more and go to school longer than the average U.S. citizen? Are gay people smarter and harder workers who deserve higher salaries? It's hard to come up with a good reason to think that sexual orientation affects talent and work motivation. Some might argue that the stigma of being gay plus fear of discrimination turns lesbian, gay, and bisexual people into overachievers. While this strategy might work for some people at work or school, the achievements of those people might have been even greater if being gay were not stigmatized, and other equally well-meaning gay people might not be able to overcome the effects of anti-gay prejudice.

Or are gay people privileged in other ways that result in better jobs? Again, this seems unreasonable when we match that argument against evidence that lesbians and gay men face discrimination in hiring and promotions and even lose their jobs simply because of their sexual orientation.

From the perspective of statisticians and social scientists who work with statistics, however, the answer to the puzzle is easy: those numbers cited in the opening quotes do not accurately describe lesbian and gay people in the United States. Using those numbers to describe *all* lesbian and gay people is misleading and, in many cases, deliberately deceptive.

Those numbers are deceptive because they come from a "biased sample" of lesbian and gay people. As the next section discusses, the people who received and answered the surveys are likely to have more education and higher incomes than most gay people, so the results are not surprising! The third part of this essay describes information about gay people that comes from more reliable surveys that are not biased in the same way. All of the evidence from better surveys shows that gay people do not earn more than straight people, and two detailed studies even show a more disturbing pattern: lesbian, gay, and bisexual people earn *less* than heterosexual people.

Where These Numbers Came From

The income and education figures come from two main sources. The first three quotes use survey data from the Simmons Market Research Bureau. That survey was commissioned by Rivendell Marketing Company, which used the survey results to sell advertising space in gay newspapers. The other source of information is from surveys done by Overlooked Opinions, a company that sells this information. Overlooked Opinions sends surveys to people on its large list of names of lesbian and gay people across the United States who read gay newspapers and magazines or who have filled out questionnaires at gay events, such as gay pride festivals or the March on Washington.

To apply information about some subgroup (the "sample") to the larger group (the "population"), the sample must be "representative" of the group. A sample is representative if each member of the larger group has an equal chance of being in the survey. Such samples are called either "random samples" or "probability samples."

The surveys done by Simmons and by Overlooked Opinions do not meet this requirement. Only those gay people who read certain magazines or attend certain kinds of events are even eligible to be in the surveys. People who buy and read newspapers and magazines tend to have more education and higher incomes. Gay events such as the 1993 March on Washington attract people who can afford travel or ticket costs.

(In addition, reader and event surveys typically have very low "response rates." The small percentage of readers who respond to the survey may not be representative of survey recipients, since they may have stronger opinions on the questions asked and are more comfortable with surveys. This could mean that respondents are better educated, which would also raise the average income found in the survey.)

While this might be a reasonable way to get information on readers of a newspaper or magazine, common sense tells us that we cannot use those results to describe the larger target group. For instance, readers of magazines aimed at African Americans are not economically similar to the typical African American. In 1989, the Simmons Market Research Bureau did a survey revealing that readers of *Ebony*, *Essence*, and *Jet* magazines earn 41% to 82% more than the typical African American.

	Men	Women
Ebony readers	$19,983	$14,361
Essence readers	$20,905	$13,894
Jet readers	$17,745	$14,028
U.S. African Americans	$12,609	$ 7,875

Sources: Simmons Market Research Bureau, 1989; *Economic Report of the President*, 1991.

	Men	Women
USA Today readers	$29,428	$17,776
Wall Street Journal readers	$42,040	$22,846
U.S.	$19,893	$ 9,624

Sources: Simmons Market Research Bureau, 1989; *Economic Report of the President*, 1991.

Obviously, as this comparison shows, the economic status of African American magazine readers does not mirror the economic reality for all African Americans.

Nor should we survey people who read *USA Today* or other newspapers with national readership to find out the average incomes of all people in the United States. As the same Simmons survey shows, people who read those newspapers earn far more than the typical American.

Representative Surveys Allow Reasonable Comparisons

Getting a random sample of gay people in the U.S. is no simple matter. Government agencies and academic statisticians spend a lot of time and money to get representative samples of the U.S. population. Unfortunately, few such surveys ask the right questions that would allow direct comparison of incomes between lesbian/gay/bisexual people and heterosexual people. Recently this situation has changed, and several surveys now make it possible to make better statistical comparisons. Detailed analyses of these surveys suggests that it is much more common for lesbian, gay, and bisexual people to earn *less* than heterosexuals.

The 1993 Yankelovich Monitor included a question on sexual orientation in its survey of consumer attitudes (Elliott, 1994). Out of 2503 people in the randomly chosen sample, 143 identified themselves as "gay, lesbian, or homosexual." The gay male respondents reported an average household income of $37,400, compared with heterosexual men's $39,300 average household income. Lesbians reported an average household income of $34,800, very close to the $34,400 household income reported on average by heterosexual women.

In the 1992 general election, exit polls of random voters revealed much the same pattern for "family income" reported by lesbian and gay voters (Cronin, 1993). Voter Research and Surveys (VRS) interviewed over 15,000 voters, 466 of whom identified themselves as gay, lesbian, or bisexual. Comparing the distribution of family income (reported as an income category) between the l/g/b voters and all voters shows that gay voters tend to be in lower income categories:

Family income	Gay men	All men	Lesbians	All women
less than $15,000	18%	12%	26%	16%
$15,000-30,000	26%	23%	26%	25%
$30,000-50,000	28%	30%	29%	29%
$50,000-75,000	16%	20%	12%	19%
more than $75,000	12%	14%	6%	11%

Source: Cronin, 1993.

Although the Yankelovich Monitor and VRS findings begin to undermine the myth of gay affluence, more important questions about the economic status of gay and lesbian people remain. Opponents of gay civil rights protection essentially argue that economic status is a measure of the degree of discrimination faced by a group, and since gay people do not show signs of economic harm, they do not need legal protection. It is certainly true that other groups facing discrimination, such as women and African Americans, have earned lower incomes because of discrimination. Analyzing whether gay people face a similar economic disadvantage requires taking into account the many different factors that determine how much people get paid. The most obvious ones that economists have identified are education and age, as well as where people live and whether they face discrimination for being black or female, for instance. To know how gay people's incomes compare to heterosexuals', we have to compare people who are similar in all of those ways.

I recently conducted the first study of that kind (Badgett, 1995). I analyzed data from the 1989-1991 versions of the General Social Survey, a national probability sample developed by the National Opinion Research Center at the University of Chicago. Questions on this survey allow the identification of people who have had sex partners of the same sex—behaviorally lesbian, gay, or bisexual people.

In this random sample, the behaviorally l/g/b people who work full-time earn less on average than behaviorally heterosexual people, even before adjusting for other differences. Lesbians earn an average of $15,056 per year compared with the $18,341 earned by the average heterosexual woman. Gay men earned $26,321, in contrast to the $28,312 earned on average by heterosexual men.

A standard statistical technique known as multiple regression separated out the effect of sexual orientation from the effects of other factors influencing people's incomes. (The same technique is often used to measure discrimination against African Americans or against women.) In this case, after taking differences in education, age, and other factors into account, behaviorally gay/bisexual men (that is, men who had sex with men) earned 11% to 27% less than similar heterosexual men. Behaviorally lesbian/ bisexual women (women who had sex with women) earned 12% to 30% less than similar heterosexual women, but that finding is not "statistically significant," i.e. the fairly small sample of lesbians in the group means that we might see this result just by chance. (In other words, a sample of this size might show an income difference this large even if there were no salary difference in the population.)

In its conclusion that gay people earn less than straight people, this study goes farther than the Yankelovich Monitor, which shows roughly equal incomes on average (without controlling for any other differences in the groups) and the Voter Research and Survey voter poll, which only asks for family income. But because the sample of l/g/b people is fairly small in the General Social Survey (81 out of the 1680 full-time workers), replication of this analysis is important. We need more research on larger sample sizes and with other ways of measuring what it means to be gay or bisexual. Early results from another very recent analysis of a different (and larger) dataset confirms that gay people might actually earn less than heterosexuals.

In the 1990 Census of the U.S. population, the Census Bureau asked unmarried people whether they had an "unmarried partner" and the gender of that partner. As a result, same sex couples can be identified, and we might presume (but cannot know for sure) that those people are likely to be lesbian, gay, or bisexual. Unfortunately, the Census data do not allow the identification of single lesbian or gay people, and judging from the low percentage of unmarried same sex couples among all households (only 0.16%) some same sex couples may have either accidentally or intentionally failed to check the unmarried partner option on the census form.

But the Census dataset is quite large, making it an important source of information. Professors Marieka Klawitter and Victor Flatt (1994) analyzed Census data for 13,000 married couples, 14,500 same sex unmarried partner couples, and 6,800 opposite sex unmarried partner couples. Their analysis again demonstrates that men and women in same sex couples do not earn more than men and women in heterosexual married couples. Overall, the average "gay male" household took in $58,366 in 1989, the average "lesbian" couple's household income was $45,166, and the average income of married heterosexual couples was $47,193. But the apparent economic advantage for gay male couples disappears when we look at individual earnings:

	Men	Women
L/G/B	$23,037	$17,497
Heterosexual	$24,949	$ 9,308

Source: Klawitter and Flatt, 1994.

Thus the reason that heterosexual married couples and lesbian couples have lower total incomes is sex discrimination: women earn less than men, so a family with two male earners will have higher-than-average incomes. After controlling for education, age, location, race, and other relevant factors, Klawitter and Flatt find that the sexual orientation individual earnings gap widens for gay men. Women in same sex couples still earn more than married women after controlling for those factors, but that is probably because Klawitter and Flatt did not take into account the fact that lesbians are likely to work more hours and weeks than married women.

Since the income differences seen in my study and in the Klawitter and Flatt study are between people who are similar in characteristics closely related to workplace productivity, the lower incomes for gay and bisexual people are likely to be the result of discrimination. These studies, which are the most reliable evidence available, directly contradict the current distorted view of the economic well-being of lesbian and gay people. That distorted view mainly results from the inappropriateness of applying results from marketing surveys to the larger group of lesbians and gay men in America.

Does this more accurate picture of lesbian, gay, and bisexual people's economic status mean that advertisers should not target gay people? Some gay and lesbian people are wealthy and, therefore, are particularly attractive targets for advertising, just as some heterosexual people are wealthy and are highly sought after by many marketers. But some gay and lesbian people are poor, and most are somewhere in the middle along with the majority of heterosexual people. As the best available academic studies show, the real economic difference comes from the harmful effects of employment discrimination against lesbian, gay and bisexual people. Those studies confirm what other groups facing discrimination also know: discrimination doesn't just hurt psychologically—it hits people in their pocketbooks.

Acknowledgments

I thank Greg Lewis and members of the National Organization of Gay and Lesbian Scientists and Technical Professionals (NOGLSTP) board for helpful comments on earlier drafts of the pamphlet.

References

Badgett, M. V. Lee, "The Wage Effects of Sexual Orientation Discrimination," *Industrial and Labor Relations Review*, Vol. 48, No. 4, July 1995, pp. 726–739.

Cronin, Anne, "Two Viewfinders, Two Pictures of Gay America," *The New York Times*, June 27, 1993, Section 4, p. 16.

Economic Report of the President, United States Government Printing Office, Washington, February, 1991. Table B30, p. 320.

Elliott, Stuart, "A Sharper View of Gay Consumers," *New York Times*, June 9, 1994, p. D1.

Klawitter, Marieka M., and Victor Flatt, "Antidiscrimination Policies and Earnings for Same-sex Couples," University of Washington, presented at the Association for Public Policy Analysis and Management annual meetings, October 1994.

Simmons Market Research Bureau, "1989 Study of Media and Markets: Publications: Total Audiences," M-1, 1989, pp. vii-viii.

7

Lesbian and Gay
Occupational Strategies

M. V. Lee Badgett and Mary C. King

What jobs do lesbians and gay men hold? Will the facts about gay people's occupations reinforce or shatter long-held stereotypes? This question is basic to understanding gay economic life, yet the answers are elusive, because large, representative sets of data rarely identify gay subjects. In this article, Lee Badgett and Mary King develop a mainstream economics model of the factors influencing gay men's and lesbians' occupational choices, then offer a glimpse of some preliminary—and in some cases surprising—data.

This essay is an initial attempt to think about whether lesbians and gay men might tend to be in different occupations than straight people, and to consider how being in different occupations might affect lesbians' and gay men's earnings. Due to discrimination, socialization, and family responsibilities, both gender and ethnicity significantly influence occupational distributions—the proportions of different groups found in different occupations (Reskin 1994; King 1992). For similar reasons, we might expect sexual orientation to influence occupational distribution. Factors that specifically affect the occupational distribution of lesbians and gay men may be roughly divided into two categories: those relating to discrimination against lesbians and gay men, and those stemming from same-sex family structures.

The first section of the essay develops an analytical framework, based on economics, with which to think about the occupational strategies of lesbians and gay men—that is, the ways that being gay is likely to affect job and career decisions. The second section presents data on the occupational distributions of gay and straight people and on the degree of acceptance of homosexuality prevailing in different occupations. The statistics in the second section are based on data from the General Social Survey (GSS), a nationally representative survey conducted by the National Opinion Research Center. Since 1989, the GSS has included several sets of questions allowing the identification of respondents' sexual orientations and attitudes toward homosexuality, along with their occupations, education, and other characteristics. The third section includes a discussion of the limitations of the work presented here and plans for further research.

Analytical Framework

Economic analysis is often conducted in the language of unfettered personal choice, as if individuals are able to make completely free choices about those aspects of their lives examined by economists, subject to "constraints" generally having to do with financial means and, sometimes, discrimination. When examining the occupational distributions of two different groups, as we do here with gay and straight people, economists are not really investigating the entire process by which anyone comes to his or her occupation, a process that includes many factors such as an assessment of what's realistically available to people of different circumstances in different places at different times. Economists in the neoclassical paradigm, which we are using, are looking for differences at the margin. In other words, we are assuming that gay and straight people face similar labor markets with similar limitations due to their class, ethnicity, location, and gender, and we are looking for differences in occupations that stem solely from differences in sexual orientation.

Using this perspective, we may expect lesbians and gay men to enter different occupations than straight women and men for two reasons: (1) the potential for discrimination against lesbians and gay men may vary in different occupations, and (2) lesbians and gay men may have different expectations than straight women and men about the way in which their work life will mesh with their family life.

Discrimination Against Lesbians and
Gay Men in Different Occupations

Beth Schneider (1986, 464) has called the need to "manage a disreputable sexual identity at the workplace" the most persistent problem lesbians and gay men face in their daily lives. The potential for discrimination against lesbians and gay men is evident from the public's ambivalent attitudes about homosexuality. A 1993 Gallup poll (Moore 1993) found that 80 percent of respondents believed that gay people should "have equal rights in terms of job opportunities," although only 46 percent favored specifically protecting gay people with civil-rights laws. In the same survey, however, 45 percent of men and 30 percent of women "prefer that homosexuals stay in the closet." Of the 818 adults surveyed in a national 1993 *Washington Post* poll (Warden 1993), 69 percent said that they "feel comfortable" working with a gay person, but 53 percent believe that "it is wrong for two consenting adults to have a homosexual relationship," a finding consistent with many previous polls (Herek 1991).

Lesbians and gay men have good reason to expect that they will be discriminated against at work if people know of their sexual orientation. A 1987–88 survey of 191 employers in Anchorage, Alaska revealed that 18 percent would fire, 27 percent would not hire, and 26 percent would not promote homosexuals (Brause 1989). A recent review of 21 surveys of lesbians and gay men found that between 16 and 46 percent of survey respondents reported having experienced some form of discrimination in employment—in hiring, promotion, discharge, or harassment (Badgett, Donnelly and Kibbe 1992). Using GSS data, Badgett (1995; also see previous chapter in this volume) finds evidence that discrimination against gay men and lesbians lowers their earnings.

However, unlike discrimination based upon easily observable characteristics such as color or gender, discrimination against lesbians and gay men is analogous to that based on religion or national origin, which depends on the knowledge or suspicion that an employee has the stigmatized characteristic. Gay people who do not reveal their sexual orientation at work can be described as "passing—that is, providing a facade of heterosexuality" (Escoffier 1975). Passing entails the need to dissemble, to hide one's personal life, to avoid discussions of families and relationships, to come alone to work-related social events, and, often, to endure derogatory conversations about lesbians and gay men (Escoffier 1975; Herek 1991; Woods 1993). When career advancement depends in part on socializing, passing may carry economic as well as psychological costs (Escoffier 1975).

Gay employees may voluntarily disclose their sexual orientation or may be unable to hide it, given military discharge records, arrests and/or convictions, marital status, residential neighborhood, or silences in conversations and gossip. Lesbians and gay men who voluntarily reveal their sexual orientation to employers or coworkers for psychological or political reasons risk loss of income and diminished prospects for career advancement. However, disclosure provides psychological relief, as it ends the need for passing, allowing people to be themselves at work. And politically, disclosure has the potential to educate people or to promote greater understanding and acceptance of homosexuality.

It makes sense to assume that lesbians and gay men will attempt to minimize the impact of antigay discrimination on their work lives. Depending on their preference for being out at work, a gay worker will avoid occupations in which either:

1. it is relatively difficult to pass as heterosexual, *or*
2. the penalties for disclosure of a gay identity are relatively high because of institutional policies or coworker attitudes.

Occupations in which it would be most difficult to pass are those that involve high levels of social interaction, either on or off the job (Escoffier 1975); examples include sales and social services (Schneider 1986).

Occupations in which it may be easier to pass but in which the penalties for disclosure are relatively high are more diverse. These include occupations that:

• explicitly exclude people who are or are presumed to be lesbian or gay, such as military occupations and some jobs requiring security clearances

- exclude gay people in historical and current practice, such as elementary school teaching and law enforcement
- require work with children, a source of public contention and fear (Schneider 1986)
- require supervision of other employees, since authority is socially as well as officially conferred (Reskin and Padavic 1994)
- are traditionally imbued with a feminine or masculine identity, such as craft work (Baron 1991)
- are occupations dominated by men, who are reported to be more hostile than women to lesbians and particularly to gay men (Herek 1991)
- require more contact with the public.

In addition, we may expect to find lesbians and gay men concentrated in:

- the "gay ghetto" occupations, i.e., those publicly associated with gay men, such as positions in the arts, interior decorators, librarians, and waiters (Escoffier 1975)
- occupations found predominantly in large cities such as New York and San Francisco, where the best known gay communities exist.

It is difficult to determine whether discrimination against lesbians and gay men is likely to be greater in the private or the public sector. Civil-service hiring procedures appear to benefit women and ethnic minorities, and might afford some protection to lesbians and gay men. On the other hand, many workplaces that have been particularly hostile to gay people are found in the public sector, including elementary schools, police and fire departments, jails, intelligence agencies, and the military. Lesbians and gay men who have been politically motivated by the experience of prejudice, discrimination, and harassment may choose to work in nonprofit organizations dedicated to social change, where we also find women and ethnic minorities overrepresented, if not overly well-paid, relative to white men (Burbridge 1994; Kleiman 1994).

Finally, Beth Schneider (1986) has suggested that penalties for coming out are higher for jobs that pay more, since an employee with a high income has more to lose, and she has presented some evidence that people with high incomes are less willing to come out at work. Schneider mentions that this might be less true for lesbians than for gay men, since occupational segregation by gender limits women's employment options. It may also be true that the decision to remain closeted is different from the decision to avoid occupations with high penalties for disclosure. In other words, gay men and lesbians in highly paid positions might be especially careful to avoid disclosure of their homosexuality without steering away from such positions altogether. However, we believe that losing a relatively poorly paid position is in fact likely to exact a relatively greater cost than losing a well-paid job. People in well-paid jobs generally have more options when looking for work and may be expected to have more financial security to weather a period of unemployment and job search. A lawyer who is fired can work as a waitress, but a fired waitress cannot work as an attorney, and lawyers usually have more physical, social, and financial resources than waitresses.

Since the package of job characteristics includes income and status as well as institutional and personal attitudes toward gay people, a gay employee will make decisions based on the whole package. Because of the importance of the workplace environment, we expect that lesbians and gay men may enter less financially rewarding occupations than they would if they were straight, trading income and status for a job in which it is easier to pass or where the penalties for disclosure are relatively low, including jobs traditionally associated with lesbians and gay men or concentrated in areas with large gay communities.

Economists would describe these occupational strategies as pursuing a compensating differential, in other words, a tradeoff a worker faces between pay and work environment—between a job with lower pay and a more pleasant work environment and one with higher pay and less pleasant work conditions. The classic example of a compensating differential is the relatively high pay of garbage collectors. Although the concept of compensating differentials is well developed, many economists question the extent to which such differentials actually exist. It's certainly easier to think of examples of pleasant, high-status jobs that pay well and unpleasant, low-status jobs that pay poorly than the reverse.

However, we can imagine that a lesbian might choose a lower-paying occupation or a job in a tolerant environment over a better-paying one in a workplace hostile to disclosure of her sexual orientation. This kind of compensating differential operates for women who leave the trades, where they face greater levels of sexual harassment, for female-dominated occupations that are relatively poorly paid (Bergmann 1986; Martin 1988). Such a differential may be said to be operating for members of ethnic minorities who have been pushed by harassment and hostility out of particular jobs and entire occupations (Hill 1985).

Of course, the compensating differential is not an intrinsic characteristic of the job, but results from coworkers' attitudes and behavior. Harassment can be seen as a tactic to reserve particular jobs and workplaces for the incumbent social group. Fire departments have provided many examples in recent years of severe harassment of people of color and white women who have attempted to work in jobs previously held exclusively by white men. It may be difficult in practice for researchers working with quantitative data to distinguish employee harassment from hiring and promotion discrimination, since both operate to keep target populations out of good jobs. Certainly management bears the responsibility for both on the job.

Occupational Strategies Related to Family Structure

Lesbians' and gay men's expectations about their future family structures might lead them to choose different occupations from those entered by straight women and men. If it is true that gay relationships are less stable than those of straight couples (Blumstein and Schwartz 1983), then gay people need to plan for more independent and autonomous futures. And regardless of the relative stability of relationships, no legal protections exist for gay partners who forgo their own career advancement in the interest of their families. Certainly neither lesbians nor gay men can currently expect to receive health and other work-related benefits through a partner, as very few employers provide benefits to domestic partners. Consequently, both lesbians and gay men might foresee the need to support themselves through adulthood and into retirement, and the need to establish benefits under their own names. Likewise, gay people must establish credit on an individual basis.

While they share all of these considerations, lesbians and gay men are likely to have different expectations about family life and its impact on their career choices. Lesbians might anticipate that their partners are likely to earn significantly less than the (male) partners of straight women, regardless of class, ethnicity, or educational level, given the significant wage gap between men and women at all levels of education and in all occupations. They would thus expect to have to earn a higher individual income than straight women to achieve a particular standard of living. Moreover, if, on average, lesbians have fewer children than straight women, then lesbians would be less likely to voluntarily work part-time, combining childrearing and paid work, as more women than men currently do. Lesbians who do have children have more incentive to work full-time in order to obtain benefits than straight women, who may obtain benefits for themselves and their children through marriage.

Many economists believe that women tend to work in female-dominated occupations because these pay best over the long run to people who work intermittently, depending upon the needs of their families (Polachek 1981), but empirical research has discredited this line of reasoning (England 1982). However, if it does retain any power to explain occupational segregation by gender, we would expect that lesbians would be less likely to choose to work in typical "women's jobs" to the extent that they are less likely to raise children. Finally, straight women may work in low-paid female occupations to retain a badge of femininity as an asset in the marriage market (Bergmann 1986), an asset that lesbians may not value.

Gay men, on the other hand, can anticipate that their partners will have higher incomes and fewer children than the partners of straight men. Except for the necessity of securing their own benefits, gay men have fewer family-based incentives than straight men to pursue well-paid work, since they are less likely to be responsible for the support of children or a partner. However, having fewer children may also free both lesbians and gay men to devote more time and energy to education, training, and work, which should result in higher pay.

Finally, it may be true that lesbians and gay men receive less support from their parents and other family members for schooling, down payments, starting a business, or emergencies; if this is so, they are likely to have less opportunity for advancement and thus need to work harder to ensure their own financial security.

In short, lesbians have greater family-based incentives than do straight women to aim for full-time, better-paid jobs with benefits, even if they violate some gender norms in the process. Thus, the influence of family considerations runs counter to the strategy most likely to help a lesbian avoid discrimination—one that gives up higher income and benefits in return for a gay-tolerant work environment.

Gay men may have less responsibility for family welfare. However, they do need to ensure their financial security independently, and they may receive less support from their families of origin. If gay men on average have less incentive than straight men to pursue highly paid work, this might be expected to amplify an occupational strategy that trades pay for lower levels of discrimination and harassment.

Empirical Evidence

Description of the Data

Finding reliable random samples of the population with information on sexual orientation as well as economic and social characteristics is very difficult. Students of the gay community have been forced to rely on small, unrepresentative data sets generated either by marketing surveys of gay publications or by snowball sampling techniques, which involve researchers interviewing all of their own contacts, then all of the contacts of their contacts, and so on. Both kinds of samples appear to overrepresent gay people who are white, professional, relatively affluent, urban, middle aged, well-educated, politically oriented, and, of course, willing to identify themselves to surveyers as gay (Larson 1992; Gluckman and Reed 1993; Badgett 1995).

One underutilized but valuable survey, the General Social Survey (GSS) conducted by the National Opinion Research Center, has collected data on a variety of economic, demographic, and attitudinal characteristics, and in 1989 began asking respondents about their sexual behavior (Davis and Smith 1991). The GSS contains no specific variables on sexual orientation or identity, but it allows respondents who have had same-sex partners to be identified. Here, then, people who have had at least one same-sex sexual partner are behaviorally identified as lesbian, gay, or bisexual, behavioral identification being highly correlated with a self-identified gay or bisexual orientation (Lever, et al. 1992). People who have had a gay period in their lives but who currently behave and may identify as straight are also included in the "gay" category. The questions on sexual behavior were self-administered, accompanied by assurances of confidentiality.

Because of the design of the GSS, not all respondents were asked all questions in each survey. After eliminating those responses without information on sex partners, attitudes, or occupation, and a few with missing data on other variables, the sample pooled from the 4,426 respondents in the 1989–91 surveys contained 996 men and 1,156 women. Of this subsample, 3 percent of the women and 5 percent of the men reported having had at least one same-sex sexual partner since the age of eighteen (our definition of behaviorally lesbian, gay, or bisexual), a proportion that falls within the range determined in studies of sexual orientation (Gonsiorek and Weinrich 1991).

In addition to data on occupation, age, education, race, sex, and place of residence, the GSS asked about attitudes toward homosexuals in two ways. One series of three questions asked respondents whether an admitted male homosexual should be allowed to speak in the respondent's community, to teach in a college or university, or to have a book in the respondent's local public library. Those answering yes to these questions were coded as "gay-tolerant." A separate question asked if the respondent thought that sexual relations between two adults of the same sex were always wrong, almost always wrong, wrong only sometimes, or not wrong at all. For this question, one coding of gay-tolerant included just those answering "not wrong at all"; another specification also included those answering "wrong only sometimes."

Are the People in Some Occupations More Tolerant?

One measure of the potential magnitude of antigay discrimination in different occupations is to assess the attitudes of people working in those occupations. Table 1 shows this cross-tabulation for two of the tolerance questions, which were consistent in their ordering with the other questions. People in the professional and technical occupations hold more tolerant attitudes, regardless of the measure, and those in craft and operative occupations are the least tolerant. The tolerance rankings are the same for men and women, with one exception: men in clerical and sales positions are more tolerant of sex between two adults of the same sex than are men in managerial positions, while women in clerical/sales and managerial positions are roughly the same in terms of tolerance.

These patterns could simply reflect the unequal distribution of occupations across regions, urban and rural areas, educational levels and age groups, or could point to particular work cultures in the different occupations, all of which might be related to tolerance. If these other factors are the main influence on tolerance, then getting more education or moving might be more important strategies than occupational choice for lesbians and gay men seeking a tolerant workplace. To see if there is a relationship strictly between tolerance and occupation, we estimated what are called probit models for the attitude measures, using race, age, education, marital status, region, urban residence, sexual orientation, and occupation as independent variables. The effect of this statistical procedure is to hold constant the effect of factors such as region and urban residence, so as to see what the separate effect of occupation is on the degree of acceptance people express toward homosexuality.

Table 1: Measures of Tolerance within Occupations

Occupation	Would allow homosexual college teacher (%)		Believe that sex between two adults of same sex is not wrong (%)	
	Women	Men	Women	Men
Professional/Technical	81.0	86.7	26.2	24.6
Managerial	67.8	73.3	16.1	15.8
Clerical/Sales	66.3	71.4	14.0	21.1
Service	63.7	63.5	12.2	14.1
Craft/Operative	54.6	54.2	9.8	5.4

Source: Authors' tabulations from General Social Survey 1989–91, in Davis and Smith 1991.

The results of the probit procedure were fairly consistent for men and women, regardless of the survey question asked. Using the effect of occupational category generated by the probit procedure, we found the ranking of occupations by the level of tolerance to be much the same as in Table 1. People in professional/technical and managerial occupations are always among the most tolerant in their answers to the first set of civil liberties questions, along with men in clerical/sales positions. People in craft and operative jobs again appear to be the least tolerant, though women in these positions are less inclined than men to feel that gay sexual behavior is wrong. These results may be due to greater numbers of men in clerical and sales positions and women in craft and operative positions who are either gay themselves or more likely to know someone who is gay, given the overrepresentation of lesbians in craft/operative work and of gay men in clerical/sales jobs (see next section) and the correlation between acquaintance with gay people and tolerance (Herek and Glunt 1993).

However, the occupational parameters are rarely statistically significant; in other words, the effects seen here could be the result of an unusual sample of people rather than some systematic effect of occupation on level of tolerance. This is evidence that the markedly different levels of tolerance evinced by people in different occupational groups summarized in Table 1 may be a smoke screen, obscuring the more important underlying relationships between tolerance and education, urban residence, and age, the three variables that appear to be the most significant for predicting tolerance. It may be, however, that a larger sample and a more detailed occupational breakdown would reveal a greater role for occupational differences as well.

Are Lesbians and Gay Men Found in Tolerant Occupations?

Lesbians and gay men do appear to be distributed differently among occupations compared to heterosexuals, even when occupations are very broadly defined, as shown in Table 2. Lesbians in this sample are significantly less likely to hold professional/technical or clerical/sales positions and more likely to be engaged in ser-

Table 2: Occupational Distribution by Sexual Orientation and Gender, 1989–91

Occupation	Women			Men		
	Lesbian/Bi	Heterosexual	All	Gay/Bi	Heterosexual	All
Prof/Technical	11.4	20.8	18.1	32.0	18.9	14.9
Managerial	11.4	10.2	11.1	12.0	16.8	13.9
Clerical/Sales	14.3	36.6	40.9	18.0	14.6	16.8
Service	34.3	17.8	17.7	12.0	8.4	9.6
Craft/Operative	28.6	14.6	12.2	26.0	41.3	44.7
N=	35	1,121		50	946	

Sources: Data by sexual orientation comes from the General Social Survey, 1989–91, Davis and Smith 1991; data for all men and women comes from *Employment and Earnings*, January 1990.

vice or craft/operative jobs than heterosexual women. Gay men are overrepresented in professional/technical, clerical/sales, and service categories and underrepresented in managerial and craft/operative positions, relative to heterosexual men.

At first glance, the concentration of lesbians in craft/operative positions would seem to confirm the prediction that lesbians are likely to trade conformity to gender roles to obtain better-paid positions with benefits. However, earnings equations performed by Badgett (1995; see also previous chapter) on these same data indicate that lesbians earn no more, and perhaps less, than comparable heterosexual women, in part due to lesbians' occupational distribution. What is odd is that lesbians appear to be in different and somewhat less conventional occupations than straight women, but they are neither earning more nor are they clustered in the more tolerant occupations; indeed, lesbians are concentrated in the least tolerant occupations. The lesbians and straight women in this sample have equal levels of education, but the lesbians are on average younger and less likely to be white. It may be that the lesbians are in relatively lower-paying occupations because of discrimination, because they have not yet trained for or been promoted to better jobs, or in order to reduce their potential losses from disclosure or discrimination, as Beth Schneider argues. A larger sample is needed to perform the sophisticated statistical analysis which could determine the relative influence of age and ethnicity on lesbians' and gay men's occupations. A larger sample would also allow us to identify particular jobs that are attractive to or problematic for lesbians, due to levels of customer contact, teamwork, or other issues. Identifying the specific jobs in which lesbians are concentrated may help us to understand why lesbians appear to be clustered in relatively poorly paying and intolerant occupations.

Gay men's occupational distribution may indicate that they are avoiding or are unable to enter craft and operative jobs, which stereotypically entail the greatest emphasis on masculinity as a prerequisite for the work (or perhaps for the work culture). Again, the gay and straight men in this sample have equal levels of education; indeed, all four groups average 13.6 years of education. Perhaps gay men with less education are concentrated in clerical, sales, and service occupations rather than craft and operative positions, because these jobs are not only outside of the masculine preserve in the labor market but are also concentrated in urban areas—as are the gay men in this sample, 55 percent of whom live in large urban areas (SMSAs) in comparison to 46 percent of the straight men.

Further, gay men are underrepresented in management, where hiring and promotion depend on very subjective assessments of ability, allowing a wide latitude for excluding people. They are overrepresented in professional/technical positions, where access is more often mediated by credential. It may be that socially subordinate groups in general find the credentialing process easier to pursue than promotion; for instance, the ratio of white women and African Americans in management compared to those in the professions is much lower than for white men (King 1992). Gay men do seem to be concentrated in the more tolerant occupational groups.

However, this sample is quite small, including only thirty-five lesbian and bisexual women and fifty gay and bisexual men, and it cannot be relied on for more than the suggestion of large patterns. Further, the sample as a whole may be slightly skewed toward professional and managerial employees, especially for men, as is indicated by the data in the columns for all working women and men, taken from the larger 1990 *Employment and Earnings* sample.

Discussion and Conclusion

Several issues complicate straightforward predictions of occupational strategies based on sexual orientation. First is the timing of one's realization of one's own sexual orientation. If, as suggested by Escoffier (1975), many lesbians and gay men do not identify as gay until their early twenties, many will already be well into an occupation or on an occupational path that has been influenced by other factors such as gender, class, ethnicity, and personal aptitudes and tastes.

Second, gender, ethnicity, and class have been shown to be very influential in sorting people into occupations, and these factors may explain some of the puzzles raised in this paper. The lesbians in this sample are younger, more likely to be nonwhite, and more likely to live in the South than the straight women, while the gay men are slightly older and more likely to live in a large urban area than the straight men. For these reasons, the lesbians in our sample have been more restricted in the occupations they could enter than the gay men. This may explain why they appear to be concentrated in less well-paid and less tolerant occupations than straight women, but not to face sexual orientation-based pay discrimination in these occupations, while gay men appear to be overrepresented in well-paid and tolerant occupations but to face sexual orientation-based pay discrimination in those occupations (Badgett 1995; see also previous chapter, this volume).

Third, we have assumed that lesbians and gay men are identical to straight women and men in every way except their sexual orientation. We have also treated lesbians and gay men as if they were the same except for their likely partners. An approach which investigated the impact of the different cultures, networks, opportunities, and experiences that combine to shape occupational distributions might contribute significantly to our understanding of gay occupational distributions.

In short, a larger sample and perhaps a more qualitative approach—including interviewing—are needed to pursue the questions raised here. With a larger sample, we could (1) see how gay and straight people are distributed among occupations defined more specifically than we were able to here; (2) use more sophisticated statistical techniques to separate the influences of education, location, age, gender, and ethnicity from the effect of sexual orientation; and (3) test the validity of our results: that lesbians are concentrated in less well-paid and less tolerant occupations, and that gay men are clustered in better-paid, more tolerant occupations but earn less than comparably situated straight men. We hope that data from the 1990 U.S. Census, a huge, nationally representative sample and the first Census in which couples could identify themselves as gay, will allow us to explore these questions in far greater depth.

Finally, the development of the gay civil-rights movement over the last few decades suggests that the occupational options for gay people have changed and will continue to change. Several examples demonstrate the tremendous possibilities. First, many explicit barriers have fallen, with openly gay and lesbian people working in government jobs or as police officers or teachers, for instance. Second, the development of the gay-rights movement has involved taking control of important institutions serving the lesbian, gay, and bisexual communities, a trend intensified by the HIV epidemic and the subsequent formation of support institutions. These trends have led to new entrepreneurial opportunities and employment options in gay bars, bookstores, restaurants, newspapers, magazines, hotels, health services, and political organizations. And third, many of the barriers related to intolerant attitudes are apparently susceptible to change. Gay workers are organizing workplace groups to fight for equal employment opportunities and equal benefits (e.g., domestic partner benefits), and much effort has gone into increasing gay visibility and directly educating coworkers and supervisors on lesbian and gay issues. If the composition of these groups' leaders is any indication, however, most of these efforts are directed at the managerial and professional levels of coworkers, increasing the tolerance level—and the attractiveness to lesbian and gay workers—of those occupations that are already relatively tolerant.

Acknowledgments

The authors would like to thank Johanna Brenner, Connie Ledbetter, Clifford Lehman, Vicky Lovell, Lisa Saunders, Harold Vatter, Bill Weber, Mary Young and our editors for their insightful comments.

References

Badgett, M. V. Lee. "The Wage Effects of Sexual Orientation Discrimination." *Industrial and Labor Relations Review*, Vol. 48, No. 4 (July 1995): 726–739.

Badgett, M. V. Lee, Colleen Donnelly, and Jennifer Kibbe. "Pervasive Patterns of Discrimination Against Lesbians and Gay Men: Evidence from Surveys Across the United States." Washington, DC: National Gay and Lesbian Task Force Policy Institute, 1992.

Baron, Ava (ed.). *Work Engendered: Toward A New History of American Labor*. Ithaca, NY: Cornell University Press, 1991.

Bergmann, Barbara. *The Economic Emergence of Women*. New York: Basic Books, 1986.

Blumstein, Philip, and Pepper Schwartz. *American Couples: Money, Work, Sex*. New York: William Morrow & Company, 1983.

Brause, Jay. "Closed Doors: Sexual Orientation Bias in the Anchorage Housing and Employment Markets." *Identity Reports: Sexual Orientation Bias in Alaska*. Anchorage, AK: Indentity Incorporated, 1989.

Burbridge, Lynn. "The Reliance of African American Women on Government and

Nonprofit Employment." Unpublished paper presented at the Allied Social Science Associations (ASSA) meetings in Boston, January 1994.

Davis, James Allan, and Tom W. Smith. General Social Surveys, 1972–1991 (machine-readable data file). Principal Investigator, James A. Davis; Director and Coprincipal Investigator, Tom W. Smith. NORC ed. Chicago: National Opinion Research Center, producer, 1991; Storrs, CT: The Roper Center for Public Opinion Research, University of Connecticut, distributor.

England, Paula. "The Failure of Human Capital Theory to Explain Occupational Sex Segregation." Journal of Human Resources, Vol. 17, No. 3 (Summer 1982).

Escoffier, Jeffrey. "Stigmas, Work Environment, and Economic Discrimination Against Homosexuals." Homosexual Counseling Journal, Vol. 2, No. 1 (January 1975): 8–17.

Gonsiorek, John C., and James D. Weinrich. "The Definition and Scope of Sexual Orientation," in John C. Gonsiorek and James D. Weinrich (eds.), Homosexuality: Research Implications for Public Policy. Newbury Park, CA: Sage Publications, 1991.

Herek, Gregory M. "Stigma, Prejudice and Violence Against Lesbians and Gay Men," in John C. Gonsiorek and James D. Weinrich (eds.), Homosexuality: Research Implications for Public Policy. Newbury Park, CA: Sage Publications, 1991.

Herek, Gregory M., and Eric K. Glunt. "Interpersonal Contact and Heterosexuals' Attitudes Toward Gay Men: Results from a National Survey." The Journal of Sex Research, Vol. 30, No. 3 (August 1, 1993).

Hill, Herbert. "Race and Ethnicity in Organized Labor: The Historical Sources of Resistance to Affirmative Action," in Winston Van Horne and Thomas Tonnesen (eds.), Ethnicity and the Work Force. Madison, WI: University of Wisconsin System, 1985.

King, Mary C. "Occupational Segregation by Race and Sex, 1940–1988." Monthly Labor Review, Vol. 115, No. 4 (April 1992): 30–37.

Kleiman, Carol. "At Non-Profit Agencies, Women Lag Men in Salary and Power." San Diego Union Tribune, Sept. 27, 1994, c-6.

Larson, Kathryn. "The Economic Status of Lesbians: The State of the Art." Unpublished paper presented at the ASSA meetings in New Orleans, January 1992.

Lever, Janet, David Kanouse, William H. Rogers, Sally Carson, and Rosanna Hertz. "Behavior Patterns and Sexual Identity of Bisexual Males." The Journal of Sex Research, Vol. 29 (1992): 141–67.

Martin, Molly (ed.). Hard-hatted Women: Stories of Struggle and Success in the Trades. Seattle: Seal Press, 1988.

Moore, David W. "Public Polarized on Gay Issue." The Gallup Poll Monthly, No. 331 (April 1993).

Polachek, Solomon. "Occupational Self-Selection: A Human Capital Approach to Sex Differences in Occupational Structure." Review of Economics and Statistics, Vol. 63, No. 1 (February 1981).

Reskin, Barbara. "Segregating Workers: Job Differences by Ethnicity, Race and Sex." Paper presented at the ASSA meetings in Boston, January 1994.

Reskin, Barbara, and Irene Padavic. *Women and Men at Work.* Thousand Oaks, CA: Pine Forge Press, 1994.

Schneider, Beth. "Coming Out at Work." *Work and Occupations,* Vol. 13, No. 4 (November 1986): 463–87.

U.S. Department of Labor, Bureau of Labor Statistics, *Employment and Earnings,* Vol. 37, No. 1 (January 1990).

Warden, Sharon. "Attitudes on Homosexuality." *Washington Post,* April 25, 1993, A18.

Woods, James D. *The Corporate Closet: The Professional Lives of Gay Men in America.* New York: Free Press, 1993.

Part II

The Contradictions of Capitalism for Lesbians and Gay Men

Some Theoretical Perspectives

8

Queer Political Economy
The Social Articulation of Desire

Richard R. Cornwall

This is an adaptation of a longer paper on queer political economy. The author conducted mathematical simulations of the way in which individuals form social networks in order to discover their desires. This approach helps explain the repression of queer desire in England and America, and lays bare the distortions of mainstream economic theory arising from its individualistic bias. See Cornwall (1996) for the mathematics of this model.

"My desire,
More sharp than filed steel, did spur me forth"
—Shakespeare, *Twelfth Night*

desidero, ergo sum

post/modern epigraph

1. Introduction

The foundation for political economy is the concept of each person's tastes or preferences, i.e., desire. In neoclassical economics, preferences are assumed to be essentially predetermined genetically for each individual—oh, all right, perhaps bent a bit *in utero* by the mother's choices and even warped a small amount shortly after birth by the "nuclear family."[1] It is these preferences that lie at the base of the celebrated First and Second Efficiency Theorems of economic theory, which provide the key logic underlying intellectual defenses of market-based systems for social guidance and control. These theorems hold that capitalism allocates tasks and consumptions to each person in such a way that it is impossible to rearrange them in any way that would make some people happier and no one less happy (this is known as the market's "pareto efficiency").[2] Marxism, in contrast, takes individual preferences as wholly socially constructed by the social relations of production. In this view, the social structure of capital-versus-labor determines all noteworthy variations in human desires.

I offer here an overview of arguments that each individual's preferences are formulated at the deepest cognitive levels through social interaction, in markets, and otherwise. This is the basis for social structures—social codes or identities—that in their formation, operation, durability, and complexity are very similar to the earth's swirl of human languages. The effect of conceptualizing these social codes is to eviscerate mainstream economics' argument for the "efficiency" or "optimality" of the market as well as the priority assigned in Marxian economics to the dichotomy between capital and labor over other social categorizations. In particular, this paper presents the first sociocognitive model of what is the central queer example of paretian inefficiency of a social system: how a substantial fraction of the population can continue to deny to themselves as well as to others their "true" tastes—i.e., to stay stuck in the closet—despite repeated social interaction that includes visible queers.

To begin this story, it is appropriate to start with the perspective of queer studies, as it focuses on describing both the social articulation of human desire[3] and the resulting vortex of social identities. It is critical to understand why identities often appear so essentially natural, so clear and durable, yet why they also appear as mirages, so insubstantial and false, mere social artifices. To make this double vision of identities tangible, consider this case from literary history.

At the rollover from the sixteenth to the seventeenth centuries, it was still possible for the two most prominent English playwrights, Shakespeare and Marlowe, to perceive and to articulate queer desire for all their audience. The first line quoted at the start of this piece was spoken by Antonio, whose urgent efforts to pursue Sebastian after their ship lands reflect the prominent role of queer desire in *Twelfth Night.*[4]

This ability simply to perceive, let alone articulate, queer desire in Shakespeare's work was lost in the intervening years so that, until Oscar Wilde started articulating rudely at the end of the last century, no one could admit to perceiving queer desire in Shakespeare's work. Only now in the mid-1990s in a few spots in this world can one readily discover how queerly Shakespeare's wordplay can be cast, thanks to such efforts as the production in the fall of 1994 of *Twelfth Night by* Danny Scheie at Theatre Rhinoceros. This was sited, significantly, in the heavily Latino/a, poor, and, yes, subversive Mission district of San Francisco.

To develop one theoretical description of this cycle from queer visibility to erasure and back to visibility, section 2 examines the process by which human desire gets expressed. It uses Keynes's notion that "we make judgments about the probability of future events without detailed numerical information"[5]—i.e., we judge based on subjective probabilities—to construct networks to articulate our desires. This story of people discovering their desires leads to an explanation of how social codes can come to falsely—"illusorily"—link desires to irrelevant human traits.

The key insight underlying this argument is that humans are totally dependent on our linguistic communities for our abilities to perceive, categorize, and articulate desires. This dependence is explored by looking at changes in the social categories of queer and straight, of lower and middle class, and of male and female, in the United States from late in the nineteenth century to the present. This historical evolution is then tied to what psychologists call illusory correlations in human cognition, correlations of the irrelevant which have been especially relevant to queers in the past sixty years. Finally, in section 6, I look at some of the implications of these ideas for the role of ideology in political economy, inspired by Oscar Wilde's and Jean Genet's efforts to subvert and appropriate individualism for queerly socialistic ends.

The mixture here of voices and of concepts from different disciplines is queer and few may feel fluent in all these languages, yet this *ver/mischung* seems essential to initiate a queer political economy. Much of the most insightful thinking about shame/abjection has been done not by political economists but by literary cultural analysts. The mathematical and political-economic strands here are made explicit in Cornwall (1996).

2. Social Articulation of Desire: Social Codes/Languages as Institutions for Parallel Processing

To understand the functioning of social codes in the formulation of desire, I have conducted mathematical simulations of the process of individual economic decision making. I began with a conceit especially popular in the previous two centuries and now deeply ingrained in economists' thinking: the solitary individual, who confronts markets completely on her/his own, but, we imagine, who has no idea of what s/he wants. Following Cyert and DeGroot (1980), McFadden (1981, 205), McFadden and Richter (1990, 165), Arthur (1991), Marimon, McGrattan, Sargent (1990), and Sargent (1993),[6] I imagined this solitary individual, Robinson Crusoe (or R.C., for short), as knowing her budget constraint but not her preferences and so making choices by intelligent randomness. I drew R.C. with the face of Mr. Magoo,[7] missing his glasses and groping quite blindly for insights as to where his goodies are. Since R.C. Magoo knows she does not know how to make himself feel good—what s/he desires, she decides to randomly sample among all her options to discover how they work. Thus we imagine that Magoo adopts a "stochastic" strategy to learn about his own desires.

Economists assume that people know their preferences and make these preferences the basis for interpreting everyone's behavior in markets. If, however, preferences are unknown (and whether or not they are fixed), an individual will find that there are significant gains to pooling information with other people about which choices are inferior to which other choices. Yet this pool of information about rankings can get seriously contaminated if people with different tastes contribute to the pool.

As a result, people can be thought to use standard statistical procedures to find variables that help them distinguish which people have the same tastes as they do and with whom they can trade information about inferior/superior choices. These networks that facilitate the articulation of desire are "homopreference" networks. Individuals within homopreference networks can often be led to conclude that a variable that is actually completely irrelevant, but that is more easily discernible than is more sophisticated evidence of another's tastes, is in fact a reliable cue to differences in tastes. Because people are persuaded that such an irrelevant, "illusory," variable is helpful in their effort to articulate their own desires through swapping information with others, everyone can end up choosing her/his network of "friends" by excluding anyone who differs in this illusory variable. This results in a biased construction of homopreference networks. Sophisticated tests of whether someone's tastes are the same as one's own can repair this bias only belatedly. Hence, the correction cannot be complete for people whose Face and preferences make their group small compared to the size of the homopreference networks (race and class bias, for instance, limits the range of a homopreference network).

In the ten simulations conducted, the consequence of reliance on an illusory trait was that approximately one-third (eleven out of thirty) of the people with the minority type of preferences were led into the "closet," i.e., led to articulate a choice as being best for them that was, in fact, significantly different from what was best for them. Only one out of sixty of the people with the majority type of preferences made such an error. This misarticulation of desire, which occurred in all ten simulations, was "pareto inefficient." Each of the people who chose as "best" a choice that in fact was inferior to another choice for them could feasibly have changed to their (hidden) best choice.

The model employed was extremely simplistic and essentialistic, taking people's "true" tastes as genetically given. These true tastes may then be distorted by sheer random chance depending on whom one "chooses" as neighbors with whom to pool information on preferences. A more complete model (Cornwall 1996) allows for a person's true tastes to be shaped, at least in part, through social interaction.

In addition, this model does not capture the important dynamics of abjection/shame that have powered homophobia for the past five centuries in western cultures. In particular, it does not pretend to offer a full explanation of the "closet."[8] Surely there are some who act straight (and so are conventionally described as being "in the closet") but who do so for very different reasons than not knowing they would prefer being intimate with their own gender. But for some of us it does hint at what delayed our sexual maturity to an age which is startling for some today.

The model assumes that cognitive codes (e.g., the idea that a different Face signifies different tastes) evolve socially, as people endeavor to distinguish others with the same tastes from those with different tastes. This evolution is analogous to the sociologically nuanced development of linguistic variation, and akin to William Burroughs' claim that "language is a virus" (Ricco 1994, 76)."[9]

The growth of these cognitive codes generates social structures known as "social identities," which are simply the labels that come, like game theory's focal points, to distinguish homopreference networks. These identities, like sociolinguistic structures, are ambiguously bordered from/overlapping with each other as well as both very durable and rather plastic. When seen as a social solution to the problem of how individuals know what they desire, these codes can be seen to be institutional "social software" coordinating the "parallel processing" of experience by multiple individuals. This in turn saves people enormously in the time required to articulate their desires. This social articulation of cognitive codes, which in my model are based on the networked evolution of each person's probabilities (i.e., his or her understanding of who is different or similar in tastes), gives one meaning to Dollimore's (1991, 244) assertion that "identity—individual and cultural—involves a process of disavowal."

It is important to stress that the extremely simplistic and essentialist model I have used to draw these conclusions is not, by itself, a model of real economies. Rather, this model aims to make tangible a deep, specific criticism of neoclassical economics: if perfectly competitive market-guided outcomes are to be superior to all other allocation of tasks and consumptions (i.e., if they are to be pareto efficient), people must know and act on their true preferences. A more useful model for political economy comprehends that we enter the world blind like Magoo about our own desires; that our understanding—articulation—of our desires is largely determined by the social structures in which we are ensnared; and that important social forces of political economy mold these social structures.

We turn next to analyses of our use and formation of categories for perception, sketching some of the forces of political economy shaping these categories.

3. Categories and (Illusory) Correlations

I use the phrase "socially articulate desires" to describe the way in which people in groups categorize each other in order to express and act on their desires. This articulation involves breaking humanity into distinct pieces; i.e., forming categories for distinguishing people according to some traits and joining these pieces together, recognizing that society includes these different types.

To understand how we form categories, we must look at human inference: how do we know? This invites epistemological complexity, but I choose queerly, instead, to follow Wittgenstein in assuming a sociolinguistic basis of "ordinary language" for "knowing" what we know.[10] Cognitive psychology has, in the last twenty years, made significant progress in mapping many contours of how individuals perceive (and also fail to perceive), encode, store, retrieve, and then express/act on perceptions. "The view that categories are invariably defined by a set of necessary and sufficient conditions for membership has by now been thoroughly discredited" (Holland, et al. 1986, 182). Instead of such a discredited "positivist" epistemological approach, Wittgenstein (1958) in philosophy and Berlin and Kay (1969) in linguistics suggested that a more useful mental model is that we form categories on the basis of prototypes and we have quite ambiguous boundaries between categories.[11]

This process for forming social categories can be thought of as the elevation of an instance of one person doing/being something into an archetype. The central metaphor/analogy here is:

figure out a problem = figuration (put a face on the problem)

The etymological roots of this linguistic associative code in English are the Latin (*figura*) and French (*la figure*) words for face. The strong analytical preference for "specific-level evidence" (i.e., specific human examples) over more abstract "base-rate information" (i.e., abstract categories) is evident in Lee Edelman's (1994) study of the cinematic focus on the face. Edelman notes how movies use faces to represent many things—concepts, feelings, language, smells, experiences, class, ethnicity, race, gender, sense of safety/violation. Political campaigns also do it (Willie Horton). It is what makes TV so powerful: faces seduce people to be viewers by capturing their attention. Even MTV's Beavis and Butthead have identifiably working faces with mouths that fart, noses that wrinkle.

The preference for specific figuration, the use of facial prototypes, over abstract categorization may be a mere statistical regularity, or may be deeply embedded within the operating systems (e.g., limbic systems) of our cognitive software and hardware by the amygdala.[12] Such figuration may only be supplemented when we have had powerfully salient experience through the use of abstract categories rather than faces.

This suggests that prosopopeia, the process by which we give a face to an idea with a figure of speech, may be more than mere metaphor for human categorization and induction. This conjecture of a central role in human cognition for facial images is strengthened by growing evidence that "the amygdala has a central role in social communication. . . . The direction of one's gaze signals the object of one's attention . . . while facial expression indicates how one is disposed to behave. When mutual eye contact is established, both participants know that the communication loop between them has been closed and for primates of all species this is the most potent of social situations" (Allman and Brothers 1994).

There is also an increasing body of evidence that cognitive access to facial images appears to be "effortless," "a rapid, automated process," and more accurate than are "deliberative, analytic retrieval processes"; e.g., sorting, matching, and elimination (Dunning and Stern 1994, 819 and 832; see also Wells, Rydell, and Seelau 1993).

Making the blatant leap of applying this description of very specific types of induction to socially mediated categorization, it is tempting to consider the "sex/gender system" (Rubin 1975, 1984) that admitted little variation, and appears to have been hegemonic, until approximately the end of the last century. It was taken for granted, as "natural,"[13] that sexual object preference was determined by gender: "In the dominant turn-of-the-century cultural system governing the interpretation of homosexual behavior, especially in working-class milieus, one had a gender identity rather than a sexual identity or even a 'sexuality'; one's sexual behavior was thought to be necessarily determined by one's gender identity (Chauncey 1994, 48)."[14] In other words, gender was determined by the dichotomy of "male" versus "female" face, which also determined sexual object choice.

The turn of the century was a time not only of increasing urbanization in this country, but also of radical changes in the roles and extents of markets and the organization of production. The rise of wage labor in this country occurred for men after the first third of the nineteenth century and was followed at the end of the century by dramatic changes for women, as wage labor became both gendered and segregated. For example, at the turn of the century bank tellers switched amazingly quickly from being an all-male occupation to a predominately female occupational category.[15] Equally momentous was the rise of factories with thousands of workers under one roof, a structure that led to enormous social upheaval as new codes and occupations for imagining/running productive enterprises were developed.[16]

This blender of changing social roles created a vortex of changing social identities:

> Working-class men and boys regularly challenged the authority of middle-class men by verbally questioning the manliness of middle-class supervisors or physically attacking middle-class boys. . . . [As one contemporary] recalled, he had "often seen [middle-class cultivation] taken by those [men] of the lower classes as "sissy." The increasingly militant labor movement, the growing power of immigrant voters in urban politics, and the relatively high birthrate of certain immigrant groups established a worrisome context for such personal affronts and in themselves constituted direct challenges to the authority of Anglo-American men as a self-conceived class, race and gender. (Chauncey 1994, 112)

These struggles over where to map key social borders led

> politicians, businessmen, educators, and sportsmen alike [to protest] the dangers of "overcivilization" to American manhood. . . . Theodore Roosevelt was the most famous advocate of the "strenuous life" of muscularity, rough sports, prizefighting, and hunting. . . . The glorification of the prizefighter and the workingman bespoke the ambivalence of middle-class men about their own gender status. . . . A "cult of muscularity" took root in turn-of-the-century middle-class culture. . . . Earlier in the nineteenth century, men had tended to constitute themselves as men by distinguishing themselves from boys. . . . . But in the late nineteenth century, middle-class men began to define themselves more centrally on the basis of their difference from women. . . . . Gender-based terms of derision (e.g., sissy, pussy-foot) became increasingly prominent in late-nineteenth-century American culture. (Chauncey 1994, 113–14)

This oversimplifies and ignores counterpressures to cover gender distinctions (e.g., Vicinus [1992] and Matthaei [1992]), but this recoding of masculinity seems to have been powerful at this time.

Closely tied to this redefinition of "male"[17] in the 1890's was redefinition of class:

> Men and women of the urban middle class increasingly defined themselves as a class by the boundaries they established between the "private life" of the home and the rough-and-tumble of the city streets, between the quiet order of their neighborhoods and the noisy, overcrowded character of the working-class districts. The privacy and order of their sexual lives also became a way of defining their difference from the lower classes. (Chauncey 1994, 35)

Just as a new "face" was being put on not-male, i.e., not-male became "female" instead of "boy," so "middle-class" became "clean face and well-laundered/mended clothes" versus the "dirty" faces of slums. A quickly judged face was put on people living in slums:

The spatial segregation of openly displayed "vice" in the slums had . . . ideological consequences: it kept the most obvious streetwalkers out of middle-class neighborhoods, and it reinforced the association of such immorality with the poor. . . . Going slumming in the resorts of the Bowery and the Tenderloin was a popular activity among middle-class men (and even among some women), in part as a way to witness working-class "depravity" and to confirm their sense of superiority. (Chauncey 1994, 26)[18]

This simultaneous redefinition of gender and class spilled over, and infected, the definition of sexual orientation that was emerging at the turn of the century:

In a culture in which becoming a fairy meant assuming the status of a woman or even a prostitute, many men . . . simply refused to do so. . . . The efforts of such men marked the growing differentiation and isolation of sexuality from gender in middle-class American culture. . . . . The effort to forge a new kind of homosexual identity was predominantly a middle-class phenomenon, and the emergence of "homosexuals" in middle-class culture was inextricably linked to the emergence of "heterosexuals" in the culture as well. If many workingmen thought they demonstrated their sexual virility by playing the "man's part" in sexual encounters with either women or men, normal middle-class men increasingly believed that their virility depended on their exclusive sexual interest in women. Even as queer men began to define their difference from other men on the basis of their homosexuality, "normal" men began to define their difference from queers on the basis of their renunciation of any sentiments or behavior that might be marked as homosexual. (Chauncey 1994, 100)

Further, "the queers' antagonism toward the fairies was in large part a class antagonism. . . . . The cultural stance of the queer embodied the general middle-class preference for privacy, self-restraint, and lack of self-disclosure" (106).

This link between the signification of economic class and of sexuality was, of course, not new at the end of the last century. "In colonial America, [convicted] sodomites were more often than not lower-class servants, and the shoring up of patriarchal power was imbricated in nascent class divisions. One has only to look to other colonial situations of the time to see that that was not the only way the category of sodomy was being mobilized; the Spaniards, for instance, prone to see sodomites among the Moors in Spain, saw native cultures as hotbeds of irregular sexual practices" (Goldberg 1994, 7). As Stallybrass and White note, "The bourgeois subject continuously defined and re-defined itself through the exclusion of what it marked out as 'low'—as dirty, repulsive, noisy, contaminating. Yet that very act of exclusion was constitutive of its identity. The low was internalized under the sign of negation and disgust" 1986, 191). This *ver/mischung* of the codifications of class, sexuality, and gender is of fundamental importance for queer political economy, which is explored further in section 4 below.

The tendency to label certain traits as "invidious," and to tie these traits to other categories, is an example of errors that are typical in human categorization of both physical and social environments. We induce categories in order to sort out who is appropriate for the homopreference networks that articulate our desires.

It is hard to overemphasize the enormity of the changes in the working and living conditions of most western humans since postindustrial society emerged at the end of the last century. Many people, especially those migrating from rural life, simply lacked categories to express what they were experiencing: migrating from living and working with kinfolk, typically in rural or small-town settings, to wage labor, sometimes in the new institution of factories. All of this depended on reduced costs of transportation and communication—as well as more superficial changes like new commodities for consumption. This significant acceleration of the velocity of social change in the postindustrial era appears to have heightened the need for new institutions to articulate desires. This need, cutting to the heart of what it is to be human, may have contributed to perceptual errors caused by the use of new illusory variables.

The seminal as well as nomenclatory work on the phenomenon of "illusory correlation" was based on discovering false correlations between homosexuality and other traits. Loren and Jean Chapman (1967, 1969; Chapman 1967)[19] surveyed several dozen clinical psychologists about which Rorschach signs distinguished their gay male clients from straight male clients. Of those surveyed, thirty-two clinicians "said that they had seen the Rorschach protocols of a number of men with homosexual problems [sic]" (1969, 273). The Chapmans concluded that

> the "popularity" of signs [as indicators of homosexuality] among practicing clinicians has little relationship to the objective clinical validity of the signs. . . . The most popular signs among practicing clinicians are the ones that have the strongest verbal associative connection to male homosexuality. Naive observers, when presented with contrived Rorschach responses arbitrarily paired with statements of symptoms of the patient who gave each response, erroneously report these same associatively based invalid signs occur as correlates of homosexuality.[20] The naive observers reported these associatively based illusory correlations even when the materials are contrived so that other [clinically] valid correlations are present. (1969, 273)

How, one might ask, can sexual orientation, given its frequent invisibility, be construed to be a "readily available cue" to illusorily correlate with other traits and, hence, to use for stereotyping?[21] The intensity of the affect associated with sexual orientation leads many to pay very close attention to any clues. For example, many men, both straight and gay, are familiar with the technique experienced by Essex Hemphill at age fourteen:

> Crip was standing. I was sitting. It happened that from where I sat I could eye his crotch with a slight upward shift of my eyes. Well, one of the times that I peeked, Crip caught me. . . . Instantly, Crip jumped forward and got in my face. "I see you looking at my dick!" he hurled at me. I felt as though he had accused me of breaking into his house and violating his mother. Immediately, all

conversation ceased and all eyes focused on me and Crip. (Hemphill 1992, 100)

Hemphill survived this humiliation without getting beaten up and limped home to shut himself in his room as soon as he could break away. He learned to survive through high school by getting a girlfriend, a "good girl," who did not want to fuck.

This story highlights the role played by watching another's gaze in making sexual orientation distinctive, and suggests why it might be a trait used in making illusory correlations, which in turn serve as the basis for the intensely biased cognitive codes underlying homophobia.[22] Feeling sexually aroused is one of the most intense affects humans ever experience. Thus anything associated with this affect, such as sexual orientation, appears highly distinctive. This recalls the tendency of European-male-dominated American culture to label both Black men and women as "hypersexual."[23] The same scrutiny is apparent in the madonna/whore dichotomy socially constructed for European-American women.[24]

To recap: How do we know what we know—or feel, or desire? Our perceptions depend on the cognitive categories with which we articulate (i.e., perceive and express) our desires and "knowledge." These categories have been created through the particular dynamics of the social networks we have been part of since birth. A survey of work by psychologists, sociologists, historians, philosophers, and sociolinguists has led to the conclusion that socially learned codes play an enormously important role in determining how we perceive others. These codes produce prosopopeic categories based on central archetypal figures. The use of archetypes renders this process surprisingly agile, but also renders it very susceptible to making false—illusory—correlations of human traits.

The false articulation of desires, described in section 2, might actually occur in one's social world through a reliance on a particular social network—on neighbors from a particular class and/or gender—to discover what choices are best for oneself. This can lead one to fail to recognize one's own "true" preferences, which are formed through social interaction but which are also socially distorted and repressed. Bray tried to make comprehensible the homosexual behavior of some people in the sixteenth and seventeenth centuries at the time of the erasure of the articulation of queer:

The individual could simply avoid making the connection; he could keep at two opposite poles the social pressures bearing down on him and his own discordant sexual behaviour, and avoid recognising it for what it was. . . . For when one looks at the circumstantial details of how homosexuality was conceived of and how it was expressed in concrete social forms, it becomes obvious how very easy it was in Renaissance England—far more so than today—for a cleavage of this kind to exist, between an individual's behaviour and his awareness of its significance. Firstly the way homosexuality was conceived of: how possible was it to avoid identifying with the "sodomite" who was the companion of witches and Papists, of werewolves and agents of the King of Spain? When the world inhabited by the conventional image of the sodomite was so distant from everyday life, it cannot have been hard. (Bray 1982, 67–68)

The sense of being socially of such a different caste if one were queer made it impossible for many to position themselves as homosexual in their internal cognitive maps. This was true for many in Renaissance England, and likewise for people maturing in the McCarthy-polluted 1950s. Anecdotal evidence suggests that this latter generation had more difficulty recognizing same-sex desire than did those either growing up before the Depression or reaching maturity in the late 1960s, especially after Stonewall.

A useful parallel to the 1950s in the United States (which followed the two queer panics, described in section 4 below) might be the pre–World War I period in England following the queer panic produced by the trial of Oscar Wilde. Both were times of dramatic queer cultural innovation (e.g., the Bloomsbury group's writing, painting, and historicizing in England, and Beat writing, Rauschenberg and Johns's painting, and Tennessee Williams's playwriting in the United States) and also of dramatic social repression of queer social structures. The ability not to articulate one's queerness in such a setting was captured well by that straddler of this sexual divide, D. H. Lawrence, writing in the suppressed prologue to *Women in Love*:

> The male physique had a fascination for him, and for the female physique he felt only a fondness . . . as for a sister. In the street it was the men who roused him by their flesh and their manly, vigorous movement. . . . He loved his friend, the beauty of whose manly limbs made him tremble with pleasure. He wanted to caress him. But reserve, which was as strong as a chain of iron in him, kept him from any demonstration. . . . He wondered very slightly at this, but dismissed it with hardly a thought. Yet every now and again, would come over him the same passionate desire to have near him some man he saw. . . . It might be any man.
> . . . How vividly, months afterwards, he would recall the soldier who had sat pressed up close to him on a journey from Charing Cross to Westerham . . . [o]r a young man in flannels on the sands at Margate. . . . In his mind was a small gallery of such men: men whom he had never spoken to, but who had flashed themselves upon his senses unforgettably, men whom he apprehended intoxicatingly in his blood. . . . This was the one and only secret he kept to himself, this secret of his passionate and sudden, spasmodic affinity for men he saw. He kept this secret even from himself. He knew what he felt, but he always kept the knowledge at bay. (1981, 103–107)[25]

We have thus far developed one story for the use of prosopopeia—of faces-as-archetypes—as the basis for our induction of social categories and for the role our social networks can play in this articulation of categories. Political and social dynamics may powerfully influence this social articulation of cognitive codes, an idea to which we now turn and which is, of course, the heart of queer political economy.

4. Our Social Site: Construction of American Social Identities since 1930

Academic analysis of the Chapmans' work on illusory correlations has ignored the central role that homosexuality has had in American culture in shaping the cognitive structures (semantic associations) of the Chapmans, of their subjects (psychoanalysts) and of the patients of these psychoanalysts at the time the Chapmans carried out their work. What makes this scholarly blindness so ironic is that the Chapmans' discovery was based on an "associative connection" enormously amplified by two "illusory" correlations of homosexuality with other, socially-feared traits—i.e., two queer panics—of which they and all subsequent commentators pretended to be blithely unaware. These panics transformed homosexuality from an exotic, possibly deplorable—or possibly intriguing—attribute (prior to the 1930s) into the worst, most "salient" human characteristic, bar none, in the 1950s and 1960s when the Chapmans did their work.

As Chauncey describes it, in the 1930s, the previously flourishing and widely known gay culture had been pushed underground into invisibility. Yet,

> the homosexual hardly disappeared from public view . . . for police bulletins and press coverage continued to make him [sic] a prominent, but increasingly sinister, figure. As America anxiously tried to come to terms with the disruptions in the gender and sexual order caused by the Depression and exacerbated by the Second World War, the "sex deviant" became a symbol of the dangers posed by family instability, gender confusion, and unregulated male sexuality and violence. A number of children's murders in the late 1930s and the late 1940s, sensationalized by the local and national press and interpreted as sexual in nature by the police, fanned a series of panics over sex crime. (Chauncey 1994, 359)

In 1950, when Commie panic was towering higher and higher, a

> chance revelation by a State Department official during congressional hearings on the loyalty of government employees led to the entanglement of homosexuality in the politics of domestic anticommunism. Facing sharp interrogation by members of the Senate Appropriations Committee, Under Secretary John Peurifoy testified on February 28, 1950, that most of ninety-one employees dismissed for moral turpitude were homosexuals. . . . In the succeeding months, the danger posed by "sexual perverts" became a staple of partisan rhetoric. Senator Joseph McCarthy . . . charged that an unnamed person in the State Department had forced the reinstatement of a homosexual despite the threat to the nation's safety. (D'Emilio 1983b, 41)

The first illusory correlation above tied homosexuality to sex crimes and the second amplified this hysteria by tying homosexuality to a threat to national security—a risk that is hard to imagine in the 1990s, as the "Evil Empire" appears totally vanquished and the fear of atomic attack has greatly receded. To understand the astounding reversal in social codes that occurred from 1930 to 1960—a seismic shift whose magnitude may well be impossible to imagine for those growing up hearing songs about a detachable penis and fistfucking—it is necessary to first try to imagine 1930, when the pansy was at least as trendy as the queer is now in alternative music mosh pits and New Year's Eve Exotic Erotic Balls. Lillian Faderman (1991, esp. ch. 2), Jonathan Weinberg (1993), and George Chauncey (1994, chs. 8–11), among others, show that during the 1920s a gay culture—ranging from a wide variety of baths to art, music, and Broadway shows—grew up with close connections to, and immediately succeeding upscale New York's modish curiosity, the Harlem Renaissance.

With the onset of Prohibition, the queer trend was amplified since the "economic pressures Prohibition put on the hotel industry by depriving it of liquor-related profits . . . led some of the second-class hotels in the West Forties [of Manhattan] to begin permitting prostitutes and the speakeasies to operate out of their premises." (Chauncey 1994, 305). Furthermore, the "speakeasies, [social reformers] feared, were dissolving the distinctions between middle-class respectability and working-class licentiousness that had long been central to the ideological self-representation of the middle class" (Chauncey 1994, 307).

Much of the evolution of queer culture has been (partially inadvertently) promoted by conventional profit-seeking entrepreneurs operating small taverns or prostitution rings, etc. (e.g., see Weeks 1979, 42; D'Emilio 1983a). But the two queer panics in the 1930s and 1950s were the result of a different type of entrepreneur, one whose central role has been detailed by numerous sociologists (just two: Michel Foucault [1978] and David Greenberg [1988]), but who has been virtually invisible in political economy generally and certainly in mainstream economics. This is the ideology entrepreneur: someone who undertakes ventures at some personal risk and some possible personal gain—though not necessarily pecuniary—to reshape the social margin. This involves amplifying some parts and suppressing other parts of existing cognitive codes and, occasionally, adding new inventions to existing codes.[26] This may be done somewhat unconsciously, or at least, indirectly, in order to expand the entrepreneur's access to economic and other social opportunities. Alternatively, it may be done with a conscious ideological goal.

Examples of such entrepreneurship abound, and can have various social consequences. It suffices to cite a few that are relevant to incidents cited above. First, as Chauncey relates, "Joseph Pulitzer's *World* and William Randolph Hearst's *Journal* pioneered in those years a new style of journalism that portrayed itself as the nonpartisan defender (and definer) of the 'public interest,' waged campaigns on behalf of moral and municipal reform, and paid extravagant attention to local crimes, high-society scandals, and the most 'sensational' aspects of the urban underworld" (1994, 39). Second, "the expanding bachelor subculture in the city's furnished-room and tenement districts precipitated a powerful reaction by social-purity forces" (136).

Only twenty-two sodomy prosecutions occurred in New York City in the nearly eight decades from 1796 to 1873. The number of prosecutions increased dramatically in the 1880s, however. By the 1890s, fourteen to thirty-eight men were arrested every year for sodomy or the "crime against nature." Police arrested more than 50 men annually in the 1910s . . . and from 75 to 125 every year in the 1920s. . . . [M]uch of [the dramatic increase in arrests] stemmed from the efforts of the Society for the Prevention of Cruelty to Children, which involved itself in the cases of men suspected of sodomy with boys. The fragmentary court records available suggest that at least 40 percent—and up to 90 percent—of the cases prosecuted each year were initiated at the complaint of the SPCC. Given the SPCC's focus on the status of children in immigrant neighborhoods, the great majority of sodomy prosecutions were initiated against immigrants in the poorest sections of the city. (140)

The ranks of the medical profession have long been filled with innovative ideology entrepreneurs. "Doctors [in the late nineteenth century] were not simply speaking up when called upon; they were actively seeking to shape society's control apparatus. Why this new involvement? Physicians came primarily from the middle class and would have shared the general sexual ideology of that class" (Greenberg 1988, 401).

These examples illustrate the diversity of ideology entrepreneurs. Joseph Pulitzer and William Randolph Hearst were choosing market niches that they apparently thought were more profitable than the alternatives they gave up. The social purity activists were, in many cases at least, pursuing ethical goals at some possible pecuniary cost to themselves. Finally, the actions of the doctors (as well as numerous other new "helping" professions in the late 1800s and early 1900s) could, in many instances, have plausibly been motivated by a desire to promote "professional standards" rather than by any immediate pecuniary purpose. These are not dissimilar from the ideologically entrepreneurial efforts of western church people, especially at the end of feudal times.

Aside from "externalities" such as environmental pollution or epidemics, the conventional ways in which economists conceptualize how social welfare is impaired is by looking at monopolistic markets,[27] or at rent-seeking "special-interest" interference with governmental regulation.[28] But the concept of social cognitive codes suggests that social welfare can be impaired in a new way: misleading conflations and oversimplifications in the cognitive categorizations through which people perceive, think about and act in the world. These conflations, such as the illusory correlations described in section 2, are encouraged by an esthetics-of-simplicity in our mental software.

A new cognitive code propagates like a virus, like a dialect. A new schema or semantic association (as highlighted by the Chapmans in their original work on illusory correlations) of what is evil and so what must be socially eradicated spreads not because of lack of competition among ideology entrepreneurs. Rather, it occurs because the spread of an idea that is tied to market-born and market-articulated inequality, like the force of a wildfire on the prairie, irresistibly engulfs all of the individuals standing in its path. Thus, as Dollimore (1991, 246) has noted, "while . . . homophobic panics [can be seen as being provoked by repressed homosexuals [in the Freudian sense], the panic may only 'take' socially, because of the other kind of repression—exclusive identity formation—as it affects a far greater number" (1991, 240). Dollimore gave this latter idea concreteness by quoting G. K. Lehne: "Homophobia is only incidentally directed against homosexuals—its more common use is against the 49% of the population which is male. . . . The taunt 'What are you, a fag?' is used in many ways to encourage certain types of male behaviour and to define the limits of 'acceptable' masculinity" (Dollimore 1991, 245).

My allusion to waves of wildfire on a prairie stands in, of course, for an analytical apparatus yet to be developed.[29] One might guess that to break into cognitive awareness, outside senders of signals must first penetrate the limbic gatekeepers of our sensory awareness. And, as retailers and advertisers have known for some time, erotic signals that open the door to the limbic system are especially powerful. These signals get attention, something that Calvin Klein, Guess jeans, and even Budweiser have proven rather effectively. The implication is clear: to get a hearing by a person as s/he articulates her/his desire, first send a strong erotic signal to catch that person's attention. Thus a new social code does not spread because each person digitally compares it with her present code. Rather, the extent to which it gets used depends on whether it sweeps in a wave, like an epidemic, through society. Studying this conjecture seems fundamental to understanding queer political economy.

The two queer panics sketched above did, indeed, have the power of social epidemics, and they are our legacy today. They got their power from the abject dependence of each individual on the social codes of her/his network/society. Because of this dependence, our most complex desires can become severely distorted. The system is "inefficient," in the sense that alternative evolutions can be conceived that would result in a better state for many. In the classic terminology of Arrow-Debreuvian welfare economics, the endogeneity of these codes introduces a possible new type of externality among all actors' actions/voices, on one hand, and their perceived preferences, on the other hand. This possibility, as the evolution of queer social identities shows, is important enough to be worthy of further attention.

5. Update to the 1990s

The spin of social codes/identities prevalent today is captured well by U2's late-1980s articulation of Desire[30] as female: "She's the candle burning in my room . . . [causing] fever when I'm beside her, Desire, Desire." Bono goes on, having absorbed the code developed during the rollover from the nineteenth century, to intertwine all irresistible (male) drives—greed, ambition, security—with strong overtones of female sin—corruption/slut/whore: "She's the dollars / She's my protection / She's the promise / in the year of election / Sister, I can't let you go / I'm like a preacher / Stealing hearts at a traveling show / For love or money, money . . . ? / Desire . . ."

U2 is answered in the 1990s by Trent Reznor's Nine Inch Nails (NIN) (a bit of bragging there?—I'd love to see) singing: "my head is filled with disease/ my skin is begging you please / i'm on my hands and knees / i want so much to believe / i need someone to hold on to / ... / i give you everything / my sweet everything / hey God, i really don't know who i am / in this world of piss."[31] NIN, preoccupied with religious codes, plays on alternating currents, seeking absolution and sanctification, through fucking a female lover: "if she says come inside i'll come inside for her / if she says give it all i'll give everything to her / i am justified / i am purified / i am sanctified."[32]

NIN's clearest articulation of desire is queerly ambiguous: "i'm drunk / and right now i'm so in love with you / and i don't want to think too much about what we should or shouldn't do / lay my hands on Heaven and the sun and the moon and the stars / while the devil wants to fuck me in the back of his car . . . but this is the only time i really feel alive / . . . / i can't help thinking Christ never had it like this."[33] This could be "justified" for straights by imagining that Trent Reznor is singing from a woman's view—until the last line where this desire is only a bottom-man's hunger. NIN's acknowledgment of fisting is explicit on *nine inch nails fixed*. These themes also arise in NIN's song of erotic boasting: "i am a big man / (yes i am) / And i have a big gun / got me a big old dick and i / i like to have fun . . . / shoot shoot shoot shoot / i'm going to come all over you / me and my fucking gun / me and my fucking gun."[34]

This is not a new metaphor, and certainly far from unknown to straight European American men since the 1970s. But it is definitely queer to articulate on major radio stations (e.g., KOME in San Jose discovered there is more profit in a phallic format in the spring of 1994), along with a song featuring a "detachable penis" and other acknowledgments of phallic eroticism. This is reinforced by noting the contrast between NIN's deeply guilt-driven naked self-absorption and the comfortably mainstream articulation of longing in U2's music.

The rapid rise to greater prominence in the 1990s of alternative voices (hip-hop, gangsta rap, and alternative), voices of cynicism after the 1980s hegemony of aerosol desire, offers a sharp variety of discourse. This spawning of market niches defined by distinct cognitive codes—the rise of cognitively coded commodities, from microbrews to culturally diverse film festivals and commercial film success—may reflect in part the rising inequality in wealth in market-guided social systems. It may also reflect increasing awareness of the market advantages of cognitive coding, combined with decreasing cost of being more flexible in production due to computerized technology.

At this close range (1995), this proliferation of diverse cognitive codes appears to be an example of a "language in process of evolution," which the seminal sociolinguist William Labov (1972, 272) asserted did not occur in a "monoglot community."[35] "Studies of current sound changes show that a linguistic innovation can begin with any particular group and spread outward and that this is the normal development; that this one group can be the highest-status group, but not necessarily or even frequently so" (Labov 1972, 286). Linguistic "change does not occur without regard to [socioeconomic] class patterns" (295). "The creation of low-prestige working-class dialects . . . embodies two major linguistic trends of the past several centuries: the decline of local dialects and the growth of vertical stratification in language" (300). Further, Labov observes that "the sexual differentiation of speech often plays a major role in the mechanism of linguistic evolution" (303). Labov ends this book by suggesting "that language diversity may have value for humans other than linguists, providing relative cultural isolation and maintaining cultural pluralism" (325). Again making a blatant transdisciplinary leap, this perspective envisioning distinct linguistic patterns in different social groups recalls the spread of new patterns in music in this decade. It also could describe the libertarian-style rise of gay (male) identity, as it emerged through the propagation of new dialect-like codes by the molly houses in Britian (i.e. gay bars in eighteenth-century England; see D'Emilio 1983a), and from the pansy craze in New York of the 1920s and early 1930s–two spells, each just before major queer panic.[36]

6. New Categories for the Social Articulation of Desire?

This notion that social evolution may arise from lower, "minor," social codes can be made more concrete by looking at a contestation, a queer struggle, that is occurring now and seems to shed light on the role of ideology in political economy—the evolution of the jack-off room. This evolution has been captured well by John Paul Ricco, an art historian, who uses the phrase "minor architecture" to describe a notion closely analogous to linguistic variation. Ricco starts from the idea of a minor aesthetic, from Deleuze and Guattari's (1986, 18) formulation of the concept of "minor literature." Ricco applies this to describe how we see sexuality through our lenses of social codes:[37]

> Designating jack-off rooms as *minor architecture* allows me to circumvent an appeal to the paradigmatic bourgeois (or *major*) binary public/private, a pair of terms not only insufficient but inappropriate to the conditions of jack-off rooms. The public/private binary[38] not only forces these spaces into un-fitting categories, it also forecloses an understanding of the politics of these spaces. The minor is situated *within* the major/majority/masterly, rather than *outside*, as this latter term is usually understood. As examples of minor architecture, jack-off rooms articulate and are articulated by queers (minorities), whose identities are anything but constant, unified, and self-evident, but rather are always in the process of becoming, changing, and being contested. Queers are here part of a collective assemblage or multiplicity of anonymous bodies, assembled within a small, dark, cramped space, touching, kissing, licking, hugging, stroking, pumping. . . . Borders between self and not-self are radically undermined. (Ricco 1993, 236–37)

Individuals, as

> bodies-of-desire, forfeit their individual subjective selves as they are re-constituted as parts of a collective assemblage. . . . A jack-off room is a space of connections, extensions and exteriorizations, all mobilized by desires. And darkness operates as a crucial collectivizing force. (239)

This articulation of bodies is

> mobilized by the collective force of *desire*, a nearly tangible device or mechanism, through which jack-off rooms-as-minor-architecture are built, and by

which they operate. Desire and erotics are potentially tremendous mobilizing and articulating forces, capable of opening up and linking particular spaces, bodies, and practices, and thereby begin to approach the kind of activ[ist] politics which many of us are pursuing. Jack-off rooms-as-minor-architecture constitute this linkage of space, bodies, and practices. They are sites for the formulation, deployment and continuous re-constitution of a post-identity sexual politics [a different network of identities].(240)

Ricco has captured a backlash to the extreme individualism that dominates so much thinking now, as he notes that in jack-off rooms, men "forfeit their individual subjective selves as they are re-constituted as parts of a collective assemblage." Such mingling of selves is, of course, familiar from looking at love across other socially constructed boundaries: "love across the racial divide . . . is thoroughly public, saturated with social and political meanings . . . the image [of interracial couples] comes to stand for a fact that none of us has any notion what to do with: the fact that each of us is a part of the other, that we are so unalterably tainted by a messy and heartbreaking history that any claim to purity or separation becomes insupportably fragile" (Scott 1994).

The loss of individuality in homodesire is central to the articulation of desire. In fact, this penetration of the social into the "deepest" innermost parts of the individual through the articulation of homodesire is as close to a universal human phenomenon as we could imagine having the arrogance to assert. In any case, it is not solely characteristic of a sexual minority. This irony, that individuality is lost through the struggle to assert one's individuality through the articulation of desire, recalls Genet's discovery of beauty in the betrayal of individual distinctness and in merger/murder/death consummating love/orgasm.[39] Indeed, *Funeral Rites* is an orgy of Genet's signifying the *in*significance of the particular person, a rite celebrating the funeral of "the individual," with its repeated, often disconcerting, shifts in voice and in the frequent avowals that Jean (Genet? he plays on an ambiguity of who Jean is) writes himself. Genet's very self-conscious articulation-of-self and his identification of writing himself/ourselves with social construction is the epitome of Oscar Wilde's "individualism as . . . 'disobedience [that] . . . is man's original virtue' "—so much so that "there comes to be a close relationship between crime and individualism" (Dollimore 1991, 8, with inner quote from Wilde 1990, p. 4).[40]

Queer art, from Stéphane Dupré to Paul Stanley and David Sprigle, and from Barbara Hammer to Isaac Julien in film, is driven by a postmodern awareness that renders modernist boundaries between individuals ambiguous. Steven Arnold,[41] especially, captures with human bodies the aesthetic of isolation/merging, flowers, erections, crucifixes, and death that Genet inscribed on our queer minds. As in mosh pits, there is a clear opposition to the possessive individualism "in which individuals are defined primarily as proprietors of their fleshly incarnation, who are consequently entitled to rights only as the owners of themselves" (Cohen (1991, 77–78).

Seventeenth-century individualism contained [a] central difficulty which lay in its possessive quality. . . . the conception of the individual as essentially the proprietor of his own person or capacities, owing nothing to society for them. The individual was seen neither as a moral whole, nor as part of a larger social whole, but as owner of himself. The relation of ownership, having become for more and more men [sic] the critically important relations determining their actual freedom and actual prospect of realizing their full potentialities, was read back into the nature of the individual. (Macpherson, quoted in Cohen 1991, 78)

This ideology of the total separateness of each "rational" individual, able to choose independently and freely, splendidly isolated by her/his libertarian shield of property rights,[42] arose along with the sanctity of property rights in the sixteenth and seventeenth centuries (coinciding with the social death of ganymedians). This evolution is the central ideological component of what is arguably the most significant sociological innovation of the last millennium: the rise from mere social niche to social dominance of the market's guidance and discipline of people.[43]

This bourgeois sense of individualism was both born by and gave birth to the market-system, and has implied a respect, by the individual, of the property/body/privacy of others. This is precisely what Wilde and Genet are contesting with their celebrations of the individual as criminal, as perverter-of-the-social, as queer. Indeed, this is their only celebration of individuality: it is a vision of a heroic (ideological) entrepreneur.[44] For many today, this crossing of ideological boundaries will be most uncomfortable, or even cognitively impossible. For example, the "death" of self in orgasm, even in mere desire, and the succeeding "treachery/betrayal" of one's orgasmic partner(s), are insights by Genet into resonances of queer sexuality. This seems to be invisible to Edmund White, writing in the introduction to *Prisoner of Love*: "Genet maintained a purported admiration for treachery that I've never comprehended. . . . I've never heard of a single charge of betrayal lodged against Genet" (1992, xiii). White concludes: "Finally I've decided that 'treachery' is Genet's code word for the incorrigible subjective voice that can never be factored into the consensus. . . . Genet seeks in [*Prisoner of Love*] to honour the collective emergency, but in the end he remains true to his equally radical . . . need for independence. Fidelity to oneself is treachery to the group; artistic quirkiness pokes holes in any political rhetoric."

In grappling to understand what Genet "means" with his use of "betrayal," White seems to be reading Genet through a mirror, reversing meanings by 180 degrees. He takes the romantic true individual, the "subjective voice," buried deep, within as requiring "betrayal" of a stale, politically charged notion of the collective. More useful is Bersani's insight that betrayal consists of seeking solitude (1995, 168) and that *Funeral Rites* "[is about] rejection . . . of relationality" (1995, 172). White's acknowledgment that "Genet's writerly neutrality and acuity . . . represent a rejection of petit bourgeois values and an affirmation of independence and a passive resistance against the forces of order" (Genet, 1992, xii), though valid, misses how extremely "Genet is an out-and-out social constructionist." (Bersani 1995, 173). Missing is Genet's rejection of what "our culture tells us to think[:] . . . sex as the ultimate privacy, as that intimate knowledge of the other on which the familial cell is built" (Bersani 1995, 165). Also missing is Bersani's insight, relevant to micro political economy, that Genet depicts "the degeneration of the sexual into a relationship that condemns sexuality to becoming a struggle for power."

Wilde and Genet display a queer ambiguity. They stake a socialist aesthetic on a celebration of what is a right-wing notion, namely, the heroic individual writing her/his own performance. At the same time, profoundly, and in very distinct ways, they elaborate the extent and power of the social construction of each of us through performative, self-enacting utterances (Judith Butler [1990, 1993] and Jonathan Dollimore [1991] make this wonderfully manifest). These two notions are feverishly grappling with each other—first, our individuality contesting the blinders imposed by our social construction, and second, our cloneness, and indeed our most intimate sense of merging with each other through homodesire. This struggle seems central to current queer contestation over the utility of notions of social identities. It is the *simultaneity* of this articulation of the individual and of the social that seems to engender much of the confusion in efforts to define, use, and contest social identities as institutions of social control. This simultaneity of the articulation of the individual and the social has been addressed better by literary cultural analysts than by most other scholars.

Is it mere happenstance that the rise of modernism with the ideology of possessive individualism coincided with the erasure of the social articulation of queer desire in western cultures? As Goldberg notes, "For the [American] colonists, as perhaps too for the tribes whose history is told in Genesis, nation-founding was inseparable from procreation, and the particular economic, social and patriarchal gender arrangements in the colonies [were] subtended by the crime of sodomy. Sodomy was . . . a crime against the family and the state, 'political sodomy,' in short" (1994, 6). The synchronicity of the rise of property-rights-individualism and the transformation of "sodomy" into a capital offense more narrowly focused on certain sexualities is worth further inquiry. The rise of modernism in England—rather analogous to cultural shifts at the end of the last century in this country—was a time of enormous change in socioeconomic institutions.

> In the sixteenth century, there was real alarm at the growth in unemployment, poverty, and crime. Vagrancy . . . became one of the most pressing social problems. . . . Social and economic dislocation was often refigured as the evil of aberrant movement. . . . [I]t is difficult for us today to recover the meaning which attached to the masterless. . . . Even more disturbing in certain respects than the masterless man was the masterless, wandering woman, perversely straying and inviting others to do the same. (Dollimore 1991, 119)

There grew "anxieties about female sexuality . . . about its relation to property, to the threat of the violation of this private place if it were to become a 'common' place . . . rather than a particular property" (Parker 1987, 105–106, as quoted by Dollimore, 1991 119–120; see also Soltan 1988).

The possible connection of the recodification of "female" to the rise of property rights as a dominant social institution offers further reason to suspect a link between the rise of property rights and the gradual erasure of queer desire from social cognitive codes. (This, as we saw at the start, erased the possibility for leading playwrights to articulate queer desire.) In fact, the effects of the rise of the sanctity of property rights may go even further than the recodification of female and of queer as dangerously perverse.[45] Contrary to Foucault, the rise of the social dominance of property rights and of possessive individualism as an institution of social discipline may, at a very deep level, have nurtured erotophobia by raising and fortifying boundaries between bodies. In this way, such ideologies may have made the liquidly lubricious permeability of sexuality not only less desired and desirable, but also less imaginable and performable. And in turn, this may have rendered much of the concreteness of sexuality less voiceable, in particular helping to erase interpersonal distinctions based on specificities of sexuality: to wit, queer distinctions. This is consonant with Judith Butler's awareness of "the dangers that permeable bodily boundaries present to the social order" (1990, 132) by raising questions about "the categories of identity that contemporary juridical structures engender, naturalize, and immobilize" (5).

Can post/modern be defined as the articulation of ambiguity in the boundaries between individual and collective?[46] Will a post/modern intellectual renaissance of desire—and of emotions generally—prompt rearticulation of the binary of individualistic vs. collective? Will it also provoke a celebration of desire on the same level as the celebration of cognition?[47]

The roles of "ideology" are much more central to cognition, and hence to the social cognitive codes that lie at the base of political economy, than even Marx imagined.[48] This is not mere "superstructure," frosting on the basic productive/technological relations of labor inputs to other inputs that ultimately determine the social relations of production.[49] Rather, "ideology" describes the deepest patterning of human mental software and, in turn, our mental hardware.[50] Indeed, the classic marxian conceptual framework may have impoverished the concept of class by denying it rich connotative connections to other social identities. More important, such a framework precludes an understanding of the agency of class in *shaping* the basic productive/technological relations of labor inputs to other inputs. In addition, it seems important for political economy to model the simultaneous determination of each human's "preferences" and the vortex of social codes and identities channeling all humans in the maelstrom/malestream of social relations. In particular, as described in sections 2 and 3, a person's perception of what is best for him/herself can be severely restricted by his or her network of "neighbors" with whom s/he articulates desires. This network, in turn, can be severely circumscribed by one's class/race at birth.

This is what the model described in section 2 attempts to demonstrate. It suggests that an idea underlying much public policy discourse—that people can "freely choose" to do or not to do things—ought to be replaced by the notion of contingent choice: each person's discovery and expression of desire is likely to be very dependent on some notion of "the other" (who has a different Face). As Dollimore reminds us: "No consideration of cultural and/or racial difference should ever neglect the sheer negativity, evil, and inferiority with which 'the other' has been conceived throughout history" (1991, 329). I have shown how this limitation on free choice by individuals led people to fail to perceive their sexual orientations, and that this failure was closely tied to the simultaneous evolutions of concepts of race, class, and gender.

For Americans who are largely blind to the hegemony of individualism due to its ubiquity, it might be helpful to consider a recent example from Japan, where, for the past century, there has been significant groping to develop cognitive codes that articulate more individualistic ideas: "There is an entire genre of words like 'my home' and 'my car,' for example, meaning individually owned cars and homes. A Japanese might ask a colleague if he is a my car commuter or takes the subway" (Kristof 1995). Further, Sony's use in Japan of the name "Walkman" for a product that did not previously exist illustrates William Burroughs's notion that languages are viruses, spreading from culture to culture rather randomly, but very powerfully as a market-driven phenomenon. The lesson from jack-off rooms, from understanding queer desire, from straight, but not strait, folks attending queer SexArt Salons, is that the hegemony of individualism-as-property-rights is being contested sociolinguistically.

7. Epilogue

The second phrase in italics at the start of this piece is a play on Descartes' epigraph, *cogito ergo sum*, which over the course of several centuries has come to signify modernist thinking that celebrates the Enlightenment.[51] I juxtapose instead the post/modern notion that we, like Shakespeare's Antonio and like all living organisms, exist in the richness of our social structures and identities because of our desires. Therefore, a significant goal for social disciplines, as well as for physical sciences (e.g., Hamer and Copeland 1994 and Damasio 1994), is to increase our understanding of the social articulation of desire.

Notes

This work is dedicated to the honor of Alan Turing and John Maynard Keynes, whose sharply contrasting social positions as intellectuals figure well the distinct possibilities for queers described here. Alan Turing's achievements birthing computers enabled the silicon simulations at the heart of this paper and his death was caused by the forces I seek to conceptualize. Maynard Keynes's queer interest in arts *and* economics inspire the disciplinary *ver/mischung* here. I want to acknowledge sabbatical support by Middlebury College as well as access as a research associate to facilities at the University of California at Berkeley, which enabled me to conduct this queer research intensively in the Bay Area and so to recover from years of near asphyxiation in the intense heterosexism at Middlebury College and, indeed, covering all of Vermont. While at Middlebury, my breathing was occasionally pushed above water by early research assistance from Jeff Spencer and by supportive reactions of a number of people to my earlier efforts to endogenize the world—which, they thoughtfully refrained from pointing out, were a bit inadequate. These people include Lee Badgett, Marion Eppler, Rhonda Williams, Nancy Folbre, Sam Bowles, Julie Matthaei, Jeff Escoffier, Michael Jacobs, Frank Thompson, Robert Anderson, and Ellen Oxfeld. It is, *bien entendu*, important not to illusorily correlate any of these people with any foolishness the reader might find in this paper.

1. There has recently been grudging acknowledgment of the social construction of *market-revealed* preferences by the high priest of the irrelevance of tastes, Gary Becker (1993).

2. For a development of these theorems, see chapter 4 of Cornwall (1984) and the references to Arrow cited there.

3. For fainthearted lesbigays in our erotophobic culture, there may be some reassurance in noting that John Dewey, in his debate with Bertrand Russell over an appropriate philosophical basis for ethics, acknowledges the primacy of desire, noting: " 'valuing' is identified with any and every state of enjoyment no matter how it comes about—including gratification obtained in the most casual and accidental manner, 'accidental' in the sense of coming about apart from desire and intent" (Dewey 1929, 53). He goes on to acknowledge implicitly that this violates disciplinary self-aggrandizement by ethicists since it makes "psychology . . . paramount, not only over logic and the theory of knowledge, but also over ethics" (95).

4. Marlowe's queer view has been well disseminated recently by Derek Jarman's film, *Edward II*. Of course, queer desire could not be shown as "licit" then, with the first sodomy statute having been adopted in 1533 (Goldberg 1994, 17), but as Greenblatt (1988, 92–93) has noted: "Though by divine and human decree the consummation of desire could be licitly figured only in the love of a man and a woman, it did not follow that desire was inherently heterosexual. The delicious confusions of *Twelfth Night* depend upon the mobility of desire." Smith (1991) makes this "mobility of desire" in Shakespeare's England wonderfully tangible.

5. This quote is from Escoffier (1995, 34), who suggests that this key innovation by Keynes was prompted by his attempt to recast the modernist (nonreligious) basis for morals that had been offered by his teacher and the leading English philosopher at that time, G. E. Moore, and which implied a disapproval of his homosexuality.

6. I thank Herb Gintis for these last two references, which he offered in response to an earlier version of this paper.

7. Of course, Magoo is an especially appropriate allegorical face to put on an actor in queer political economy since Magoo, a.k.a. Jim Backus, was the father of James Dean (in "*Rebel Without a Cause*").

8. To appreciate my effort to simplify my model, contrast it with Eve Sedgwick's (1990) rich model of the closet.

9. This recalls the apparent prevalence, in any catalogue of human societies, of cultural codes in which types of homosexuality are significant, even if this was invisible to notable western anthropologists, as surveyed by Greenberg (1988, ch. 2). It might be conjectured that the current worldwide hegemony of homophobia may be significantly due to the edge given western homophobia-infected (Christian) culture by the rise of market-guided societies, which engendered the rise of powerful technology in the West, which then contaminated other cultures (e.g., Native American, Hindu, and Moslem), which are now significant in any tabulation of world cultural patterns.

10. See also Celia Card (1994) and Kenny (1994).

11. For a useful summary, see Holland, (1986), ch. 6. This identification of categorization as being based on archetypes or typical instances has become so unproblematic for some social psychologists that it is taken as the *definition* of categorization. See, for example, Fiske and Pavelchak (1986, 171).

12. See Allman and Brothers (1994) for an excellent overview as well as Damasio (1994, esp. p. 133), who calls the amygdala "the key player in preorganized emotion." From work in the 1950s finding that "light touch to the skin could be an extremely potent stimulus for driving amygdala neurons" in cats (Allman and Brothers 1994, 613) to work in the 1970's which started mapping intricate patterns of "single neurons (in the amygdala of monkeys) that responded to dimensions of the social environment" (Allman and Brothers 1994, p.

614), work on humans has been slow due to the difficulty of finding people with injury just to their amygdalas who can be compared with others. For work pointing to the role of the amygdala in finely perceiving social cues in our faces, see Adolphs, et al. (1994) and Young, et al. (1995). See also Kuhl (1993) for related research and theory.

My extremely loose analogy between the limbic system and a computer's operating system would, no doubt, be contested by Damasio (1994, 250) and in no way is meant to contest his strong assertion that the whole body is an integral part of the "mind."

13. Note that this appearance of being "natural" lies at the heart of the Gramscian notion of "hegemony" as defined, e.g., by Comaroff and Comaroff (1991, p. 23). See also Gramsci (1971).

14. As Foucault has powerfully argued, this too appears simplistic due to being biased by our view from our social site in North America in the 1990s, a view that threatens to impose a teleological reading of history so that any multiplicity of sexual identities that preindustrial people might have perceived is easily lost to our view.

15. For an excellent overview of the rise of gender-segregated wage labor, see Amott and Matthaei (1991), 315–48.

16. This brief sketch does not indicate the magnitude of the social changes occurring then. For more detail, check Edwards (1979), Montgomery (1987), and Brody (1980).

17. This focus on "male" is revealing of our cultural categories. See also Faderman (1991), D'Emilio and Freedman (1988), Vicinus (1992), and Matthaei (1992).

18. Sounds similar to Halloween in the Castro in San Francisco which, in 1994, had become the largest annual event in the City, with an estimated 400,000 people attending. It is no longer a queer event celebrating gender-fuck, but is rather a lesbian/gay hosted party where well over half the participants appear to be strait gawkers, most not in costume and a few extremely threateningly armed. Analogous comments apply to the social position of "street-people" in our cities today as props for a middle-class sense of superiority.

19. Homosexuality was the focus of the third paper by the Chapmans (1969) with the second giving great, but not exclusive, emphasis to homosexuality phrased indirectly in instructions to the experimentees ("He is worried about how manly he is"). The first looked at people's perceptions of correlations between word pairs having no connection to homosexuality. More detail on the Chapmans' work is given in Cornwall (1995b).

20. They offer as an example of the format of the word-pairing game thirty-four undergraduates played for them in order to measure *verbal associative connection* (1969, 274):

The tendency for "homosexuality" to call to mind "rectum" and "buttocks" is

a. Very strong
b. Strong
c. Moderate
d. Slight
e. Very slight
f. No tendency at all.

21. This was evidently the case for the U.S. Court of Appeals for the Sixth Circuit ruling on 12 May 1995: "No law can successfully be drafted that is calculated to burden or penalize, or to benefit or protect, an unidentifiable group or class of individuals whose identity is defined by subjective and unapparent characteristics such as innate desires, drives and thoughts. Those persons having a homosexual 'orientation' simply do not, as such comprise an identifiable class" (*New York Times,* 14 May 1995, A10). As the Associated Press

report printed in the *San Francisco Chronicle* (13 May 1995, A4) noted: "sexual orientation is not 'an identifiable class' worthy of inclusion in (Cincinnati's) human rights ordinance alongside gender, race and age" which, presumably for this court, are entirely unproblematic.

22. Goldberg's (1994, 1–22) superb introduction offers a quick overview of the diverse distortions these codes have assumed over recent centuries as they articulated "sodometries."

23. Page 76 of E. Francis White (1990).

24. See D'Emilio and Freedman (1988).

25. Dollimore (1991, 273) led me to this picture of willful suppression of desire.

26. This conjecture of a role for conscious (possibly "self-interested") human agency in the evolution of social cognitive codes is a divergence from the analogy I have thus far drawn to sociolinguistics as formulated by William Labov, who has written that

> "[L]anguage structure . . . is a largely mechanical system, out of the reach of conscious recognition or adjustment by its users. . . . It therefore seems odd that we are not free to adjust this system to maximize its efficiency in conveying information. . . . One possible explanation is that the efficiency of language depends upon its automatic character, and that a phonological or grammatical structure that was open for conscious inspection and manipulation would necessarily operate very slowly. Therefore our efforts to change language consciously must be confined to higher-level stylistic options: the selection of words, and the construction of phrases and sentences within a narrowly limited set of choices. The linguistic changes that have been discussed here [i.e., in Labov's book] operate well outside the range of conscious recognition and choice." (Labov 1994, p. 604)

It is possible that a similar notion of "higher" and "lower" levels of change in social cognitive codes is also valid, with what I am calling "ideology entrepreneurs" merely tweaking the given cognitive codes—possibly for great profit and/or power—and with "deeper," "more basic" changes in social cognitive codes operating only unconsciously with *every*one in the society acting as a miniideology-entrepreneur. This speculation awaits future exploration.

27. There seems to be almost free entry in ideological entrepreneurship: everyone manipulates ideology to some extent in many social interactions. To joke or insinuate that certain traits imply other human traits is the easiest source of humor, bonding, personal position, etc. This role might be termed "ideology manipulation." Ideology entrepreneurship might be reserved for the operation of a "business" that produces "new" articulations of human perceptions by gathering information on the distribution of traits/behaviors and using this "information" to "justify" new associations of traits. These "businesses" can range from single proprietorships—like Richard Epstein at the University of Chicago Law School promoting simplistic ideas for a complex world or the author of this piece promoting cognitive complexity, just for example—to the Heritage Foundation and many corporations. The "product" produced by ideological entrepreneurs will, since "knowledge" is a public good, have to be "sold" by being tied to another good, a good which typically involves facilitating access to such "knowledge." Examples range from William Randolph Hearst's journalism early in the twentieth century to the rise of the *New York Times* as a national newspaper. What these profit-maximizing examples share is the production of *cognitively coded commodities*: goods whose market niche is based on appeals to combinations of characteristics known/appreciated by people sharing certain key language in their cognitive codes. Do differential costs of providing access to such "knowledge" open possibilities for new types of analysis of barriers to entry?

28. An example of the government responding/using, rather than creating, social cognitive codes is the inability of Edmund Burke and Jeremy Bentham to mitigate, even ever so slightly, the barbaric, savage homophobia infecting England in the eighteenth and nineteenth centuries. This savagery is indicated more by the frequent use of the pillory than by the relatively infrequent hangings for sodomy, since "standards of proof were high in sodomy cases: until 1828, courts required evidence both of penetration and emission." Instead of seeking convictions for sodomy when the difficult-to-obtain evidence was missing, the social control system convicted men

> of the lesser offense of "assault with the attempt to commit sodomy." This charge might be based on nothing more than a solicitation invited by a plain-clothes man who had gone to some homosexual rendezvous for the purpose of entrapping men. Convicted men were placed in the pillory and exposed to the wrath of the mob, who were allowed to pelt them. Such events attracted thousands, sometimes tens of thousands of spectators. The pelting of the men often took on an organized form under the supervision of the police. There was a tradition that women of the street—fishwives, vendors of produce, and "Cyprians" (as the press euphemistically called prostitutes)—should have pride of place in these orgies of ill-will, and some of the most abused members of British society revenged themselves for the contempt they received from others by the violence with which they attacked the helpless sodomites." (Crompton 1985, 21–22)

> In 1780, an exceptionally grim episode led [Burke] to utter a unique protest [in Parliament]. On April 10 of that year, a coachman named William Smith and a plasterer named Theodosius Reed had been exposed in the pillory at St. Margaret's Hill in London for attempted sodomy. Though their punishment did not take place until nearly noon, nevertheless . . . according to one newspaper: "A vast Concourse of People had assembled upon the Occassion, many by Seven o'Clock in the Morning, who had collected dead Dogs, Cats, &c. in great Abundance, which were plentifully thrown at them; but some Person threw a Stone, and hit the Coachman on the Forehead, and he immediately dropped on his Knees, and was to all Appearance dead." Smith did, in fact, die though there was some uncertainty whether the cause of his death was the violence of the crowd or the tightness of the pillory about his neck. . . . Burke protested that the pillory existed to expose men to contempt and not to kill them by a punishment "as much more severe than execution . . . as to die in torment, was more dreadful than momentary death." . . . Burke had the satisfaction of seeing the undersheriff for Surrey tried for murder [in another case]; not surprisingly, the jury acquitted him. Burke himself . . . suffered much abuse in the press for his stand. . . . [P]rejudice ran high at the popular level and affected most of the intelligentsia. (31–33)
>
> The leading example of the impotence of an intellectual in the eighteenth–nineteenth centuries is Jeremy Bentham, who was the inventor of utility-theoretic modeling of desire.

> In light of [the British] . . . bias toward silence [about homosexuality], Bentham's voluminous analyses are . . . remarkable. Bentham first jotted down about fifty pages of notes in 1774 when he was twenty-six. In 1785 he completed a somewhat longer formal essay. In 1814 and 1816 he filled almost two hundred pages with another impassioned indictment of British attitudes. Two years later he produced several hundred more pages of notes on homosexuality and the Bible, and in 1824, eight years before his death at the age of eighty-four, he wrote a final short synopsis of his ideas

on sodomy law reform. All in all, this adds up to a sizable book on a subject that British jurists usually dismissed in a paragraph or page. (Crompton 1985, 20)

Bentham was clear that utilitarianism, with what we now think of as a libertarian conceptual base, implied sodomy should be decriminalized. But he was realistic in his fear that for him to publicly acknowledge this "would have given (his) opponents a powerful weapon for discrediting his whole program of [prison] reform" (Crompton 1985, p. 30). In particular, Bentham was aware of homophobia's modus operandi as a metanorm: "There is a kind of punishment annexed to the offence of treating [this crime] with any sort of temper, and that one of the most formidable that man can be subjected to, the punishment of being suspected at least, if not accused, of a propensity to commit it. (47–48). "Bentham's rough notes give a vivid picture of conscience at war with discretion. Discretion won out." (31). Bentham wrote about his turmoil: "To other subjects . . . it is expected that you sit down cool: but on this subject if you let it be seen that you have not sat down in a rage you have *given judgement against* yourself at once. . . . I am ashamed to own that I have often hesitated . . . [to] expose my personal interest so much to hazard as it must be exposed to by the free discussion of a subject of this nature" (47). In the end, Bentham's writings on homophobia were—and still are—not published except for Crompton's glosses.

The social forces that led to Burke's and Bentham's impotence parallel closely those described above for the United States: newspapers using fascination with condemned erotica to whet sales and readers' bloodlust, as noted earlier. There were private alliances of ideological entrepreneurs working for social purity: the Society for the Reformation of Manners (founded in 1691 "to wage the first important morals campaign since the Puritan Revolution, aimed . . . at countering the freedom of the Restoration period" (Crompton 1985, 57); the Society for the Reformation of Manners ended in 1738, but in 1788 the Proclamation Society—then became the Society for the Suppression of Vice, which "pursued a vigorous course in Georgian and Victorian England" (61–62)—and connections to xenophobia were used by governmental leaders. Crompton notes:

Bentham, for all his perspicuity, failed to understand how English xenophobia intensified English feelings about sodomy. In particular, he failed to see its peculiar connection with English Protestantism (and violent anti-Catholicism). . . . [T]he temptation to reaffirm the traditional association of sodomy with Italy was too powerful for Protestant polemicists to resist. . . . [T]he hanging, pillorying, and ostracism of homosexuals were incontrovertible facts to which the nation could point to assure itself of its superiority to Catholic Europe in at least one respect. In this way, as in Spain under the Inquisition, intolerance became a badge of virtue and brutality a point of national pride." (Crompton 1985, 53, 60)

29. Thus Labov (1985, 317) notes in trying to understand linguistic change: "There is comparatively little that can be said about the particular social or linguistic events that trigger a particular change." He then goes on to offer "a typical life history of a sound change. The change first appears as a characteristic feature of a specific subgroup, attracting no particular notice from anyone. As it progresses within the group, it may then spread outwards in a wave, affecting first those social groups closest to the originating group. . . . As the linguistic feature develops within the original group of speakers, it becomes generalized in several senses. Over the course of time (three or four decades) a wider range of conditioned subclasses may be involved, and more extreme (less favored) environments." (319–320)

30. Bono, "Desire," *Rattle and Hum*, Island Records, 1988.
31. Trent Reznor, "Terrible lie," *pretty hate machine*, TVT Music, Inc., 1988.
32. Trent Reznor, "Sanctified," *pretty hate machine.*
33. Trent Reznor, "The only time," *pretty hate machine.*
34. Trent Reznor, "big man with a gun," *the downward spiral*, leaving hope/TVT Music, Inc., 1994.
35. Words in quotes are cited by Labov as Martinet's ideas, which Labov is disputing.
36. Recall also the origins of "house dancing" and "punk" with gay African American teenagers.
37. See also Bolton, Vincke, and Mak (1994, 257–259) for a good description of the paucity of scholarly consideration of gay baths and for survey evidence that baths are socially desirable to promote safer sex.
38. This footnote added to Ricco: For a more accessible discussion of how this dichotomy has misled lesbians and gay men in our thinking going back to 1982, see Califia (1994, 71–82).
39. This is expressed most clearly in Genet's *Funeral Rites.* See Bersani (1995) and Dollimore (1991).
40. An illuminating current example of "extreme individual" (his teammate, Jack Haley's description) as "hardened criminal" (description by his team's assistant coach, Dave Cowens) is Dennis Rodman of the San Antonio Spurs basketball team, who has vanilla-colored hair topping chocolate skin, rides a Harley-Davidson (spraining his shoulder), and who took his wife and Haley and his girlfriend to a gay bar to a show of male dancers in G-strings (Friend 1995).
41. Steven Arnold, "Lust: The Body Politic," *The Advocate*, pp. 81–85 (1991).
42. For example, see Nozick (1981).
43. For example, see North (1981).
44. Wilde often reads as being as essentialistic as Gide, extolling as great "he who is perfectly and absolutely himself" (Wilde 1990, 12) and who avoids "thinking other people's thoughts" (13)—this last, in a typically Wildean irony, adapted from Ralph Waldo Emerson, thus redeeming himself from any suspicion of being unworthy of *Dorian Gray*. His avowal of socialism as a simple end of property rights sounds especially quaint with our view of the rise and fall of such national politics in the century since he wrote.
45. Note that the concept of perversion in western thought goes back at least to Augustine, as explored by Dollimore (1991).
46. I follow Dollimore (1991, 25, n. 2) in using the "typographically pretentious" (32) "/" to indicate an ambiguity, at our close vantage point, of any boundary between modern (or post-Renaissance) and postindustrial thinking.
47. Hamer and Copeland (1994) and LeVay (1993) are examples of such a renaissance in the biological sciences. Damasio's strong argument for the essential, often unconscious, role of emotions (through what Damasio terms "the somatic-marker hypothesis" involving "dispositional representations," which are located in the "hypothalamus, brain stem, and limbic system" (1994, 104)) in promoting, as well as sometimes confounding, rationality indicates the breadth of this intellectual renaissance. The connection between recognition of a "cognitive" role for emotions, on one hand, and ambiguity of boundaries between individual and collective is supported by Damasio's suggestion that impairment of the brain's processing of emotions can "compromise" a person's "free will." He also repeatedly alludes to a role for social construction of "secondary emotions" (134–136) and "feelings," which he distinguishes from emotions: feelings are our perceptions of our emotions (145). Damasio asserts that our "social environment" plays an important role (251, 260–67) but

never sketches how this happens except for surprisingly naive references to "sick culture" (178–179), "healthy culture" (200), "culture of complaint" (247), a deepening "spiritual crisis of Western society" (257), and "increasingly hedonistic cultures" (267). These references to populist concepts in social analysis with no indication of their being problematic, belie the shallowness of his consideration of social interactions—this despite Damasio's carefully crafted contingent assertions not only in his area of expertise of neurobiology but also about medical practice and physical sciences generally and his thoughtful use of literary illustrations.

48. Cornwall (1996) offers further discussion of Marx's insightful discussion of the social embeddedness of humans and of how misleading is economists' use of the trope of "Robinson Crusoe" to represent all humans.

49. Althusser (1971) hints, but does not explicitly recognize, that ideology is much deeper than the codes promoted by what he calls "ideological state apparatuses" ("churches, parties, trade unions, families, some schools, most newspapers, cultural ventures" [137]) by arguing that ideologies represent a human's "relation to [their real] conditions of existence" in the real world (154). "The existence of ideology and the . . . interpellation of individuals as subjects are one and the same thing" (163; see also 167–170). But his postscript arguing that "[t]he ideology of the ruling class does not become the ruling ideology by the grace of God, nor even by virtue of the seizure of State power alone. It is by the installation of the [ideological state apparatuses] in which this ideology is realized and realizes itself that it becomes the ruling ideology" (172) is too simplistic and is not much of an advance over attributing ideologies to "a small number of cynical men" or to "the material alienation which reigns in the conditions of existence of men themselves" (154), which Althusser wisely rejects.

50. There is evidence that patterns of perception that are learned become, rather quickly, permanent structures in our minds that then limit/channel our subsequent perceptions: Werker (1989), Kuhl, et al. (1992), and Kuhl (1993).

51. Dollimore (1991, 281) notes that Jacques Lacan made a postpsychoanalytic (postdiscovery of the unconscious) reformulation of Descartes' epigram which serves as an intermediary between Descartes' and my versions: "I think where I am not, therefore I am where I do not think. Words that render sensible to an ear properly attuned with what elusive ambiguity the ring of meaning flees from our grasp along the verbal thread. What one ought to say is: I am not wherever I am the plaything of my thought; I think of what I am where I do not think to think" (Lacan 1977, 166). Damasio (1994, 248–52) offers useful insights on Descartes' epigram also.

References

Adolphs, R., D. Tranel, H. Damasio, and A. Damasio. "Impaired recognition of emotion in facial expressions following bilateral damage to the human amygdala." *Nature* 372 (15 December 1994): 669–672.

Allman, John and Leslie Brothers, "Faces, fear and the amygdala," *Nature* 372 (15 December 1994) pp. 613–614.

Althusser, Louis. "Ideology and ideological state apparatuses." in *Lenin and Philosophy and Other Essays*, translated by Ben Brewster, pp. 123–73 London: NLB, 1971.

Amott, Teresa, and Julie Matthaei. *Race, Gender, and Work: A Multicultural Economic History of Women in the United States.* Boston: South End Press, 1991.

Arthur, W. Brian. "Designing economic agents that act like human agents: a behavioral approach to bounded rationality." *American Economic Review* 81, 2 (May 1991): 353–59.

Arnold, Steven, "Lust: The Body Politic," *The Advocate*, 1991.

Becker, Gary S. "Preference formation within families." Presented at the meeting of the American Economic Association, 6 January 1993, Anaheim, CA.

Berlin, B., and P. Kay. *Basic Color Terms: Their Universality and Evolution.* Berkeley: University of California Press, 1969.

Bersani, Leo. *Homos.* Cambridge: Harvard University Press, 1995.

———. "Is the rectum a grave?" In *AIDS: Cultural Analysis, Cultural Activism*, edited by Douglas Crimp. Cambridge: MIT Press, 1988. Reprinted in Goldberg, (1994).

Bolton, Ralph, John Vincke, and Rudolf Mak. "Gay baths revisited: an empirical analysis." *GLQ: A Journal of Lesbian and Gay Studies* 1, 3 (1994): 255–73.

Bray, Alan. *Homosexuality in Renaissance England.* London: Gay Men's Press, 1982.

Brody, David. *Workers in Industrial America: Essays on the Twentieth Century Struggle.* New York: Oxford University Press, 1980.

Butler, Judith. *Gender Trouble: Feminism and the Subversion of Identity.* New York: Routledge, 1990.

———. "Imitation and gender insubordination." pp. 13–31. In Fuss (1991), pp. 13–31.

———. *Bodies that Matter: On The Discursive Limits of "Sex".* New York: Routledge, 1993.

Card, Celia (ed.). *Adventures in Lesbian Philosophy.* Bloomington: Indiana University Press, 1994.

Califia, Pat. *Public Sex: The Culture of Radical Sex.* Pittsburgh and San Francisco: Cleis Press, 1994.

Chapman, Loren J. "Illusory correlation in observational report." *Journal of Verbal Learning and Verbal Behavior* 6 (1967): 151–55.

Chapman, Loren J., and Jean P. Chapman. "Genesis of popular but erroneous psychodiagnostic observations," *Journal of Abnormal Psychology* 72 (1967): 193–204.

———. "Illusory correlation as an obstacle to the use of valid psychodiagnostic signs." *Journal of Abnormal Psychology* 74 (1969): 271–280.

Chauncey, George. *Gay New York: Gender, Urban Culture, and the Making of the Gay Male World, 1890–1940.* New York: BasicBooks (HarperCollins), 1994.

Cohen, Ed. "Who Are 'We'? Gay 'Identity' as Political (E)motion (a Theoretical Rumination)." In Fuss (1991), 71–92.

Comaroff, Jean, and John Comaroff. *Of Revelation and Revolution: Christianity, Colonialism, and Consciousness in South Africa* Chicago: University of Chicago Press, 1991.

Cornwall, Richard, *Introduction to the Use of General Equilibrium Analysis.* New York: North-Holland, 1984.

———. "deconstructing silence: the queer political economy of the social articulation of desire." (1996).

Crompton, Louis. *Byron and Greek Love: Homophobia in 19th-Century England.* Berkeley: University of California Press, 1985.

Cyert, Richard M., and Morris H. DeGroot. "Learning applied to utility functions." In *Bayesian Analysis in Econometrics and Statistics: Essays in Honor of Harold Jeffreys,* edited by Arnold Zellner. New York: North-Holland, 1980, pp. 159–68.

Damasio, Antonio R. *Descartes' Error: Emotion, Reason, and the Human Brain.* New York: Grosset/Putnam, 1994.

Deleuze, Gilles, and Felix Guattari. *Kafka: Toward a Minor Literature.* Minneapolis: University of Minnesota Press, 1986.

D'Emilio, John. "Capitalism and gay identity." In *Powers of Desire: The Politics of Sexuality,* edited by Ann Snitow, et al. New York: Monthly Review Press, 1983a.

———. *Sexual Politics, Sexual Communities: The Making of a Homosexual Minority in the United States, 1940–1970.* Chicago: University of Chicago Press, 1983b.

———. "The homosexual menace: the politics of sexuality in cold war America." In *Passion and Power: Sexuality in History,* edited by Kathy Peiss and Christina Simmons, pp. 226–40. Philadelphia: Temple University Press, 1989.

D'Emilio, John, and Estelle B. Freedman. *Intimate Matters: A History of Sexuality in America.* New York: Harper & Row, 1988.

Dewey, John. *Experience and Nature.* LaSalle, IL: Open Court Press, 1929.

Dollimore, Jonathan. *Sexual Dissidence: Augustine to Wilde, Freud to Foucault.* Oxford: Clarendon Press, 1991.

Dunning, David, and Lisa Beth Stern. "Distinguishing accurate from inaccurate eyewitness identifications via inquiries about decision processes." *Journal of Personality and Social Psychology* 67, 5 (November 1994): 818–35.

Edelman, Lee. *Homographesis: Essays in Gay Literary and Cultural Theory.* New York: Routledge, 1994.

Edwards, Richard. *Contested Terrain: The Transformation of the Workplace in the Twentieth Century.* New York: Basic Books, 1979.

Elster, Jon. *The Cement of Society—A Study of Social Order.* New York: Cambridge University Press, 1989.

Escoffier, Jeffrey. "Sexual revolution and the politics of gay identity." *Socialist Review* 15 (July–October 1985): 119–153, 1995.

———. *John Maynard Keynes.* New York: Chelsea House Publishers, 1995.

Faderman, Lillian. *Odd Girls and Twilight Lovers: A History of Lesbian Life in Twentieth-Century America.* New York: Columbia University Press, 1991.

Fiske, Susan T., and Mark A. Pavelchak. "Category-based versus piecemeal-based affective responses: developments in schema-triggered affect." In *Handbook of Motivation and Cognition: Foundations of Social Behavior,* edited by Richard M. Sorrentino and E. Tory Higgins, 167–203. New York: Guilford Press, 1986.

Foucault, Michel. *The History of Sexuality, Vol. 1: An Introduction.* New York: Vintage Books, 1990 (originally 1978).

Friend, Tom. "A nonconformist in a league of his own." *New York Times.* 20 April 95, B7.

Fuss, Diana (ed.). *inside/out: lesbian theories, gay theories.* New York: Routledge, 1991.

Genet, Jean. *Funeral Rites.* New York: Grove Press, 1969.

————. *Prisoner of Love.* Translated by Barbara Bray and with introduction by Edmund White. Hanover, NH: University Press of New England, 1992.

Goldberg, Jonathan (ed.). *Reclaiming Sodom.* New York: Routledge, 1994.

Gramsci, Antonio. *Selections from the Prison Notebooks.* New York: International, 1971.

Greenberg, David F. *The Construction of Homosexuality.* Chicago: University of Chicago Press, 1988.

Hamer, Dean, and Peter Copeland. *The Science of Desire: The Search for the Gay Gene and the Biology of Behavior.* New York: Simon & Schuster, 1994.

Hamilton, David L., and Steven J. Sherman, "Illusory correlations: implications for stereotype theory and research." In Daniel Bar-Tal, et al. (eds). *Stereotyping and Prejudice—Changing Conceptions.* New York: Springer-Verlag, 1989.

Hemphill, Essex. *Ceremonies—Prose and Poetry.* New York: Plume, 1992.

Holland, John H., Keith J. Holyoak, Richard E. Nisbett, and Paul R. Thagard. *Induction: Processes of Inference, Learning and Discovery.* Cambridge: MIT Press, 1986.

Kenny, Anthony. *The Wittgenstein Reader.* Oxford: Blackwell, 1994.

Kristof, Nicholas D. "Japan's favorite import from America: English." *New York Times,* 21 February 1995, A15.

Kuhl, Patricia. "Innate predispositions and the effects of experience in speech perception: the native language magnet theory." In *Developmental Neurocognition: Speech and Face Processing in the First Year of Life,* edited by Bénédicte de Boysson-Bardies, Scania de Schonen, Peter Jusczyk, Peter McNeilage, and John Morton, pp. 259–74. Boston: Kluwer, 1993.

Kuhl, Patricia K., Karen A. Williams, Francisco Lacerda, Kenneth N. Stevens, and Björn Lindblom. "Linguistic experience alters phonetic perception in infants by 6 months of age." *Science* 255 (31 January 1992): 606–608.

Labov, William. *Sociolinguistic Patterns.* Philadelphia: University of Pennsylvania Press, 1992.

————. *Locating Language in Time and Space.* New York: Academic Press, 1980.

————. *Principles of Linguistic Change. Vol. 1. Internal Factors.* New York: Blackwell, 1994.

Lacan, Jacques. *Écrits: A Selection.* Translated by Alan Sheridan. London: Tavistock, 1977.

Lawrence, D. H. *Phoenix II: Uncollected, Unpublished and Other Prose Works.* Edited by Warren Roberts and Harry T. Moore. London: Heinemann, 1981.

LeVay, Simon. *The Sexual Brain.* Cambridge: MIT Press, 1993.

Lorde, Audre. *Sister Outsider.* Freedom, CA: Crossing Press, 1984.

Marimon, Ramon, Ellen McGrattan, and Thomas J. Sargent. "Money as a medium of exchange in an economy with artificially intelligent agents." *Journal of Economic Dynamics and Control* 14 (1990): 329–73.

Matthaei, Julie. "The sexual division of labor, sexuality, and lesbian/gay liberation: towards a Marxist-feminist theory of sexuality in U.S. capitalism." Presented at URPE session entitled "The economics of sexual orientation: theory, evidence, and policy," at the Allied Social Science Association Meetings, 5 January 1992, Anaheim, CA.

McFadden, Daniel. "Econometric models of probabilistic choice." *Structural Analysis of Discrete Data with Econometric Applications*, edited by Charles F. Manski and Daniel McFadden, pp. 198–269. Cambridge: MIT Press, 1981.

McFadden, Daniel, and Marcel K. Richter. "Stochastic rationality and revealed stochastic preference." In *Preferences, Uncertainty, and Optimality*, edited by John S. Chipman, Daniel McFadden, and Marcel K. Richter, pp. 161–86. (1990) San Francisco: Westview Press, 1990.

Montgomery, David. *The Fall of the House of Labor: The Workplace, the State, and American Labor Activism.* Cambridge: Cambridge University Press, 1987.

North, Douglass. *Structure and Change in Economic History.* New York: W. W. Norton, 1981.

Nozick, Robert. *Anarchy, State, and Utopia.* New York: Basic Books, 1981.

Parker, Patricia. *Literary Fat Ladies: Rhetoric, Gender, Property.* London: Methuen, 1987.

Ricco, John Paul. "Jacking off a minor architecture." *Steam* 1, 4 (Winter 1993): 236–43.

———. "Queering boundaries: semen and visual representations from the Middle Ages and in the Era of the AIDS crisis." *Gay and Lesbian Studies in Art History*, edited by Whitney Davis, pp. 57–80. New York: Harrington Park Press, 1994.

Rubin, Gayle. "The traffic in women: notes on the 'political economy' of sex." In *Toward an Anthropology of Women*, edited by Rayna R. Reiter, pp. 157–210. New York: Monthly Review Press, 1975.

———. "Thinking sex: notes for a radical theory of the politics of sexuality." In *Pleasure and Danger: exploring female sexuality*, edited by Carole S. Vance, pp. 267–319. London: Pandora, 1984.

Sargent, Thomas J. *Bounded Rationality in Macroeconomics: The Arne Ryde Memorial Lectures.* Oxford: Clarendon Press, 1993.

Saslow, James M., *Ganymede in the Renaissance: Homosexuality in Art and Society.* New Haven, CT: Yale University Press, 1986.

Scott, Darieck. "Jungle fever? Black gay identity politics, white dick, and the utopean bedroom." *GLQ: A Journal of Lesbian and Gay Studies* 1, 3 (1994): 299–321.

Sedgwick, Eve Kosofsky. *Epistemology of the Closet.* Berkeley: University of California Press, 1990.

Smith, Bruce R. *Homosexual Desire in Shakespeare's England.* Chicago: University of Chicago Press, 1991.

Soltan, Margaret. "Night errantry: the epistemology of the wandering woman." *New Formations* 5 (1988): 108–119.

Stallybrass, Peter,. and Allon White. *The Politics and Poetics of Transgression.* London: Methuen, 1986.

Tversky, Amos, and Daniel Kahneman. "Belief in the law of small numbers." *Psychological Bulletin* 2 (1971): 105–110.

———. "Judgement under uncertainty: heuristics and biases." *Science* 185 (1974): 1124–31.

Vicinus, Martha. " 'They wonder to which sex I belong': the historical roots of the modern lesbian identity." *Feminist Studies* 18, 3 (1992): 467–98.

Weeks, Jeffrey. *Coming Out: Homosexual Politics in Britain, from the Nineteenth Century to the Present.* New York: Quartet Books, 1979.

Wells, Gary L., Sheila M. Rydell, and Eric P. Seelau. "The selection of distractors for eyewitness lineups." *Journal of Applied Psychology* 78, 5 (October 1993): 835–44.

Werker, Janet F. "Becoming a native listener." *American Scientist* 77 (1989): 54–59.

White, E. Frances. "Africa on my mind: gender, counter discourse and African-American nationalism." *Journal of Women's History* 2, 1 (Spring 1990): 73–97.

Wilde, Oscar. *The Soul of Man and Prison Writings.* Edited by Isobel Murray. Oxford: Oxford University Press, 1990.

Wittgenstein, Ludwig. *Philosophical Investigations.* Translated by G.E.M. Anscombe. Oxford: Blackwell, 1981.

Young, Andrew W., John P. Aggleton, Deborah J. Hellawell, Michael Johnson, Paul Broks, and J. Richard Hanley. "Face processing impairments after amygdalotomy." *Brain* 118 (1995): 15–24.

9

The Political Economy of the Closet
Notes toward an Economic History of Gay and Lesbian Life before Stonewall

Jeffrey Escoffier

Jeffrey Escoffier sketches out some of the most significant characteristics of the economic life of lesbians and gay men in the years immediately preceding Stonewall. He describes this life as a highly constrained one, shaped by the stigma against homosexuality and by its illegality. He also speculates on both the significance and the limitations of the gay economy that has sprung up in the United States since 1969.

The market process has often played an important role—both positive and negative—in the development of gay and lesbian communities. The bar is one example of an economic institution that has occupied an immense part in gay and lesbian life. A great deal of thought and scholarship has gone into understanding the development of lesbian and gay communities, but other than practical studies such as those done for marketing purposes, little has been devoted to understanding the homo/economy.[1] Now, more than ever, it is imperative that we begin to explore the interdependencies as well as the tensions that exist between the growth of lesbian and gay markets and our goals as communities.

I believe that there have been four broad periods or phases in the post–World War II economic history of homosexual communities, although with considerable overlapping of some of the elements of each phase. The first period was the *Closet Economy*. Its primary economic institutions were bars, baths, adult bookstores and heavily coded mail order services, most of which operated on the margins of legality. The second period was initiated by Stonewall and might be called the *Liberation Economy*. Its dominant economic institutions were the proliferating retail businesses—bars, bookstores, baths and consumer services that emerged from the confines of semi-legality. Political and other voluntary organizations also provided previously unavailable public services. The third phase of the homo/economy was the *Territorial Economy* of the late seventies, marked by the spread of gentrification and neigborhood development. This process was cut short by the emergence of AIDS and development of the *AIDS Economy*, a period in which the largest economic institutions of the homo/economy are those that provide AIDS services as well as educational and other non-profit organizations. Currently, gay communities are in transition to a new phase—one of hyper-commodification, as mainstream corporations target the homo/market niche with consumer goods and advertising.[2]

In this essay I want to sketch out some of the economic aspects of gay and lesbian community life, in particular in the period of the Closet Economy before the emergence of visible gay and lesbian communities in American cities, roughly between 1945 and 1969. We have only the barest sense of the economic history of the lesbian and gay communities. Certainly the history is marked, like the economic lives of many oppressed populations, by the economic domination of outsiders, and—by virtue of the hegemony of the closet—by an existence on the borders of legality. And the homo/economy has always catered more to men than to women, for reasons having to do with men's greater opportunities for employment, income, and mobility. But for the most part, the economic history of lesbian and gay collective life is unknown. Economic research on gay and lesbian life suffers from the virtual non-existence of empirical information. No systematic or periodic social surveys have ever been undertaken, nor have statistics on gay and lesbian life been routinely collected. This is because homosexuals, historically stigmatized, have been invisible to "the gaze" of the random sampling methodology of American social science.

Nevertheless, economic research about lesbians and gay men has slowly accumulated. Since the mid-seventies, a growing number of social surveys and market research surveys have begun to provide some economic information about homosexuals.[3] Economists, lawyers, and other social scientists have begun to study the effects of economic discrimination, especially in the workplace.[4] A number of writers have also explored the impact of economic change on the emergence of gay and lesbian identities.[5]

Historians of gay and lesbian life have shown that homosexual communities have existed in some U.S. cities at least since the end of World War II.[6] This implies that an economic history is conceivable, since it is impossible for the shared activities of communal life to take place without using economic resources and without community members engaging in economic decision making. The economic history of homosexual communities has to be pieced together on the basis of fragments and anecdotes embedded in personal narratives, historical work, or older sociological research.[7] Like an archaeologist or paleontologist, the homo/economic historian has to imagine and identify larger economic forces on the basis of the slenderest of factual threads. Almost all homo/economic research is today at a stage that requires ingenuity and speculation—and, of course, "a little data." So, I will try to sketch the outlines of gay and lesbian communal history by bringing together some of these historical fragments and by drawing on the theory of institutional development in the work of economic historians and theorists.[8]

The Economic Consequences of the Closet

Before Stonewall, two decisive factors shaped the social and economic contours of gay and lesbian life. The first was the social stigma attached to homosexuality, a stigma so severe that millions of homosexual men and women feared even to engage in sexual relations with the people who attracted them sexually and appealed to them emotionally. Over thirty years ago, Erving Goffman devised a general theory of stigmas that delineates well some of the social structural consequences of being homosexual.[9] He identified two different kinds of stigmas that had radically different effects on the social organization of the people stigmatized. One sort of stigma was visible, for example, race. People often respond to visible stigma by feeling tension, and therefore the main problem facing those whose stigmas were visible was, according to Goffman, "the management of tension." As history demonstrates, social tension provoked by racial difference has proven to be the spark of violence frequently directed at African Americans.

The other sort of stigma that Goffman identified was the stigma that is not obvious or visible. Such a stigma poses an altogether different challenge; it is the harm that a piece of discrediting information can cause that has typically made members of such a group vulnerable to intimidation and threats of blackmail. Thus, "the management of information" is the strategy open to this group.

For a vast majority of those who experienced homosexual desire, homosexuality was not a visible stigma, although this was not true for everyone. Drag queens and butch lesbians were visible representatives of the homosexual population, and, like racial or other minorities whose stigma is visible, they were constantly confronted by tense social situations that frequently resulted in violence. But drag queens and butch lesbians formed a vanguard (as open homosexuals *and* as targeted victims) that mapped the outer perimeter of tolerance by which society was able to contain homosexuality. During the late 1940s and through at least the 1950s, the closet was constructed for most homosexuals by the dialectic between the management of information and the threat of violence posed by visibility.

The second factor shaping gay and lesbian life in this time was simple: homosexuality was not only the basis of a non-visible social stigma, it was also an illegal activity throughout the United States. Like liquor during Prohibition or street drugs today, the provision of goods and services and the related social institutions of the homo/economy were shaped by the underground channels through which they flowed. These two factors, the social stigma and the criminalization of homosexuality—both of which reinforced the necessity of homosexuals themselves controlling information—contributed to the construction of what we now call "the closet."

The economic repercussions of social stigma and criminalization vary considerably, of course, in different historical periods, or in diverse communities, or in varied geographical regions; or for various characteristics like age, gender, physical traits, class or race. But organizing a social world around a stigmatized and illegal identity generates a number of predictable outcomes: one is that, in order to manage secrets,[10] individuals' lives are shaped around the bifurcation between public and private space and time; a second is that many people with strong homosexual desires tend to migrate to large cities, which, because of their anonymity,[11] offer an expanded space for the stigmatized private dimension of homosexual life; a third is that whatever social life exists takes place in the shadow of protection rackets; and a fourth is the necessity of coded cultural representations.[12] All of these dimensions of lesbian and gay life in the postwar period had economic consequences.

The High Cost of a Double Life

Until 1969, the severe stigma attached to homosexuality led homosexual activity to take place in a profoundly asocial manner—that is, without very many social institutions of its own as well as outside the institutional framework of mainstream society.[13] In the vast majority of cases, male homosexuals engaged in sexual relationships with other isolated individuals in social spaces that were either private or anonymous, while lesbians often formed isolated couples or small social circles. Nonetheless, homosexuals were able to find one another and to establish certain shared social patterns and institutions.[14]

Before Stonewall, the overwhelming power of the stigma fostered homosexual social institutions that were premised on the segregation of information between the gay and the straight worlds. One could participate in such institutionalized homosexual social life as existed while continuing to remain in the closet, but this meant living a double life. Lesbians and gay men divided themselves between two worlds—one in which they maintained the appearance of being "straight" at work, with their families, and while in public, and another world where it was possible to engage in same-sex sex, where some women could dress and act like men and some men could dress and act like women, where people often knew one another only by their first name, perhaps even a false name, and where no one knew where others lived or worked. They lied to their families and straight friends, and they often lied to their sexual partners. These deceptions, along with the strict separation of the social, family, and work components of their lives, imposed an enormous burden of emotional stress on lesbians and gay men.

The closet had an enormous impact on gay men's and lesbians' work lives in particular. Lesbians and gay men did not take their lovers to the company Christmas party, nor did they discuss their vacations with coworkers or the boss. To the degree that these kinds of personal conversations and acquaintanceships in the workplace help grease the wheels and lead to employment and promotion opportunities, gay men and lesbians lost out.[15] If they were not married, they failed to win certain promotions. Many homosexuals responded to these limitations by scaling back their career expectations and, thus, their earning potential.

Being in the closet also tended to imply the strict separation in *time* and *space* of lesbian and gay life: social/sexual life was completely sequestered from work, "friends" and lovers were hidden from one's family and employers, and gay or lesbian gathering places such as bars or bathhouses were often quite distant, geographically, from the location of one's residence or job. It was this dramatic segmentation of private life from public life that made the "transaction costs" of everyday life much greater for homosexuals than for heterosexuals.

These high transaction costs—essentially the costs of concealing one's homosexuality—imposed by the closet meant that closeted homosexuals expended more of their individual income and resources than heterosexuals on routine adult activities. Such costs included transportation, liquor, multiple sets of clothing, and even the expense of maintaining separate households instead of living with one's lover. These costs created obstacles to realizing stable sexual/emotional relationships, managing an ambitious career, or developing political and social organizations. Of course, while the closet in this period generated substantial transaction costs, there were also tremendous costs of a different kind if one were out and known (particularly if one was a butch lesbian, a drag queen, or even an effeminate gay man), on top of the stress of managing a public identity as a homosexual. In strictly economic terms, the costs of being out probably exceeded the costs imposed by the process of concealment.

Certain of these costs could be reduced by living in or migrating to large cities that had socially and ethnically diverse populations. Such large cities offered a heterogeneous population to blend into as well as a certain degree of anonymity. The population density and scale of large cities also allowed for spatial separation of homosexual activities from residential and workplace locations.

The Protection Business: Bars, Baths, and Bookstores

The most significant factor in the development of early lesbian or gay social institutions was the fact that homosexual behavior was illegal. As long as anti-homosexual laws were enforced, they not only imposed severe psychological and social burdens on bisexuals, gay men and lesbians but also economic ones. In the 1950s and '60s, police raids of bars, tearooms, and parks not only led to arrest, legal fees, and public humiliation but also the loss of jobs, the plague of blackmail, and physical harm—all of which added to the economic burden of being homosexual.[16]

The bar stood at the center of communal gay or lesbian life and therefore of its economic life in the period between 1945 and 1969, although baths and certain same-sex venues also provided institutional contexts for homosexual socializing, sexual activity, and the establishment of relationships.[17] While bars were often raided, they also afforded some protection against entrapment, physical assaults, and blackmail. Since gay and lesbian bars catered to people who were stigmatized or who engaged in "criminal acts," the owners of the bars in most American cities were forced to pay the police and/or organized crime for protection. This made drinks more expensive, because the bar owners sought to recover these costs, but any business that catered to gay men and lesbians implicitly promised its customers freedom from harassment and was thus likely to have to pay for protection.[18]

Men's greater social freedom during this period as well as their ready access to public space led to the emergence of an institutionalized social world for male homosexuals earlier than for lesbians. For women, same-sex social situations enabled lesbian socializing, primarily in places such as all-female rooming houses, shops, girls' schools, and women's colleges, while men tended to transform certain public spaces into sexual cruising venues: gyms, Ys, public parks, and restrooms. The social and economic costs of gay male cruising (time, riskiness, and inconvenience), however, were probably critical factors in promoting the emergence of relatively protected environments such as bars.

The bifurcation of homosexual life, along with the necessity of protection, often meant that gay and lesbian bars, bathhouses or other businesses sought to be as inconspicuous as possible. Their outside appearances were often muted, their signs cryptic or insignificant. They were located in neighborhoods that were segregated from everyday business and residential activities—industrial areas, red light districts, among bars catering to sailors, or on isolated roads in rural areas.[19] Bouncers often screened customers in order to minimize the intrusions of hostile outsiders or undercover police.

While the bars may have been economic institutions because they served a market of lesbians and gay men, they provided few jobs and little income to homosexuals. Businesses catering to lesbians and gay men were essentially black-market operations; they operated under the guise of being some other legitimate business (neighborhood bar, men's health club, women's residence, bookstore) and were rarely owned by lesbians or gay men. In part, the ownership of businesses selling alcohol to an illegal population would have made the homosexual owners vulnerable to both legal and illegal pressures. (The pattern of bar ownership did, however, vary from one region or city to another. In the East, bars tended to be owned and controlled by organized crime, "the Mafia," while in cities like San Francisco, perhaps 25–30 percent of the gay bars in the mid-sixties were owned, according to Bob Damron, by gay men and lesbians.[20]) Thus, most of the profits and income generated by the gay and lesbian customers went to straight owners and did not get reinvested in the satisfaction of other lesbian or gay needs or in the development of communal institutions. Bars, despite their importance as homosexually oriented business activities, actually contributed little to the creation of the gay and lesbian community's own economic surplus.[21]

Extortion was ubiquitous in gay and lesbian economic life, ranging from crude attempts at blackmail to the refined protection provided by a gay bar's payoffs to police and organized crime. In response, a strong social norm emerged among lesbians and gay men against revealing the names and identities of fellow homosexuals.[22] The effectiveness of the norm frequently broke down under the pressure of arrests, raids, and STD contact tracing.[23] Nevertheless, it represented a powerful obstacle to the development of more open communal economic or political institutions. Only when coming out was protected by a political process could the norm of concealment—along with the transaction costs of the double life—become less of an obstacle to the organization of a socially and psychologically rich gay and lesbian life.

The Production of Desire: Codes and Commodification

Many early commentators on "the homosexual community," which was slowly emerging in the fifties and sixties, challenged whether lesbians and gay men actually had anything that could be called "gay culture." Even observers as sympathetic as Gagnon and Simon adopted a thesis of cultural impoverishment, based on the belief that "community members often have only their sexual commitment in common."[24]

Indeed, the impact of the stigma and the closet's discipline meant that very few public representations of homosexuality circulated within the mainstream culture. In 1926, for instance, the British government banned Radclyffe Hall's novel *The Well of Loneliness* for obscenity, even though it was a serious literary exploration of lesbianism as a social problem and even though it contained no sexually explicit passages. Because of such repressive measures, homosexual themes in published works were often heavily coded and operated through euphemism and double entendre.

However, certain art works and erotic commodities were produced and circulated even before the existence of well-developed communities. Erotically suggestive and sexually explicit drawings and photographs had been purchased by and circulated among men in Europe and North America since the nineteenth century. Such forms of pornography not only satisfied the need for sexual fantasy; they also stimulated, defined, and multiplied those fantasies. The businesses formed to market cultural commodities to homosexuals—whether it was the sale of erotic photographs and drawings in the early twentieth century or the adult bookstore selling nude magazines, cheap pornographic fiction and sex toys beginning after World War II—tended to operate within the same margin of illegality within which bars and bathhouses functioned.

The cultural impoverishment thesis not only underestimated the value and significance of even limited sexual representations, but it also overlooked coded cultural representations that circulated in mainstream culture: Walt Whitman's Calamus poems, Tennessee Williams's *Cat on a Hot Tin Roof*, Colette's Claudine novels, *The Killing of Sister George*, Emily Dickinson's poems, Judy Garland's singing. Members of homosexual audiences, in the midst of their personal struggles to interpret their own desires, were frequently able to identify the homosexual leitmotifs in mainstream culture, which helped them to recognize their erotic desires and perhaps to come to identify as homosexual.

Eventually, the creation of homosexual social institutions and businesses provided an economic framework for the production and distribution of cultural goods and the creation of a homosexual market. In *The Mattachine Review, One* and *The Ladder*, the publications of the early homophile organizations, this market was first identified; consequently, a series of mail-order businesses developed that catered to these customers. But one of the most ambiguous characteristics of capitalism is its capacity to stimulate and shape the cultivation of desire in addition to just exploiting it.[25] In this way, the supply of any gay- and lesbian-oriented commodities, services, and cultural products contributed to the discursive process of identity formation.

The Economic Origins of the Gay Ghetto

The ghetto, whether considered in its historical origins in Jewish history or in more modern forms such as racially segregated communities in the United States, is a spatial and socioeconomic form of containment. In other words, it tends to function as a collective closet. The development of gay ghettoes in large American cities was a historical process that has been spread out over the past fifty years. As a complex of social and economic institutions, the gay ghetto only reached its maturity in the Territorial Economy of the late seventies. However, it owed its economic foundations to the spatial dynamics of gay and lesbian social institutions in the period before Stonewall—the location of homosexually oriented businesses in industrial, shipping, red-light, or immigrant neighborhoods somewhat distant from middle-class residential areas.

A number of factors came together to establish the spatial concentration later called the "gay ghetto." The demographic basis for the economic and social development of the gay and lesbian communities was created by the massive social dislocations occasioned by World War II. Young men enlisted or were drafted into the armed services, and young women moved to the cities to work in the war plants. As these young men and women left their small towns and cities and their families, they entered into new social relations outside the purview of their families and local communities. The young men moved into military housing, and the young women often set up sex-segregated households with other young women. These circumstances created the social conditions that set the stage for many young men and women to explore their sexual and affective capabilities. The wartime developments only reinforced other long-term trends, including falling family size and an increase in the number of one-person households and small households of unrelated adults.[26]

Within the constraints imposed by the need for protection, a cluster of bars, baths, adult bookstores and cruising areas developed in certain districts or neighborhoods. Sometime during the fifties and early sixties, in cities like New York and San Francisco, homosexuals began to reside in certain bohemian neighborhoods (Greenwich Village, North Beach), which offered higher degrees of tolerance as well as proximity to gay or lesbian gathering places. This process of spatial concentration reduced some of the everyday transaction costs imposed by the closet. The coming together of residential and social institutions permitted a slightly greater degree of openness; thus certain lesbian and gay cultural traits became more visible within those neighborhoods.[27]

In capitalist societies, markets can only develop when adequate information exists about the number and location of customers, the potential goods and services that can be sold, and the profits that can be made. Customers who conceal important information about their needs, identities, and whereabouts pose significant obstacles to the organization of an economic life and, for similar reasons, to the organization of a community life in general. Thus these early gay neighborhoods only developed into full-fledged gay ghettos as their economies were transformed from black-market or protected operations to conventional markets. The proliferation of political organizations, nonprofit service organizations, gay churches, cultural institutions, and community newspapers and other publications in the period after Stonewall enabled the lesbian and gay communities to make the transition to an open, "out" economy. In this transition, gay men and lesbians gained greater economic control of community institutions and businesses from outsiders.[28]

Identity Politics and Public Goods

The emergence of a gay and lesbian political movement in the wake of the Stonewall riots decisively transformed the organization of the homo/economy. The centerpiece of the new movement's political strategy was the encouragement of coming out—the personal disclosure of one's homosexuality. Most of the movement's efforts went (and still do, to a great extent) toward gaining legal and social protection for being openly homosexual. Such a strategy struck at the black-market character of the homo/economy, mitigating the extortionist dimension in bars and bathhouses and lessening the police harassment, all of which have slowly declined as important elements in many of the largest urban gay and lesbian communities. The weakening of the closet's extortion economy fostered greater social solidarity within the lesbian and gay communities. Political mobilization also had a substantial impact on the level of transaction or concealment costs in the lives of many lesbians and gay men.

Thus the gay and lesbian movement dramatically changed the framework within which lesbian and gay economic decisions would be made. In the terms of economic analysis, the movement became a provider of public goods, that is, intangible goods and services that can be enjoyed by more than a single individual without excluding others. National defense, police services, and public parks are typical examples of the public goods provided by governments. The primary public good that the gay and lesbian movement sought to provide was "protection" for openly-identified homosexuals. The degree to which it has became easier (and cheaper, without the old, exorbitant transaction costs) to start businesses and organizations (for example, nonprofit counseling services) that cater to the gay and lesbian communities is a measure of its success. Similarly, it has become more comfortable to purchase goods and services specifically addressing homosexual needs—clothing and jewelry, books and magazines, dildos and sex toys, vacations and travel. Thus another economic consequence of the political movement has been the reorganization of the homo/economy into a full-fledged gay ghetto. This reorganization has, however, created new and complex tensions between community and market. Organizing to create protection for all lesbians and gay men across the board has reinforced a sense of community; at the same time, the gay market, like markets in general, tends to segment the gay and lesbian community by income, by class, by race and by gender. And the irony of the transformation is that the ghetto is another sort of closet.

Despite these radical changes in the organization of gay and lesbian economic life, the historical economics of the closet is not a remote and irrelevant piece of arcane knowledge. Even today, the closet continues to play an important role in the political limitations that lesbians and gay men encounter. The enemies of homosexual emancipation want to push lesbians and gay men back into the closet. "Don't ask, don't tell" is the contemporary formulation of concealment, and, not insignificantly, the reimposition of an economic burden. The visible existence of gay and lesbian communities is an important bulwark against the tide of reaction; the economic vitality of contemporary lesbian and gay communities erodes the ability of conservatives to reconstruct the closet. The closet is the specter that haunts lesbian and gay politics—and lurks in every social and political action that seeks to isolate and contain lesbian and gay communities.

Notes

This essay was both very difficult and a lot of fun to write. I am grateful for the encouragement of the editors of this volume, Amy Gluckman and Betsy Reed, which allowed me to write such a speculative essay. The comments of my friends Terrence Kissack, Regina

Kunzel, Matthew Lore, Molly McGarry, Kevin Murphy, and Michael Rothberg were encouraging and helpful.

1. For a survey of economic issues see my article "Homo/Economics: A Survey of Issues," in *Out in All Directions: The Almanac of Gay and Lesbian America*, edited by Lynn Witt, Eric Marcus and Sherry Thomas, (New York: Warner Books, 1995) and the paper by M. V. Lee Badgett, "Thinking Homo/Economically" presented at "Homo/Economics: Market and Community in Lesbian and Gay Life," a conference sponsored by the Center for Lesbian and Gay Studies at The City University of New York, May 7, 1994. On employment discrimination see M. V. Lee Badgett, "The Wage Effects of Sexual Orientation Discrimination," *Industrial and Labor Relations Review*, Vol. 48, No. 4 (July 1995) and for an early discussion see Jeffrey Escoffier, "Stigma, Work Environment and Economic Discrimination Against Homosexuals," *Homosexual Counseling Journal*, Vol. 2, No. 1 (January 1975). For a discussion of the gay market see Amy Gluckman and Betsy Reed, "The Gay Marketing Moment: Leaving Diversity in the Dust," *Dollars and Sense*, November/December 1993 and Grant Lukenbill, *Untold Millions: Gay and Lesbian Markets in America* (New York: HarperCollins, 1995).

2. The term "hyper-commodification" was suggested to me by Regina Kunzel.

3. See work cited above by Gluckman and Reed, "The Gay Marketing Moment" as well as Lukenbill, *Untold Millions*.

4. See the section on employment discrimination in William Rubenstein, ed., *Lesbians, Gay Men and the Law* (New York: The New Press, 1993), pp. 243–375. There is now a series of books dealing with gay men and lesbians in the workplace, for example, James Woods with Jay Lucas, *The Corporate Closet: The Professional Lives of Gay Men in America* (New York: Free Press, 1993).

5. John D'Emilio, "Capitalism and Gay Identity" in Ann Snitow, Christine Stansell, and Sharon Thompson, eds., *The Powers of Desire: The Politics of Sexuality* (New York: Monthly Review Press, 1983) and Jeffrey Escoffier, "Sexual Revolution and the Politics of Identity," *Socialist Review*, Vol. 15, Nos. 82/83, (July–October 1985).

6. See John D'Emilio, *Sexual Politics, Sexual Communities: The Making of a Homosexual Minority* (Chicago: University of Chicago Press, 1983); Elizabeth Lapovsky Kennedy and Madeline D. Davis, *Boots of Leather, Slippers of Gold: The History of a Lesbian Community*, (New York: Routledge, 1993); Esther Newton's *Cherry Grove, Fire Island: Sixty Years in America's First Gay and Lesbian Community* (Boston: Beacon Press, 1993); Gayle Rubin, "The Valley of the Kings: San Francisco's Gay Male Leather Community," dissertation in anthropology, 1994, University of Michigan and the recent dissertations on Philadelphia by Marc Stein (University of Pennsylvania) and on San Francisco by Nan Boyd (Brown University).

7. There are a growing number of recent studies that in the course of reconstructing the history of gay and lesbian communities have begun to provide a portrait of gay and lesbian economic life. See Martin Duberman, *Stonewall* (New York: Dutton, 1993), especially the chapter on the Stonewall bar (pp. 181–190) and the work cited above by Madeline Davis and Elizabeth Kennedy, Esther Newton, and Gayle Rubin.

8. Mancur Olson, *The Logic of Collective Action: Public Goods and the Theory of Groups* (Cambridge: Harvard University Press, 1965); Douglass C. North and Lance Davis, *Institutional Change and American Economic Growth* (Cambridge: Cambridge University Press); Douglass C. North, *Structure and Change in Economic History* (New York: W.W. Norton, 1981); Douglass C. North, *Institutions, Institutional Change and Economic Performance* (Cambridge: Cambridge University Press, 1990).

9. Erving Goffman, *Stigma: Notes on the Management of Spoiled Identity* (Englewood Cliffs, NJ: Prentice-Hall, 1963).

10. Georg Simmel, "The Secret and the Secret Society," in *The Sociology of Georg Simmel* (New York: The Free Press, 1950), pp. 307–378.

11. Georg Simmel, "The Stranger" and "The Metropolis and Mental Life," in *The Sociology of Georg Simmel* (New York: The Free Press, 1950), pp. 402–427.

12. Harold Beaver, "Homosexual Signs (In Memory of Roland Barthes)," *Critical Inquiry* Vol. 8, No. 1, (Autumn 1981).

13. Maurice Leznoff and William Westley, "The Homosexual, Community," *Social Problems*, Vol. 3 (April 1956), pp. 257–263.

14. This predated World War II; see George Chauncey, *Gay New York: Gender, Urban Culture, and the Making of the Gay Male World, 1890–1940* (New York: Basic Books, 1995).

15. See Escoffier, *Homosexual Counseling Journal* and the discussion of the role of informal social networks in getting jobs in Mark Granovetter, *Getting a Job: A Study of Contacts and Careers* (Cambridge: Harvard University Press, 1974).

16. Blackmail and extortion have been features of homosexual life as long as it has been stigmatized. For an account from the early twentieth century, see Edward Stevenson, *The Intersexes: A History of Similisexualism as a Problem in Social Life* (privately printed, 1908; reprinted New York: Arno Press, 1975), p. 478. See also the example of police harassment in Jonathan Weinberg, *Speaking for Vice: Homosexuality in the Art of Charles Demuth, Marsden Hartley and the First American Avant-Garde* (New Haven: Yale University Press, 1993), p. 57. Homophile publications such as *One* and *The Mattachine Review* frequently referred to the extortionist aspects of gay and lesbian life. I owe this piece of information to Kevin Murphy. See also the chapter on blackmail in Jess Stern, *The Sixth Man* (New York: Doubleday & Co., 1961), pp. 176–188.

17. See the chapters on bars in Donald Webster Cory and John LeRoy, *The Homosexual and His Society: A View From Within* (New York: The Citadel Press, 1963) pp. 105–129; and Evelyn Hooker, "The Homosexual Community" in John Gagnon and William Simon, eds., *Sexual Deviance* (New York: Harper & Row, 1967).

18. For an good general discussion of the social norms and behavior in bars see Sherri Cavan, *Liquor License: An Ethnography of Bar Behavior* (Chicago: Aldine, 1966).

19. For a good discussion of the role of protection (as well as other topics) see Martin S. Weinberg and Colin J. Williams, "Gay Baths and the Social Organization of Impersonal Sex" in *Social Problems*, Vol. 23, No. 2 (December 1975), pp. 124–136.

20. Damron, the publisher of a national gay bar guide, estimated that 70–80 percent of San Francisco's gay bars were gay-owned—see Wayne Sage, "Inside the Colossal Closet," *Human Behavior* (August 1975), reprinted in Martin P. Levine, ed., *Gay Men: The Sociology of Male Homosexuality* (New York: Harper & Row, 1979).

21. Christopher Gunn and Hazel Dayton Gunn, *Reclaiming Capital: Democratic Initiatives and Community Development* (Ithaca: Cornell University Press, 1991), pp. 3–6.

22. For a discussion of the relationship between economic behavior and social norms see Jon Elster, *Nuts and Bolts for the Social Sciences* (Cambridge: Cambridge University Press, 1989), pp. 113–123.

23. Theorists have classified such social situations under the name of "the prisoner's dilemma." In the economic theory of games the prisoner's dilemma is about two people who have been arrested and are being questioned separately. They cannot communicate with one another but they must choose whether or not to betray the other. Each would seem to benefit individually from giving away the other, but if they both choose to protect

the other they would both go free. For a brief discussion of this famous game see Jon El-ster, *Nuts and Bolts for the Social Sciences,* p. 29.

24. The argument is made in John Gagnon and William Simon, *Sexual Conduct* (Chicago: Al-dine, 1967), pp. 153–154, and in Kenneth E. Read, *Other Voices: The Style of a Homosex-ual Tavern* (Novato, CA: Chandler & Sharp, 1980), pp. xvii–xviii. For a discussion see Joseph Harry and William B. DeVall, *The Social Organization of Gay Males* (New York: Praeger, 1978), pp. 151–154.

25. In particular see Karl Marx, "Economic and Philosophical Manuscripts" in *Early Writings,* Quinton Hoare, ed. (New York: Vintage Books, 1975), and Carol Gould, *Marx's Social Ontology* (Cambridge: MIT Press, 1976).

26. See Francis E. Kobrin, "The Fall in Household Size and the Rise of the Primary Individ-ual in the United States", *Demography,* Vol. 13 (February 1976), pp. 127–138 and John D'Emilio, "Capitalism and Gay Identity."

27. This process is analyzed and empirically tested in Martin P. Levine, "Gay Ghetto," in Martin P. Levine, ed., *Gay Men: The Sociology of Male Homosexuality* (New York: Harper & Row, 1979) and by Joseph Harry and William B. DeVall in their chapter on "Urban-ization and the Development of Homosexual Communities" in *The Social Organization of Gay Males,* pp. 134–154.

28. Even before Stonewall, gay and lesbian bar owners in San Francisco formed their own business association, the Tavern Guild.

10

The Sexual Division of Labor, Sexuality, and Lesbian/Gay Liberation
Toward a Marxist-Feminist Analysis of Sexuality in U.S. Capitalism

Julie Matthaei

Unquestionably, gay life in the twentieth century owes a debt to capitalist development, as John D'Emilio argued in 1983. Here, economist Julie Matthaei extends the historical analysis of the relationship between sexuality and the economy in new directions. In order to understand the history of modern lesbians as well as modern gay men, she analyzes the sexual division of labor as it evolved through the nineteenth and twentieth centuries, showing how it has shaped both homosexuality and heterosexuality.

In this paper, I will try to draw out some of the ways in which the economic sphere—especially the division of labor between the sexes—has contributed to the construction of sexuality during the past century and a half in the United States. I will show how economic forces have helped create both heterosexual and homosexual relationships—with emphasis on the latter, which have received very little attention from economists. I will also argue that the late twentieth century emergence of a lesbian and gay political movement—and of a feminist movement in which lesbians have played key roles—constitutes a direct challenge to the sexual division of labor and gender. Since I cover a broad sweep of history, this analysis will be, of necessity, sketchy. In particular, I will not be able to address adequately the class and racial-ethnic variations in sexuality. Nor can I integrate the many noneconomic factors that have contributed to the changing construction of sexuality. However, I hope to be able to show that the economy has played an important part in shaping and transforming sexuality.[1]

This paper builds predominantly upon the work of historians of sexuality, and on basic feminist theory. There is little recent work on sexuality written from a Marxist or radical economics perspective. Marxist economic theory essentially ignores the family and sexuality; when necessary, it assumes heterosexuality. Marxist-feminist theory has focused on the institution of heterosexuality as key to patriarchy; it has shown how the sexual division of labor, and in particular the exclusion of women from high-paying jobs, has forced women into unequal marriages with men, which include the provision of unpaid domestic labor to their husbands.[2] However, these analyses essentially equate sexuality with marriage, and usually ignore homosexuality.[3] Furthermore, as Ann Ferguson (1989, 1991) has pointed out, these analyses have utilized a "rational self-interested" view of the individual, which cannot comprehend either "unconscious libidinal motivations" or the motivations of individuals by "symbolic definitions of gender, racial, sexual and family identity," all of which are key to understanding gender and sexuality (Ferguson 1989: 32). Rhonda Gottlieb's path-breaking article, "The Political Economy of Sexuality" (1984), examined some of the basic aspects of sexuality in capitalism, including the male-centeredness of heterosexual sex, the grounding of heterosexuality and male-defined sexuality in the sex-typing of jobs, and the egalitarian aspects of many homosexual relationships. Unfortunately, there has been no response to it (not one citation in the *Social Science Citation Index*!). Here I will try to address the topic of economics and sexuality from a radical economics framework, as does Gottlieb, but with a more historical focus.

I find this to be a difficult topic, and it is one in which I am by no means an expert. However, I think that it is important that economists, especially Marxist-feminists, along with feminist social scientists in general—all of whom have remained more or less silent on the subject—begin to include an analysis of sexuality in their work. In not accounting for sexuality, they relegate it to an extrasocial given. One result is that they end up assuming heterosexuality and erasing homosexuality. For example, Marxist-feminist and feminist analyses of the family, of housework, and of reproduction almost always assume a heterosexual family. In doing so, they erase gays and lesbians, thereby contributing to our oppression. It has been gay and lesbian studies, centered in history and the humanities, that has done the most both to recognize the existence of homosexuality and to analyze sexuality itself (including heterosexuality) as a social construct.

Sexuality as Socially, and Economically, Constructed

One of the most valuable insights of Marxist economics is the recognition that individuals are constructed—i.e., produced and reproduced as social beings—by the relationships that they enter into with other members of their society. Economic relationships constitute a key part of this social production of the individual. Not only is a certain type of person constructed by a certain type of economy—for example, advanced capitalism constructs an individuated, consumption-oriented, self-seeking person—but also, economic relationships differentiate people, for example by class, race-ethnicity, and gender. This social constructionist view of the individual is the polar opposite of the prevailing neoclassical view, which starts with a predetermined individual whose preferences, along with those of other isolated individuals, determine the economy (for a neoclassical analysis of sexuality, see Posner 1992[4]).

The social constructionist view of sexuality or sexual preference, in turn, rejects biological explanations of sexual desire, behavior, and identity. Jeffrey Weeks, a historian of sexuality and a leader in the development of the social constructionist school, has written:

> We tend to see sexuality as a protean force, drawing on the resources of the body, providing the energy for myriad manifestations of desire, and having unique effects. But the more we explore this "special case" of sex, the more variegated, ambivalent and racked by contradiction it seems. There is, I would argue, no simple relationship between "sex" and "society" . . . no easy fit between biological attributes, unconscious fantasy and desire, and social appearance and identity. The mediating elements are words and attitudes, ideas and social relations. The erotic possibilities of the human animal, its generalized capacity for warmth, intimacy and pleasure, can never be expressed "spontaneously" without intricate transformation; they are organized through a dense web of beliefs, concepts and social activities in a complex and changing history. (Weeks 1985: 4)

A social constructionist view of sexuality views it as neither genetically/naturally determined nor as a purely self-conscious moral choice. Social institutions and practices not only direct and restrict one's sexual behavior, but also give this behavior its content and meaning. "Each society seems to have a limited range of potential storylines for its sexual scripts," as Stephen Epstein has noted (1987:24).[5] Theorizing about sexuality involves studying the social construction of a constellation of possible sexual behaviors at a particular place and time. Thus, neither heterosexuality nor homosexuality is either "natural" or universal; both are socially produced. Even if biologists were able to identify a genetic marker that appeared to be correlated with homosexual behavior of some sort (which they have not), this marker could not in any way be understood to determine or create homosexuality as a culturally specific set of social concepts and practices.[6]

Time and Place Matter: Sexuality as Historical and Cultural

The growth of the gay liberation and feminist movements in the 1970s engendered the development of the field of lesbian and gay history. The earliest studies were essentially searches for the lesbians and gay men of all times and places whose sexuality had been obscured by earlier historians. However, as the field developed breadth and sophistication, the rising social constructionist school criticized such studies as "essentialist" for incorrectly positing a cross-historical lesbian or gay identity. Indeed, historians of sexuality have criticized the very idea of "gay history," since the concepts that construct sexuality have varied so greatly across time.[7]

As far as I know, there are no universals about human sexuality that hold true for all time periods and societies. In the United States, sexual practices have changed very rapidly in the past 150 years, along with capitalist development; the very concepts of heterosexual and homosexual persons did not even arise until the early twentieth century, as we will discuss below. Neither is homophobia/heterosexism—prejudice against and fear of homosexuals/homosexual behavior—a universal given throughout human history. Consider, for example, the oft-admired Greeks, who viewed man-boy love (including sex) as one of the highest forms of love. Or certain Native American nations, including the Kaska and Navajo, in which lesbians were highly valued (Amott and Matthaei 1991: 37). Neither is there an unambiguous one-to-one correspondence between the economic system that characterizes a society and its sexual practices—compare the tolerance for homosexuality in the Netherlands with the repression presently practiced in Great Britain.

These historical and cross-cultural differences make difficult any historical study of sexuality (or indeed, of any social construct, be it the family, gender, or whatever). In this study, I try to stake out a conceptual middle ground between the extremes of total historical specificity (which precludes meaningful cross-historical comparison) and of universalization (which falsely projects the present social practices onto the past).

An additional problem one encounters when analyzing sexuality, even within a particular historical period, is the variation of sexuality across race-ethnicity, gender, and class. A person's sexuality is not, in the metaphor of Elizabeth Spelman (1988), a discrete "pop-bead" on his or her necklace of identity that takes the same form regardless of the gender, class, or race-ethnicity it is combined with. We are all aware of the significant interconnections between sexuality and gender—indeed, few would presume to discuss sexuality without specifying the genders of the participants. However, race-ethnicity and class also differentiate sexuality in important ways. For example, in the nineteenth century, white middle- and upper-class women were constructed as relatively asexual, endangered by the lust of Black men (for which the latter were lynched), while free Black women, viewed by the dominant white society as oversexed and "loose," were not allowed to protest against their rape by white men (hooks 1981: ch. 2). Where I can, I will specify the class and racial-ethnic aspects of the sexualities studied; unfortunately, the available literature upon which I have based this paper usually slights or simply ignores the sexual practices of those who are poor or of color.

The Sexual Division of Labor, the Social Construction of Gender, and Homophobia

Economic institutions, in particular the organization of work into men's and women's work, have played an important role in the social construction of family and sexuality. Until very recently, it was simply accepted that individuals could not and would not be permitted to perform the work of the "opposite sex." God-given, biological differences in abilities between the sexes, it was argued, made only males fit for men's work, and only females fit for women's. For example, only females/women were seen to possess the "maternal instincts" necessary for the raising of small children.

This sexual division of labor, present in all previously known societies, has assigned the biological sexes (males, females) to different and complementary work activities, men's work and women's work, respectively. In general, women's work has centered on caring for children within the family, while men's work has been focused outside of the family, involving interfamilial relationships, such as market-oriented production or political activity. When wage labor developed, jobs were typed either men's or women's work—if not in general, then at least within a particular region or workplace (Matthaei 1982: ch. 9). Among European Americans in the United States, the sexual division of labor has always involved the political and economic domination of women by men; among certain Indian nations, on the other hand, the gender differences it constructed did not involve the subordination of women to men (Amott and Matthaei 1991: ch. 3).

The sexual division of labor plays a key role in constructing gender identity—masculinity and femininity, or manhood and womanhood—because preparation for and involvement in different and complementary work activities makes the sexes into different and complementary genders, masculine men and feminine women. However, this division of labor is only one part of the social construction of gender, which begins much earlier. One's gender identity is assigned at birth, according to one's perceived biological sex, and is imprinted upon the infant and child's personality at every level, from clothing to recreation to vocabulary and way of speaking. Most people, then, by the time they are adults, accept their assigned gender identities as given and immutable parts of themselves—and actively attempt to prove and reprove them to others by doing things appropriate to their gender and by distancing themselves from behaviors attributed to the "opposite sex."[8]

While gender roles have been viewed, by society, as emerging naturally out of the biological differences between the sexes, they are in fact social constructs that are achieved only through a great deal of limiting and molding of a person's being (Hubbard, Henifin, and Fried 1982). This limiting and molding is not always successful. For example, females and males whose physiques and characters predispose them for the incorrect gender role (e.g., large, strong, and aggressive females, or small, slight, sensitive males) may find it difficult to become women and men, respectively. They may even find themselves criticized and taunted by parents and schoolmates for their deviant-for-their-sex looks or behavior. While such social ostracism may work to pressure some people into heightened efforts to "fit in," it can also succeed in convincing others that their efforts to conform to their correct gender roles are doomed—that they are really "men in women's bodies" (or vice versa) or belong to some in-between gender.[9] Some individuals, especially females as we will see, consciously choose to reject their gender roles for those of the opposite sex. Those who cross gender lines in this way often take up the sexuality connected with their new gender roles, forming heterogenderal (cross-gender) but homosexual (same-sex) relationships: for example, a masculine female with a feminine female, or an effeminate male with a masculine male.

The Sexual Division of Labor, Marriage, and Sexuality in the Nineteenth Century

An essential part of gender identity has been the social requirement to marry and form a family with a member of the opposite sex and gender. Women marry only men, and men only women. The sexual division of labor has provided much of the incentive for marriage, as well as the glue keeping these marriages together, since it makes the genders economically and socially complementary and in need of one another. In this way, gender, and the sexual division of labor that accompanies it, can be seen as involving "compulsory heterosexuality," i.e., as forcing males and females to marry one another (Rich 1980).

As capitalism developed in the United States, the sexual division of labor concentrated income in the hands of men within each racial-ethnic group and class (with the exception of enslaved African Americans). Within each of these groups, men's jobs were much higher paying than women's, and the work of homemaking and child care was assigned to wives, daughters, and domestic servants (mostly female). Hence, most women needed fathers or husbands to provide them with sufficient income to survive and support their children, while most men needed wives to take care of their children and their homes.[10] Once women were married, their inability to survive financially without their husbands placed them in a subordinate position, forced to serve their husbands in whatever ways necessary to "keep them." In this sense, a husband became a woman's "meal ticket," and many women were constrained from leaving unhappy or even dangerous marriages by their financial dependence upon their husbands. So although chosen marriages based in love increasingly replaced marriages arranged by parents (Matthaei 1982: 116–118), women did have to consider a man's financial position before deciding whether to accept a marriage proposal.

If economic forces pressured adults to marry the opposite sex, organized religion both propounded the necessity of marriage and attempted to restrict sexuality to it. Nineteenth-century Protestantism defined "good sex" as being only procreative sex within marriage. All other kinds of sexuality—from fornication (sexual intercourse between unmarried members of the opposite sex) to sodomy (any erotic physical relations that could not result in pregnancy, including anal sex between same- or opposite-sex partners, masturbation, and oral sex)—were assumed to be sins that tempted individuals, especially men, but that should be resisted (D'Emilio 1983: 104; Katz 1983: 140–5; Weeks 1977: 4, 12). Birth control and abortion were illegal. Further, love was not linked with sexual passion; indeed, the white middle- and upper-class idea of "true love" at this time involved nothing erotic—it was an "affinity between two disembodied souls," which could be of the same or opposite sexes (Snitow, Stansell, and Thompson 1983: 14).

However, other factors reduced the incidence of marriage and the confinement of sexual acts to marriage. First, a variety of economic and social forces made it difficult for many to marry. The social practice of marrying within one's class and race (laws against "miscegenation" were on the books in many states until the 1950s!), combined with regional imbalances in the numbers of men and women, limited the availability of potential partners. The migration to the West Coast, among both whites and Asians, was disproportionately male, restricting opportunities for marriage; in California in 1850, there were twelve men for every woman, and the imbalance was much greater among Asians (Amott and Matthaei 1991: 201). Among African Americans, the problem was not the sex ratio but their status as property; marriages of enslaved African Americans had no legal recognition, and were often broken up by profit-seeking owners. For American Indians, this period was one of displacement and genocide, clearly disruptive of marriage relationships (Amott and Matthaei 1991: 16–7). In 1890, 16 percent of women and 28 percent of men between the ages of 25 and 44 were reported to be single and never married; almost 22 percent of women and 30 percent of men were reported to be single, widowed, or divorced (U.S. Department of Commerce 1976: 21); substantial numbers were also married, but separated.

Second, the sexual division of labor provided less financial incentive for men to marry than it did for women. Given their access to higher wage jobs, most men were able to live independently off of their earnings, purchasing in the market most of the services which a wife provided, from meals to laundry to sex and companionship.[11] Indeed, some men chose never to marry, a choice they could make much more easily than could women, who often remained single for lack of a marriage proposal.

Third, sexuality within marriage was restricted, at least among the most-studied white middle and upper classes. Much has been made of the Victorian view of white women's sexuality—i.e., their lack of sexual feelings—and certainly this view was present, if not omnipresent. Historians have also pointed out the objective reasons that married women had for trying to limit their sexual relations with their husbands, factors that may have contributed to the ideology of woman's sexlessness. For one thing, birth control was illegal and difficult to obtain, and many women feared the dangers of miscarriage and pregnancy as well as the extra work of each additional child. In addition, the construction of marital sexuality, within the patriarchal power relations of marriage, was around the husband's sexual gratification (Gottlieb 1984: 144–50); women often found it brutish, even violent, and far from sexually arousing—an unpleasant duty to be performed. Furthermore, since men commonly exposed themselves to venereal diseases through their relations with prostitutes, wives often feared contracting these dreaded illnesses from sexual intercourse with their husbands. Indeed, nineteenth-century feminists formed a "Voluntary Motherhood" movement, centered on the assertion of every woman's right to say no to sex with her husband (and hence to the possibility of pregnancy and motherhood) (Degler 1980: ch. II; Gordon 1976: ch. 5). The lesser interest of women in sexuality—plus the concentration of income in men's hands—helped fuel men's pursuit of sex outside marriage from prostitutes.

The Sexual Division of Labor and Female and Male Prostitution

The nineteenth-century view of sexuality as either procreation or sin, however, was not successful in restricting it to marriage. As we have seen above, many people were not married. And while unmarried women were expected to remain "chaste" or risk losing their marriageability and being saddled with "illegitimate" children, unmarried men were expected to need and seek out sexual outlets—to "sow their wild oats"—even if this was viewed as sinful. Even though married women were expected to be sexual only with their husbands, married men were actively encouraged, if backhandedly, toward sexual relations outside marriage. The social construction of masculinity as driven by sexual desires, or lust, for sexual objects; the practice of men paying for their fiancees' and wives' expenses, i.e., purchasing women's sexual services; the restriction of sex within many marriages; and the gender and class differences that distributed money unevenly—all of these factors contributed to the establishment of sexuality as an industry, i.e., prostitution, that catered to men and employed a class of women who became unmarriageable (Gilfoyle 1992).

The existence of women prostitutes who serviced men of all classes is well documented. If sex within marriage was to be passionless, rare, and aimed at procreation, then men could appease their sexual desires outside of marriage with "bad" girls. And for working-class girls and women who lacked good marriage prospects or simply chose not to marry, prostitution offered much higher pay than the pittance they could earn at the other jobs that were open to them. Many working-class girls became professional prostitutes, especially within the cities; others, called "charity girls" in the nineteenth century, provided sexual favors to men in exchange for gifts, meals, and entertainment that were otherwise out of their financial reach (Peiss 1983). Among whites, prostitution was very common in the cities, as well as in all parts of the woman-scarce West. Free Black women, whose job opportunities were especially restricted, often turned to prostitution in southern cities, where they served both Black and white clientele (Amott and Matthaei 1991: 150). The sex imbalance in Chinese and Japanese immigration (25 men to 1 woman among Japanese immigrants, for example, in 1900) made for a very profitable prostitution business: women were sold or kidnapped in their home countries, sent to the United States, and kept as slaves/prostitutes (Amott and Matthaei 1991: 201, 219).

What is perhaps less well known is that male prostitution was also very common (indeed, the word "gay" in the nineteenth century referred to a prostitute [Weeks 1977: 42]). Weeks estimates that about half of the prostitutes in Europe in the late nineteenth-century cities were young men; I have not found comparable data for the United States, but male prostitution appears to have been common, especially in large cities. Weeks points out the continuity between male heterosexual and homosexual sex/prostitution: the interest was in sex; encounters were usually casual, not long term; the prostitute was a sex object, performing sexual services in exchange for money or gifts; the client was a man with money to spend.

Male prostitutes were very similar to female ones: young; working class; interested in pay that was many times what they could earn at their jobs; servicing their clients' sexual needs, usually by bringing them to orgasm. Some were full-time "professionals," who worked out of brothels or "boy-houses"; they often dressed like women. Detective Gardener describes a New York brothel in 1892: "In each room sat a (male) youth, whose face was painted, eye-brows blackened, and whose airs were those of a young girl. Each person talked in a high falsetto voice, and called the others by women's names." German sexologist Magnus Hirschfeld wrote of meeting, in Chicago, "a Negro girl on Clark Street who turned out to be a male prostitute" (Katz 1976: 63, 77).

There were also many part-time male prostitutes, who were working-class youth employed in low-wage jobs: sailors, soldiers, laborers, newspaper boys, messenger boys, and the like (Weeks 1989: 207; Katz 1976: 64, 78). For this group, prostitution was a way to supplement very low-wages or, like the charity girls, to give them access to "the better life." A gay academic wrote Hirschfeld a long letter describing the homosexual life, including this description of part-time male prostitutes:

> In the vicinity of Denver there is a military fort with a force of a few hundred men. Last summer a soldier from there propositioned me on the street in Denver. I've heard that this happens quite frequently in San Francisco and Chicago. I recall meeting a soldier who was a prostitute long ago in San Antonio, Texas, and last summer I met a young sailor from Massachusetts. The latter was on leave and looking for homosexual intercourse out on the street late at night. In all of these cases it was difficult to tell whether the soldiers were really homosexual or just prostitutes, or whether they went with men for lack of anything better. It's never easy to draw the line, and things are so expensive nowadays that someone could easily be moved to earn a little pocket money in one way or the other. (Katz 1976: 78)

Some men may have become male prostitutes because it gave them a way to live out aspects of the feminine gender role to which they were attracted—feminine dress, a desire to be a passive sexual partner, erotic attraction to a man. In a sense, they wanted to be women, and were doing "women's work" of prostitution. In some cases, such effeminate males actually "treated" their sexual partners: one study of Newport, Rhode Island, sailors in 1919 found that a gang of effeminate sailors would "take a sailor to a show or to dinner, offer him small gifts, or provide him with a place to stay when he was on overnight leave; in exchange, the sailor allowed his host to have sex with him that night, within whatever limits the sailor cared to set." Some of these gay sailors provided sexual services to civilian men in exchange for money, while others had steady relationships with masculine men they referred to as their "husbands" (Chauncey 1990: 299, 303).

While most sexuality in nineteenth-century capitalism involved the cash nexus, either overtly in prostitution, or covertly in marriage, casual male homosexual relations also could take the form of a sexual encounter in which both partners satisfied sexual needs and no exchange of money or gifts was necessary. After all, men were constructed as lustful beings, who desired sex for its own sake. Plus, there was no problem of unwanted pregnancy as in heterosexual sex. The male homosexual subculture that emerged in this period involved "cruising places" where men could meet—certain streets, beaches, woods, bars, or bath houses—to engage in mutually satisfying casual sex. Often, relationships crossed class lines. Gender roles were often involved, including "balls" where males dressed as women. Sometimes race differences were played on: one sexologist discovered, in St. Louis, a group of Black male butlers, cooks, and chauffeurs, who dressed as women for their encounters with white, masculine males (Katz 1976: 66–67, 75–76).

Females Who Lived as Men: Lesbianism as a Response to Gender Inequality and Oppression

While the sexual division of labor helped pressure women into heterosexual marriage, its rigid confines also led some females to reject womanhood and heterosexuality.[12] Some of these rebels worked as feminists to challenge gender roles in society at large. Others rebelled privately by becoming men: they dressed as men, did men's work, and married women. Many "passed" so effectively that they were not found out until their deaths, at which time their femaleness was cause for great surprise and, often, media attention. Murray Hall became a well-known New York City politician; his death, and femaleness, were covered in the *New York Times* and the New York *Daily Tribune*. One of Hall's acquaintances was quoted as saying: "While he was somewhat effeminate in appearance and talked in a falsetto voice, still his conduct and actions were distinctively masculine. This revelation [of Hall's femaleness] is a stunner to me and, I guess, to everybody else who knew him" (Katz 1976: 356).

Accounts of the lives of passing women indicate that many if not most of them were driven into passing by the inequality and oppression involved in the sexual division of labor—in particular, by the gender-typing of jobs and the restriction of females/women to low-paid jobs. Many passing women directly referred to their inability to survive on women's wages in explaining their decisions to take up the masculine gender. A female who called herself Charles Warner wrote in the 1860s:

> When I was about 20 I decided that I was almost at the end of my rope. I had no money and a woman's wages were not enough to keep me alive. I looked around and saw men getting more money and more work, and more money for the same kind of work. I decided to become a man. It was simple, I just put on men's clothing and applied for a man's job. I got it and got good money for those times, so I stuck to it (Berube 1979:1).

According to the *Day Book* tabloid newspaper of Chicago, Cora Anderson, an American Indian, studied nursing with Marie White, who was white, at the Provident Hospital in Chicago. The two formed a relationship but found it difficult to survive on nurses' wages—and Cora was unwilling to accede to sexual harassment: "Two-thirds of the physicians I met made a nurse's virtue the price of their influence in getting her steady work. Is it any wonder that I determined to become a member of this privileged sex, if possible?" The two moved to Cleveland as the Kerwinnieos, with Cora becoming the husband, Ralph. "This disguise also helped me to protect my chum as well as myself. She could stay in the home, and believe me, as long as society, with its double code and double standards of morals, is as it is now, the only place for a woman is in the home." Ralph worked as a bellboy and later for a manufacturer. Later, Ralph left Marie to marry another woman. Marie responded by exposing Ralph as a passing woman, and Cora/Ralph was charged with "disorderly conduct" (Katz 1976: 385–90).

Another passing woman, Caroline Hall, decided to live as "Mr. Hall," according to a *New York Times* story in 1901, because of her "belief that women were not afforded as many opportunities in the world as men." She was an artist who was "an excellent rifle shot," and, as a man, traveled in Italy as a painter, entering and winning several rifle contests. She/he met and became domestic partners with Giuseppina Boriani (Katz 1976: 365–68).

It appears that passing women were from all classes and races. Edward Stevenson wrote of a group of about ten women, most likely African American, who passed as men to work as porters, train agents, switchmen, and cooks for the New York Central Railway in 1903 (Katz 1976: 378–79). Mary Fields, an ex-slave, passed and found employment as a stagecoach driver (Faderman 1991: 44). It was also common for women who wished to fight in wars to pass as men; many were found out when they were wounded in battle. One Civil War expert estimated that 400 females fought as men in that war; one such female, accepted as a man, was a spy who "posed" as a woman! (Katz 1976: 323, 345–46, 363, 909–910). I have found references to females passing as men to practice medicine in the early 1800s (U.S. Dept. of Labor 1974: 21–23) and in the early 1900s (Faderman 1991: 317), and to female (passing as men) sailors (Katz 1976: 905–914).

Sometimes daughters started the process of gender switching at the behest of their parents. For example, Lucy Ann Lobdell, the only child of a farm couple, took on men's work to help her parents, both of whom were disabled by illness. When she reached adulthood, she decided to actually take up life as a man. As she explained:

> First, my father was lame, and in consequence, I had worked in-doors and out [on the farm, and hunting]; and as hard times were crowding upon us, I made up my mind to dress in men's attire to seek labor, as I was used to men's work. And as I might work harder at house-work, and get only a dollar per week, and I was capable of doing men's work, and getting men's wages, I resolved to try . . . to get work away among strangers. (Katz 1976: 333)

During her life as a man, Lucy (who took the name of Joseph) supported herself as a hunter and trapper, and married a woman who had been abandoned by her husband and was living on charity. Lucy/Joseph had to work to hide her femaleness. While changing one's gender wasn't acceptable in her society, in contrast, among the Canadian Kaska nation, it was common and accepted for families lacking sons to urge one of their daughters to become a man (Amott and Matthaei 1991: 37).

While anecdotal evidence points to many passing women who formed long-term relationships with other women, the evidence leaves many questions unanswered. For example, we cannot determine whether it was the economic disadvantage of being a woman or the potential for partnering with another woman that was more likely to be the primary impetus for a woman to pass. And what of the female/women partners of passing women? Some, it appears, were not aware that their husbands were female.[13] Others married "men" they knew to be females, because of love or perhaps because of bad experiences they had with male men.[14] Males passing as women seem to have been much less common, probably because of the clear loss in economic power and social status that this involved.

Similars Attract: The Gender Divide, Romantic Friendships, and "Gay" Jobs

Even for those who did not reject their assigned gender role, the rigid sexual division of labor of the nineteenth century tended to spawn intimate homosocial (and perhaps homosexual) relationships, especially between women, because of the vast social chasm it opened up between the sexes. Men's and women's work and social lives were so disparate, their interests and sensibilities so opposed, that real intimacy between them was difficult to achieve, and usually not expected. As Carroll Smith-Rosenberg writes:

> If men and women grew up as they did in relatively homogeneous and segregated sexual groups, then marriage represented a major problem in adjustment. From this perspective we could interpret much of the emotional stiffness and distance that we associate with Victorian marriage as a structural consequence of contemporary sex-role differentiation and gender-role socialization. With marriage, both women and men had to adjust to life with a person who was, in essence, a member of an alien group. (Smith-Rosenberg 1979: 331)

In contrast, members of the same gender had a good deal in common; they could understand one another's feelings, thoughts, and experiences, and hence achieve emotional and intellectual intimacy.

Not only did the rigid sexual division of labor make the genders so different as to seem alien to one another, but also the nineteenth-century idea of love, as a nonsexual meeting of souls, was easily applied to same-sex relationships. What historians have called "romantic friendships" were common between middle- and upper-class women in the late nineteenth and early twentieth centuries; all of the documented examples I have seen appear to have been among white women, but it is probable that they also occurred among other racial-ethnic groups. Unlike the relationships between a passing woman and another woman, these relationships were homogenderal: that is, these (female) women were attracted to a person of their same, feminine, gender. These women had intense, emotionally and physically intimate love relationships with other women before and during their marriages with men (Smith-Rosenberg 1979; Faderman 1981). For most of these women, their "romantic friendships" were more passionate and intimate than their marriages; for example, "rural women developed a pattern of . . . extended visits that lasted weeks and sometimes months, at times even dislodging husbands from their beds and bedrooms so that dear friends might spend every hour of every day together" (Smith-Rosenberg 1979: 319).

Close friendships among men—also viewed as love relationships—were also common, given the gulf between the genders. While there has been less attention paid to these relationships, they were probably widespread. Discussions of love between men were common in mid-nineteenth-century popular novels, letters, and diaries, in which "American men loved each other, sought verbal and physical forms for the expression of that love, located it in a tradition, and worried about its place in a social order" (Martin 1990: 170). The celebrated poet Walt Whitman spoke of "adhesiveness," love between men, as coexisting with "amativeness" between the sexes, but finessed the question of sexuality (Weeks 1977: 34, 52–53); the German sexologist Hirschfeld wrote in 1914, "Strongly sublimated homosexuality is also common in America; a good example is provided by the poet of comradely love, Walt Whitman" (Katz 1976: 77). Not pressured by financial need into marriage, men could remain bachelors or maintain their friendships after marriage.

The rigid sexual division of labor also created homosexuality in another way: jobs that isolated the employee with his/her coworkers tended to spawn homosocial and homosexual relationships, as did the sex segregation of other social institutions. Military and maritime employment, cattle herding (cowboys), and other men's employments in the woman-scarce West encouraged close relationships and sexuality among men. Prostitution, which marginalized and isolated women from the mainstream and from marriage, as well as exercised their sexuality, generated loving relationships that were often sexual among women: "They spent all their free time together, traveled together, protected each other, loved each other" (Faderman 1991: 37; see also Nestle 1987: 157–77). The sex-segregated schools that were viewed as preparation for segregated gender roles also, because of their homosocial environment, encouraged homosexual relationships, as did the sex-segregated prison system (Faderman 1991: 19–20, 36–37). Interestingly, women in reform schools formed same-sex relationships across racial (Black-white) lines in which "the difference in color . . . [took] the place of difference in sex," with Black women taking the masculine role (Otis, quoted in Faderman 1991: 38).[15]

Lesbian Career Women and Boston Marriages: A Variation on the Romantic Friendship Theme

In the nineteenth and early twentieth centuries, women whom historians have called "social homemakers" worked to expand woman's traditional work of homemaking and, indeed, the boundaries of womanhood; some of these social homemakers were explicitly feminist. While few directly attacked the sexual division of labor, these activists did argue for (middle class) women's right to a college education (to prepare themselves better for motherhood), and for women's claims on emerging professions that they viewed as naturally feminine—teaching, social work, librarianship, and nursing, as well as social activism/social homemaking itself. Black as well as white women participated in this movement and in the emerging women's professions, although Black women encountered virulent discrimination in both (Matthaei 1982: 173–86; Amott and Matthaei 1991: 152–54). As Lillian Faderman has pointed out (1991: ch. 1), access to such jobs gave educated, middle-class females the economic wherewithal to live with other females as life partners, without one member of the couple having to pass as a man (an opportunity working class-women did not have). Indeed, "Many of the leaders of this [social homemaking] movement, including Jane Addams, Vida Scudder, and Frances Willard, not only rejected marriage, but lived with women in intense emotional (and probably sexual) love relationships" (Amott and Matthaei 1991: 125). One suspects that their rejection of heterosexual marriage in favor of relationships with women was a factor underlying their commitment to expanding women's professional options.

Not only did education and career open up women's possibility of nonmarriage, but they also restricted a woman's marriage options: in white middle-class society, paid careers were seen to be incompatible with the full-time dedication to homemaking and mothering expected of wives. (Indeed, marriage bars—employer policies to fire female employees upon marriage and/or refuse to hire married women—were common, especially in teaching and clerical work, through the 1940s [Goldin 1990: 160–71]). Thus, the movement for women's college education, and the participation in feminine careers it encouraged and made possible, discouraged those women from heterosexual marriage (Matthaei 1982: ch. 11). Because a college education prepared women for labor force careers, rates of nonmarriage were much higher among college graduates than among nongraduates; one study found that 35 percent of women college graduates born before 1897 had not married by the age of 50, compared to 8 percent of nongraduates (Matthaei 1982: 259).

Thus, the development of women's education and careers both reduced women's opportunities for marriage and increased their ability to form live-in relationships with one another. Women who had formed close emotional (and maybe sexual) relationships in college no longer had to subordinate these "romantic friendships" to marriage, as in previous times, but could set up households together (Faderman 1991: ch. 1; Matthaei 1982: ch. 11). As Jessie Taft, a sociologist, wrote in 1916:

> Everywhere we find the unmarried woman turning to other women, building up with them a real home, finding in them the sympathy and understanding, the bond of similar standards and values as well as the same aesthetic and intellectual interests, that are often difficult of realization in a husband. . . . One has only to know professional women to realize how common and how satisfactory is this substitute for marriage. (Quoted in Matthaei 1982: 260)

Such arrangements were so common in the East that they were called "Boston marriages."

It is interesting to note that these relationships, like the romantic friendships that preceded them, were homogenderal and were usually with members of the same class and race. Sometimes, both women were professionally employed. For example, Katharine Coman (professor of economics) and Katharine Lee Bates (professor of English, and writer of the words to "America the Beautiful"), lived and worked together at Wellesley College (my employer); Katharine Lee Bates wrote a book of poetry to Katharine Coman, entitled *Yellow Clover* (1922), whose dedication reads, in Latin, "How can it be wrong to love one so dear?" (Schwartz 1979). However, it appears that it was more common for one woman to take on the role of primary provider, and for the other to take on a wifely/motherly role (Vicinus 1992: 482–83; Faderman 1981: ch. 5). The same-class, same-race quality of these relationships contrasts with the prevalence of cross-class and cross-race sexual liaisons among male homosexuals.

The Twentieth Century:
The Emergence of Heterosexuals and Homosexuals

Two important and related changes in the social conceptualization of sexuality occurred as the nineteenth century gave way to the twentieth: the growing connection of sexuality to pleasure and love, and the emergence of "homosexuals" and "heterosexuals." These changes can be connected, at least indirectly, to the process of capitalist development: in particular, as we will see, to the rise of consumerism and to the emergence of a secular and scientific view of the world. Figure 1 lists some of the key aspects of this new view of sexuality, and contrasts it with the nineteenth-century view.

Historian Jonathan Katz (1983) notes that the view of sex as a pleasurable activity for both sexes accompanied the rise of consumerism and the decline of the work ethic that characterized advanced capitalism in the early-twentieth-century United States. Pleasure was to be sought after, through sexuality as well as consumption. The growing acceptance of birth control signified the acceptance of sexual intercourse for its own sake, not for procreation. While all sexual behavior was not seen as involving

	19th Century	Early 20th Century	Late 20th Century
System of Conceptualization	Religious	Medical	Lesbian/Gay Liberationist
"Good" Sex	Procreative	Heterosexual	Safe, informed, consensual
"Bad" Sex	Nonprocreative	Homosexual	Unsafe, nonconsensual, uninformed
View of Homosexual Desire	Felt by all, but not to be acted upon because evil	Only felt by minority of "homosexuals," as result of illness or congenital defect	Can coexist with heterosexual desire; differing views of origins (biological vs. socialization vs. choice)
Problem with Homosexual Sex	Nonprocreative, hence sinful	An illness, requiring treatment by medical profession	Not a problem

Figure 1: Contrasting Views of Sexuality

love, true love now was thought to properly include both sexual passion and the friendship/companionship of the earlier era.

One would think that this revolutionary shift would have eased if not eliminated the stigmatization of homosexual sexual relations—which are intrinsically nonprocreative, and hence clearly centered on pleasure and love. But this was not the case. Instead, the seeking of pleasure through homosexual sexual relations was in the process of being pathologized by "sexologists" in the medical profession, who attempted to analyze such relations scientifically.

In the late nineteenth century, the expanding medical profession began to develop the concept of "inversion" to describe individuals who took on the gender role of the opposite sex, and engaged in heterogenderal, homosexual sexual relations. Among males, the "invert" was the one who acted or dressed in feminine ways, including those who took the "feminine" role in homosexual sexual encounters—i.e., men who were "cocksuckers" or who liked to be anally penetrated. (Men who looked and acted masculine, and who played the "masculine" role in sex with men were not similarly labeled and pathologized.) Similarly, the female invert was the passing woman, the female who dressed like a man and took on the masculine gender role, including an active role in sexuality—and not her partner, if the latter took a feminine role (Chauncey 1989).

By the early twentieth century, medicine's focus began to shift from gender role transgression in general to sexual object choice: "homosexuality" was the illness from which *all* engaged in same-sex sexual relations were thought to suffer, regardless of the gender role they took in those relations or in life in general (Chauncey 1989). Thus, sex-object choice became a key aspect of an individual's identity. One was either heterosexual and normal, or homosexual and abnormal. The latter identity was seen as the result of illness or congenital flaws, and required treatment by the medical profession, especially by its emerging field of psychiatry. In this way, love and/or sexual relationships with members of one's own sex were increasingly viewed as the behavior of a minority of physically "deviant" homosexuals, anathemas to the vast majority of "normal" heterosexuals (Katz 1983: 142–55). Increasingly, then, individuals who felt emotionally close or who were sexually attracted to members of their own sex—and/or were emotionally or sexually indifferent to or alienated from members of the opposite sex—would begin to accept this new view, define themselves as homosexual, and look for support in the growing homosexual subculture.

The new view of sexuality was tightly tied into gender roles, the sexual division of labor, and heterosexual marriage. Sexually healthy individuals were thought to feel sexual passion for members of the opposite sex, passion that they eventually consummated in love-based heterosexual marriage (although nonprocreative heterosexual sex outside of marriage was increasingly accepted) (Katz 1983: 147–50). Conversely, those who engaged in homosexual sex were not viewed as real women or men, no matter how tightly they conformed to other aspects of their gender roles; they became a sort of "third sex," a new kind of person. This tight connection between sexuality and gender increased pressures on all individuals to conform to other, nonsexual aspects of their gender roles, for fear of being stigmatized as lesbian or gay (Goodman et al. 1983: 36).

While the sexual division of labor remained a cornerstone of heterosexuality during this period, it still contained contradictions that ended up encouraging homosexual behavior. The genders continued to be constructed as "opposite," so that emotional intimacy and mutually satisfying sexuality were difficult to achieve between the genders; at the same time, common experiences and world views—and, for women, common oppression by men—continued to draw together members of the same gender. Many females were unwilling to swallow women's roles "whole hog," given the financial insecurities, subordinate position, and risk of harassment and spousal abuse that were involved. Many males, in turn, found the responsibility of supporting a wife and children overwhelming and unappealing. Others probably simply did not "feel" masculine or feminine enough to consider themselves "normal heterosexuals," especially when another category, homosexual, was defined and connected in the public mind to deviance from assigned gender roles. Indeed, homosexuality, now seen as an identity and way of life (even if a stigmatized one), provided a way to escape restrictive gender roles, as did growing subcultures which supported and validated these choices (Weeks 1991: 69–75). A massive rural-to-urban migration supported these emerging communities by bringing gays together and providing them with relative anonymity.

To establish sexual relationships with members of the same sex, gender roles had to be subverted, amended, played with, or simply rejected. Some females continued to pass as men. Jazz musician Billy Tipton started passing in the 1930s in order to play with the all-male swing bands of that era, and was not "found out" until her death in 1989 (Faderman 1991: 317). Ester left her husband and grown sons in Puerto Rico and moved to New York City, where she took up life as a man taxi-cab driver and lived with her female lover, a prostitute, during the 1950s (Nestle 1987: 40–41).

However, increasing numbers of females who rebelled against womanhood, especially those from the working class, identified themselves not as men but as gay women who were "butch"; modified versions of "passing women," they tried to find jobs where they could dress in pants (such as truck or cab driver, or factory worker), and formed relationships with "fems" who dressed like women. In the working-class lesbian subculture's version of heterogenderality, both women were usually employed, but other aspects of masculine/feminine difference were taken on (Faderman 1991: ch. 7; Kennedy and Davis 1993: 64–65).

Among middle- and upper-class women, romantic friendships and Boston marriages continued. However, the passionate love involved in such same-sex relationships became increasingly suspect and viewed not as a complement to heterosexual marriage but rather as an unacceptable "homosexual" substitute. "Throughout most of the twentieth century . . . the enriching romantic friendship that was common in earlier eras is thought to be impossible, since love necessarily means sex and sex between women means lesbian and lesbian means sick" (Faderman 1981: 311).[16] In contrast to working-class lesbian culture, most lesbian career women seemed to prefer androgynous roles and homogenderal relationships (Faderman 1991: 178–87).

Male homosexuality appears to have been more prevalent than lesbianism: Kinsey found in 1948 that over one-third of his sample of men had had sex to orgasm with a man after adolescence (D'Emilio and Freedman 1988: 291). D'Emilio suggests that the greater prevalence of homosexuality among men was due to their greater economic independence and, hence, their greater ability to live outside of marriage (1983: 106). While long-term, monogamous relationships have become increasingly common (especially after the onset of the AIDS epidemic), a large part of gay male life has revolved around casual sex, available at cruising spots, bars, and baths to both married and single men. As Richard Mohr points out, "[male] homosexual relations cut across all social classifications but gender," creating an equalizing or democratizing tendency in the subculture they create (1992: 198).[17] And men's demand for homosexual sex has continued to provide employment for some young gay males; for example, a recent *Boston Globe* article described the division of turf into the "boys' block" (male prostitutes), the "girls' block" (male transvestites and transsexuals), and the "real girls" area (female prostitutes) (Jacobs 1992: 20).

Labor Demand and Sexuality During the Depression and World War II

I have argued that the restriction of women to lower-paid jobs has provided a major economic motive for heterosexuality among women. Lillian Faderman provides an interesting, economically based analysis of the restriction of lesbianism and encouragement of heterosexual marriage in the 1930s. During this decade, high male unemployment generated a groundswell of anger against employed women —particularly against career women or women living independently of men—generating discrimination against women in jobs that could be filled by men "who had families to support." Even the dean of one women's college (Barnard) actively discouraged graduates from paid employment, claiming that this sacrifice would provide a service to their community. Professional women were increasingly portrayed as unwomanly, and their numbers dropped by over 50,000 between 1930 and 1940, even though the female labor force grew by over 500,000 during that period (U.S. Census 1930: 279; U.S. Census 1940: 75). In sum, during the depression years, both economic and social pressures toward heterosexual marriage were strengthened for middle-class young women.

At the same time, Faderman found that some middle- and upper-class married women, both Black and white, maintained lesbian relationships, one of the most famous being Eleanor Roosevelt.[18] And lesbianism was not uncommon among the substantial numbers of working-class women who dropped through the economic cracks into poverty and homelessness; living the life of hobos, they wore pants, joined with other women for protection, and formed intimate relationships that were sometimes self-consciously lesbian (Faderman 1991: 94–99).

The war economy during World War II shifted the balance between homosexuality and heterosexuality. In dire need of soldiers, the military established a secret policy of toleration of homosexuality in its ranks, as long as it was private and not disruptive. Young men were drafted in large numbers; most gay men appear to have been able to slip through the crude examination that was supposed to screen out homosexuals. Many more "came out" in homosexual relationships within the intimate, high-pressure atmosphere of the barracks (Berube 1990; D'Emilio 1992: 65–66).

In stark contrast to the 1930s, employers now actively recruited women into high-paid war-industry jobs in the cities. This facilitated the development of lesbian relationships: "As wage earners working in well-paying defense jobs, wearing men's clothes to do 'men's work,' and living, working, and relaxing with each other, many women for the first time fell in love with other women, socialized with lesbians, and explored the gay nightlife that flourished in the crowded cities" (Berube 1990: 384–85). Women wearing pants to war-industry jobs began to legitimize that practice among women, making it easier for masculine lesbians to "pass" as heterosexual (Faderman 1991: 125–26), while the absence of men from city streets made it safe for women to be out together without male escorts (Kennedy 1994). Some women enlisted in the Women's Army Corps, which both attracted women-loving women and put women in intimate contact with one another. A WAC lecture to officer candidates explained that, in this work situation, it was natural for women to have relationships "that can become an intimacy that may eventually take some form of sexual expression. It may appear that, almost spontaneously, such a relationship has sprung up between two women, neither of whom is a confirmed active homosexual" (Berube 1990: 385–86).

The 1950s: Government-Sponsored Antigay Discrimination

If World War II exerted major pressures against the traditional sexual division of labor and toward women's paid employment, lesbianism, and male homosexuality, the immediate postwar period brought a major backlash consciously aimed at reversing all of these trends. As historian Allan Berube describes:

> Churches, the media, schools, and government agencies conducted a heavy-handed campaign to reconstruct the nuclear family, to force women back into their traditional roles, and to promote a conservative sexual morality. A tactic of this campaign was to isolate homosexual men and women and identify them, like Communists, as dangerous and invisible enemies (Berube 1990: 391).

The military conducted antigay witch hunts, purging thousands of lesbians and gay men from its ranks. Antigay hearings were held in the U.S. Senate, in which it was argued that homosexuals were unfit to be federal employees because they were "generally unsuitable" (due to being abnormal and lacking in emotional stability and moral fiber) as well as because they were "security risks" in certain positions (because they could be blackmailed on the basis of their homosexuality, due to the federal policy of firing them!). President Eisenhower signed an Executive Order barring homosexuals from federal jobs; firing was allowed on the basis of anonymous, unsubstantiated accusations; no appeal was allowed beyond the employee's department. Many state governments followed suit, as did private employers and colleges and universities. Gay and lesbian bars were not a refuge: police raided them and released the names of those arrested to the newspapers, which commonly published them (D'Emilio and Freedman 1988: 292–95; Faderman 1991: ch. 6; Berube 1990: 391–93).

Many lesbians and gay men lost their jobs and careers; those who did not struggled to hide their gayness "in the closet" and lived in perpetual fear of being discovered; many probably chose to give up their gay lifestyles, and many others were deterred from even considering homosexuality. Whether gay or heterosexual, women workers lost their jobs to returning GIs. The pressure on both sexes to "be straight" was strong. Women married and sought happiness in caring for husbands and children; men married and shouldered the provider role, anxious to show they were not among the 50 percent of men who Kinsey had found were attracted to their own sex. But a small and brave group of men and women insisted on living gay lives, mostly in cities, and even founded groups that constituted the beginning of the lesbian and gay movement (D'Emilio 1992: 78–79; Kennedy and Davis 1993).

The Decline of the Sexual Division of Labor and the Attenuation of the Economic Basis of Heterosexuality

Cyclical and war-related ups and downs in women's labor-force participation in the '30s, '40s and '50s did not prevent an overall, secular increase in the entrance of women into the paid labor force full- or part-time—from less than 20 percent of all women in 1900 to 69 percent in 1991 (Matthaei 1982: 142; U.S. Census Bureau 1993: 394). This change was the result of a variety of factors. The growth of needs and consumerism from the 1920's on drew homemakers into the labor force as part of their job of filling family needs. Middle-class women entered higher education as training for homemaking, but this education inadvertently prepared them for paid careers and spawned the career woman. The rapid growth of jobs that had been typed feminine, especially clerical jobs, also helped draw women into the labor force (Matthaei 1982: Part 3). After 1970, the movement of women into the labor force gained further momentum as men's average real wages began a long-term decline. As a result, a major part of the sexual division of labor in marriage—the assignment of wage-earning to the husband and only the husband—began to break down to the point that by 1993, 59 percent of married women held paid jobs (U.S. Census Bureau 1993: 399).

The movement of married women into the paid labor force has been accompanied by a second major change in the sexual division of labor. As women began to spend more years of their lives in the paid labor force, and hence to view their jobs not as temporary stints before marriage but as lifelong careers, they began to challenge women's exclusion from the higher paid and higher status "men's jobs" more vigorously. The demand for access to these jobs—i.e., for an end to gender discrimination in employment—became a key demand of the feminist movement, as did a demand for men to share in women's traditional work of homemaking and childrearing (Matthaei 1982: Part 3).

As an increasing share of women are employed, and more of these are in better paid jobs, more and more women have become able to support themselves, and even their children, independently of husbands or fathers. For example, in 1992, 11 million women—almost one third of the women who were employed full-time—held managerial or professional jobs; their median earnings of $562/week exceeded the overall median earnings for full-time employed men, which were $505/week (U.S. Census Bureau 1993: 426). Two million of the women who headed families with children but without husbands—one-quarter of the total—lived on annual family incomes of above $25,000 (U.S. Census Bureau 1993: 464).

The increase in the numbers of women who are economically independent of men has had an important effect on sexuality. The economic pressure toward heterosexual marriage has decreased for growing numbers of women, as has the pressure to remain in unhappy marriages. Concurrently, men's overall sense of economic responsibility for women in marriage has declined (Ehrenreich 1983), further fueling women's increasing participation in and commitment to the labor force. The divorce rate has sky-rocketed; the share of women who were married dropped from 71 percent in 1970 to 60 percent in 1992, and the share of those who were either divorced or never married rose from 16 percent to 30 percent (U.S. Census 1993: 53).[19]

At the same time, economic independence from men made it economically feasible for some women to structure their lives around lesbian relationships. A 1989 random phone survey, for example, found the median income for full-time full-year workers was $19,643 among all employed women, but $26,331 among employed lesbians (Badgett 1993: 19).[20] This could be both because higher incomes allow women to live without men, and because women who are lesbians expect to have to support themselves and/or their lovers, and hence invest in more training and stay on the job longer than comparable heterosexual women.

Feminism, Lesbian/Gay Liberation, the Attack on the Sexual Division of Labor and Gender, and the Conservative Response

There have been many noneconomic factors contributing to the rise of the feminist and lesbian/gay liberation movements, including the continued persecution of gays and lesbians, the legacy of the civil-rights movement, and the growing secularization of U.S. society. Here I want to focus on the relationship between these movements and the sexual division of labor.

The feminist movement of the 1970s and 1980s was closely linked to lesbianism. On the one hand, lesbians had a higher stake than heterosexual married women in accessing well-paid jobs, since lesbians did not have access to "family wages" through husbands. Furthermore, lesbians had already crossed gender lines in other ways—dress, choice of sexual partner—and were less fearful of losing their "womanhood" and attractiveness to men if they took on "men's jobs" than were heterosexual women. Thus lesbians made up a disproportionate part of the ranks of feminists among all class and racial-ethnic groups. Indeed, French feminist Monique Wittig has argued that feminism has provided lesbian activists with a closeted way of pushing their agenda of dismantling the sexual division of labor and gender roles.[21]

Furthermore, feminist analysis and the movement—especially its radical feminist, socialist feminist, and lesbian feminist components (e.g., Koedt, Levine, and Rapone 1973; Sargent 1981; and Johnston 1973, respectively)—have resulted in the "coming out" of many involved. First, feminists developed a critique of the sexual division of labor and of gender roles as being both restrictive to all and oppressive to women. Second, they directly criticized heterosexual marriage because of its subordination of women to men as unpaid servants and sexual objects. Third, many feminists put forth lesbianism as a viable alternative—even, some argued, *the* appropriate feminist choice, a form of resistance to patriarchy that is more symmetrical and egalitarian than heterosexuality (e.g., Johnston 1973; Radicalesbians 1973; Rich 1980). Many of the leading early feminist theorists—such as Adrienne Rich, Andrea Dworkin, Gayle Rubin, Charlotte Bunch, Mary Daly, Audre Lorde, Barbara Smith, Cherrie Moraga, and Susan Griffin—were "out" lesbians. Fourth, feminism has brought like-minded women together as coparticipants in support and action groups, providing them with potential sexual/love partners.

In other words, feminist movement[22] has encouraged women to challenge and even deviate from traditional gender roles; it has highlighted the oppressiveness of traditional heterosexuality; it has supported and even advocated lesbianism as an option for women; it has encouraged women to pursue "men's" jobs (and fought to open these higher-paying jobs to women), jobs that allow them to survive economically without men; and it has brought women in close and cooperative contact with other like-minded women. When criticized as being lesbian or proslesbian, some feminist groups (such as the early NOW) tried to distance feminism from lesbianism. However, most feminist groups have instead responded by openly supporting their lesbian members and by adding the demand for lesbian and gay civil rights to their platforms.

Meanwhile, the 1969 Stonewall rebellion against a police raid of a gay bar began a growing, out-of-the-closet movement of gay men and lesbians that has asserted our rights to live and love. While the early movement was tied into radical feminism and to the Left, it has become increasingly centered on a liberal agenda of gaining rights and protection from discrimination for lesbians and gays (Seidman 1993). By the early nineties, the movement had succeeded in making antigay discrimination illegal in a number of states. Gay and lesbian couples are demanding and beginning to win recognition as families, with access to spousal benefits and the right to parent. This extension of rights and legal protections to lesbians and gays is gaining increasing public acceptance as a logical extension of civil rights and antidiscrimination principles central to the U.S. ethical/legal system.[23]

Indeed, during his 1992 presidential campaign, Clinton courted the lesbian/gay vote by promising to end discrimination in the military. He reneged on this promise once in office, in the face of vociferous opposition from the military and Congress, and instead compromised with a modest reform: under the new "don't ask, don't tell" policy, the military agreed not to investigate a service member's sexuality, but service members are prohibited from being "out" on their jobs. The terms of the debate on the issue also represented a minor step forward in public discourse. Those who argued against the proposed changes did not use either the religious argument (gays are immoral) or the medical one (gays are mentally or physically compromised). Rather, they argued that the presence of "out" gays in the military would "threaten unit cohesion," an argument centered on the inefficiencies caused by homophobia rather than by homosexuals themselves.

A new, "social" view of sexuality is being put forward by lesbian/gay and feminist movements, in which "bad" sex is sex that creates unwanted children, sex that exposes the participants to disease (especially AIDS), or sex into which either participant has been forced against his/her will (see Figure 1). Our society, it is argued, has the responsibility to support "good" sex by educating us all about sexuality, including reproduction, birth control options, and safe sex; by exposing, condemning, and punishing rape and child sexual abuse; and by supporting an individual's right to engage in homosexual (as well as heterosexual) sex if she/he so chooses, through education, antidiscrimination, and other measures.

In these ways, then, feminism and the lesbian and gay movements, encouraged by and combined with economic developments, have attacked the core of the sexual division of labor—the assignment of individuals to men's or women's work, on the basis of their sex—as well its main corollaries—gender identity as given by sex, and marriage as the union of different and complementary genders. Gender differences are themselves being eroded, as each gender's work and sexual options are expanded, so that gender now has less and less consistent meaning beyond biological sex. If a female/woman can do anything that a male/man can do and still be a woman (and vice versa), then woman is not any different from man, other than biologically.

New principles are arising. The right to choose from among all jobs for which one is qualified, regardless of one's gender. The notion that full individuality (for both males and females) involves participation in family, economy, and polity. The conception of marriage as a union of socially similar beings, be they of the same or opposite sexes (Matthaei 1982: ch. 13, Conclusion; Matthaei 1988). The new concept of "sexual preference," which suggests that sexual orientation is not inborn but rather a choice between two desirable options, a choice that *all* individuals make. The category of bisexual: individuals who refuse to acknowledge an exclusive sexual preference. If gender further fades into sex, we can expect an entirely new set of sexual categories, perhaps not even called "sexual," to emerge (see Figure 1).

The radical nature of these changes, both won and proposed, has called forth a strong conservative reaction, a reaction that has coalesced in the religious and "pro-family" arms of the "New Right." Their goal is to roll back the gains of the feminist and gay movements and to reestablish the "traditional family": a heterosexual married couple with children, in which the husband/breadwinner commands and the wife/full-time homemaker submits. As they see it, "the homosexual movement is nothing less than an attack on our traditional, pro-family values" (Schwartz and Rueda 1987: 8). Key to their ideology is a religious view of sexuality that virtually replicates the nineteenth-century view we have discussed above: homosexual acts, as well as birth control and sex outside of marriage, are seen as sinful because they prevent or cannot lead to the birth of legitimate children; abortion is viewed as murder, pure and simple.[24] In the fall of 1992, the religious right won passage in Colorado of an amendment that prevented state agencies from protecting lesbians and gay men from discrimination; the amendment was later overturned by the courts. A similar but stronger measure was put forward in Oregon that, besides banning nondiscrimination policies, also required government-funded organizations to represent homosexuality as "abnormal, wrong, unnatural, and perverse"; the measure was narrowly defeated. For the 1994 elections, the religious right backed antigay initiatives in ten states; however, only two made it onto ballots (Idaho and Oregon), and both were defeated by voters. However, the Republican take-over of the House and Senate has brought a heightened threat of federal antigay legislation. Meanwhile, the religious right has also been active in local school board elections, their goal being to block or roll back progressive curricular reform, such as the inclusion of gay and lesbian families in New York City's "rainbow curriculum." With the backing of a number of semi-independent, well-financed organizations that have trained thousands of committed activists, and with powerful allies in the now-dominant Republican Party, the New Right poses a real threat to the realization of the goals, both liberal and radical, of the feminist and gay rights movements (Cagan 1993; *Gay Community News* 1994: 5–6; Hardisty 1993; *Momentum* 1994: 1).

Acknowledgments

I would like to thank Sumangala Kailasapathy for research assistance. An earlier draft of this paper was presented at "The Economics of Sexual Orientation: Theory, Evidence, and Policy" panel, sponsored by the Union for Radical Political Economics (URPE) at the annual Allied Social Science Associations (ASSA) meetings in Anaheim, California in January 1993. I have benefited from comments made at that session, and at presentations of the paper at the Washington, DC, Economic History Seminar and at the Homo-Economics Conference in the spring of 1994. I would also like to thank the members of the Wellesley Faculty Seminar on Lesbian and Gay Studies, and Laurie Nisonoff, Jayati Lal, and Ann Davis—the reviewers at *The Review of Radical Political Economics*—for their comments and help.

Notes

Reprinted with permission, with minor changes, from *The Review of Radical Political Economics*, June 1995.

1. A short note regarding my methodology is in order here. My method of argument is an historical and dialectical one, and may discomfort those who think in linear terms, as it did one reviewer. For example, I argue simultaneously that the sexual division of labor is a main force in cementing heterosexual marriage, and that it contains contradictions that help construct homosexual relationships. I do not believe that historical processes can be adequately analyzed through an econometric logic according to which each "independent variable" is thought to have a consistent effect.
2. See, for example, Hartmann (1979), Folbre (1982), and Delphy (1984).
3. Walby (1990) is an exception, as is Ehrlich (1981); neither was trained as an economist. Ferguson (1989), whom I discuss next, is a philosopher.
4. Building on Becker, Posner (1992) argues that an individual's sexual behavior is deter-

mined by a combination of genetic predisposition (along Kinsey's range from purely homosexual to purely heterosexual) and rational choice. The latter is then influenced by a
number of factors, from sex ratios in the population to urbanization to social policy.

5. As also quoted in Vicinus (1992: 469).

6. See LeVay and Hamer (1994) and Byne (1994) for a recent rehashing of the "gay gene"
debate.

7. For more on the constructionist-essentialist debate, see Stein (1990) (especially the essay
by Boswell), Vance (1991), and Escoffier (1992).

8. The concept of gender identity, including the difference between sex and gender, is key to
women's studies; see, for example, Oakley (1972). The sexual division of labor is a central
concept in the work of Marxist-feminist economists and feminist anthropologists; see, for
example, Hartmann (1979), Rosaldo and Lamphere (1974), and Amott and Matthaei
(1991: ch. 2). More recently, queer theorist Judith Butler has analyzed gender as "an identity tenuously constituted in time, instituted in an exterior space through a *stylized repeti-
tion of acts*" (1990: 140). These "acts and gestures, articulated and enacted desires create
the illusion of an interior and organizing gender core" (136).

9. See, for example, Morris (1975), the eloquent autobiography of a male who underwent a
sex change operation to realize his feminine identity; and Feinberg (1993), in which the
main character is taunted and ostracized for not being feminine enough, eventually finds
an identity as a butch lesbian, and thinks of herself as a "he-she." Kennedy and Davis
(1993) report that "butch identity was based in various combinations of masculine inclination and sexual interest in women" (327).

10. This differs from the neoclassical analysis of the sexual division of labor in marriage. The
latter argues that utility-maximizing individuals freely choose marriage and specialization
because it increases their total utility. Specialization results either from different innate
preferences, from different relative abilities to do home and market work, and/or from sex
discrimination (women receiving less return than men to their human capital invest-
ments).

11. Indeed, historian John D'Emilio (1983) argues that the development of capitalism and
wage labor enabled homosexuality, especially male homosexuality, by enabling individuals to provide for their needs outside of a traditional family context. In my opinion, this
argument is much stronger for men than it is for women.

12. For a discussion of the historical antecedents of the passing woman, see Vicinus (1992).

13. For example, Dr. Eugene de Savitsch wrote in 1958 of the case of Nicholas de Raylan, a
female who passed as a man, in the early 1900s. His/her second wife wept at his death,
"declaring that talk of his being a woman was nonsense." The postmortem showed him to
be female. "An imitation penis and testicles made of chamois skin and stuffed with down
were suspended in the right place by means of a band around the waist" (Katz 1976: 380).

14. For example, the July 25, 1863, *Fitcher's Trades' Review* had a story on a "Curious Married
Couple."

> In 1731, a girl named Mary East was engaged to be married to a young man for
> whom she entertained the strongest affection; but upon his taking to evil courses, or,
> to tell the whole truth, being hanged for highway robbery, she determined to run no
> risk of any such disappointment from the opposite sex in future. A female friend of
> hers having suffered in some similar manner, and being of the like mind with her-
> self, they agreed to pass for the rest of their days as man and wife. . . . The question
> of which should be the husband was decided by lot in favor of Mary East. (Katz
> 1978: 343–44).

15. The women were physically segregated by race to some degree within the reform schools.
16. Recent analysts note that even in the mid- and late-nineteenth century, romantic friendships, while acceptable, were viewed as involving potential threats to traditional marriage (Martin 1990; Vicinus 1992).
17. Mohr (1992) quotes Paul Goodman as writing, "Its [queer life's] promiscuity can be a beautiful thing. . . . I have cruised rich, poor, middle class, and petit bourgeois; black, white, yellow and brown; scholars, jocks, Gentlemanly C's, and dropouts; farmers, seamen, railroad men, heavy industry, light manufacturing, communications, business, and finance; civilian, soldiers and sailors, and once or twice cops (1977: 219–21)."
18. Faderman's and others' claims that Eleanor had a homosexual relationship with Lorena Hickock have been hotly disputed or, more commonly, simply ignored by many mainstream biographers.
19. These data were standardized by age. This is not to say that all women have become economically independent. For a substantial share of women, the choice to stay single or to divorce is still a choice to live in poverty; indeed, over one third of all women heading households without husbands present lived in poverty in 1991 (U.S. Census 1993: 471). Many of these women were divorced or abandoned by their husbands. Thus, while a larger share of women is economically independent from men, overall, women's per capita access to resources has declined (Albelda 1988).
20. In this volume, Badgett reports a later research finding showing no significant difference between the average incomes of straight women and lesbians. She also discusses the limitations of all research to date on lesbian and gay incomes, given the paucity of data.
21. Talk by Wittig at Wellesley College in the mid-1980s. Clearly it is impossible to accurately ascertain the numbers of lesbians in different parts of the feminist movement, due to so many of them being in the closet; however, my personal experiences in many parts of the feminist movement over the past fifteen years, as well as my reading on the subject, lead me to this conclusion.
22. I use the term "feminist movement" instead of "the feminist movement" to emphasize the many different forms feminist organizing has taken, as suggested by bell hooks in her *Feminist Theory: From Margin to Center* (1984).
23. A Gallup poll of Americans reported in *Newsweek* on September 14, 1992, p. 37, found that 67 percent approved of health insurance for gay spouses, 70 percent approved of inheritance rights for gay spouses, and 58 percent approved of Social Security for gay spouses. Significant minorities approved of legally sanctioned gay marriages and adoption rights for gays (35 percent and 32 percent, respectively).
24. One difference, however, is that they do not seem to assume that all feel attractions to members of their own sex. For example, Schwartz and Rueda (1987: 8) write of homosexuality as a "disordered sexual condition" that leads to evil acts in *Gays, AIDS and You* (quoted in Hardisty 1993: 3).

References

Albelda, Randy, et al. 1988. *Mink Coats Don't Trickle Down: The Economic Attack on Women and People of Color.* Boston: South End Press.

Amott, Teresa, and Julie Matthaei. 1991. *Race, Gender and Work: A Multicultural Economic History of Women in the United States.* Boston: South End Press.

Badgett, M. V. Lee. 1993. The Economic Well-Being of Lesbians and Gay Men: Pride and Prejudice. Paper Presented at a Union of Radical Political Economics-sponsored Session of the 1993 Allied Social Science Associations Meetings. Anaheim, CA.

Bates, Katharine Lee. 1922. *Yellow Clover: A Book of Remembrance*. New York: E. P. Dutton.

Berube, Alan. 1979. Lesbian Masquerade. *Gay Community News*. November 17, 1979.

———. 1990. Marching to a Different Drummer: Lesbian and Gay GIs in World War II. In *Hidden from History: Reclaiming the Gay and Lesbian Past*, edited by Duberman, Vicinus, and Chauncey, pp. 383–94. New York: Penguin.

Butler, Judith. 1990. *Gender Trouble: Feminism and the Subversion of Identity*. New York: Routledge.

Byne, William. 1994. The Biological Evidence Challenged. *Scientific American* 270(5): 50–55.

Cagan, Leslie. 1993. Community Organizing and the Religious Right: Lessons From Oregon's Measure Nine Campaign. An Interview with Suzanne Pharr. *Radical America* 24(4): 67–75.

Chauncey, George. 1989. From Sexual Inversion to Homosexual: The Changing Medical Concept of Female "Deviance." In *Passion and Power: Sexuality in History*, edited by K. Peiss, et al., pp. 87–119. Philadelphia: Temple University Press.

———. 1990. Christian Brotherhood or Sexual Perversion? Homosexual Identities and the Construction of Sexual Boundaries in the World War I Era. In *Hidden from History: Reclaiming the Gay and Lesbian Past*, edited by Duberman, Vicinus, and Chauncey, pp. 294–317. New York: Penguin.

Degler, Carl N. 1980. *At Odds: Women and the Family in America from the Revolution to the Present*. New York: Oxford University Press.

Delphy, Christine. 1984. *Close to Home: A Materialist Analysis of Women's Oppression*. Amherst: University of Massachusetts Press.

D'Emilio, John. 1983. Capitalism and Gay Identity. In *Powers of Desire: The Politics of Sexuality*, edited by Snitow, Stansell, and Thompson. New York: Monthly Review Press.

———. 1992. *Making Trouble: Essays on History, Politics and the University*. New York: Routledge.

D'Emilio, John, and Estelle Freedman. 1988. *Intimate Matters: A History of Sexuality in America*. New York: Harper & Row.

Duberman, Martin, Martha Vicinus, and George Chauncey, Jr. (eds.). 1990. *Hidden from History: Reclaiming the Gay & Lesbian Past*. New York: Penguin.

Ehrenreich, Barbara. 1983. *The Hearts of Men: American Dreams and the Flight from Commitment*. Garden City, NY: Anchor Press/Doubleday.

Ehrlich, Carol. 1981. The Unhappy Marriage of Marxism and Feminism: Can It Be Saved? In *Women and Revolution*, edited by Lydia Sargent. Boston: South End Press.

Escoffier, Jeffrey. 1992. Generations and Paradigms: Mainstreams in Lesbian and Gay Studies. In *Gay and Lesbian Studies*, edited by Minton, pp. 7–88. New York: Haworth Press.

Epstein, Stephen. 1987. Gay Politics, Ethnic Identity: The Limits of Social Constructionism. *Socialist Review* 17(3&4): 9–54.

Faderman, Lillian. 1981. *Surpassing the Love of Men: Romantic Friendship and Love between Women from the Renaissance to the Present.* New York: William Morrow.

———. 1991. *Odd Girls and Twilight Lovers: A History of Lesbian Life in Twentieth-Century America.* New York: Penguin.

Feinberg, Leslie. 1993. *Stone Butch Blues.* Ithaca, NY: Firebrand Books.

Ferguson, Ann. 1989. *Blood at the Root: Motherhood, Sexuality, and Male Dominance.* London: Pandora.

———. 1991. *Sexual Democracy: Women, Oppression, and Revolution.* San Francisco: Westview Press.

Folbre, Nancy. 1982. Exploitation Comes Home: A Critique of the Marxian Theory of Family Labour. *Cambridge Journal of Economics* 6(4) : 317–29.

Gay Community News. October. 1994. "Bigot Busters V. Religious Right: Bigot Busters Win" 20(3) : 5–6.

Gilfoyle, Timothy. 1992. *City of Eros: New York City, Prostitution, and the Commercialization of Sex, 1720–1920.* New York: W. W. Norton.

Goldin, Claudia. 1990. *Understanding the Gender Gap: An Economic History of American Women.* New York: Oxford University Press.

Goodman, Gerre, et al. 1983. *No Turning Back: Lesbian and Gay Liberation for the '80s.* Philadelphia: New Society Publishers.

Goodman, Paul. 1977. The Politics of Being Queer. *Nature Heals: The Psychological Essays of Paul Goodman.* Edited by Taylor Stoehr, pp. 216–25. New York: Free Life Editions.

Gordon, Linda. 1976. *Woman's Body, Woman's Right.* New York: Grossman Publishers.

Gottlieb, Rhonda. 1984. The Political Economy of Sexuality. *Review of Radical Political Economics* 16: 143–66.

Hardisty, Jean. 1993. Constructing Homophobia: Colorado's Right-Wing Attack on Homosexuals. *The Public Eye: A Publication of Political Research Associates* (March): 1–10.

Hartmann, Heidi. 1979. Capitalism, Patriarchy, and Job Segregation by Sex. In *Capitalist Patriarchy and the Case for Socialist Feminism,* edited by Z. Eisenstein, pp. 206–247. New York: Monthly Review Press.

hooks, bell. 1981. *Ain't I A Woman: Black Women and Feminism.* Boston: South End Press.

Hubbard, Ruth, Mary Sue Henefin, and Barbara Fried (eds.). 1982. *Biological Woman—The Convenient Myth: A Collection of Feminist Essays and a Comprehensive Bibliography.* Cambridge, MA: Schenkman.

Jacobs, Sally. 1992. Cruising and Losing: Young Men Barter Flesh, Dismal Future. *Boston Sunday Globe,* December 20, pp. 1, 20.

Johnston, Jill. 1973. *Lesbian Nation: The Feminist Solution.* New York: Simon and Schuster.

Katz, Jonathan. 1976. *Gay American History: Lesbians and Gay Men in the U.S.A.* New York: Discus/Avon Books.

————. 1983. *Gay/Lesbian Almanac*. New York: Harper & Row.

Kennedy, Elizabeth. 1994. Codes of Resistance in the Buffalo Lesbian Community of the 1950s: Class, Race and the Development of Lesbian Identity. Talk Given at Wellesley College, February 22.

Kennedy, Elizabeth, and Madeline Davis. 1993. *Boots of Leather, Slippers of Gold: The History of a Lesbian Community*. New York: Routledge.

Koedt, A., A. Levine, and A. Rapone (eds.). 1973. *Radical Feminism*. New York: Quadrangle/The New York Times.

LeVay, Simon, and Dean Hamer. 1994. Evidence for a Biological Influence in Male Homosexuality. *Scientific American* 270(5): 44–49.

Martin, Robert K. 1990. Knights-Errant and Gothic Seducers: The Representation of Male Friendship in Mid-Nineteenth-Century America. In *Hidden from History: Reclaiming the Gay and Lesbian Past*, edited by Duberman, Vicinus, and Chauncey, pp. 169–82. New York: Penguin.

Matthaei, Julie. 1982. *An Economic History of Women in America: Women's Work, the Sexual Division of Labor, and the Development of Capitalism*. New York: Schocken Books.

————. 1988. Political Economy and Family Policy. In *The Imperiled Economy, Book 2*, edited by Robert Cherry, et al. New York: Union for Radical Political Economics and Monthly Review Press.

Momentum: The Newsletter for Members of the Human Rights Campaign Fund. " '94 Voters Reject Anti-Gay Discrimination" (Winter 1994): 1.

Mohr, Richard. 1992. *Gay Ideas: Outing and Other Controversies*. Boston: Beacon Press.

Morris, Jan. 1975. *Conundrum*. New York: New American Library.

Nestle, Joan. 1987. *A Restricted Country*. Ithaca, NY: Firebrand Books.

Oakley, Ann. 1972. *Sex, Gender, and Society*. San Francisco: Harper & Row.

Peiss, Kathy. 1983. "Charity Girls" and City Pleasures: Historical Notes on Working-Class Sexuality, 1880–1920. In *Powers of Desire*, edited by Snitow, Stansell, and Thompson. New York: Monthly Review Press.

Posner, Richard A. 1992. *Sex and Reason*. Cambridge: Harvard University Press.

Radicalesbians. 1973. The Woman-Identified Woman. In *Radical Feminism*, edited by Koedt, Levine and Rapone. New York: Quadrangle/The New York Times.

Rich, Adrienne. 1980. Compulsory Heterosexuality and Lesbian Existence. *Signs: Journal of Women in Culture and Society* 5(4) : 631–60.

Rosaldo, Michelle, and Louise Lamphere (eds.). 1974. *Woman, Culture, and Society*. Stanford, CA: Stanford University Press.

San Francisco Lesbian and Gay History Project. 1990. "She Even Chewed Tobacco": A Pictorial Narrative of Passing Women in America. In *Hidden from History: Reclaiming the Gay and Lesbian Past*, edited by Duberman, Vicinus, and Chauncey, pp. 183–94. New York: Penguin.

Sargent, Lydia (ed.). 1981. *Women and Revolution: A Discussion of the Unhappy Marriage of Marxism and Feminism*. Boston: South End Press.

Schwartz, Judith. 1979. Yellow Clover: Katharine Lee Bates and Katherine Coman. *Frontiers* 4 (1) : 59–67.

Schwartz, Michael, and Enrique Rueda. 1987. *Gays, AIDS and You.* Old Greenwich, CT: Devin Adair Company.

Seidman, Stephen. 1993. Identity and Politics in a "Postmodern" Gay Culture: Some Historical and Conceptual Notes. In *Fear of a Queer Planet,* edited by Michael Warner, pp. 105–42. Minneapolis: University of Minnesota Press.

Smith-Rosenberg, Carroll. 1979. The Female World of Love and Ritual. In *A Heritage of Her Own: Toward a New Social History of American Women,* edited by Nancy F. Cott and Elizabeth H. Pleck, pp. 311–342. New York: Simon and Schuster.

Snitow, Ann, Christine Stansell, and Sharon Thompson (eds.). 1983. *Powers of Desire: The Politics of Sexuality.* New York: Monthly Review Press.

Spelman, Elizabeth. 1988. *Inessential Woman: Problems of Exclusion in Feminist Thought.* Boston: Beacon Press.

Stein, Edward (ed.). 1990. *Forms of Desire: Sexual Orientation and the Social Constructionist Controversy.* New York: Garland Publishing.

U.S. Department of Commerce. Bureau of the Census. 1930. *Census of Occupations. Occupations: General Report.* Washington, D.C.: GPO.

———. 1940. *Census of the U.S. Population: Vol. III: The Labor Force. Part I: U.S. Summary.* Washington, DC: GPO.

———. 1975. *Historical Statistics of the U.S.: Colonial Times to 1970.* Washington, DC: GPO.

———. 1993. *Statistical Abstract of the United States.* Washington, DC: GPO.

U.S. Department of Labor. 1974. *Nontraditional Occupations Women of the Hemisphere—The U.S. Experience.* Washington, DC: GOP.

Vance, Carol. 1991. Anthropology Rediscovers Sexuality: A Theoretical Comment. *Social Science Medicine* 33(8) : 876–84.

Vicinus, Martha. 1992. "They Wonder to Which Sex I Belong": The Historical Roots of the Modern Lesbian Identity. *Feminist Studies* 18(3) : 467–98.

Walby, Sylvia. 1990. *Theorizing Patriarchy.* London: Basil Blackwell.

Weeks, Jeffrey. 1977. *Coming Out: Homosexual Politics in Britain, from the Nineteenth Century to the Present.* New York: Quartet Books.

———. 1985. *Sexuality and its Discontents: Meanings, Myths, and Modern Sexualities.* London: Routledge and Kegan Paul.

———. 1989. Inverts, Perverts, and Mary-Annes. In *Hidden from History: Reclaiming the Gay and Lesbian Past,* edited by Duberman, Vicinus, and Chauncey, pp. 195–211. New York: Penguin.

———. 1991. *Against Nature: Essays on History, Sexuality and Identity.* London: Rivers Oram Press.

11

Do Gay Men Have a Stake in Male Privilege?
The Political Economy of Gay Men's Contradictory Relationship to Feminism

Michael P. Jacobs

This essay, originally written in 1985, never published, and revised for this volume, confronts a difficult question for the gay and feminist movements: Can gay men's political sympathies with women be counted on, even as feminism challenges the economic privilege they enjoy?

Ever since the near-concurrent emergence of the gay liberation and modern feminist movements in the late 1960s, many gay leftists as well as radical and socialist feminists have asserted the critical importance of linking the oppression of women and the oppression of gay men and lesbians; it has become conventional wisdom. In her essay "Socialism, Feminism, and Gay/Lesbian Liberation," Christine Riddiough argued in favor of an expanded definition of feminism, "aimed at the liberation of women and gay people and at sexual self-determination for all people" (1981, 75–76). In the mid-1980s, journalist Laura Cottingham made a parallel point at a conference of gay activists; deploring the fact that only one speaker had explicitly connected gay oppression to sexism, she asked, "If homophobia isn't connected to women's oppression, then where the hell does it come from?" (1985, 16)

The presumed affinity of gay liberation with feminism is based not merely on the commonality of the two groups' enemies. Theoretical explanations of the connection of homophobia to women's subordination generally highlight either the political and economic importance of the heterosexual, nuclear family or the relationship of society's gender norms to the enforced dominance of heterosexuality. In the former group of theories, the nuclear family is seen as an ideal or even structurally necessary institution in capitalist and/or patriarchal societies, depending on the particular theory, and as a common oppressor of women and gay people. The two groups are thus seen as having a common interest in fighting the social dominance and oppressiveness of this institution. In criticism focusing on gender and sexuality, the emphasis is on the social processes that construct both gendered and heterosexual identities, and on the role of homophobia in enforcing conformity to prescribed gender roles. Both of these modes of thought generally assume that the interests of gay people in confronting the heterosexual norm and of women in challenging gender roles are highly complementary and essential for each other's success.

Gay men thus would appear to be natural allies of feminism. And indeed, many gay and bisexual men do consider themselves feminists and are supportive of women's empowerment, broadly defined, perhaps to a greater extent than heterosexual men. Yet many others respond to women's political activism with indifference, discomfort, or even hostility. These latter responses suggest that the relationship of gay men to feminism is more complicated than conventional wisdom acknowledges. This essay reexamines the theoretical foundations for linking gay liberation and feminism, through an analysis of recent changes in both the economic structure of women's subordination and in the relationship of gender to sexual identity.

Women and gay men have a common stake in securing livelihoods outside of the heterosexual, nuclear family, which is a *private* sphere of women's oppression. But in *public* spheres, such as the labor market, their concerns diverge, because gay men's economic interests are aligned more with other men than with women. As economic and social forces have led to an increase women's employment outside the home and a decrease in the number of people living in two-adult, heterosexual nuclear families, feminist political economists have noted a shift in the site of women's economic inequality away from the private and toward the public sphere. As a result, the continuing importance of the heterosexual nuclear family to the maintenance of either capitalist or patriarchal inequalities has been called into question. With the weakened role of the nuclear family and the greater significance of the labor market and public policy structuring women's oppression, areas of common interest between women and gay men have thus declined in importance, while structural conflicts between them have heightened.

Changes in the relationship of the social construction of sexuality to gender roles, generated in part by the gay movement, may be giving these conflicts greater political expression. In the culture at large and within peoples' identities, sexual orientation is less often seen as determining one's gender identity and vice versa. Literature on the social construction of sexuality suggests that enforced heterosexual norms and homophobia cannot be viewed simply as functional products of gender role formation and gender hierarchy, but rather that they are somewhat autonomous social forces. If this autonomy increases in the future, struggles against gender roles and against privileged heterosexuality will become even less closely related.

In short, theoretical arguments that connect women's and gay people's oppression and highlight their common interests frequently overlook structural conflicts between gay men and women.[1] While common interests exist, economic and social forces have placed gay men in an increasingly contradictory relationship to feminism, and this in turn suggests that the link to feminism might not provide a sufficient basis for either gay or feminist political activism.

Feminism, Gay Liberation, and the Dominance
of the Heterosexual Nuclear Family

Both feminists and gay liberationists have been critically concerned with the dominance of the nuclear family in advanced industrial societies. While feminists have focused on the family as a site of the oppressive relations between men and women, gay liberationists have stressed, as John D'Emilio has put it, that "Gay men and lesbians exist on social terrain beyond the boundaries of the heterosexual nuclear family" (1983, 110). The three theoretical writings summarized in this section each point to women's and gay people's common interest in challenging the dominance of the family. These analyses differ, but each overlooks possible conflicts of interest between the two groups.

David Fernbach's (1980) functional analysis of gay oppression and capitalism is an early example of a theoretical consideration of the family by a gay leftist.[2] Fernbach asserts that the nuclear family, in which women have primary responsibility for childrearing and men have preferential access to the wage in order to fulfill their primary roles as wage earners, is the simplest, most direct arrangement for the reproduction of a working class necessary to capitalism. The family is a site of social as well as biological reproduction, in which psychological processes produce masculinity in boys and femininity in girls and, simultaneously, involve a repression of homosexuality. These processes sometimes do not succeed, creating a homosexual minority that, in Fernbach's view, serves the maintenance of the nuclear family by becoming the focus of the aggression of those marginally "successful" heterosexuals who must repress their own homosexual feelings.

Fernbach views the family as a primary site of gay oppression, but he contends that, until recently, the reproduction of the working class under capitalism also required a state policy against homosexuality. In the past, he argues, individuals' heterosexuality cultivated by the family came into conflict with capitalist society's interest in postponing the marriage of prospective parents until they could afford children; this interest compelled the capitalist state to attempt to restrain premarital heterosexuality. In this view, state proscriptions against homosexuality were a necessary "ancillary" to such an attempt, in order that the pent-up sexual energies of unmarried heterosexuals, especially males, not "burst through the psychological barriers erected against homosexuality" (Fernbach 1980, 152). With the spread of modern forms of birth control breaking the causal link between heterosexuality and procreation, Fernbach believes that governmental policies against premarital sex and homosexuality were rendered obsolete. Stating that the state's willingness to grant gay rights is almost assured, Fernbach maintains that gay liberation is concomitant with feminism's undermining of familial gender roles yet is incapable of becoming a viable, independent political force. Fernbach reasons that gay people cannot contribute to this process, because they exist outside of the family and so cannot participate in the struggle against familial structures. Capable of merely "cashing in" on the progress of the women's movement (157), gay men are natural though passive allies of feminism.

Christine Riddiough's (1981) analysis of the nuclear family's relationship to gay and women's oppression offers a different assessment of gay people's political potential, though she echoes Fernbach's view of the family as the site of heterosexism. Citing Antonio Gramsci's argument that the stabilization of sexual relations within the nuclear, monogamous family was of critical importance in creating an efficient and obedient work force, Riddiough asserts that the family is the fundamental unit of civil society and that sexual puritanism is its underlying basis.[3] The family's hierarchical relations between men and women and the repression of sexuality teach the young that gender roles and the bond between sexuality and reproduction are natural. Because the existence and specific sexual behavior of lesbians and gay men contradicts these lessons of the nuclear family, society is keenly interested in keeping gay people invisible and using homophobia to marginalize those who manage to become visible.

Consequently, in Riddiough's view, open gay life challenges both homophobia and the dominance of the nuclear family, which is vital for both women's liberation and socialism. In this analysis, gay people have a particularly important role to play in women's liberation, and the common interests of gay men and women with respect to the family are clear.[4]

D'Emilio is also concerned with the oppression generated by the dominance of the nuclear family, but unlike Fernbach and Riddiough he does not view the family as merely functional to capitalism. Instead, D'Emilio regards capitalism's relationship to the family as contradictory, creating the potential for the liberation of both gay people and women.

Distinguishing homosexual *behavior*, which evidence indicates men and women have always engaged in, from homosexual *identity*, in which homosexual desire is a central component of personal identity, D'Emilio argues that this identity is "based on the ability to remain outside the heterosexual family and to construct a personal life based on one's attraction to one's own sex" (1983, 105). Capitalist development has created economic opportunities for such nonfamilial life. Before the economic development and attending urbanization of the nineteenth century, most production in the United States took place in patriarchal families whose survival depended on all family members working together to produce the goods they consumed. But subsequent economic development undermined the material basis of the patriarchal family, as large numbers of people began to make their living independent of household production, earning wages as employees of businesses. Significantly, those who could survive economically outside of the family also had the opportunity to construct a social life independent of the nuclear family and, possibly, a gay identity.

But while capitalism undermined the material basis of the nuclear family, its ideology "enshrined the family as a source of love, affection, and emotional security, the place where our need for stable, intimate human relationships is satisfied" (D'Emilio 1983, 108).[5] In D'Emilio's view, this contradiction takes its toll on women and gay people: "Materially, capitalism weakens the bonds that once kept families together so that their members experience a growing instability in the place they have come to expect happiness and emotional security. . . . [L]esbians, gay men, and heterosexual feminists have become the scapegoats for the social instability of the system" (109).

A political strategy of gay liberation for D'Emilio is one that defends and expands the social and economic terrain outside the nuclear family in order to enable more people to form a gay identity, and to make sure that future generations are not socialized so thoroughly by the family's heterosexist norms.[6] The non-exclusive list of issues that he believes the gay movement should endorse—"the availability of abortion and the ratification of the Equal Rights Amendment, affirmative action for people of color and for women, publicly funded daycare and other essential social services, decent welfare payments, full employment, the rights of young people"— clearly indicates his belief that gay men's interests are aligned with many feminist and progressive economic goals.

Despite the insights of these and other writers in connecting female and gay subordination to the dominance of the nuclear family in capitalist societies, the authors fail to recognize the conflicting interests of women and gay men. This common failure is due not merely to political oversight or optimism but also to an incomplete consideration of women's lack of power within the family and other economic spheres.

Though all three writers recognize women's subordination in the family, they do not explicitly acknowledge the way in which women's work within the household provides goods and services enjoyed by men, whose work is for the most part wage-earning employment outside of the family. The authors also fail to consider ways in which all men, whether family patriarchs or not, benefit from the maintenance of women's inferior status outside of the family. Political-economic analyses of earnings differentials and occupational segregation by gender, and of the increasingly public nature of patriarchal economic relations, point to conflicts of interest outside of the family between women and men, including gay men.

Earnings Differentials, Occupational Segregation, and Public Patriarchy

While many feminist economists have focused on gender inequalities within the nuclear family, others have turned their attention to earnings differentials by gender in the labor market. In the early 1990s, full-time, year-round female workers earned only about 70 percent as much as their male counterparts did (McCrate 1993). Ten years earlier, this earnings gap was somewhat greater, though the degree to which women's earnings increased relative to men's in the 1980s was less than one might expect from the significant increases in the percentage of women employed in the labor force and in the percentage of the total labor force that is female.[7]

The inequality of incomes between women and men reflects, in large part, the extent to which they are concentrated in different occupations with disparate earnings.[8] The lower the pay of an occupation, the more likely it is to have a higher percentage of female job holders (Treiman and Hartmann 1981).

There are competing explanations for this in the economics literature (for an overview, see Treiman and Hartmann 1981). While neoclassical economists stress individual choice in the matter (i.e., women choose jobs that happen to pay poorly), feminist and radical economists focus on the formal and informal means by which women are effectively excluded from better-paying jobs or firms. Comparable-worth advocates argue that the work women perform tends to be underpaid precisely because women's work in the labor market, as in the home, is undervalued. Whichever analysis is the most telling, it is clear that male workers benefit from women being concentrated in low-paying jobs, since this lessens competition for more desirable jobs. This conflict over access to better-paying jobs has been exacerbated by a widening discrepancy in the earnings of high- and low-paying jobs, a relative decline in the number of middle-income jobs, and a growing disparity in income and wealth in society at large.

All men in the labor market benefit from the institutions and social customs that hinder female entry into certain jobs, including traditional notions that women should be committed to domestic life and not to market labor. In this regard, it is important to include gay men among the beneficiaries. Because they usually exist or want to exist independently of their families of origin, and because they are more likely than the general population to be physically, socially, and economically isolated from other family members and their communities of origin, gay adults are more dependent than others on their own wage-earning labor power. As a result, gay men might correctly value access to greater wages as the means to economic independence and a life more fully integrated with other gay people.[9]

While it can be argued that gay people tend to have higher disposable incomes since they are more likely to be childless, this does not confute the argument that gay people are more dependent on wage income and susceptible to its loss than others, other factors being equal.[10] Recent empirical data do not support the common contention that gay men earn far more than straight men (Badgett, 1993), and there is evidence of significant downward mobility among gay people who migrate to more tolerant urban areas and work environments (Rubin 1984).

To the extent that gay men perceive their extra dependence on wage income, one would expect some of them to value their preferential access (as men) to those earnings and to look favorably on the social attitudes and public policies that contribute to such privilege. In the workplace, some gay men have exhibited a belief that they are more deserving of a job or promotion than female counterparts, while in the voting booth many opt for conservative candidates who support neither feminist nor progay policies.[11] For gay men who have secured or are struggling to secure their conditions of existence outside the heterosexual nuclear family, traditional notions about women's role in the family and appropriate occupations for them in the labor market may no longer seem so contrary to their own interests, however much these notions are premised on a heterosexual model of the family that seems at odds with gay liberation.

Feminist economists and others have attempted to keep in focus the economic benefits to men of women's oppression by conceptually separating male-dominated or patriarchal economic relations—both within the family and in the public sphere—from capitalist relations, even though each type may be influenced by the other. Many suggest that the public realm has become an increasingly important site of patriarchal relations, a shift that has significant implications for gay men's stake in male privilege.

In her seminal discussion of the need for distinguishing between capitalist and patriarchal conflicts, Heidi Hartmann (1981) identified men's control over women's labor power as the material basis of patriarchy. Occupational segregation by sex, which enforces lower wages for women and limits their ability to live independently of a male wage earner, has been critical for the maintenance of patriarchal control in the capitalist era (Hartmann 1976). The primary beneficiaries of the patriarchal economy, Hartmann argues, are husbands who enjoy their wives' production of goods and provision of services and benefit from their labors in bearing and raising children. Yet all men, whether married or not, benefit from patriarchy in other ways; directly, through women's low-wage provision of services for businesses; and indirectly, through occupational segregation. In this regard, unmarried men, including gay men, benefit from patriarchal economic relations.

The increasingly nonfamilial activities and structures of male domination have been termed *public patriarchy*. Interest in public patriarchy has been motivated by the noticeable growth in recent decades in the number of female-headed households and the impoverishment of many of these families.[12] While motherhood is a key factor associated with the impoverishment of female-headed households, the number of children is also an important determinant of the likelihood of poverty.[13] Because of the association of mothering with single women's poverty, many depictions of public patriarchy focus on the disproportionate share of child-rearing costs that women bear in contemporary society.

Carol Brown (1981) argues that as capitalism developed, children became less of an economic asset and more of a burden to families and patriarchs, making divorce and desertion of families by men more common. As women's job of childrearing became less important to their husbands, the products and services of other kinds of domestic labor became more available as commodities, making such labor "less necessary for a man's survival and comfort" (Brown 1981, 245). Over time, the relationship of men's income to women's labor has become increasingly mediated by a public patriarchy that guarantees the appropriation of women's service labor for men through women's subordinate position in the economy. The result is a decrease in individual men's control over individual women but an increase in men's collective control over all women.

Since the private sphere of patriarchy has become less valuable to individual men, an implication of Brown's analysis is that in the contemporary economy, unmarried men, including gay men, have as much at stake as do married men in the maintenance of patriarchal relations. Because the development of public patriarchy has made gay men's economic interests diverge from women's interests and converge toward other men's, it would not be surprising if gay men's attitudes about their privileged relation to women were to become increasingly similar to that of other men.

Nancy Folbre's (1985) discussion of public patriarchy provides an additional reason why gay men's interests are served by patriarchal economic relations. Looking at child rearing in advanced capitalist economies, which have established programs such as Social Security to provide economic support for elderly citizens who no longer work, Folbre observes that children have become "public goods" (1985, 75) who benefit all workers, since a share of their future earnings will be transferred to the older generation. Such programs have largely replaced transfers of income that used to center on the patriarchal family (5–6).[14] Because the public transfer of income is facilitated by women raising children without remuneration from the state, employers, or, in many cases, individual fathers, the system relies on the relatively costless use of women's labor to the benefit of men and other wage earners who have not raised children. The implication of Folbre's analysis is that gay men benefit, as do other groups of the wage-earning childless.

Heterosexual nuclear families have become less predominant in society, yet if the analysis of public patriarchy is correct, this has not jeopardized either patriarchal or capitalist relations. Public patriarchy limits the cost to the state and to capitalist firms of producing future workers, while at the same time facilitating a transfer of income that disproportionately benefits men. Thus the heterosexual nuclear family is less critical to maintaining a patriarchal, capitalist economy than has been asserted by those attempting to link gay and feminist political agendas.

The relationship of gay and feminist interests with respect to the heterosexual nuclear family has been further complicated by changes in gay people's oppression and their relationship to their families of origin. The increasing number of unmarried people in society has made existence outside of a traditionally defined family less deviant than in former years, giving breathing space to gay men and lesbians, among others. As marital status recedes as a defining personal characteristic, the public sphere appears to have become more significant as a site of gay people's oppression and political struggles. This is indicated by the proliferation of antigay discourses that allege gay people's higher incomes and economic privilege (see Badgett 1993), and that define legal protections for gay people from discrimination in employment, housing, and other arenas as schemes for granting "special rights." These discourses have been used to promote ballot initiatives to overturn and/or prohibit the enactment of local antidiscrimination ordinances in many areas (e.g., Colorado and Oregon), particularly where economic distress has made many resentful of groups they perceive, correctly or not, to be economically advantaged.

While gay people's existence outside of a heterosexual, nuclear household is no longer so unusual, the characterization of gay men's and lesbians' lives as "nonfamilial" is less accurate. In recent decades, it has become more common for gay men and lesbians to establish their own families, in various alternative forms,[15] and to attempt to become socially accepted by their families of origin. Gay families need not be modeled on the social norm of a two-adult household, but for gay male couples who do form a two-income household, the benefit of men's generally higher wage earnings is doubled. This amplifies income differentials by gender within the gay community[16] and perhaps makes gay men more conscious of the economic benefits of male privilege and less comfortable with an agenda that challenges this privilege. To the extent that their efforts to integrate into their families of origin are successful as well, many gay men may no longer find the social dominance of the family particularly oppressive and thus may not respond favorably to a political rhetoric that describes it that way.

It can be argued that the ways in which gay men benefit from women's economic oppression—women's occupational segregation, lower wages, and disproportionate burden of society's childrearing—are relatively short-term and limited in importance, compared to the more vital and long-run interest that gay men share with women in overcoming the heterosexual nuclear family's social dominance. Indeed, gay men and lesbians have increasingly undertaken important political struggles to enlarge the definition of the family to include gay families, while right-wing political activists have promoted a "profamily" agenda that explicitly excludes gay people. Among the contested issues are the rights of gay people to raise children and to adopt, to obtain health insurance and other benefits through their employed partners, to obtain legal protections in housing and other areas as domestic partners, and to marry. The value to gay liberation of a political program aimed at the defense and expansion of gay families' rights and interests has been subject to much debate.[17] To the extent that this program advances the establishment of alternatives to the heterosexual nuclear family for women in general as well as for gay people, it contributes to women's liberation. But the fight for alternative families does not confront the structures of women's economic oppression that have become increasingly significant with the development of public patriarchy, and thus it does not threaten gay men's economic privilege with respect to women.[18]

The Social Construction of Sexuality and Gender

Theoretical considerations of the social constructions of sexuality and gender have also suggested a link between gay liberation and feminism. Feminists have been critically concerned with the social processes through which the people of the two biological sexes are transformed into gender-identified men and women. Similarly, gay liberationists and others have been concerned with the social processes that transform people who have physiological capacities for a wide variety of sexual activities into individuals with specific sexual practices, so as to refute notions that heterosexual beings are more natural and less socially molded than homosexual ones. For many feminist and gay theorists, the social constructions of gender and sexuality are intimately connected, which suggests that challenges to gender roles and to the belief that heterosexuality is the norm should be complementary.

This section first reviews several works that explicitly link the social constructions of gender and sexuality, and then examines whether sexual orientation has become less closely tied to gender identity in recent years. If so, the personal and cultural identities of gay men have become less at odds with masculinity. This in turn may give greater political expression to the economic conflicts of women and gay men, which further complicate the relationship of gay men to feminism.

In "Compulsory Heterosexuality and Lesbian Existence," Adrienne Rich contends that both sexes are naturally attracted to women, since mothers provide the "earliest sources of emotional caring and physical nurture for both female and male children" (1983, 182). Conflict between men and women over access to women is the result, with men exercising power by private and public means that deny women a sexuality independent of men and that enforce heterosexuality "as a means of assuring male right of physical, economical, and emotional access" (191).[19] The variety of ways in which women throughout history have resisted patriarchal control is termed by Rich the "lesbian continuum,"[20] with "lesbian existence"—as a "breaking of a taboo and the rejection of a compulsory way of life"—being a particularly valuable element of that continuum (192). While Rich's influential essay strongly identifies the fight against obligatory heterosexuality with feminism, it cannot serve as a guide to gay liberation, since its analytical framework precludes an understanding of male homosexuality and thus denies a political role for gay men. While she recognizes that male homosexuality is stigmatized, it's not clear whether Rich believes that feminist struggle against coerced heterosexuality will somehow benefit gay men or will conflict with their culture and interests.

Others have attempted to analyze the oppression of gay men by focusing on the relationship between homophobia and gender roles, especially masculinity. Writers associated with the Movement for a New Society[21] (MNS) been have particularly notable in such attempts. While Bruce Kokopeli and George Lakey (1984) consider the imbalance of power between men and women as a defining feature of patriarchy, their central concern is patriarchy's creation of two gendered character ideals. Patriarchy prescribes gentleness, emotionalism, nurturance, and passivity for women; and competitiveness, productiveness, emotionlessness, and aggression for men, placing greater value on the male characteristics.[22] Competitive masculinity results in an aggressive, dominating, and ultimately violent sexuality and an inability to relate emotionally to other men, all of which is depicted as being at odds with homosexual expression. Because women and gay men fail to live up to the masculine standard, Kokopeli and Lakey argue that they have a common interest in struggling against patriarchal gender roles.

The role of homophobia in enforcing the masculine/feminine dichotomy is a theme of other MNS writers. Noting that assertive women and nurturing men are suspected of homosexuality whether or not they are gay, Goodman, et al. reason that "homophobia . . . helps keep the masculine/feminine dichotomy in place which deprives individuals of wholeness and maintains men's power over women" (1983, 4). The immediate focus of MNS political strategy is the promotion of an androgyny that embraces and synthesizes the best characteristics of the two gender roles (see Killinger 1980). MNS writers clearly perceive a strong link between the social construction of sexuality and gender norms, and they and others place great political value on reconstructing that connection.[23]

Many gay and feminist critics focus on the family as a site where gendered and heterosexual individuals are produced. In Fernbach's account, boys and girls learn gender norms from fathers and mothers; girls learn to sublimate their erotic needs to care for children and men, while boys are raised to be aggressive and to objectify women. Fear and repression of homosexuality in men follow, as homosexuality signifies being an object rather than a subject of male aggression, as well as losing one's gender privilege (Fernbach 1980, 150). In Fernbach's view, feminism must undermine the nuclear family's psychological processes, as the constructions and deconstructions of gender and sexuality are one and the same.

Ann Ferguson's (1989) analysis of mothering and women's subordination is a less mechanistic, economic account of the dynamics of sexuality and gender formation. Central to Ferguson's approach is the notion that the production of children, affection, and sexuality is as vital to human existence as the production of physical goods, and she terms such production "sex/affective production." Ferguson believes that women are generally exploited in sex/affective production, because of an unequal exchange of goods and labor in which "women receive less of the goods produced than men, and typically work harder, that is, spend more time producing them" (1989, 132). But she details important historical changes in the social organization of labor and exchange in sex/affective production. In the United States, two earlier modes of sex/affective production[24] have been succeeded, for the most part, by a "capitalist public patriarchy" in which there has been "a relative transfer of power from individual husbands over wives to male professionals . . . and to women's male bosses in wage labour" (110).

Ferguson believes that the family remains an important site of sex/affective production. However, she argues that in recent years, the erosion of familial systems of patriarchal control and the increasing importance of public media representations of sexuality that contain contradictory messages have "unravelled the automatic recreation of patriarchal compulsory heterosexual desire (and its attendant sexual symbolic codes) in the family" (1989, 117). Furthermore, by creating material conditions that have lessened women's "emotional, economic and sexual dependence on personal relations with men," capitalist public patriarchy generates more possibilities for lesbian identity than before (204). In short, Ferguson believes the modern economy of sex/affective production is in disarray, especially with respect to its sexual symbolic codes, giving feminists and others an opportunity to undermine male dominance. But she does not consider effective opposition to compulsory heterosexuality to be sufficient or particularly key to women's liberation; nor does she presume that, in areas other than sexuality, feminist political goals will coincide with gay men's interests.

Gayle Rubin (1984) also argues that in advanced, capitalist societies, there has been an increasing separation between the social processes by which sexuality is constructed and those that shape gender identity. In contrast to societies in which family and kin networks structure both sexuality and gender (see Rubin 1975), industrialization and urbanization since the nineteenth century have created the conditions for sexual desires and behaviors to become a base for identities, lesbian and gay identities being the primary examples. With these identities there has developed, according to Rubin, a modern sexual system that arranges various sexual acts and relations in a hierarchical order of value. Groups within the system "engage in political contests to alter or maintain their place in the hierarchy," and individuals with low standing in the sexual system "are subjected to the presumption of mental illness, disreputability, criminality, restricted social and physical mobility, loss of institutional support, and economic sanctions" (Rubin 1984, 270).[25]

Though gender oppression affects, and is manifested in, this sexual system, Rubin asserts that "the system of sexual oppression cuts across other modes of social inequality, sorting out individuals and groups according to its own dynamics" and is not reducible to the dynamics of gender oppression (1984, 293). On this basis, she argues that political goals in regard to sexuality should be formulated independently of gender politics, and be aimed at the general abolition of hierarchical valuation of sexual behavior and erotic desire rather than at a feminist reordering of that sexual hierarchy.

In addition to being inappropriate sexuality politics, Rubin contends that such a reordering won't significantly affect gender oppression: "A good deal of current feminist literature attributes the oppression of women to graphic representations of sex, prostitution, sex education, sadomasochism, male homosexuality and transsexualism. What ever happened to the family, religion, education, child-rearing practices, the media, the state, psychiatry, job discrimination, and unequal pay?" (1984, 302). In criticizing Rich and others who view compulsory heterosexuality as the key mechanism perpetuating male domination, Ferguson makes a similar though more specific point about the insufficiency of lesbianism as a means to resist male domination, given the political and economic dimensions of women's oppression.[26]

To distinguish the social construction of sexuality from the social construction of gender, as Ferguson, Rubin, and others have done, is not to submit that changes in gender roles do not affect sexuality norms, and vice versa. Rather, it is to conceive of the two processes as both intertwined and distinct, with complex influences on one another. If heterosexual norms are not the critical component of patriarchal relations, and if gender roles are not the sole basis of enforced heterosexuality, the effectiveness of either Rich's or MNS's strategy against patriarchy and compulsory heterosexuality is questionable, especially if the relative autonomy of gender and sexuality has increased.

Jeffrey Escoffier (1985) contends that gay people and the modern gay movement have played a critical role in the breakdown of automatic connections between gender identity and sexuality. The central concept employed in his analysis is the "principle of consistency," Barbara Ponse's (1978) description of how sexuality and gender are culturally tied together. This principle links the "sexual anatomy" of individuals to their private awareness of themselves as male or female ("gender identity"), which in turn is linked to learned gender behavior ("gender role"), which, finally, is linked to "sexual object choice"—same sex or opposite sex. The principle of consistency represents as "natural" a functional relationship within each link, so that, for example, anatomical males will have a male identity, which results in their learning masculine behavior; their masculine role, in turn, implies a female sexual object choice. The principle also dictates that a reversal or "inversion" of any of these elements yields a consistent inversion of the other elements. Thus, "a woman who wears men's clothes (or indeed chooses to pass as a man) must be a man either biologically or psychologically ('a man's spirit in a female body') and also a lesbian" (Escoffier 1985, 136).

As part of the dominant ideology of gender and sexuality, the principle of consistency has structured the understanding of homosexuality by "experts" such as medical professionals,[27] and by homosexuals themselves. Prior to the mid-twentieth century, the sexual behavior of gay men was generally viewed as either the result of a feminine man acting out a natural attraction to the masculine (i.e., gender inversion along the lines of the principle of consistency) or as fulfilling a heterosexual need (e.g., in prison situations). In either case, the sexual meaning of the act was "heterosexual" (Marshall 1981). Escoffier argues, however, that the development of lesbian and gay identities since World War II has weakened the principle of consistency. Such identities have implied attraction to someone of the same sex, not someone with opposite sex/gender characteristics, thus straining the rigid link between gender behavior and sexual attraction that the principle demands.[28]

Escoffier examines lesbian and gay subcultures of the last fifty years to chart the disintegration of the principle of consistency as homosexual identities developed. In the repressive years after World War II, when most U.S. homosexuals were "passing" as heterosexual in public, an "urban homosexual subculture was created by the routine activities of women and men in search of sexual partners" (1985, 137–38). Given society's presumption that all people were heterosexual, and the stigma that was placed on homosexuality, lesbians and gay men devised tactics of identifying sexual partners that involved a re-interpretation of the principle of consistency. Lesbians' butch and femme roles were neither a repudiation nor an exaltation of traditional gender roles, but a vehicle that "allowed women to play with and to extend the range of possible behavior within a firm personal sense of female gender identity" (1985, 140). Similarly, Escoffier argues that through the conscious and exaggerated feminine mannerisms of camp, gay men played with interpretations of their sexuality as inverted.[29] Through subcultures that questioned the naturalness of the world around them, gay men and lesbians weakened the grip of the principle of consistency on their own identities.

The 1969 Stonewall Rebellion and subsequent political activity of gay people further undermined the principle of consistency in the public mind. The gay liberation movement after Stonewall attached considerable importance to coming out as a political act, which facilitated the creation of political, social, and commercial institutions to serve a range of gay people's needs. The visibility of these institutions in turn challenged society's prior assumptions about homosexuality, further relaxing the perceived connection between gender roles and sexual preference.

In lieu of the principle of consistency, Escoffier suggests that what is emerging is "the combinatorial principle—in that the social relations will be more fluid" and which allows hetero- and homosexuals alike the ability to construct their own "recipes for being" (1985, 148). Escoffier warns that gay politics as a politics of unity, in which men and women are politicized together on the basis of a common identity and oppression, may have reached its limits. He cites the controversies over sexuality within the lesbian and gay male communities in the 1980s as evidence that this new, looser sex/gender system will result in political conflicts and divisions among gay people.

Escoffier doesn't consider whether the emerging politics of difference will divide gay people by gender with respect to more mundane matters such as affirmative action and comparable worth, child care and education funding, Social Security, taxation, and budgetary cutbacks.[30] With the breakdown of the principle of consistency, gay men are more able to construct identities that are not at odds with masculinity, a recipe for being that can accommodate a desire not to compromise male privilege. Gay men are thus increasingly able to identify and articulate their interests as men, interests that in the economic sphere often conflict with feminist goals.

A great deal of casual evidence from gay male culture indicates a popular desire to identify with and valorize masculinity. Commenting on the fact that some gay bars deny admission to effeminate men, Altman worries that "the message that it's okay to be a fag provided you're also a man suggests some of the ambivalence felt about the changes" brought about by political activity in the decade following Stonewall (1982, 14).[31] Perhaps this ambivalence should be viewed with the benefits associated with masculinity in a patriarchal society more clearly in focus. Rather than reflecting insecurity about being gay, the bars' actions may bespeak discomfort with the possible loss of gender status, conferred by public patriarchy, that would occur if the principle of consistency persisted in identifying gay men with women.

Conclusion

A political-economic analysis of gay men's relationship to feminism reveals a contradiction. On the one hand, feminist attacks on the dominance of the traditional, heterosexual nuclear family are in the interest of gay men, as are feminist challenges to the social construction of rigidly heterosexual, gendered identities. On the other hand, the growing significance of the nonfamilial structures of women's economic subordination have brought gay men's economic interests more into line with those of other men, and into greater conflict with those of women in general. Gay men's willingness to articulate these interests is increasing as sexuality is perceived as less of a determinant of gender identity. If this trend continues, the contradictory relationship of gay men to feminism can be expected to gain even greater political expression.

In spite of their affinity with feminism, it would be misleading to view gay men as feminists' natural allies. This does not mean that gay men are more likely than other men to be antifeminist or to play a special role in antifeminist political activity. For some gay men, the connections of homophobia to other forms of oppression, especially women's, are meaningful, and they outweigh any narrow economic interests that might suggest otherwise. But many other gay men, who are more attuned to such interests, may not be particularly supportive of feminist goals, particularly in the economic sphere. Even some of those who welcome political activity on a variety of issues of importance to gay people are likely to be less than enthusiastic about a gay liberation ideology that challenges both sexuality norms and male privilege.[32]

Certainly, the gay political movement should neither endorse male privilege nor appeal to sexism (or racism or class privilege) in order to motivate men. However, if one of the aims of gay political activism is to motivate large numbers of gay men to participate, a program that defines its goals in terms of feminism is less likely to succeed than one that focuses more directly on homophobia and on expanding the possibilities for gay people's lives and livelihoods.

It is likely, unfortunately, that a program of gay rights in and of itself will yield more immediate benefits to men, as well as to the affluent, white, and able-bodied. Though it can minimize the degree to which white men benefit first, one cannot expect such a program to achieve feminist or other worthy goals. Given its inherent limitations, gay activism should neither be conflated with, nor attempt to substitute for, a strong political movement that confronts women's subordination in all its forms.

Rubin likens the discussion of whether an analysis of gender and patriarchal relations provides a complete understanding of sexuality to an earlier discussion within the women's movement about whether Marxism could fully explain women's oppression. She cautions against assuming that either Marxism or feminism has "the last word in social theory" and argues for theoretical and political pluralism (1984, 308–309). As part of this political pluralism, the worth of feminism must not be measured in terms of the degree to which it contributes to anticapitalist struggle, as this diminishes the validity of fighting women's oppression in and of itself. Similarly, the worth of the gay movement should not be measured in terms of how much it contributes to feminist struggle, for the oppression of gay men and lesbians is substantial enough to be worthy of political struggle in and of itself. Regarding the feminist and gay liberationist movements as variations on the same political theme has obscured real conflicts between women and gay men. The important ends of both movements, however complementary in the long run, will be better served if their immediate conflicts are acknowledged.

Notes

This essay has benefited from the thoughtful comments of John Calhoun, Kim Christensen, Nancy Folbre, Desma Holcomb, Kate Oser, Betsy Reed, and Bob Sutcliffe. It is dedicated to the memory of Gary Lucek, whose spirit, intellect, and quest for a just world are greatly missed.

1. The common distinction between homosexual behavior and gay identity is referred to at various points in this essay. The term "homosexual," as a noun or adjective, is used here to define groups of people on the basis of behavior rather than identity. "Gay men," "lesbians," and the inclusive "gay people" are all used to mean people whose sexual attraction to members of their own sex is a strong though not necessarily exclusive basis of personal identity. While this definition of gay identity formally subsumes bisexual men and women, it is not intended to deny bisexuals distinctive identities, and what is argued here concerning gay men and feminism is not presumed to extend automatically to bisexual men.
2. Fernbach's essay was written in 1973.
3. She applies Antonio Gramsci's concept of "civil society"—the set of institutions such as schools, churches, and the family, whose structures and activities generate and recreate "an entire system of values, attitudes, beliefs, morality, etc. that is in one way or another supportive of the established order and the class interests that dominate it" (Boggs 1976, quoted in Riddiough 1981, 78).
4. Specifically, Riddiough supports an emphasis on legislative and judicial action by the gay movement as a vital first step to protect the rights of those who come out, and suggests that such struggles will not be easily won. She also advocates using gay counterculture to present to the rest of society "alternative ways of looking at human relations" essential to effecting the demise of the hegemony of family life (1981,87).
5. D'Emilio notes that the exaltation of the family as the preeminent sphere of social life provides a structure of childrearing and reproduction of workers necessary for capitalist production; it also is a structure in which the young generation internalizes "a heterosexist model of intimacy and personal relationships" (1983, 109).
6. D'Emilio argues that the left should "create structures beyond the nuclear family that pro-

vide a sense of belonging" so that the family as a focus of emotional significance will fade, to the benefit of all people (1983, 111). Since lesbians and gay men have had to create freely chosen networks of support other than the family, D'Emilio believes they are especially suited to play an important role in this project.

7. The narrowing of the earnings gap in the 1980s followed a couple of decades in which women working full-time outside the home earned on average about 60 percent as much as men; the earlier period comprised years in which women's orientation to wage-earning work, as indicated by their labor force participation rate and their share of the labor force, greatly increased. McCrate points out that the recent overall decline of earnings inequality has occurred in the context of greatly increasing inequality in the U.S. economy as a whole and thus masks considerable differences among women in their economic fortunes (1993).

8. Treiman and Hartmann's survey of empirical work found that studies that focus on occupational segregation explain a greater proportion of the wage differential by gender than do those that employ individual worker characteristics as explanatory variables (1981, ch. 2).

9. Many of those interviewed for Weston's study of gay people's relationships to families took care to establish financial independence before coming out to parents (1991, 62).

10. Class, race, and sex are factors as important as, and often more important than, sexual identity in determining an individual's dependence on wage labor and vulnerability to a loss of earning power.

11. Despite the Republican Party's rightward shift, in the 1994 elections self-identified gay men and lesbians voted for its candidates in greater numbers and more openly than ever before; almost one-third of gay people's votes were captured by the G.O.P., "one-and-a-half times the percentage who voted Republican in 1990 and 1992" (Miller 1995, 61). It would be interesting to know if gay men were more likely than lesbians to vote Republican and, if so, whether this gender gap in voting was greater or less than that for the entire electorate.

12. In her article that coined the term "the feminization of poverty," Pearce pointed out that between 1959 and 1976, the percentage of households that are female-headed rose from 10.1 percent to 14 percent; during the same period, the percentage of families below the poverty line that were female-headed doubled (1979, 103–104). In the 1980s poverty rates for female-headed households were roughly five times that of husband-wife families (Amott 1985, 7). Both the percentage of families headed by women and the rate of poverty of female-headed households vary widely among racial-ethnic groups; a significantly higher share of African American and U.S. Puerto Rican families are headed by women; in addition, a higher percentage of American Indian and Chicana female-headed families have poverty-level incomes (Amott and Matthaei 1991, 311–13).

13. The U.S. Civil Rights Commission reported that "nearly 31.3 percent of white women [maintaining families] with 1 child under 18 were poor, compared to 33.8 percent for mothers of 2 children and 58.8 percent for three children. For Black women, the poverty rates rises from 45.1 percent for 1 child to 72.6 percent with three children" (Amott 1985, 7). Folbre notes the relatively high income of female-headed households without children (1985, 76).

14. In addition to increasing the costs of raising children, capitalist economic development has provided more opportunities for wage labor independent of families, limiting parental authority over children and making it less certain that children will support their aged parents. Folbre (1985) contends that the response to this uncertainty is the establishment of programs like Social Security, which structure and ensure a public intergenerational transfer of income.

15. Weston (1991) terms gay men's and lesbians' self-established networks of friendship, kin-

ship, and love "families we choose," to differentiate them from families of origin. Without a presumption of the "procreative imperative," these chosen families take many forms and generally are not modeled on the heterosexual, nuclear family (210).

16. When considering men and women with average earnings for their genders, in absolute (though not relative) terms the income disparity between a male couple and a female couple is greater than that between a single man and a single women; it also is greater than the income differential between a male couple and a two-income, heterosexual couple.

17. Evaluating the arguments for and against gay people focusing their political efforts on issues of concern to gay families is beyond the scope of this paper; see Weston for a discussion of the politics of gay families (1991, ch. 8).

18. Though they would reduce the economic inequality of gay and nongay families, reforms that would confer economic advantages, such as domestic partner and tax benefits, to alternative families might increase the inequality between those gay people who are members of families and those who are not. Moreover, to the extent that those gay people who form couples choose a partner of a similar socioeconomic background, in the absence of efforts to reduce preexisting inequalities by gender, race, and class, gay people's increased membership in families would reinforce inequalities among gay people.

19. Public manifestations of compulsory heterosexuality include the sexualization of male-female relations in the workplace and pornographic and commercial representations of women's sexual desires.

20. The continuum comprises "women-identified" experiences that may or may not contain "consciously desired genital experience with another woman" (Rich 1980, 192).

21. An outgrowth of Quaker-based political activism in the early 1970s, Movement for a New Society (MNS) was a secular organization with a multifaceted agenda of social change through nonviolent action; it existed until the late 1980s. In addition to nonviolence training and organizing on a wide variety issues, MNS members established cooperative work environments and income- and work-sharing living collectives.

22. "Patriarchy creates a character ideal — we call it masculinity — and measures everyone against it" (Kokopeli and Lakey 1984, 4).

23. Writing a few years after the Stonewall Rebellion, Altman asked if gay liberation, as part of a wider movement challenging the cultural norms that form the basis for individual identity in capitalist societies, eventually might result in the end of homosexual-identified individuals. He concluded, "one hopes that the answer lies in the creation of a new human for whom such distinctions [of hetero- or homosexuality] no longer are necessary for the establishment of identity. The creation of this new human demands the acceptance of new definitions of man- and womanhood such as are being urged by gay and women's liberation" (Altman 1973, as quoted in Escoffier 1985, 144).

24. The first mode, "father patriarchy," coincided with rural, family-based economic production and was characterized by fathers' coercive control over the family's resources and labor (Ferguson 1989, 102–104). The subsequent development of wage-earning and entrepreneurial opportunities for men outside the family led to a "husband patriarchy," which featured a split between capitalist and home production in which the latter was defined as the domain of women's work (104–106).

25. Rubin notes the hierarchy is made all the more powerful and pernicious by the "excess of significance" placed upon sexual acts in a sex-negative western culture (1984, 279).

26. She writes,

Though forms of compulsory heterosexuality are certainly some of the mechanisms that perpetuate male domination they surely are not the single or sufficient ones.

Others such as the control of female biological reproduction, male control of the state and political power and economic systems involving discrimination on grounds of class and race (systems which divide women by other forms of social dominance, thus weakening the possibilities for unified resistance to male power) are analytically distinct from coercive heterosexuality yet are social structures which support and perpetuate male dominance." (Ferguson 1989, 190)

27. A notable example of the principle's influence is found in the work of Magnus Hirschfeld, a German doctor who based his early twentieth-century campaign for homosexual rights on a theory that homosexuals were an "intermediate sex" that incorporated psychological qualities of both males and females.
28. While the historical development of homosexually identified people is usually placed in the late nineteenth century (e.g., Weeks 1981), Marshall (1981) believes that most homosexual men did not unambiguously understand their own behavior as homosexual, as opposed to gender inversion, until the middle of this century, and thus argues that this later date is a more accurate indicator of the emergence of a modern gay identity. For Escoffier, this emergence marks the breakdown of the principle of consistency.
29. "Camp was built on the assumption that gender behavior is a 'role,' something that can be adopted, changed, or dropped" (Escoffier 1985, 140).
30. Gray (1992) does touch upon these issues in her analysis of how gender-blind, "queer" identity and its accompanying political activity subordinates lesbians' needs to gay men's.
31. More recently, a similar message is imparted by movies, such as *Philadelphia* and *The Sum of Us*, in which gay male characters are emphatically depicted as ordinary men and masculinity is a key indicator of their ordinariness and worth (Cunningham 1995).
32. Similar arguments can be made in regard to racial and class-based economic privilege that some gay people enjoy and would not wish to compromise through political activity. Though this essay does not pursue these arguments, the effect on gay people's political activity of racial/ethnic and class differences should not be underestimated.

References

Altman, Dennis. *The Homosexualization of America.* Boston: Beacon Press, 1982.
———. *Homosexual: Oppression and Liberation.* New York: Avon Books, 1973.
Amott, Teresa. "Race, Class and the Feminization of Poverty." *Socialist Politics*, No. 3, April 1985.
Amott, Teresa and Julie Matthaei. *Race, Gender and Work: A Multicultural Economic History of Women in the United States.* Boston: South End Press, 1991.
Badgett, M. V. Lee. "The Economic Well-Being of Lesbians and Gay Men: Pride and Prejudice." Paper presented at The Economics of Sexual Orientation, Theory, Evidence, and Policy panel, sponsored by Union for Radical Political Economics, at the meetings of the Allied Social Science Association in Anaheim, CA, January 1993.
Boggs, Carl. *Gramsci's Marxism.* London: Pluto Press, 1976.
Brown, Carol. "Mothers, Fathers and Children: From Private to Public Patriarchy." In Lydia Sargent, ed., *Women and Revolution.* Boston: South End Press, 1981.

Cottingham, Laura. "Chainsaws, Motherhood and A.A." *New York Native*, No. 115, May 6–19, 1985.

Cunningham, Michael. "Straight Arrows, Almost." *New York Times*, May 7, 1995, Section 2.

D'Emilio, John. "Capitalism and Gay Identity." In Ann Snitow, Christine Stansell, and Sharon Thompson, eds., *Powers of Desire: The Politics of Sexuality*. New York: Monthly Review Press, 1983.

Escoffier, Jeffrey. "Sexual Revolution and the Politics of Gay Identity." *Socialist Review*, Vol. 15, Nos. 4 & 5 (Nos. 82/83), July–October 1985.

Ferguson, Ann. *Blood at the Root: Motherhood, Sexuality and Male Dominance*. London: Pandora Press, 1989.

Fernbach, David. "Towards a Marxist Theory of Gay Liberation." In Pam Mitchell, ed., *Pink Triangles*. Boston: Alyson Publications, 1980.

Folbre, Nancy. "The Pauperization of Motherhood: Patriarchy and Public Policy in the United States." *Review of Radical Political Economics*, Vol. 16, No. 4, Winter 1985.

Goodman, Gerre, George Lakey, Judy Lashof, and Erika Thorne. *No Turning Back: Lesbian and Gay Liberation for the 80's*. Philadelphia: New Society Publishers, 1983.

Gray, Natasha. "Bored With the Boys: Cracks in the Queer Coalition." *NYQ*, No. 26, April 26, 1992.

Hartmann, Heidi. "The Unhappy Marriage of Marxism and Feminism." In Lydia Sargent, ed., *Women and Revolution*. Boston: South End Press, 1981.

———. "Capitalism, Patriarchy, and Job Segregation by Sex." *Signs*, Vol. 1, No. 3, Pt. 2, Spring 1976.

Killinger, Marc. "Lesbian and Gay Oppression in the 80's: Androgyny, Men and Power." In Pam Mitchell, ed., *Pink Triangles*. Boston: Alyson Publications, 1980.

Kokopeli, Bruce, and George Lakey. "More Power than We Want: Masculine Sexuality and Violence." In *Off Their Backs . . . and on Our Own Two Feet*. Philadelphia: New Society Publications, 1984.

Marshall, John. "Pansies, Perverts and Macho Men: Changing Conceptions of Male Homosexuality." In Kenneth Plummer, ed., *The Making of the Modern Homosexual*. London: Hutchinson Press, 1981.

McCrate, Elaine. "Closing the Pay Gap." *Dollars and Sense*, No. 183, January/February 1993.

Miller, Mark. "Is It Good for the Gays?" *Out*, March 1995.

Pearce, Dianna. "Women, Work and Welfare: The Feminization of Poverty." In Karen Walk Feinstein, ed., *Working Women and Families*. Beverly Hills, CA: SAGE Publications, 1979.

Ponse, Barbara. *Identities in the Lesbian World: The Social Construction of Self*. Westport, CT: Greenwood Press, 1978.

Rich, Adrienne. "Compulsory Heterosexuality and Lesbian Existence." In Ann Snitow, Christine Stansell, and Sharon Thompson, eds., *Powers of Desire: The Politics of Sexuality*. New York: Monthly Review Press, 1983.

Riddiough, Christine. "Socialism, Feminism and Gay/Lesbian Liberation." In Lydia Sargent, ed., *Women and Revolution*. Boston: South End Press, 1981.

Rubin, Gayle. "Thinking Sex: Notes for a Radical Theory of the Politics of Sexuality." In Carole Vance, ed., *Pleasure and Danger: Exploring Female Sexuality*. Boston: Routledge and Kegan Paul, 1984.

———. "The Traffic in Women: Notes on the 'Political Economy' of Sex." In Rayna R. Reiter, ed., *Toward an Anthropology of Women*. New York: Monthly Review Press, 1975.

Treiman, Donald J., and Heidi I. Hartmann, eds. *Women, Work, and Wages: Equal Pay for Jobs of Equal Value*. Washington, DC: National Academy Press, 1981.

Weeks, Jeffrey. *Sex, Politics and Society*. New York: Longman, 1981.

Weston, Kath. *Families We Choose*. New York: Columbia Univ. Press, 1991.

12

Homosexual Liberation
A Socialism of the Skin

Tony Kushner

As Log Cabin Clubs of gay Republicans were cropping up across the country, and as new gay pundits called for the gay movement to whittle down its political demands, Tony Kushner, the playwright who penned *Angels in America*, offered an expansive view of the meaning of gay liberation in this piece, which appeared in *The Nation*.

Is there a relationship between homosexual liberation and socialism? That's an unfashionably utopian question, but I pose it because it's entirely conceivable that we will one day live miserably in a thoroughly ravaged world in which lesbians and gay men can marry and serve openly in the army and that's it. Capitalism, after all, can absorb a lot. Poverty, war, alienation, environmental destruction, colonialism, unequal development, boom/bust cycles, private property, individualism, commodity fetishism, the fetishization of the body, the fetishization of violence, guns, drugs, child abuse, underfunded and bad education (itself a form of child abuse)—these things are key to the successful functioning of the free market. Homophobia is not; the system could certainly accommodate demands for equal rights for homosexuals without danger to itself.

But are officially sanctioned homosexual marriages and identifiably homosexual soldiers the ultimate aims of homosexual liberation? Clearly not, if by homosexual liberation we mean the liberation of homosexuals, who, like most everyone else, are and will continue to be oppressed by the depredations of capital until some better way of living together can be arrived at. So then are homosexual marriages and soldiery the ultimate, which is to say the only achievable, aims of the *gay rights movement*, a politics not of vision but of pragmatics?

Andrew Sullivan, in a provocative, carefully reasoned, moving, troubling article in *The New Republic* a year ago, arrived at that conclusion. I used to have a crush on

Andrew, neocon or neoliberal (or whatever the hell they're called these days) though he be. I would never have married him, but he's cute! Then he called me a "West Village Neil Simon," *in print*, and I retired the crush. This by way of background for what follows, to prove that I am, despite my wounded affections, capable of the "reason and restraint" he calls for at the opening of his article, "The Politics of Homosexuality."

Andrew divides said politics into four, you should pardon the expression, camps—conservative, radical, moderate, and liberal—each of which lacks a workable "solution to the problem of gay-straight relations." Conservatives (by which he means reactionaries, I think, but he is very polite) and radicals both profess an absolutist politics of "impossibilism," which alienates them from "the mainstream." Moderates (by which he means conservatives) practice an ostrich-politics of denial, increasingly superseded by the growing visibility of gay men and lesbians. And liberals (moderates) err mainly in trying to legislate, through antidiscrimination bills, against reactive, private-sector bigotry.

Andrew's prescription is that liberals (with whom he presumably identifies most closely) go after "pro-active" government bans on homosexual participation in the military and the institution of marriage. Period. "All public (as opposed to private) discrimination against homosexuals [should] be ended and . . . every right and responsibility that heterosexuals enjoy by virtue of the state [should] be extended to those who grow up different. And that is all." Andrew's new "liberal" gay politics "does not legislate private tolerance, it declares public equality. . . . Our battle is not for political victory but for personal integrity."

The article is actually a kind of manifesto for gay conservatism, and as such it deserves scrutiny. Every manifesto also deserves acolytes, and "The Politics of Homosexuality" has earned at least one: Bruce Bawer, who appeared this year in *The New Republic* with "The Stonewall Myth: Can the Gay Rights Movement Get Beyond the Politics of Nostalgia?" Bruce, however, is no Andrew. He's cute enough; he looks rueful and contemplative on the cover of his book, *A Place at the Table*, though if you've read it you'll know Bruce doesn't like it when gay men get dishy and bitchy and talk sissy about boys. He thinks it makes us look bad for the straights. Bruce is *serious*, more serious even than Andrew, as the big open book in the cover photo proclaims: He's read more than half of it! (Lest anyone think I habitually read *The New Republic*, the playwright David Greenspan gave me Andrew's article, and Andrew Kopkind among others drew my attention to Bruce's.)

Bruce is not only more serious than Andrew, he's more polite, no easy trick; he's so polite I almost hate to write that he's also much easier to dismiss, but he is. His article is short and sloppy, and he has this habit of creating paper tigers. Take the eponymous "Stonewall Myth," to which "many gay men and lesbians routinely" subscribe: According to Bruce, these "many" believe that gay history started with Stonewall and regard the riot as "a sacred event that lies beyond the reach of objective discourse." Huh? I don't know anyone who believes that, and I've never encountered such a ridiculous statement in any work of gay criticism or reportage or even fiction. But Bruce goes on for pages tilting at this windmill and the "politics of nostalgia" that accompanies it. He's also, and I mean this politely, a little slow. It took him five years to figure out that maybe a gay man shouldn't be writing movie reviews for the viciously homophobic *American Spectator*. In his book he is anguished: "Had I been wrong to write for so reactionary a publication? If so, then how did one figure out where to draw the line? Should I refuse to write for the *Nation* because its editors frequently appeared to be apologists for Communism," etc.

In the article Bruce decides that our real problem is a fear of acceptance, fear of failure, a "deep unarticulated fear of that metaphorical place at the table," and so we march in front of TV cameras in our underwear, confirming for all the world that we really are sick. (Clothes, worn and discarded, are always bothering Bruce; spandex and leather, business suits and bras, his writing is littered with the stuff.) I'll focus mostly on Andrew's meatier, seminal (oops!) text. (For a polite but mostly thorough reaming of *A Place at the Table*, read David Bergman in the Spring '94 issue of *The Harvard Gay and Lesbian Review*.)

In "The Politics of Homosexuality," Andrew concedes quite a lot of good will to those farthest to the right. He draws an odd distinction between the "visceral recoil" of bigots and the more cautious discomfort of homophobes—those who "sincerely believe" in "discouragement of homosexuality," who couch their sincere beliefs in "Thomist argument," in "the natural law tradition, which, for all its failings is a resilient pillar of western thought." Bigotry, too, is a resilient pillar of Western thought, or it was the last time I checked. Andrew realizes bigotry "expresses itself in thuggery and name-calling. But there are some [conservatives] who don't support anti-gay violence." Like who? George Will, Bill Buckley, and Cardinal O'Connor have all made token clucking noises about fag-bashing, but the incommensurability of these faint protests with the frightening extent of the violence, which has certainly been encouraged by the very vocal homophobia of "conservatives," might force one to question the sincerity of their admonitions and, further, to question the value of distinguishing "Thomist" homophobes from the "thugs" who in 1993 attacked or killed more than 1,900 lesbians and gay men (at least those are the hate crimes we know about).

Andrew takes a placid view of people on the reactionary right because he is convinced their days are numbered. But does he really believe that Pat Buchanan is now "reduced to joke-telling"? Such a conclusion is possible only if one ignores the impressive, even terrifying, political energies of the religious right. Since Andrew decides political discourse can countenance only "reason and restraint," he of course must exclude the Bible-thumpers, who are crazy and *loud*. But the spectrum is more crowded, and on the right less well-behaved, than a gentleman like Andrew cares to admit. His is an endearing reticence, but it is not wise.

Andrew is at his best describing the sorts of traumas homophobia inflicts on its victims (though to nobody's surprise he doesn't care for the word "victim"), yet despite his sensitivity, he's alarmingly quick to give up on the antidiscrimination legislation of those he calls liberals. "However effective or comprehensive anti-discrimination laws are, they cannot reach far enough." They can't give us confidence, and they only "scratch the privileged surface." "As with other civil-rights legislation, those least in need of it may take fullest advantage: the most litigious and articulate homosexuals, who would likely brave the harsh winds of homophobia in any case."

It's unclear whether Andrew opposes such legislation, which, it seems to me, is worthwhile even if only moderately effective. I assume that in limiting the gay rights movement's ambitions to fighting "pro-active" discrimination, he is arguing against trying to pass laws that impede "reactive" discrimination, though I can't find anything in his very specific article that states this definitively. (In any case, his distinction between "reactive" and "pro-active" discrimination falls apart as soon as one considers adoption laws or education or sexual harassment.) Perhaps he's vague because he knows he hasn't much of a case. What worries him especially is that the right will make effective propaganda out of the argument that "civil rights laws essentially dictate the behavior of heterosexuals, in curtailing their ability to discriminate." And he believes further that this argument contains "a germ of truth."

The argument is unquestionably good propaganda for homophobes, but it's identical to the NRA's argument for giving every nutbag in the country access to a semi-automatic. We have to argue such propaganda down, not run away from the legislation that inspired it. As for the "germ of truth," Andrew writes:

> Before most homosexuals have even come out of the closet they are demanding concessions from the majority, including a clear curtailment of economic and social liberties, in order to ensure protections few of them will even avail themselves of. It is no wonder there is opposition.

This is a peculiar view of the processes by which enfranchisement is extended: Civil rights, apparently, are not rights at all, not something inalienable, to which one is entitled by virtue of being human or a citizen, but concessions the majority makes to a minority if and only if the minority can promise it will use those rights. Antidiscrimination laws are seen as irrelevant to creating a safer environment in which closeted or otherwise oppressed people might feel more free to exercise their equality; laws apparently cannot encourage freedom, only punish transgressions against it.

The argument that antidiscrimination laws violate "majority" freedoms has already been used to eliminate the basis of most of the legislation from the civil-rights movement. Affirmative action, housing and employment laws, and voter redistricting can all be said to curtail the freedom of bigots to discriminate, which is, of course, what such measures are supposed to do. The connection that such legislation implies between gay rights and other minority rights displeases Andrew, who resists the idea that, as forms of oppression, homophobia and racism have much in common.

With homosexuality, according to Andrew, "the option of self- concealment has always existed," something that cannot be said about race. (I could introduce him to some flaming creatures who might make him question that assessment, but never mind.) "Gay people are not uniformly discriminated against; openly gay people are." Certainly there are important differences of kind and degree and consequence between racism and homophobia, but the idea that invisibility exempts anyone from discrimination is perverse. To need to be invisible, or to feel that you need to be, is to be discriminated against. The fact that homophobia differs significantly from racism—and, loath as I am to enter the discrimination olympics, I'd argue that the consequences of racism in America today are worse than those of homophobia—does not mean that people engaged in one struggle can't learn from another, or that the tools one oppressed people have developed can't be used to try to liberate others.

Andrew is joined by Bruce in his anxiety to preserve the differences among various kinds of oppression, but they both seem less interested in according each group its own "integrity," as Andrew rightly calls it, than in keeping gay rights from being shanghaied by the radical left. "The standard post-Stonewall practice . . . indiscriminately link[s] the movement for gay equal rights with any left-wing cause to which any gay leader might happen to have a personal allegiance." (this is Bruce). "Such linkages have been a disaster for the gay rights movement: not only do they falsely imply that most gay people sympathize with those so-called progressive movements, but they also serve to reinforce the idea of homosexuality itself as a 'progressive' phenomenon, as something essentially political in nature." Andrew, meanwhile, warns against the "universalist temptation," which exercises "an enervating and dissipating effect on gay radicalism's political punch."

Gay radicalism's political punch is not something either Andrew or Bruce wishes to see strengthened. Conservative gay politics is in a sense the politics of containment: Connections made with a broadly defined left are what must be contained. The pair predicts the emergence of increasing numbers of conservative homosexuals (presumably white—in both Andrew's and Bruce's prophecies they come from the suburbs) who are unsympathetic to the idea of linking their fortunes with any other political cause. The future depends not on collectivity and solidarity but on homosexual individualism—on lesbians and gay men instructing the straight world quietly, "person by person, life by life, heart by heart" (Andrew), to "do the hard, painstaking work of *getting* straight Americans used to it" (Bruce).

Like all assimilationists, Andrew and Bruce are unwilling to admit that structural or even particularly formidable barriers exist between themselves and their straight oppressors. And for all their elaborate fears that misbehaving queers alienate instead of communicate, nowhere do they express a concern that people of color or the working class or the poor are not being communed with. The audience we are ostensibly losing is identified exclusively as phobic straights, "families" (which one suspects are two-parent, middle-class), and gay teenagers.

Bruce and Andrew are very concerned about young gay people. Watching a "lean and handsome" fifteen year old leaf through *The Native* at the start of his book, Bruce worries that queer radicalism, sexual explicitness, and kink frighten gay kids and the families from whence they come. Probably it is the case that teenagers are freaked by photo ads for *The Dungeon*. But *The Native* is not produced for teenagers. Images of adult lesbian and gay desire can't be tailored to appeal to fifteen year olds and their straight parents. Our culture is the manifest content of our lives, not a carefully constructed recruiting brochure. True, there aren't readily available, widely circulated images of homosexual domesticity or accomplishment or happiness, but I'm more inclined to blame the homophobic media than gay radicalism for that. Nor does the need for such images mandate the abandonment of public declarations of the variety of sexual desire, the public denial and repression of which is after all The Problem. Lesbian and gay kids will have less trouble accepting their homosexuality not when the Gay Pride Parade is an orderly procession of suits arranged in monogamous pairs but when people learn to be less horrified by sex and its complexities.

Out of the great stew of class, race, gender, and sexual politics that inspirits the contentious, multiplying, endlessly unfixed lesbian and gay community in America, gay conservatism manages to make a neat division between a majority that is virtually indistinguishable in behavior and aspirations and *Weltanschauung* from the straight world, and a minority of deviants and malcontents who are fucking things up for everyone, thwarting the only realizable goal, which is normalcy.

Andrew says up front that politics is supposed to relieve anxiety. I'd say that it's supposed to relieve misery and injustice. When all that can be expected from politics, in the way of immediate or even proximate social transformation, are gay weddings and gay platoons, the vast rest of it all, every other agony inflicted by homophobia, will have to be taken care of by some osmotic process of quiet individualized persuasion, which will take many, many, many years. It's the no-government, antipolitics approach to social change. You can hear it argued now against school desegregation, or any attempt to guarantee equal education; you can hear it argued against welfare or jobs programs. It's the legacy of trickle-down, according to which society should change slowly, organically, spontaneously, without interference, an approach that requires not so much the "discipline, commitment, responsibility" that Bruce exhorts us to—we already practice those—but a great, appalling luxury of time (which maybe the editor of *The New Republic* and the erstwhile movie critic of *The American Spectator* can afford), after the passage of which many, many, many more miserable lives will have been spent or dispensed with. I am always suspicious of the glacier-paced patience of the right.

Such a politics of homosexuality is dispiriting. Like conservative thought in general, it offers very little in the way of hope, and very little in the way of vision. I expect both hope and vision from my politics. Andrew and Bruce offer nothing more than that gay culture will dissolve invisibly into straight culture, all important differences elided.

I think both Andrew and Bruce would call this assessment unfair, though I don't mean it to be. Andrew's politics may be roomier than Bruce's; Andrew is more worldly and generous (except, apparently, when it comes to the theater). Both men have a vision. They see before them an attainable peaceable kingdom, in which gay men and lesbians live free of fear (of homophobia, at least), in which gay kids aren't made to feel worthless, or worse, because they're gay.

But what of all the other things gay men and lesbians have to fear? What of the things gay children have to fear, in common with all children? What of the planetary despoilment that kills us? Or the financial necessity that drives some of us into unsafe, insecure, stupid, demeaning, and ill-paying jobs? Or the unemployment that impoverishes some of us? Or the racism some of us face? Or the rape some of us fear? What about AIDS? Is it enough to say, Not our problem? Of course gay and lesbian politics is a progressive politics: It depends on progress for the accomplishment of any of its goals. Is there any progressive politics that recognizes no connectedness, no border crossings, no solidarity or possibility for mutual aid?

"A map of the world that does not include Utopia is not worth even glancing at, for it leaves out the one country at which Humanity is always landing." This is neither Bruce nor Andrew, but that most glorious and silly gay writer, Oscar Wilde. Because this is the twenty-fifth anniversary of Stonewall, that mythic moment that lies beyond all objective discourse (just kidding, Bruce!), we are all thinking big. That's what anniversaries are for, to invite consideration of the past and contemplation of the future. And so, to lift my sights and spirits after the dour, pinched antipolitics of gay conservatism, I revisited Oscar, a lavish thinker, as he appears in political drag in his magnificent essay, "The Soul of Man Under Socialism."

Oscar, like our two boys, was an individualist, though rather more individual in the way he lived, and much less eager to conform. It would be stretching things to say Oscar was a radical, exactly, though if Bruce and Andrew had been his contemporaries, Lord knows how they would have tut-tutted at his scandalous carryings-on.

Oscar's socialism is an exaltation of the individual, of the individual's immense capacities for beauty and for pleasure. Behind Oscar's socialist politics, wrote John Cowper Powys, is "a grave Mirandola-like desire to reconcile the woods of Arcady with the Mount of Transfiguration." What could be swoonier? Or, with all due deference to Andrew and Bruce's sober, rational politics of homosexuality, what could be more gay?

Powys wrote that Oscar's complaint against capitalism and industrialism is "the irritation of an extremely sensitive skin . . . combined with a pleasure-lover's annoyance at seeing other people so miserably wretched." If there is a relationship between socialism and homosexual liberation, perhaps this is it: an irritation of the skin.

"One's regret," Oscar tells us, "is that society should be constructed on such a basis that man has been forced into a groove in which he cannot freely develop what is wonderful, and fascinating, and delightful in him—in which, in fact, he misses the true pleasure and joy of living." Socialism, as an alternative to individualism politically and capitalism economically, must surely have as its ultimate objective the restitution of the joy of living we may have lost when we first picked up a tool. Toward what other objective is it worthy to strive?

Perhaps the far horizon of lesbian and gay politics is a socialism of the skin. Our task is to confront the political problematics of desire and repression. As much as Bruce and Andrew want to distance themselves from the fact, Stonewall was a sixties thing, part of the utopian project of that time (and the sixties, Joan Nestle writes, is "the favorite target of people who take delight in the failure of dreams"). Honoring the true desire of the skin, and the connection between the skin and heart and mind and soul, is what homosexual liberation is about.

Gay rights may be obtainable, on however broad or limited a basis, but liberation depends on a politics that goes beyond, not an antipolitics. Our unhappiness as scared queer children doesn't only isolate us, it also politicizes us. It inculcates in us a desire for connection that is all the stronger because we have experienced its absence. Our suffering teaches us solidarity; or it should.

References

Bawer, Bruce. *A Place At the Table: the Gay Individual in American Society.* New York: Poseidon Press, 1993.

————"The Stonewall Myth: Can the Gay Rights Movement Get Beyond the Politics of Nostalgia?" *The New Republic,* March 1994.

Sullivan, Andrew. "The Politics of Homosexuality." *The New Republic,* May 1993.

Part III
Arguments and Activism

13

Where Has Gay Liberation Gone?
An Interview with Barbara Smith

Barbara Smith has been active as a Black Lesbian feminist organizer and writer since the 1970s, always articulating the need for a broad Left agenda. In this interview, conducted by the editors in June 1995, she continues to argue passionately for the gay movement to be a full-fledged social justice movement that will work to end class oppression, racism, and sexism, both within itself and in the world at large.

Would you say a little bit about where you think gay politics is at right now, and what you think some of its dilemmas or contradictions are?

It depends on what segments of the movement you're looking at. I think the image of the lesbian and gay movement that predominates is one that is the glitziest, and the most media driven, and the most affluent, and the whitest, and the most male. So it depends on who you're asking about. If you're asking about the people who hobnob in Washington, that's one part of the movement, and it's the one that gets the most coverage. I have always been much more involved in the Left, progressive parts of our movement, and centrally involved in the organizing of lesbians and gays of color. So, if the question was, what's going on with lesbians and gay men of color, it's a very different answer than what's going on in the movement as a whole.

I don't know if we're actually at a watershed as far as the direction of our movement is concerned, because I feel that those of us who are not upper class and white and male have so little impact upon the agenda, that it's almost like we don't exist. It's not like anybody is sitting around thinking, "We've really got to decide which way we're going to go; are we going to have a multi-issue movement that includes all of the diversity of the lesbian and gay community, or are we just going to continue to do business as usual." I don't think those guys are really thinking about that stuff. Those guys—and those women who practice that kind of politics even though they don't have the gender identity or the gender privilege that the men do. I don't think that anybody is really on pins and needles, except for those of us who are in parts of the movement that I consider to be dispossessed.

The links between homophobia and sexism have been analyzed a lot, but the linkages between homophobia and other forms of oppression, especially class and race oppression, haven't been thought about or analyzed as much. What connections do you see between, first of all, gay oppression and our economic system, and issues of class?

I think that's really a very complicated issue. I often say that, unlike racial oppression, lesbian and gay oppression is not economically linked, and is not structurally and historically linked, to the founding of this country and of capitalism in the United States. This country was not founded on homophobia; it was founded on slavery and racism and, before that, prior to the importation of slaves, it was founded on the genocide of the indigenous people who lived here, which also had profound racial consequences and rationales. I think that sometimes, certain lesbians and gay men get very upset when I and others—I'm not the only person who would say it—put that kind of analysis out because they think it means that I'm saying that lesbian and gay oppression is not serious. That's not what I'm saying at all.

Do you think that extends into the future? In other words, would you say that capitalism could go along its merry way and assimilate gay people and provide gay rights, but otherwise remain the same?

It's not likely. I'm talking about the past. I'm talking about the history, the basis, the bedrock of the country. I'm not talking about now, I'm not even talking perhaps about a few decades ago, and I certainly am not talking about the future.

As with all groups, I think that our economic system has the most implications for lesbians and gay men when their class position makes them vulnerable to that economic system. So in other words, it's not that in general being lesbian or gay puts you into a critical relationship to capitalism, it's that a large proportion of lesbians and gay men are poor or working class, but of course they're completely invisible the way the movement's politics are defined now.

So much of this society is about consumerism. As long as lesbians and gay men are characterized as people who have huge amounts of disposable income and who are kind of fun and trendy—nice entertainment type people, k. d. langs and Martinas, just a little on the edge but not really that threatening—as long as they're characterized in that way, probably capitalism can incorporate them. If they begin to think about how extending lesbian and gay rights fully might shake up the patriarchal nuclear family and the economic arrangements that are tied to that, then that might be the point at which capitalists would say, "Well no, I don't think we can include that." As long as it's about k. d. lang and Cindy Crawford on the cover of *Vanity Fair*, capitalism doesn't have any problem with that because that's nothing but an image. Haven't people read Herbert Marcuse; haven't they read Marshall McLuhan?

Another article in the book discusses how right-wing organizations have used inflated income information about gays and lesbians to try to drum up homophobia, which is almost a direct appeal to people's economic frustration. As an organizer, have you encountered that? To what extent do you think that the backlash against lesbian and gay rights has to do with the degree to which people in this country under capitalism are economically exploited and might seek a hateful outlet for that?

What they say is that these people do not qualify as a disenfranchised group because look at their income levels, as if the only way you could be disenfranchised is by income or lack of access to it. When they tell the untruth that all of us are economically privileged, of course that fans it. I can't say that I have personally seen that myth being picked up. When I come into contact with straight people, it's usually Black people. And it's usually around Black issues.

I don't know that the economic thing is such an issue for heterosexual Black communities; I think it's the moral thing. It's not so much that those white gays are rich, it's that those white gays are sinners, they're going against God. And they're also white, so they must be racist. And if you are a Black lesbian or gay man, then you must be a racial traitor. Those are the kinds of things that I hear, not so much that they're so rich. But I think there's an assumption on the part of most people of color that *most* white people are better off than we are anyway. It's an assumption that in some cases is accurate and in some cases is a myth that is perpetuated to keep people apart who should be in solidarity with each other because of class. It's a myth that keeps people away from each other, because there are some real commonalities between being white and poor and being of color and poor.

It's interesting that you're saying that. I think the people who made the film Gay Rights, Special Rights *perhaps should have gotten you on as a consultant, because they really took the opposite tack. That film is clearly divided into a Black half and a white half, and the Black half is not about sexual morality. The Black half is all about the economic statistics: gays are wealthy and privileged, and they're trying to usurp civil rights protection that you deserve but they don't. Which might have been their racism, to think that sexual morality was not an issue for a Black audience.*

Oh, yes. That's right. Because we're all so degenerate as it is. That's really interesting.

Can you say more about the links that you see between racism and gay oppression?

All of the different kinds of oppression are tied to each other, particularly when it comes to the kinds of repression and oppression that are practiced against different groups of people. When you look at a profile of how people who are oppressed experience their oppression, you see such similar components: demonization, scapegoating, police brutality, housing segregation, lack of access to certain jobs and employment, even the taking away of children—custody. They have done that to poor women of color and to poor women from time out of mind. This is not a new phenomenon that women who had children couldn't keep them because the state intervened. It's just that this group of people—lesbians and some gay men—are now experiencing the same thing. There are many similarities in what we experience. And also the same people who are hounding the usual scapegoat target groups, they're hounding the lesbian and gay community too. Our enemies are the same. That to me is the major thing that should be pulling us together.

The militant right wing in this country has targeted the lesbian and gay community, but they have targeted other groups, too. And they're really being quite successful during this time period. Does the Oklahoma City bombing have anything to do with the fate of the lesbian and gay community? Absolutely it does! The Oklahoma bombing epitomizes what dire straits the country is in as a whole, and if we had a responsible lesbian/gay/bisexual/transgendered people movement, it would be asking questions like, "Okay, what is our movement supposed to be doing now, post–Oklahoma City?" That really should have been a wake-up call.

We need to look at why those people are so antigovernment. The press never explains; all it gave us after the bombing was, "They're antigovernment and they're very upset over Waco." The reason those people are so antigovernment is that they think this government is a Zionist conspiracy that privileges Black savages. That's what they think. It's never explained that the reason they're so antigovernment is because they're white supremacists, they're anti-Semitic, they're homophobic, and they're definitely opposed to women's freedom too.

You asked about race and lesbian and gay oppression. One of the things that I wanted to say early on is that the clearest responses that I have to that are out of my own experience as a person who has those identities linked. I think that the clearest answers come from those of us who simultaneously experience these oppressions; however, identity politics has been so maligned during this period that I almost hesitate to bring it up, because I don't want people to think I'm saying that the only reason it makes a difference is because it's bothering *me*. Of course, I am concerned about these issues because in my own life and experience I know what struggle is about, I know what oppression is about, and I have seen and experienced suffering myself.

That's not the only reason I am an activist, though. I care about everyone who is under siege. Some people think that because I'm so positively pro-Black and because I speak out against racism at every turn, that I don't really care if white people are suffering. Quite to the contrary. I care about all people who are not getting a fair shake, who are not getting an equal chance to fulfill their maximum potential and to live without fear and to have the basic things that every human needs: shelter, clothing, quality health care, meaningful and fairly compensated work, love and caring and freedom to express and to create, all those things that make life worth living. How limited would my politics be if I was only concerned about people like me! Given who I am as a Black woman and a lesbian and a person from a working-class home who is a socialist opposed to the exploitation of capitalism, well maybe that isn't so narrow. But what if I only cared about other Black lesbians? I would be sitting on the head of a pin.

The best heroes and the best heroines that we have throughout history have been those people who have gone beyond the narrow expectations that their demographic profile would lead you to expect. I was talking about John Brown the other night, and I was saying that of course we don't have any holidays for him; we don't even know when his birthday is. In the best of all possible worlds, that's who we'd be celebrating, not those guys we celebrate in February.

Not only that, but I've run into many people who thought that John Brown was Black.

Right. Because he cared about what was happening to Black people, then he had to be Black. That's so deep. A race traitor, that's "race traitor" in quotes.

Those privileged, white gay men you mentioned that you view as setting the agenda currently—suppose homophobia could be eased in some ways. What stake do they have in other forms of oppression being ended?

The systems of oppression really do tie together. The plans and the strategies for oppressing and repressing our various groups are startlingly similar, and a society that is unjust, it's like cancer or a bleeding ulcer or something. You can't contain it. I guess it was Martin Luther King who said that when you have injustice anywhere, you really have it everywhere. It poisons the body politic of the society as a whole, and therefore you can't have singular solutions. Those white gay men who have disposable income and who think that all they need to do is get rid of the most blatant homophobia in corporate, government, and military settings, in the legal system and on TV, and everything else will fall into place, that they'll have a nice life in their little enclaves—they're dreaming. Let's say they got rid of homophobia in those places that I mentioned—which is not really getting rid of homophobia, it's getting rid of it in places that make their lives difficult—but suppose they were able to do that. If they were living in or near a city that has imploded, like Los Angeles, because of racial and economic exploitation and oppression, then how free are they going to be? I don't know why people can't understand how interconnected our fates are as creatures on the planet.

For some of those people, I guess success would be comprised of proximity to power, like getting photographs taken with various presidents, not getting anything tangible as a result, but just being in the room with them. It would be positive images on TV and in the media and on the covers of slick magazines; it would be some legislative stuff; and it really wouldn't necessarily get at the bedrock of why homophobia exists.

You were saying that instead of there being a crisis in the gay movement, that the mainstream gay movement really has abandoned the interests of a lot of the diverse members of the community . . .

. . . who would also be the logical comrades in coalitions. "We don't want to be associated with those others." As they see affirmative action, for example, being eroded, they say, "Well, why would we want to be associated with those people? They look like they're losing now, so let's not deal with losers, let's deal with winners."

Have there been specific instances of that? Have leaders in the gay movement actually distanced themselves in specific ways?

Andrew Sullivan, who was editor of *The New Republic,* was on the Charlie Rose show that I appeared on last year for Stonewall, on a different panel. He said on the show, to paraphrase, "Why would we want to be involved with the Black community? After all, they're so much more homophobic than whites." After the taping, I got right in his face and I hit the roof, because he said that on national TV. So that's an example. Here's a general example that I always give: that famous, famous refrain, that when the people of color, the working people, the women who are for reproductive freedom, the union people involved in labor organizing come into the room asking a gay group, "Will you support and get involved in this struggle?" the answer from members of the group is, "That's not our issue." It's like a cliche. And what they mean is, "It's not affecting me. I'm concerned only about AIDS and gay rights." Or just AIDS. Or just gay rights. Each of the issues in a broader gay agenda may not be *their* issue as they understand it, but as lesbians and gays of color, as women, it's definitely *our* issue, and are we not lesbians, are we not gay?

Andrew Sullivan is not the only person who has focused in recently on homophobia in the Black community—either real or imagined. Do you have any thoughts about Black homophobia becoming an "issue" in the gay movement?

I think that racist white lesbians and gay men like to pretend that people of color are more homophobic than white people as an excuse for not working with people of color or working on issues of concern to people of color. The fact that the right wing is more than 99 percent white doesn't seem to make any difference in their assessments. Institutionalized homophobia in this society is definitely a white monopoly. And when we do see examples of homophobia in people-of-color contexts, what that should motivate people to do is to increase the level of solidarity with gay men and lesbians of color so that we can challenge homophobia wherever it appears.

One of the arguments people make for single-issue activism is that the gay community is too diverse to agree on an entire multi-issue agenda. They say, "We'll never get anywhere if we have to agree on everything else, so we're just going to work on one thing that we do agree about."

That's LCD politics—lowest common denominator politics. What they don't take into account, though, is the dehumanization and the disempowering of those of us for whom a single issue isn't going to get it. They pretend that it's unifying, but it's not. I'm a lesbian, but what if I'm concerned about the fact that in the state of New York, from now on they're going to be fingerprinting welfare recipients. That bothers the hell out of me. You see, I could have been one, and I could be one still. The criminalizing of primarily women—they think it's primarily women of color, although proportionately and in truth it's not—but the demonizing of women on welfare has everything to do with the demonizing of women of color, although who actually receives welfare may indeed be different. I see that as an issue that affects me directly, because I'm a woman of color. I may not be on welfare right now, but I could be, and I could have been. And whether I ever am, I know right from wrong. I may be a lesbian, but I may be very concerned about the fact that my children don't have decent schools to go to, and with school lunch programs being cut, they won't have anything to eat when they get there.

If gay rights were put in place tomorrow, my behind would still be on fire. I would still be in ultimate danger here, because racism is still in the saddle. And so is class oppression, and so is sexual oppression. So getting a middle-of-the-road, mainstream gay rights agenda passed, how's that going to stop me from being raped? How's that going to help me not get breast cancer? How is it going to help the environment not get poisoned? How is it going to help the children of my community to have a chance for a decent life?

This whole response of "That's not a gay issue; that's not our issue" is so dismissive. It's *so* dismissive because it's basically saying, "And it's not a very important issue, either. You can deal with *that* over *there*." Bernice Reagon writes about it in "Coalition Politics: Turning the Century" [in *Home Girls: A Black Feminist Anthology*, New York: Kitchen Table Women of Color Press, 1983]. She says to beware of people who say "This is not our issue" and who won't let you bring your issues into the room. A lot of people love that piece and will comment to me about how much they love it. You can always tell where somebody's coming from if they like that article.

I want to talk a little bit about leadership of lesbians and gay men of color. We're not allowed to be leaders. In recent years there have been some signal exceptions to that, but we don't get to determine the agenda of this movement. We're not consulted when priorities are being arrived at. And if we are invited, it's made sure that we are not leftists or radicals, so that we go along with the kind of Democratic-Party-faithful view of how we get our rights.

At this point, then, it makes sense to ask about your agenda for gay politics. In what specifics would it be different from what's going on now?

First of all, the issues would be defined in such a way that lesbian, gay, bisexual, and transgendered people of all classes and races would be central to the direction of the movement. It would be a Left agenda and a multi-issue agenda; we would be dealing with housing, we would be dealing with health care, we would be dealing with affirmative action, we would be dealing with immigration. We would be dealing with violence against women. Racism would be very high on the agenda, as opposed to nowhere on the agenda. We would actually have an antiracist practice and strategy that would be different from tokenizing people.

In terms of "gay-specific" issues, I'm not interested in domestic partnership at all because I think that it's a bourgeois issue in many ways. Domestic partnership is about looking at the society the way we know it and saying: "I want some of that, it's not fair that I don't have it. I want access to my partner's insurance policy." Of course, this assumes the partner *has* health insurance. It's a way of getting the benefits that certain people get under this system. As long as we live under this system, all people should have access to the same benefits regardless of sexual orientation. But I think people should take that system apart and examine it. Except for some lesbian feminists, nobody really questions the desirability of getting our relationships recognized by the state, with the benefits and problems that come along with that recognition. Are we working for relationships that parrot heterosexual patriarchal marriage, which has not really been a very positive institution for women? No one is saying, "How does this relate to traditional marriage? Are we just trying to establish something that has discriminated against women for eons?" Domestic partnership is a reform measure; it's not a revolutionary demand.

An issue that I would see as being very important would be violence against lesbians and gay men. That would still be high on the list. Violence is the most extreme manifestation of the hatred against lesbians and gay men, of our not living with equality. Also high on the list would be helping people—both gay and straight people—to have a much more sound and accurate understanding of sexuality in general. The reason that we have so much pressure and horror around gay existence is the fact that our society is so incredibly distraught about sexuality across the board. A sexual revolution— we never had one even though they said we did—would demolish those repressed expectations around sexuality. People would be much more free to be who they are without having to pay the price of violence, ostracism, or unequal access to basic human rights and needs. AIDS research and services would also still be high on the list.

What wouldn't be high on the list would be trying to become clones and functionaries and lackeys of the corrupt social, political, and economic order that we're under presently. There wouldn't be a move for assimilation, there would be a move for justice. The major priority would be to create a society in which it was possible for people to be free, which would mean a new society.

So far we have mainly been referring to the mainstream, sometimes conservative side of the gay movement, but there is also a so-called queer part of the movement that definitely does not view itself as conservative. In an article last year in Gay Community News, *you wrote about an encounter between your political group in Albany and the Lesbian Avengers, who were planning an action in Albany. Can you say something about the differences there around political style or political focus? How well suited do you think queer-style activism is for working in low-income communities and communities of color?*

Queer-style activism in general doesn't really respect the oppressions that other people face. The first thing that Queer Nation came out with was a manifesto entitled "I hate straights"—even though the straight person might be sleeping on a grate and the gay person might be sleeping in a renovated Victorian palace. Theirs is certainly not a materialist view of how the world works. Of course, there are exceptions to every statement, so certainly there are some people in queer politics who have a much broader view. But structurally this kind of politics makes it very hard to move against racism, sexism, or class oppression, because it doesn't offer an analysis of how those things connect. *Out* magazine recently had an article, "Our Shindler's List," about victims of homophobic violence. Alan Shindler was the gay man in the Navy who was murdered a few years ago. I don't know overall how many of the gay people who are murdered are Black, but this article had pictures of many gay murder victims, and a lot of them were Black men. Was it just homophobia that ended these men's lives, or was it also racism? Hattie Mae Cohen was a Black lesbian who was murdered in Oregon in 1992. Her house was firebombed by skinheads. I was told by someone from Oregon that racism was just as much of an issue in her case as homophobia. But in the queer way of looking at things, race is not an issue, only homophobia.

Is there also a cultural clash there?

Yes, it's entirely white. That's a cultural clash. The conflict in Albany happened because the Lesbian Avengers were so disrespectful of the priorities of lesbians of color as we stated them. It didn't make any difference that we wanted to maintain political relationships that we had worked very hard to achieve. Suzanne Pharr makes a distinction between organizers and activists. Her perspective is that an organizer is a person who is in a certain context for a long time, who works in a particular locality for the long haul, and who does that patience-requiring work of building a base and building institutions so that you can really achieve social change. This includes building relationships with a variety of people who are also committed to the struggle. In the organization that I am a part of in Albany, the Feminist Action Network (FAN), we are committed to making a long-term difference in the community in which we are doing the work, and we want to make—and have made—links with people of various sexual orientations and races and nationalities around issues that commonly concern us.

One of those issues right now is the case of Mumia Abu Jamal, who is on death row in Pennsylvania. If a Black political prisoner who has been imprisoned for his beliefs is put to death for a crime where there hasn't been a fair trial to prove he committed it, then it's not a safe society for gay people either. If we have a system of unequal and uneven criminal justice, then we're not in a safe environment because the pendulum can swing against anyone. But neither the mainstream, white gay movement nor the queer, in your face, anti-establishment gay movement has prioritized the issue that he get a fair trial. Tony Kushner has, but he's also a leftist. Queers United in Support of Political Prisoners—QUISP—has worked on this case. But generally, neither of those segments of the gay movement has prioritized this issue, and as far as I'm concerned, this is the issue of the summer [in 1995]. This is not to say that no individual lesbians or gay men have been involved; many have, often not known as such. Some of us have been out. Others were afraid that their credibility would be undermined if they were out. I think some white lesbians and gay men are nervous about being out in a Black-led political movement, perhaps because they feel that they can't read the signals and that they don't know quite what is okay.

You wrote in The Nation *a couple of years ago that when you first got involved in the gay liberation movement, you felt that it was a liberation movement and there was something magical happening where the different identities that you're a part of were coming to-*

gether. You said that you thought that has shifted, that the movement has lost its edge. In your work, do you see specific examples of that? For example, do you see ways that the funding priorities have concretely shifted, so that money that might have gone one place in the gay community ten years ago is going somewhere else now?

The National Lesbian and Gay Funding Partnership had an initiative to try to increase lesbian and gay funding in local communities, by making grants to community foundations who in turn would fund lesbian and gay activities in their areas. Only about a dozen out of hundreds of these community foundations around the country applied for these funds. I sat on the advisory board for this program at the Capital District Community Foundation in Albany. One of the things about this funding partnership is that it's all aimed at service organizations. I and a couple others tried to explain that there are groups who do not deliver services, nor are they involved in lobbying, that there are political groups too. And the response was, "Well, we can't give to them because they're not 501(c)(3)s [tax-exempt nonprofits] so they must be involved with lobbying and electoral politics." We said, "No, no, these are grassroots political groups that are not involved in lobbying or electing candidates or passing legislation, but they are doing political work." We might as well have been speaking some lost, ancient language. That was the degree of comprehension that we got.

We also tried to explain to them that there are groups like the Feminist Action Network that have no interest in being 501(c)(3)s because that's not what we're involved in. We're not trying to build a not-for-profit infrastructure of staffed organizations. It's like an old-fashioned lesbian-feminist group that just meets every few weeks to figure out what work we want to do. And whatever money we need for what work we do—we don't really pick projects that are capital intensive—somehow we manage to get that little bit of money together. They couldn't even understand that.

Another thing: every city where this money has been received has to go through the same process, and the first step is a needs assessment. I was on the needs-assessment committee, and one of the things I kept saying was that this needs-assessment thing just assumes that you're delivering services to a client population. It's a social service model. I want to find out something about the lesbian and gay community in Albany that doesn't have to do with the delivery of services. I don't know where the questionnaire is at now; it has gone through a number of incarnations. I hope that it's going to get at some of that information that I consider to be absolutely as crucial as, "Do you need this? Do you need that?" I mean, what needs does a Feminist Action Network serve? Making revolution in our lifetime? Can we write that down as a felt need? One of my major needs is to abolish segregation, to desegregate the lesbian and gay community in Albany with all deliberate speed. That's one of my needs, and that was a need of many of us who got involved. But I don't know if you can put that in a needs- assessment survey.

There is a phenomenon that we talked about at the first lesbian and gay left dialogue in 1993 called the 501(c)(3)-ing of the movement. In other words, whereas you used to have the kind of group that I mentioned, the FAN, Combahee, the Abortion Action Coalition in Boston that I was a part of, the Committee to End Sterilization Abuse before that, these were not 501(c)(3)'s. These were women meeting on a regular basis because something needed to be done about something. You did whatever you needed to do; you took whatever strategy to get whatever accomplished. For example, we formed the Abortion Action Coalition in response to the Hyde Amendment, in 1977 or 1978. I remember that summer; it seemed like we were holding a demonstration almost once a week. We really made quite an effort, and we didn't have any 501(c)(3). I don't know what we did for money.

Can you explain how FAN is an example of the kind of organization you're talking about—in other words, a political group that does not provide services and is not involved in lobbying or electoral politics?

FAN was founded in 1989. It is a varied group of women that has a commitment to always have 60 percent women of color and 60 percent lesbians. So that means that this is a women of color and lesbian-led organization at all times. Instead of being tokenized and marginalized, we get to set the agenda. It's kind of refreshing. And the women who are white and/or straight recognize that this is a positive way to do organizing. We have done AIDS organizing, targeting the Black community. More recently we have been doing a project in conjunction with the NAACP to open a serious dialogue about homophobia and the right wing in the Black community.

For many years, your primary work has been as a publisher at Kitchen Table: Women of Color Press. From an economic perspective, it's clear that the publishing marketplace was not doing something that you tried to do.

We started Kitchen Table in 1980. It began as a telephone conversation between Audre Lorde and myself. From that day to this, Kitchen Table has been an integral part of my life. As you perhaps know, I'm no longer the publisher of Kitchen Table, which is the reason I think I look a lot younger this year than I did last year. At the time that we started Kitchen Table, the concept of women of color writers was not even on the map. We knew that there was a vital literature being created by women of color of various nationalities, ethnicities, and sexual orientations, but the thing is that nobody else knew. Now it's a growth industry, it's absolutely a growth industry. And it's so ironic that this little press that has never had the economic resources that it's needed was really the catalyst for the trend. Now mainstream presses publish women of color. Louise Erdrich, Isabel Allende, Maxine Hong Kingston, Amy Tan, many Black women, and more and more Latinas. Sandra Cisneros, who started with independent presses. Now you can actually find those books published by mainstream presses, but when we started, nobody was interested in that writing. Now we have Toni Morrison, Nobel prize winner. There were some of us who were teaching her novels in the early and mid-70s, because we knew.

I think some of the same things are happening with gay culture. Mainstream presses are now publishing a handful of gay titles. Do you feel that that's a cause for satisfaction?

Not necessarily. Because the mainstream is never going to publish what the independents do. There are a few presses that take risks and do books that most publishing houses might never consider. I'll never forget when I lived in Boston, having meetings with a very wonderful editor at Beacon Press. My sister Beverly would come to those meetings as well. We told her that what needed to be done first was an anthology. If you're dealing with a constituency whose voices have never been really heard or gathered, why would you start with one voice? And she said, "Well, anthologies just don't sell," etc. etc. Subsequently, of course, so many wonderful anthologies have been done in independent press contexts, often of writing by women of color. Well, now the mainstream presses do anthologies, amazingly, because they have discovered that for certain kinds of subject matter, certainly for classroom use, anthologies can be really quite lucrative.

No, I don't think it's that positive. I guess I feel a little better about women of color being published by mainstream presses than I do about lesbians and gays. Do you know why? Because the quality of writing by some of those women of color is so high, that by any means necessary, let's get it out. Their books are precious. I think that often the decisions being made about gay books are not as astute, and that a lot of the gay books that are being published are really not of a huge amount of quality. It's not really necessarily the writers' faults either; it's the crass corporate publishers who just want to get something on their list.

What about if we look at this as a symbol of the larger process of assimilation? What do you see that's lost in that process? A lot of people are critical of working toward social acceptance of lesbian/gay life styles, because that means that something is left behind in a lot of cases— some of the distinctions, the aspects that are the most radical. Do you see that as a trend?

Oh yes. I think that there has been such a mainstreaming of lesbian and gay life. It's so ironic. There's a part of me, too, because of coming from the old days, that feels amazement and some degree of pleasure that there is a lesbian kiss on *Roseanne*. I watch television, and I love sitcoms. Not all of them, but there are certain ones that are very witty. There's a wonderful episode of *Frasier*, for example, that focuses on his gay boss. It was hysterical. It made me laugh, and anything that makes me laugh without denigrating people, I'll go a long way to support it. Yes, that's a delight, but it doesn't mean that we have found freedom. It just means that there are enough gay people in the entertainment industry in this country, and enough enlightenment in the entertainment industry whether the people are gay or not, to write a few episodes of a few sitcoms. It doesn't mean that the material conditions of lesbians and gays have markedly changed, or that we're any closer to real freedom. Because at the very same time, people are getting fired from their jobs, being kicked out of their apartments, don't have benefits, can't extend health benefits to their partners, are losing their children, and, most importantly, are being physically assaulted and murdered on a daily basis. I love entertainment; I think everybody needs to have outlets, to enjoy the culture. But you have to counter the heterosexual woman on a sitcom who jokes, "Gee, I wish I was a lesbian" with the newsletter from the New York Anti-Violence Project that reports all of the homophobic violence—you've got to have all of those things in mind at one time. We're nowhere near declaring the millennium.

I think people are much more assimilationist now. I came out about five years after Stonewall. There was a real "in your face", anti-establishment ethos in political
movements, including the gay movement—the "gay liberation" movement at that
time—that really has diminished. I think if it's anywhere, it's in the organizing and
the politics of progressive lesbians and gays of color. We maintain that. People ask
me, "How can you have stayed involved for so long? How can you keep at it?" Well,
I do the same kind of political work now that I did in the 1970s. I was at a meeting
about Mumia Abu Jamal yesterday—I could have done that in the 70s. In the 70s, I
was going to meetings about Ella Ellison and Joanne Little and Willie Sanders, who
was accused of raping several white women in Brighton. It's in a different historical
period, with different constraints, but . . . I'm still an organizer because I still believe
in the same kinds of things that I did in the 70s. You can't stop me.

14

The Hoax of "Special Rights"
The Right Wing's Attack on Gay Men and Lesbians

Jean Hardisty and Amy Gluckman

This essay was adapted for this volume from Jean Hardisty's article "Constructing Homophobia: Colorado's Right-Wing Attack on Homosexuals," which originally appeared in Political Research Associates's newsletter *The Public Eye* in March 1993. Based on PRA's extensive collection of primary and secondary materials on the right wing, the essay describes how and why the Right is now focusing its political spotlight on gay men and lesbians, and analyzes the role that economic misinformation plays in the Right's antigay discourse.

> History, despite its wrenching pain,
> Cannot be unlived, but if faced
> With courage, need not be lived again.
> —Maya Angelou, "On The Pulse of Morning"

In Colorado, in Oregon, in tens of other states and localities around the United States, nagging questions now plague the everyday lives of lesbians, gay men, and bisexuals. Did the kindly person who just gave me her parking place vote for Amendment 2? Did my landlord vote for Measure 9, knowing that I am gay? Will gay rights be pushed back to the days before Stonewall? Who or what is behind this hate?

In recent years, these states and localities have seen struggles over a host of ballot questions, all of which aim in one way or another to restrict the civil rights of lesbians, gay men, and bisexuals. The earliest such referendum was in Boulder, Colorado, in 1974, where a municipal gay civil-rights law was repealed. In the 1970s and 1980s, local gay civil-rights laws were overturned by referenda in Duluth and St. Paul, Minnesota; Eugene, Oregon; Wichita, Kansas; Houston, Texas; and a number of other cities and towns. Since 1990, the pace has accelerated, with varying results. In St.

Paul and San Francisco, where earlier gay civil-rights ordinances had been overturned by referenda, new rights laws were upheld. Colorado's antigay Amendment 2 passed in November 1992; however, statewide antigay initiatives have been defeated in Oregon (in 1992 and again in 1994), Idaho, and Maine. At the same time, antigay forces in Oregon seized the initiative at the local level, passing antigay ballot questions in twenty-six (mostly small) towns in 1993 and 1994.

By the time this reaches print, no doubt more states and localities will have witnessed struggles over new antigay legislation; some of the legal challenges to successful antigay ballot questions will percolate up to the Supreme Court; and the map of local pro- and antigay legislation will look quite different. It would be nice to be able to predict that the right-wing campaign of homophobia that has been responsible for many of these local and state battles will be on the wane. However, a close examination of that movement—its institutions, its ideologies, and its strategies—does not support such optimism, for the antigay Right has succeeded in building a powerful organizational machine that has tapped into strong currents in American political ideology.

In this article, we outline the history of the Right's antihomosexual movement beginning in the 1970s and describe the well-coordinated organizational structure of this movement today, using the Amendment 2 campaign in Colorado as a case study. While these ballot battles are often portrayed as spontaneous, localized, antigay "uprisings," they are actually pieces in a centralized, well-coordinated national campaign. The right wing's religious underpinnings are clear, as a close look at its history shows. But to attract a wide audience, some groups have downplayed religious claims, shifting toward economic caricatures of the gay community and political arguments about so-called special rights. And economic and political factors, including right-wing organizations' need for new followers and new funds, have a lot to do with the very considered choice that right-wing groups have made to place homophobia at the top of their current agenda.

Historical Background to the Right's Antigay Movement

The gay-rights movement in the United States is often traced to June 27, 1969, in New York City, when police raided a Greenwich Village bar, the Stonewall Inn, and bar patrons rebelled in protest. Seven years later, in Dade County, Florida, Anita Bryant led the first religious campaign against gay rights, which opposed a new Dade County ordinance prohibiting discrimination against gay men and lesbians in housing, public accommodations, and employment. Bryant promoted a successful referendum to repeal the county commissioners' vote, and her campaign gained strength and notoriety outside the county.

In 1977, Bryant inspired a similar campaign in California, where California State Senator John Briggs, who had worked with her in Miami, sponsored the "California Defend Our Children Initiative." The Briggs Initiative, which did not pass, provided for charges against school teachers and others advocating or publicly engaging in homosexuality; it would have prohibited the hiring and required the firing of homosexual teachers if the school board deemed them unfit.

Bryant's antihomosexual campaign ended in 1979 with the collapse of her two organizations, Anita Bryant Ministries and Protect America's Children, which were hampered by a lack of political sophistication. Contemporary techniques now used to influence the political system—direct mail, computer technology, religious television ministries—were not available to Bryant. At that time, too, few religious fundamentalists and evangelicals were interested in the political sphere, and Bryant herself was plagued by personal problems.

At the end of the 1970s, a political movement that incorporated conservative Christian fundamentalists and evangelicals as full partners—the New Right—was born. Now there were tremendous political resources available to the religious right, and the success and influence of Christian fundamentalists in the spheres of public policy and popular opinion grew dramatically. Under the nurturing tent of the Reagan administration, the New Right and its religious right component flourished. Several major leaders emerged, their individual fortunes rising and falling, but their collective political clout reaching new heights.

The Second Right-Wing Antihomosexual Campaign

The "second" antihomosexual campaign, born within the New Right in the early 1980s, has been far more sophisticated and successful than the first. At least fifteen large national organizations have worked together to plan and carry it out, using an in-depth understanding of the political system as well as the most refined computer technology. It has succeeded in exerting influence the first movement only dreamed of.

In the mid-1980s, right-wing organizations began to recognize that antigay themes—particularly when tied in with the fear surrounding the onset of AIDS—had great potential to contribute to the overall success of their movement. In 1987, the Free Congress Foundation (FCF) published *Gays, AIDS and You* by Michael Schwartz and Enrique Rueda, a seminal work in the Right's analysis of homosexuality in the context of the AIDS crisis. The book's introduction defined the links between AIDS and the "pro-family" and "no special rights" rhetoric of the recent spate of antigay initiatives:

> The homosexual movement is nothing less than an attack on our traditional, pro-family values. And now this movement is using the AIDS crisis to pursue its political agenda. This, in turn, threatens not only our values but our lives. . . . They are loved by God as much as anyone else. This we believe while affirming the disordered nature of their sexual condition and the evil nature of the acts this condition leads to, and while fully committed to the proposition that homosexuals should not be entitled to special treatment under the law. That would be tantamount to rewarding evil.[1]

The book also served as a fundraiser for FCF and other right-wing groups. Paul Weyrich, head of the Free Congress Foundation, was more astute than many in the New Right in his early appreciation of the potential of antigay themes, but he was not alone. As early as 1978, Tim LaHaye—"family counselor," husband of Beverly La-Haye (president for life of Concerned Women for America), and prominent leader in both the pro-family and religious right components of the New Right—published *The Unhappy Gays*. In 1983, Jerry Falwell's Moral Majority sent out at least three mailings that highlighted the threat of homosexuality and AIDS. In a similar vein, Robert G. Grant's organization, Christian Voice, used homosexuality as a major theme in a fund-raising letter that began, "I am rushing you this urgent letter because the children in your neighborhood are in danger."[2]

As the 1980s unfolded and the New Right achieved substantial gains on economic, military, and foreign policy issues, its religious right and pro-family sectors devoted their most passionate organizing to the antiabortion crusade, which had significant successes. The campaign against homosexuality was not a major focus in the mid-1980s, though it was always in the background as a goal of right-wing organizing. New Right organizers shared a sense of alarm and loathing over the gains made by the gay-rights movement.

The Current Antihomosexual Campaign

In the late 1980s, three issues reinvigorated the New Right's antihomosexual activism and focused renewed attention at the national level. The first issue was school curriculum reform plans and school counseling programs that reflected a greater acceptance of gay men and lesbians; for example, Project 10 in southern California. The second was public funding for homoerotic art. The third was the passage of gay-rights ordinances, bills, and initiatives at the local and state levels. According to the National Gay and Lesbian Task Force, in 1996 nine states have civil-rights laws protecting gays and lesbians, at least eighteen states have executive orders, and at least eighty-seven cities or counties have civil-rights ordinances that include protection on the basis of sexual orientation.

The Right has portrayed its organizing efforts on each of these fronts as grassroots efforts, mounted by outraged citizens stirred to action by local manifestations of "gay power." In fact, while local groups did and do exist, their power and effectiveness is enormously enhanced by the technical assistance and nationwide coordination provided by national New Right organizations. According to People for the American Way, a Washington, DC organization that monitors the right wing:

> The Religious Right's anti-gay vendetta is not, as its leaders often claim, a spontaneous outpouring of concern about gay issues. Theirs is a carefully orchestrated political effort, with a unified set of messages and tactics, that is deliberately designed to foster division and intolerance.[3]

Colorado provides a case study of the effective involvement of national right-wing groups at the local level. Amendment 2, an amendment to the Colorado constitution, was passed by the state's voters in 1992. If enacted, it will prohibit the state as well as any of its localities from providing civil-rights protection to lesbians, gay men or bisexuals; it will repeal gay civil-rights ordinances already on the books in Denver, Boulder, and Aspen. (In January 1993, a Colorado court issued a preliminary injunction delaying the implementation of Amendment 2 until court challenges were completed. In May 1996, the U.S. Supreme Court, in a six-to-three decision, overturned the Amendment, finding that it denied gay men and lesbians the constitutional guarantee of equal protection.)

Colorado for Family Values, the local group that sponsored Amendment 2 originally, was cofounded by Coloradans Kevin Tebedo and Tony Marco and is headed by Colorado Springs car dealer Will Perkins. CFV has maintained adamantly that its strategy was not coordinated by national religious or political groups.[4] It promotes itself as a grassroots group, but its tactics, success, and power are largely the result of support from national New Right organizations. In 1992, five national right-wing organizations were represented on the executive or advisory boards of CFV: Traditional Values, Focus on the Family, Summit Ministries, Concerned Women for America, and Eagle Forum. Pat Robertson's Christian Coalition was not officially represented on the board of CFV, but has a strong presence in Colorado (and is ubiquitous in antigay organizing nationally). Here we profile these organizations and their involvement in the Colorado campaign.

Traditional Values

Traditional Values (often called the Traditional Values Coalition), headed by Rev. Louis Sheldon and based in Anaheim, California, has taken a leadership role in the religious right's antihomosexual campaign. In October 1989, Rev. Sheldon led a "West Coast Symposium on Homosexuality and Public Policy Implications" in Orange County, California. In January 1990 he convened a conference in Washington, DC, billed as a "national summit meeting on homosexuality." One of the two dominant themes of the conference was that homosexuals have, since the 1960s, been seeking "special protection over and above the equal rights already given to all Americans." This theme would later appear in Colorado as the focus of CFV's publicity for Amendment 2.

In 1992, Barbara Sheldon, then chair of the Traditional Values Coalition of Colorado, was on the executive board of Colorado for Family Values. (She is not related to Rev. Louis Sheldon.)

Focus on the Family

The 1991 arrival in Colorado Springs of Dr. James Dobson and his national organization, Focus on the Family, was an important catalyst for Colorado for Family Values, which had already led a successful campaign against a local gay-rights ordinance. Focus on the Family, however, brought to Colorado Springs a tremendous influx of resources and sophisticated political experience. It arrived with 750 employees (and has since added another three hundred) and an annual budget of nearly $70 million, including a $4 million grant from the El Pomar Foundation to buy fifty acres in Colorado Springs. While it has no official ties to CFV, it has offered "advice" to CFV, and several Focus on the Family employees, such as public policy representative Randy Hicks, sat on CFV advisory boards in 1992.[5] Focus on the Family has given an in-kind donation worth $8,000 to CFV.[6]

Dr. Dobson's organization has been heavily involved in antihomosexual organizing. In 1988, Focus on the Family merged with the Washington, DC–based Family Research Council, headed by Gary L. Bauer. The Family Research Council distributed a "homosexual packet," available through Focus on the Family, which contained the lengthy document "The Homosexual Agenda: Changing Your Community and Nation." This detailed guide includes instructions on how to start an antigay initiative. In October 1992, the Family Research Council separated from Focus on the Family in order to protect the latter organization's tax-exempt status, though the two organizations remain ideologically united.

Summit Ministries

Summit Ministries of Manitou Springs, Colorado, is a little-known religious right organization whose work is national in scope. It is a thirty-year-old Christian group specializing in educational materials and summer youth retreats. Summit Ministries' president, Rev. David A. Noebel, formerly a prominent preacher in Rev. Billy James Hargis's Christian Crusade, is on the advisory board for CFV.

Summit was founded in 1962 as a retreat and anticommunism summer college,[7] a part—along with the Christian Crusade and the John Birch Society—of the "old right." Summit's relationship with the John Birch Society (JBS) is deeper than mere ideological affinity. In fact, in 1983, a donor responding to a John Birch Society fund-raising letter sent in a check made out to Summit Ministries and received a thank-you letter from Robert Welch of the JBS.[8] Rev. Noebel was a member of the John Birch Society until at least 1987, and for many years Summit Ministries took out full-page advertisements for its summer youth retreats in *Review of the News* and *American Opinion*, two JBS publications.

Summit Ministries is also politically close to Dr. James Dobson and Focus on the Family. Dr. Dobson leads seminars at Summit Ministries, and his endorsement of Summit's work was prominent in the ministry's material promoting its thirtieth anniversary.

Concerned Women for America

Touting itself as the largest women's organization in America, Beverly LaHaye's Concerned Women for America (CWA) claims a membership of 600,000, a number disputed by many. CWA was founded in 1979 as "the Christian women's answer to the National Organization for Women." It is based in Washington, DC and organizes its member chapters through prayer circles and LaHaye's monthly newsletter, *Family Voice.*

In 1992, the president of Concerned Women for America's Colorado chapter, Bert Nelson, sat on the CFV advisory board. CWA remains involved in promoting Amendment 2 as it makes its way to the Supreme Court. Beverly LaHaye, in a passionate fund-raising letter dated August 1995, warned that: "This year Colorado 2 [sic] could give legal sanction to forcing homosexuality into the fabric of our nation." Later in the same letter, LaHaye boasted: "We've been involved from the very beginning."

Eagle Forum

Phyllis Schlafly's Eagle Forum, with offices in Washington, DC, St. Louis, and Alton, Illinois, is another national organization whose local affiliate is represented on the advisory board of Colorado for Family Values. Phyllis Schlafly is perhaps best known for her successful campaign against the Equal Rights Amendment. During that campaign she used the threat of homosexual and lesbian privileges as a central argument to support her opposition to the ERA. She argued that the ERA would promote gay rights, leading to the legitimization of same-sex marriages, the protection of gay and lesbian rights in the military, the voiding of sodomy laws, and protection of the rights of persons with AIDS.[9] Eagle Forum continues to oppose gay and lesbian rights.

These five organizations, represented on the boards of Colorado for Family Values, are national organizations that have been participating for a number of years in a coordinated national antihomosexual campaign by the religious and political right. Together, they have played a critical role—with their money, contacts, resources, sophistication, and experience—in local antihomosexual efforts such as Amendment 2.

Other national groups did not play as direct a role in the Colorado Amendment 2 campaign as these five but have been active in the overall right-wing antihomosexual campaign. Among these, the most prominent is Pat Robertson's Christian Coalition. Reverend Pat Robertson, long-time host of the cable television program *The 700 Club* and currently the most prominent leader within the religious right, ran unsuccessfully in the Republican presidential primaries in 1988. In October 1989, Robertson used the 1.9 million names he had collected from his 1988 campaign to identify 175,000 key activists and donors and to launch the Christian Coalition, whose stated goal was "to build the most powerful political force in American politics."

Opposition to homosexuality has always been a commitment of the Coalition. However, it was a 1990 political battle over a gay-rights initiative in Broward County, Florida, that moved the antihomosexual agenda to prominence within the organization. In its literature, the Christian Coalition took credit for "spearheading" the defeat of the initiative. It claims to have "led the charge" and "won a major political victory." Robertson has called on Christian Coalition members to "duplicate this success in your city and state and throughout the nation."[10] By 1992, the organization had grown dramatically; Ralph Reed, its executive director, claimed to have 250,000 members in forty-nine states and $13 million in the bank.

Colorado for Family Values is not an affiliate of, nor is it funded by, the Christian Coalition. However, the Oregon Citizen's Alliance, the group that spearheaded Oregon's antigay initiative Measure 9, is a Christian Coalition affiliate. And in Colorado, the Christian Coalition played an indirect but important role in supporting the Amendment 2 campaign. The National Legal Foundation of Chesapeake, Virginia—a conservative Christian legal organization founded by Pat Robertson and funded by Robertson's Christian Broadcasting Network, but no longer affiliated with Robertson—gave advice to Colorado for Family Values as early as 1991, long before Amendment 2 was on the ballot. The consultation was intended to help CFV formulate ballot language that would survive legal and political challenges.[11] By the end of 1992, the National Legal Foundation had taken over much of the legal work of CFV.

Several other right-wing organizations are active in the antigay movement. These include the Berean League, based in St. Paul, Minnesota, whose antigay publications were used in both the Colorado and Oregon ballot campaigns; Rev. Donald Wildmon's American Family Association, based in Tupelo, Mississippi; the Rutherford Institute of Manassas, Virginia, a rightist nonprofit legal defense group associated with the far-right fringe of the religious right; the John Birch Society; and Lyndon LaRouche, a far-right political extremist with whom many New Right groups avoid any official alliance.

Coordination and Networking in the Pro-Family Movement

Since its earliest days in the late 1970s, the New Right has actively sought to develop networks among its members. The Religious Roundtable, the Free Congress Foundation, the Heritage Foundation, Christian Voice, the Conservative Caucus, the Moral Majority, Eagle Forum, and Concerned Women for America, among others, have held frequent conferences, published in each other's journals and newsletters, and worked together to promote legislation.

The antihomosexual campaign nests within a sector of the New Right known as the pro-family movement. The major national gathering for the pro-family movement in the 1980s was the Family Forum Conference, held annually from 1981 through 1988. The conference was usually sponsored by the Moral Majority (now defunct), the Free Congress Foundation, and other right-wing groups focused on "family values." These conferences were emblematic of the extensive coordination and networking that characterize the right's organizing strategy. A 1984 promotional letter for Family Forum III aptly described the issues of concern to the pro-family movement: "important moral issues such as: the economic survival of the family, parents' rights in education, the homosexual movement, personal charity, child pornography, and abortion."[12]

Reflecting the New Right leadership's shared opposition to homosexuality, the

Family Forum conferences nearly always featured an antihomosexual speaker. With the arrival of the AIDS epidemic and the publication of *Gays, AIDS and You*, the antihomosexual focus sharpened. We see the fruits of a decade of organizing by the pro-family movement in the many current challenges to the rights of gay and lesbian people, through bills, initiatives, and referenda across the country.

Camouflage of the Christian Agenda

Three of the four national New Right organizations that played the most visible roles in organizing in support of Colorado's Amendment 2 are explicitly Christian. The central role played by these organizations demonstrates the religious (specifically Christian) motivations and goals that undergird their antihomosexual political activities, but the groups state this only when they are targeting fellow Christians. When organizing in the wider political arena, antigay organizing is cast in the secular terms of "family values" and "defense of the family."

This is an important aspect of the religious right's organizing strategy. Since the mid-1980s, when the heavy-handed style of Jerry Falwell's Moral Majority lost popularity, the Christian right has formulated its slogans and campaigns in terms not so obviously linked to the Bible. Ralph Reed of the Christian Coalition has referred to the soft-pedaling of the religious message in his own organization's work as a "stealth campaign." Referring to the Coalition's electoral campaigning in 1992, he told one reporter, "I do guerrilla warfare. I paint my face and travel at night. You don't know it's over until you're in a body bag. You don't know until election night."[13]

Though these organizations disguise the religious basis of their antihomosexual fervor, occasionally it surfaces. On February 10, 1992, Bill McCartney, then the head football coach at the University of Colorado and founder of Promise Keepers, an evangelical men's organization, said at a press conference that homosexuality was a "sin" that is "an abomination of almighty God."[14] McCartney is a member of the advisory board of Colorado for Family Values. Former U.S. Representative William Armstrong of Colorado, who describes himself as having had a "life-changing experience" when he became religious, is chairman of the advisory board of CFV.[15] But then–CFV Executive Director Kevin Tebedo offered the clearest statement of the religious basis for CFV's work at the First Congregational Church in Colorado Springs on August 23, 1992. In this setting, Tebedo stated that Amendment 2 is "about authority." He went on to say, "It's about whose authority takes precedence in the society in which we live . . . is it the authority of God? The authority of the supreme King of Kings and Lord of Lords? You see, we say we should have the separation of church and state, but you see, Jesus Christ is the King of Kings and the Lord of Lords. That is politics; that is rule; that is authority."[16]

In spite of the obvious preeminence of Christian principles in the values of its national organizational supporters and some of its advisory board members, the literature of Colorado for Family Values does not refer to Christianity, biblical admonitions on homosexuality, or religious principles. A large CFV packet of information dated January 9, 1992, does not mention a religious basis for CFV's work. Finally, there is no mention of religion in the CFV Mission Statement.

The History of "No Special Rights"

Another area of deception in the public face of the antihomosexual campaign is its assertion that lesbians and gay men are seeking "special rights" or "special protections." This was the guiding premise behind Anita Bryant's campaign, Enrique Rueda raised it again in *The Homosexual Network* and *Gays, AIDS and You*, and it eventually emerged as the major slogan of the antigay ballot campaigns in Colorado, Oregon, and across the country.

The use of "no special rights" is purposefully misleading. Gay-rights initiatives do not provide "special rights," but rather a guarantee of equal rights for lesbians and gay men. Amendment 2 would deny equal protection against discrimination only to this group. CFV's decision to use "no special rights" only in its public material and *not* in the legal language of the Amendment itself was a decision made on the advice of its legal counsel, the National Legal Foundation. A June 1991 letter from Brian McCormick of NLF advised CFV to stay away from the "no special rights" language in its legal formulations, but to use it as the centerpiece of its publicity campaign.[17] The Amendment 2 campaign bombarded Coloradans with advertisements and flyers, all drumming home the message that Amendment 2 did nothing but reverse the unfair granting of "special rights" through gay-rights initiatives.

Other antigay initiatives have continued to use the successful slogan "no special rights." This was easily predictable, because the cohesiveness of the right's antihomosexual campaign virtually guarantees that local initiatives will follow the lead of national organizations.

An Economic Appeal for Homophobia

Antigay activists no doubt created the "No Special Rights" slogan both to appeal to a broad audience and to serve as a special trigger for those Americans who have been a part of the civil-rights movements of the past four decades. The slogan implies—and much of the right's homophobic literature claims—that the movement to ensure civil rights for lesbians and gay men is usurping and destroying the African American civil-rights agenda.

Recently, a new stereotype has crept into the antihomosexual literature of the right. In addition to being portrayed as immoral, disease-ridden child molesters, gay men and lesbians are now described as superwealthy, highly-educated free spenders. The economic arguments that have begun to appear in the past few years are an important part of the same strategy: to split the gay community off from what might have appeared to be its natural allies in a broad, progressive civil-rights movement.

Colorado for Family Values co-founder Tony Marco, for example, offered up these stereotypes in an article published by Focus on the Family in the months leading up to the Amendment 2 vote.[18] Arguing that lesbians and gay men do not meet the criteria that define a "disadvantaged minority," Marco's first claim is that "homosexuals have an average annual household income of $55,430, versus $32,144 for the general population and $12,166 for disadvantaged African-American households." He goes on to cite related marketing statistics: gay men and lesbians are three times more likely to have a college degree, three times more likely to hold a professional or managerial job, and four times more likely to travel overseas than the average American. The argument is bolstered by quotes from gay publications asserting the marketing muscle of the gay community.

The video *Gay Rights, Special Rights* purveys these same data. Produced in 1993 by a group calling itself Citizens United for the Preservation of Civil Rights, it has been widely distributed by Rev. Sheldon's Traditional Values organization through churches and community groups as well as to members of Congress and other policy makers. Although in many ways a seamless example of antigay propaganda, the video is strangely divided into two very distinct parts. The producers saved titillating descriptions of "perverted" gay sex for the second half of the video, which features an all-white cast of "experts" and spokespeople. But the first half, which showcases a number of African American spokespeople, does not touch on sex explicitly at all. Instead, it opens with footage of Martin Luther King Jr. delivering the "I Have a Dream" speech at the 1963 March on Washington, then cuts to Larry Kramer addressing the 1993 national gay rights march and paraphrasing Dr. King. It continues along the same lines as Marco's article, describing gay men and lesbians as a powerful, well-off community trying to muscle in on the civil-rights accomplishments of African Americans. In case any African American viewer has missed the point, the video cuts to images of a nameless ghetto. The voiceover is Rev. Sheldon saying, "Homosexuals are not . . . homeless people, under bridges, in food lines. These are high-income people who want to push their agenda." Apparently, the video's creators assume that claiming the gay community is too wealthy and powerful to merit civil-rights protection would appeal to an African American audience, while depicting gays as child molesters and perverts would appeal to a white audience.

Gay Rights, Special Rights is just one piece of a broad outreach effort that some religious-right groups have begun making to the African American and Latino communities. The Christian Coalition and other groups are now explicitly trying to recruit people of color through churches, through the kinds of topics they're discussing on Christian TV talk shows, and through the kinds of issues they are choosing to organize around.[19] And the decision to organize in opposition to gay rights is a keystone of this divide-and-conquer strategy. Fighting against the gay civil-rights bill in California in 1991, TVC lobbied African American legislators the most intensively. Director Sheldon stated, "Very clearly the black community realizes that the homosexual agenda is a parasite within the true civil rights movement."[20]

The data that Marco and *Gay Rights, Special Rights* present on gay incomes are just plain wrong when used to describe the "average" gay man or lesbian, because they are based on surveys of narrow, nonrepresentative groups such as the readers of particular gay magazines. In fact, recent research suggests that the average income of gay men is lower than that of straight men, and that lesbians' and straight women's average incomes are comparable, holding education and other relevant variables constant. Clearly, many gay men and lesbians have been subject to intense discrimination on the job; others have limited their career expectations in order to hold jobs where they could be openly gay. (See Badgett, "Beyond Biased Samples" and Badgett and King, "Lesbian and Gay Occupational Strategies," this volume.)

However inaccurate, these kinds of data are evidently effective, and have become an important part of the Right's case against homosexual rights. The organizations leading the charge against gay rights seek to veil the religious roots of their homophobia when outside their fundamentalist Christian circles. Unlike attacks on the supposed sexual immorality of gay life, portraying the gay community as wealthy and politically well-connected appears to be an entirely secular line of argument. This portrayal becomes a way to expand the appeal of homophobia, both to those who are basically nonreligious in outlook and to African Americans who, whether religious or not, are likely to be suspicious of the Right's traditional kind of discourse because of its long history of racism. And whipping up economic envy may be an effective form of outreach to low- and moderate-income people of all ethnicities, whose attention needs to be deflected from the conservative economic policies of the Right.

Since the 1980s, opposition to gay rights has become a sexy, successful fund-raising issue for many of the organizations discussed above. For example, in 1991 People for the American Way tracked the fund-raising letters from three of these groups—Concerned Women for America, the American Family Association, and the National Association of Christian Educators—and found gay rights to be the focus in eleven out of fifteen letters. Another clear example is the Free Congress Foundation-sponsored book, *Gays, AIDS and You*, which was planned from the start as a fund-raising tool. FCF provided bulk copies of the book to different right-wing organizations to use as donor premiums. FCF also offered the book as part of an $18.75 "Action Kit" to "Fight the Gay Lobby":

> FCF considered the kits "central to our marketing strategy for *Gays, AIDS and You*. We will clear about $8 to $9 per kit—Concerned Women for America will simply give us the orders and we will have the names forever" for FCF's direct mail fundraising list.[21]

Most of these fund-raising appeals use lurid descriptions of gay sex, not economic data, to excite the attention of their donors. But they do repeatedly assert that lesbians and gay men have "enormous political clout." And to the extent that right-wing organizations can portray themselves as battling a well-funded gay "conspiracy," their fund-raising efforts around this issue can only be enhanced.

Conclusion

Homophobia is a bedrock value in our society, one that crosses class, race, and even gender. Our Calvinist attitudes toward sex, based in religious teaching that sex is only for procreation, and a macho culture that is threatened by any breakdown of rigid sex roles, all combine to create a culture that has traditionally been able to deal with homosexuality only in the artistic and commercial spheres. The gay-rights movement has pushed homosexuality out of the artistic and commercial worlds and into the political and social spheres. This is almost guaranteed to create a backlash while society absorbs and adjusts to new values.

While that backlash may be inevitable, it can be tamped down or fanned by political forces. Deprived of its old enemies—particularly communists—and needing a new issue to promote, the Right's antihomosexual organizing is rank opportunism. The antigay backlash is in large part a creation of the Right. It is generating funds, keeping alive right-wing organizations that were in danger of complete eclipse, and generating the all-important evidence of political power—media attention. Many additional New Right and "old right" organizations are climbing on the antihomosexual bandwagon as the issue becomes more prominent. Tony Marco himself has started two new antigay organizations since leaving CFV in 1992—DoveTail Ministries, the parent organization, and America for Family Values—in order to take the Colorado campaign, and his career, to the national stage.

The threat this backlash represents is very real. Violence is its most blatant manifestation, but the litany of pain and waste caused by homophobia is all too long. It takes time, energy, and money away from the work necessary to bring about reforms to guarantee equal rights for lesbians and gay men. It also distracts large sectors of the public from seeking out the real causes of their social and economic insecurity.

In the United States we must decide what role religious institutions and religious tenets are going to play, especially when those tenets are in conflict with the Constitution and the Bill of Rights. If we are truly a society in which church and state are separate, then the prohibitions of church dogma cannot overrule the protections provided by the Constitution. And the Constitution, to paraphrase Justice McKenna in the 1910 case of *Weems v. U.S.*, is progressive and is not fastened to the obsolete but may acquire meaning as public opinion becomes enlightened by a humane justice.

Notes

1. Schwartz and Rueda, *Gays, AIDS, and You*, p. viii.
2. Crawford, *Thunder on the Right*, p. 146.
3. "The Religious Right's Anti-Gay Campaign of Hate: A Strategy for the 1990s" (Washington, DC: People for the American Way), no date, p. 2.
4. Michael Booth, "Legal Defense Dropped by CFV," *Denver Post*, December 10, 1992, p. 3B.
5. Peggy Lowe, "Ideas clash in focus on family values," AP story, November 15, 1992.
6. "Amendment 2 Opponents Outspent Backers 2–1," *Denver Post*, December 12, 1992, p. 10B.
7. "Anti-Red Buys Hotel at Manitou," *Denver Post*, May 27, 1962, p. 11A.
8. Correspondence on file at Political Research Associates, Cambridge, MA.
9. Phyllis Schlafly, "Why Congress Must Amend the E.R.A.," *The Phyllis Schlafly Report*, November 1983, pp. 1–4.
10. Christian Coalition direct-mail letter, 1990.

11. Booth, "Legal Defense Dropped by CFV."
12. Family Forum III, direct-mail letter dated June 13, 1984, p. 1. Family Forum III is a project of the Free Congress Foundation, Washington, DC.
13. Fred Clarkson, "The Christian Coalition: On the Road to Victory?" *Church and State*, January 1992, pp. 4–7.
14. John Gallagher, "Colorado Coach's Antigay Comments Spark Dispute," *The Advocate*, March 24, 1992, p. 29.
15. Virginia Culver, "Armstrong Credits Religion for Changes," *Denver Post*, February 20, 1992, p. 4B.
16. Transcript of taped talk by Kevin Tebedo, First Congregational Church, Colorado Springs, CO, August 23, 1992.
17. The letter is described in detail in Booth, "Legal Defense Dropped by CFV."
18. Tony Marco, "Oppressed Minority, or Counterfeits?" *Focus on the Family Citizen*, April 20, 1992.
19. See Sara Diamond, "Change in Strategy," *The Humanist*, January/February 1994, pp. 34–36.
20. Bruce Mirken, "Hell-Raiser," *Los Angeles Reader*, August 2, 1991, p. 8.
21. Chip Berlet, "Marketing the Religious Right's Anti-Gay Agenda," *Covert Action*, Spring 1993, p. 47.

References

Crawford, Alan. *Thunder on the Right*. New York: Pantheon, 1980.

Dannemeyer, William. *Shadow In The Land: Homosexuality in America*. San Francisco: Ignatius Press, 1989.

Diamond, Sara. *Spiritual Warfare: The Politics of the Christian Right*. Boston: South End Press, 1989.

LeHaye, Tim. *The Unhappy Gays*. Wheaton, IL: Tyndale House Publishers, 1978.

Magnuson, Roger. *Are Gay Rights Right?* Portland, OR: Multnomah Press, 1990.

Noebel, David. *The Homosexual Revolution*. Tulsa, OK: American Christian College Press, 1977.

———. *Understanding the Times: The Story of the Biblical Christian, Marxist/Leninist and Secular Humanist Worldviews*. Manitou Springs, CO: Summit Ministries, 1991.

Noebel, David, Wayne C. Lutton, and Paul Cameron. *AIDS: Acquired Immune Deficiency Syndrome: A Special Report*. Manitou Springs, CO: Summit Ministries, 1986.

Rueda, Enrique. *The Homosexual Network*. Old Greenwich, CT: Devin Adair Co., 1982.

Schwartz, Michael, and Enrique Rueda. *Gays, AIDS and You*. Old Greenwich, CT: Devin Adair Co., 1987.

15

Lavender Labor
A Brief History

Duncan Osborne

Stereotypes of hostile, antigay blue-collar workers abound, while gay men and lesbians are painted as the consummate capitalists. Yet while some labor unions have clashed with gay groups, today the labor movement has a visible gay and lesbian presence, and union leaders have joined gay and lesbian activists in key political struggles.

It was 1974 when Allan Baird, an organizer from the International Brotherhood of Teamsters, Chauffeurs, Warehousemen and Helpers of America, approached Harvey Milk, who would become San Francisco's first openly gay elected official, for help on the Coors beer boycott.[1]

Born and raised just blocks from Castro Street, the heart of San Francisco's gay community, Baird had watched as the ranks of the gay community had swelled, and he suspected that its political and economic power had grown as well. The Teamsters' local was striking six distributors who were refusing to sign a proposed contract. Baird had already recruited a federation of Arab grocers and a second group of Chinese grocers to refuse deliveries from scab drivers. Signing on San Francisco's gay bars would tip the balance. Milk agreed to organize the Coors boycott in San Francisco's gay community, but only if Baird would find "gay" jobs in the Teamsters. They had a deal. This was the first time an elected labor leader had taken a public stand in favor of gay rights.

Although a gay/labor alliance was also emerging on the East Coast and in pockets elsewhere in the country, in 1974 San Francisco saw the formal inauguration of the Lesbian/Gay Labor Alliance (though the name did not become official until 1982). In October of 1976, this alliance demonstrated its political might when the Bay Area Gay Liberation Labor Committee and twenty-two local unions—including the Teamsters, the Building and Trades Council, and the International Longshoremen—held a press conference to announce their unified opposition to eight antilabor ballot initiatives before San Francisco voters. For their part, the unions pledged to support gay-rights clauses in future contracts. The press conference knocked national news stories off the front pages of local San Francisco papers.[2] Subsequently, the alliance helped defeat the Briggs initiative, a 1978 statewide ballot proposal that would have banned lesbian and gay teachers in California's public schools.

By late 1982, the gay and lesbian presence in the labor movement had increased dramatically. The six million members and thirty-four unions of the AFL-CIO's Industrial Unions Department—the "hard hat" unions—called for an end to discrimination "based on sexual preference in public accommodations and employment."[3] Several large unions had openly gay senior officers, and AFL-CIO President Lane Kirkland marched side-by-side with longtime gay labor activist Howard Wallace in San Francisco's Labor parade. In 1983, the national convention of the AFL-CIO gave its unanimous endorsement to gay rights, well ahead of most states and cities that now have gay-rights legislation. It was the culmination of years of coalition building and education. A statement from the Lesbian/Gay Labor Alliance called the action a "great historic milestone—our movement's greatest advance since the defeat of Briggs." The policy was reaffirmed in 1991. So despite popular notions that unionists and gay activists have little common ground, in fact recent history shows that the labor movement has lent its organizational muscle to the fight for gay rights.

Gay/Labor Affinity in the Nineties

In April 1993, one day before the March on Washington, several hundred gay and lesbian union activists gathered in the main lobby of the Washington, DC, headquarters of the AFL-CIO. John Sweeney, an AFL-CIO executive board member (now the federation's president) and the president of the 1-million member Service Employees International Union, received an award for his "support and solidarity" with the gay and lesbian labor movement. Also honored was Gerald McEntee, another executive board member and the president of the 1.2-million member AFSCME. For the gay and lesbian trade unionists, the reception was deeply symbolic. The very presence of Sweeney and McEntee spoke volumes about the strength of gay men and lesbians in the labor movement.

Following the 1993 March on Washington, lesbian and gay unionists from across the country convened a meeting to organize the founding convention of the National Lesbian and Gay Labor Organization (NLGLO), a national network of gay and lesbian union members. The NLGLO—some 350 union members from around the country—met at the AFSCME offices in New York City prior to the "Stonewall 25" march and rally in June of 1994.

Today, there are labor networks scattered around the country, according to Howard Wallace and Harneen Chernow, a member of Service Employees International Union Local 285 in Boston. New York City and Boston have had networks since 1986. Colorado, Utah, New Mexico, and the mid-Atlantic states have them as well. Another has emerged in Florida's Dade County. Gay and lesbian organizers have begun "some work in the Midwest," Chernow said in an interview, adding that there is "a proliferation of lesbian and gay caucuses in unions around the country." Across the country gay and lesbian union members can tap into the existing communications networks and the organizing skills of unions. And they have won substantial acceptance from the union higher-ups.

Lesbian and gay union members have called on the "people power" of the labor movement to great effect. The unions were an important part of the coalition of groups that defeated Oregon's virulently antigay Measure 9 in 1992, according to Beckie Capoferri, a staff member of the Oregon Public Employees Union and SEIU Local 503. In the early days of the "No on 9" campaign, organizers grew concerned that they were only talking with the "friendlies," Capoferri said in an interview. The question became how to carry their message to the general public.

"Union members are the general public," said Capoferri. "No on 9" organizers and union activists convinced many unions to both embrace and publicize their position. Though Capoferri concedes the effort was not as far-reaching as she would have liked, the activists ultimately won over SEIU, AFSCME, and the Communications Workers of America, among others.

The unions also showed their support when the Oregon Citizens Alliance (OCA), the Measure 9 sponsor, attempted to pass antigay initiatives of a milder tone at the county level. In June 1993, Lane Kirkland sent the AFL-CIO affiliates in Oregon a letter reminding them of the 1983 progay resolution, advising them to help defeat any antigay measures.

Unions also assisted in the resistance to the OCA 1994 campaign to enact a second antigay initiative—Measure 13. "Labor's involvement was as extensive as it was [in 1992]. We had labor on our leadership committee, and they gave money," said Julie Davis, executive director of the "No on 13" campaign, in an interview. "They were right out there in front."

Similarly, in Idaho, where the Idaho Citizens Alliance (ICA) successfully placed the antigay Proposition 1 on the state ballot in 1994, labor weighed in early behind gay rights. In June 1993, the state convention of Idaho's AFL-CIO unanimously adopted—without debate—a resolution opposing the proposed antigay initiative sponsored by the ICA. With labor representatives serving on its executive board, Idaho's "No on 1" campaign defeated the proposition in a tight 205,754 to 202,681 vote.

Gay men and lesbians, as workers, also owe a debt to unions for a significant advance: the establishment of domestic partner benefits at some institutions. In 1982, the *Village Voice*, a New York–based unionized weekly newspaper, became the first employer, either public or private, to extend domestic partnership benefits to employees. Since then, both union and nonunion employers have begun to extend domestic partner benefits [see Robert Anderson's "Domestic Partner Benefits: A Primer for Gay and Lesbian Activists," in this volume], but in the case of the *Voice*, it was only after the union brought the demand to the bargaining table that it prevailed.

The Troubles

Some antigay prejudice among union members persists, though gay people in the labor movement contend that it's not as virulent as often depicted. "There is certainly homophobic action from individual members, but not in the overall movement," said Van Sheets, coordinator of AFSCME's Washington, DC–based political action committee, in an interview.

Still, there have been some disturbing instances of antigay union policy-making. Across the country, at least six union health plans have eliminated or capped lifetime benefits for people with AIDS at amounts ranging from $5,000 to $25,000. One case, *Mason Tenders District Council Welfare Fund v. Terrence P. Donaghey et al,* earned the Carpenters' Union national publicity and a poor reception in the gay and lesbian community. Mason Tenders eliminated all coverage for HIV or AIDS-related illnesses, though Donaghey's attorney could not say for certain that the move was motivated by antigay sentiment.

"In our case, and certainly in others, the unions claimed they were having terrible financial trouble," said Cary LaCheen, staff attorney with New York Lawyers for the Public Interest, who represented Donaghey and a second man. "But I do believe that bigotry and stereotyped notions are responsible for these actions. . . . I know that one of our clients believed he was treated differently by the union in lots of ways based on his sexual preference."

For its part, the gay political movement has not had a stellar record recently in supporting labor. A significant breach occurred in 1994, and ironically in Oregon. As the OCA mounted another unsuccessful effort to pass a statewide antigay initiative, Oregon's 180,000 public unionized employees were also facing threatening initiatives—as many as half of the eighteen on the ballot—that promised to have a dramatic impact on their lives if enacted.

Measure 5, which would have required voter approval of all new taxes, tax increases, and fees, could have bankrupted the state. The same could be said of Measure 20, an "equal tax" initiative that would have substituted a single flat tax for all of Oregon's current taxes had it passed. The most onerous was Measure 8, which would have required public employees to pay 6 percent of their salaries toward their pensions.

Yet when AFSCME approached Oregon's gay lobbying group Right To Privacy for support on these campaigns, the union was told that the group's mission statement prevented them from weighing in on any issue that did not relate to equal or reproductive rights, gender equality, or AIDS. "This is the first election cycle in which we said 'We need you' and they walked away," said Mary Botkin, AFSCME's political director in Oregon. "I am very angry. This is a group that I advocated for at my personal and professional risk."

According to Botkin, her membership, including the gay and lesbian members, were "outraged." Right To Privacy has since reviewed its qualifications for endorsements. "We're investigating whether or not it's time for us to change our criteria," said executive director Greg Jackson. For AFSCME's Sheets, Right To Privacy's action comes as no surprise. Gay organizations tend to be responsive to their donor base—"rich, white males," not working-class people. "When they set their agenda, they set it without looking at working-class folks," Sheets said. "It was easy to buy into the view that government costs too much."

While many gay groups and leaders have merely remained silent on issues of importance to labor, others have actively clashed with unions. In San Francisco in 1994, City Hall was contending with a $200 million budget gap. So City Supervisor Carole Migden, an out lesbian, sponsored a charter amendment to allow City Hall to cut city workers' salaries by declaring a fiscal emergency if local money from the state or national government were to decline by 5 percent or more. Previously, she had voted to uphold a veto of a $140 million union contract that included raises and new benefits for city workers. Migden had won her seat with substantial union support in 1990, but her actions won her the anger of the public employee unions.

In New York City, the roughly 250 employees at Gay Men's Health Crisis, the nation's oldest and largest AIDS service organization, sought to be represented by Local 1199 of the National Health and Human Service Employees Union in a petition filed with the National Labor Relations Board in July 1993. The workers faced an acrimonious, seven-month battle with management, which culminated in the staff voting 72 to 28 against joining Local 1199 in February 1994. A second group of professional employees opted for Local 1199 representation in a 10 to 8 vote. The management's antiunion stance left Local 1199 staffers, who had worked closely with GMHC previously, bitter and angry.

Distressing as they are, these stories do not signal an erosion of the long-standing relationship between labor and gay groups; networks, commitments, and strategies cementing the ties on a broad scale remain securely in place. In addition, some of these conflicts are labor struggles in the conventional mold, rather than evidence of gay/labor strife. The GMHC fight falls into this category, according to Stacie Spector, director of Americans Against Discrimination, a project of the Human Rights Campaign, a Washington, DC–based gay lobbying group. "I see that more as a management-employee issue," Spector said. "I don't see that as a gay/labor issue. . . . I've spent the past ten-and-a-half months working with labor unions about these antigay initiatives, and the response has been very positive."

In response to experiences of friction, activists in both gay and labor circles predictably call for more communication between the two groups. Yet some go beyond this, pointing to the need for compromise, especially as this coalition is tested by shrinking government budgets and politically motivated attacks. "We may have to look at our missions and do some bending," said "No on 13's" Davis. "It's a part of what we have to learn about working outside our issue. . . . The times we live in require us to go outside ourselves. If we don't we are going to be standing by ourselves."

Notes

1. See Randy Shilts, *The Mayor of Castro Street: The Life and Times of Harvey Milk* (New York: St. Martin's Press, 1982).
2. *The Advocate*, November 1976.
3. *Bay Area Reporter*, November 1982.

16

Laboring for Gay Rights
An Interview with Susan Moir

Gay labor activist Susan Moir, in this June 1995 interview conducted by Amy Gluckman, offers a personal view of the accomplishments and problems of the union-based gay-rights movement. Moir has been active for many years in the Boston-area Gay and Lesbian Labor Activists Network. She candidly discusses some of the conflicts she has witnessed between the gay and labor movements; ultimately, she argues, the gay movement has a lot to gain from a more consistent alliance with organized labor.

Can you tell me a little bit about your own history in the gay labor movement and about the Gay and Lesbian Labor Activists Network (GALLAN)?

I began my union activism with the school bus drivers, Steelworkers Local 8751. The School Bus Drivers Union was organized by a coalition of progressive people that included lesbians. One of the early presidents of the union was an out lesbian, and a lot of the women leaders in the union were lesbians.

When was that?

I started there in 1979. I became a steward and did union work. I was out at work, but we didn't organize around lesbian and gay issues. We already had antidiscrimination language in our contract. Partner benefits weren't an issue; nobody was looking for them back then.

My involvement in lesbian/gay activism within the labor movement was in conjunction with the formation of GALLAN around 1987. I wasn't involved in calling the first meetings. Three people got together and decided that there would be a meeting of lesbians and gays, a lot of us who were seeing each other at different union events. At the time, some of the people involved in GALLAN had been involved in union campaigns like the one at Berklee School of Music—very close or losing campaigns in workplaces where there were a lot of gay people, particularly gay men, out gay men. One of the early discussions we had was the class implications in a workplace where there were a lot of gay men who didn't have traditional family responsibilities, who didn't have traditional career paths, and who often seemed to ally themselves with management and to think of the jobs they were in—potentially union jobs—as instead a transition place for moving up the ladder.

In 1989 we had what we called our coming out party. The first activity we undertook was to stage a benefit for the United Farm Workers (UFW) and the Fenway Community Health Center [a community health center in Boston with a special focus on serving gay men and lesbians]. The idea was to bring together the UFW Grape Boycott and the issues that the farm workers were raising about health with lesbian and gay health issues and to raise money for the Fenway. We called it "United for Health/Allies for the 90s."

The event itself was an incredible success. We practically filled New England Life Hall, which was a union hall; we got straight union guys to work in the hall with us. The production was very gay and very union. As part of the production, we had this solidarity thing for the United Farm Workers. Union members had gone to their unions and asked for endorsements for this event and for the grape boycott. We had a big banner stretched out on the stage. All the unions were called up one at a time and their representatives came up and signed the banner. We had a hundred people on the stage including Cesar Chavez, the head of the Boston Building Trades Council, and a couple of drag queens. We had music while this was happening. It was a very exciting event; people really loved it!

But one of the more interesting things that went on behind the scenes that is not as well known is that we were raising money for the Fenway to build their new building. It wasn't just that evening; a lot of fund-raising went on outside—a program book and so forth. Just as we were trying to line up all of these endorsements, the Fenway told us, "Oh sorry, we're going to build this building with nonunion labor." We basically shut down the planning for the event for a couple of weeks and sought to convince the Fenway of the value of using union labor in terms of prevailing wage benefits, safety training, and the effect on the economy. We committed to them that we would work with the unions to get lesbian and gay workers on that site. Not all, but we would have gotten maximum employment of any out lesbian and gay construction workers who wanted to work on that site. We negotiated that agreement with them, we held the benefit, and then the Fenway reneged. They built the building nonunion, with scab labor. Substandard wages, no benefits, extremely cheaply. It was a real betrayal on the part of the Fenway and, in addition to that, it was totally unnecessary. The building had no mortgage; they totally fund-raised all the money for the building and built it with cash. They had the money to pay decent wages to the workers who built that building.

Just about the time that happened, we found out that the Haymarket People's

Fund [a small progressive foundation in Boston] was also building. They had bought an old building that they were rehabbing, and they were doing it with nonunion labor. We went into a series of negotiations with Haymarket, but they too chose to build their building with nonunion labor.

What Fenway did really symbolizes how working-class interests often lose out when in conflict with the interests of the gay and lesbian community narrowly defined, generally by those from more privileged classes. And it compromised our integrity with the Building Trades people that we had brought on board for this benefit. The Building Trades people were very good about it, though. They knew that we were sticking our necks way out to try and get the building built union.

Between the benefit and the two struggles, even though we had lost, it gave us a strong internal sense of what we were about. There wasn't any question among the people at GALLAN that this was absolutely the right thing to do. We never questioned that we should compromise the wages of the workers in order to build a community resource more cheaply in either of these cases. So, we came out more unified and really clear on what we were doing and who our best allies were.

What we're doing is bringing lesbian and gay issues to the union community and bringing working-class and union issues to the lesbian and gay community. It is much easier in the union community than it is in the lesbian and gay community. We've certainly had our bumps in the unions, but when it comes to the bottom line, people within the unions understand solidarity. They understand that an injury to one is an injury to all; that's not true in the lesbian and gay community.

Let's jump to that. In terms of educating union members about gay and lesbian issues and creating that alliance within the union movement, is this a completed task? What is it in union culture that has appeared to be so successful in overcoming homophobia?

I don't mean at all to paint this as easy because it has not been. But my experience has been that with the unions, you go through the struggle and you get someplace. You arrive at either a point of agreement or a point of principled disagreement. When I've gone through those struggles in the lesbian and gay community, people don't understand class. You end up someplace where you still don't understand each other because people don't understand class. I find that much more frustrating.

But there are a lot of union people who didn't start out understanding sexual orientation.

Yes, but it doesn't matter, because we're talking about oppression and they understand oppression. A lot of union people don't understand it intellectually and are not going around talking about it, but they recognize that in society there are winners and losers and that the losers don't stand a chance if they're not united against the winners. Not every individual union member understands that, but unions organizationally understand it because it's a part of the culture and the ideology of unions.

That's what happened with Briggs back in the 70s. [The Briggs Initiative in 1978 would have prohibited lesbians and gay men from working as teachers in the state of California; it was defeated.] Maybe it took all summer to convince individuals within the union movement, but when it came down to it, the decision went the right way because union people knew that Briggs was an attack on teachers. An attack on queer teachers was an attack on teachers, and teachers are workers.

Are you saying there's a gap between union leadership and union rank and file on this issue?

No. I don't really think that's the case, because whether you're in the leadership or the rank and file, homophobia cuts across all communities and across the union movement, too. In the leadership you might have more sophistication; people in the leadership obviously have a greater level of experience and commitment to what union principles are. So that might make a difference. But there are homophobes at all levels. However, in the unions there's a context for discussing why gay rights is an important issue.

Let me tell you a story, because I don't want to paint this as too rosy. Today, the union movement is in a huge period of change, which is signified most obviously and nationally by the Service Employees International Union's John Sweeney pushing Lane Kirkland not to run again for president of the AFL-CIO. The lesbian/gay movement is part of this. When Sweeney talks about diversity, everybody knows he's talking about bringing lesbians and gay men and workers of color into this organization. Everybody knows exactly what he's talking about. He's been asked, directly, "Will you continue in the AFL-CIO the level of support for lesbian and gay activism in unions and leadership in unions that you have promoted in the SEIU?" He has said, "Yes, absolutely."

So in his last-gasp efforts to hold on to the dinosaur leadership of the AFL-CIO, Kirkland held regional meetings throughout the country in May [1995]. There was one held in Boston. I wasn't there, but during the question period, Tom Barbera, a member of GALLAN, stood up and asked a question regarding the support of the AFL-CIO for lesbian and gay issues. When he said, "As a gay man, I want to ask you . . . ," there was a rumble of boos from one section of the audience. Tom continued to ask his question, and there were more boos in the crowd—a lot of them. When he finished, there was a standing ovation from the rest of the audience, the people who did not boo.

The majority of the people in that audience were on our side. And labor can't turn around without us. We're not an interest group like the mainstream, Washington-based folks who want a place at the table. We don't see ourselves as a bloc of votes that someone needs. Sweeney doesn't need our bloc of votes to win or lose. All he needs are a few key unions that have large memberships. We're not a bloc like that. What we are is representative of the new coalition that's going to make this country more progressive. We don't just represent ourselves as lesbian and gay labor. We represent poor people. We represent working people. We represent women on welfare. We represent people of color. We represent immigrant workers. Because we're all in the same boat.

[*Editor's Note: In October 1995, John Sweeney was elected international president of the AFL-CIO. In May 1996, a progressive and pro-gay candidate, Andy Sterns, won election as Sweeney's successor at SEIU.*]

Is this a critique of identity politics?

I don't think it is. And the reason I don't is because I take identity politics back to the Combahee River Collective Statement—the Combahee River Collective was a black feminist group that began meeting in Boston in the early 1970s—and the work of Barbara Smith and other lesbians of color. I know that other people have interpreted this idea of identity politics in other ways. But what I took from the roots of these kind of politics is that I can understand the position of an immigrant because I understand my own oppression. I understand my oppression as a lesbian so I can identify with low-wage service workers. That's what I mean by identity politics. We have a sense of common identity from our oppression under the current economic and social system.

I'm not an altruist or a liberal. I'm not out there for immigrant workers simply because I think it's the right thing to do. I'm not out there for janitors in L.A. because I think it's the right thing to do. I'm out there because they and I share a common oppression that may be different in its details but the effect is exactly the same and because banded together, we have a chance of winning. That's a class perspective. I think altruism is shortsighted; it's the emotional basis of liberalism, and that's what got us here.

Where do middle-class and upper-middle-class lesbians and gay men fit into that politic?

Middle-class people need to get educated about working-class issues. Often, I think, the kind of interaction that goes on between middle-class progressives and working-class people is a helping thing, trying to transfer their privilege, when in fact we don't need that privilege. When given the opportunity and exposed to the kind of collective experience we can have in our unions, we can have incredible privilege. You can see the society much more clearly from the bottom than you can from the top. That's why we need our unions; they are the social institutions we need in order to come together to collect our cultural identity around us.

To get back to GALLAN, does GALLAN involve itself in specific workplace contract negotiations and so forth?

No, GALLAN doesn't. What we do is to try to provide support for members or contacts of members.

Can you mention a few specific situations where that kind of involvement has produced contract gains?

I don't know if we've had that many. Some of the unions that we are the closest to have had nondiscrimination language for a long time. Right now I'm involved with organizing a chapter in a local SEIU that is not progressive. We put domestic partnership and spousal and family benefits on the table, and it looks like we're going to get them although the guy from the local gulped big when I put this issue on the table. I think it's the first chapter within this local to even put it on the table.

The other thing that we've done is that certain GALLAN members have been very instrumental in getting antidiscrimination language out of [Massachusetts Gov. William] Weld. There is a myth that Weld granted domestic partnership rights for state employees right after he came into office. Well, by executive order he did grant nonunion managers working for the state a bare-bones package that doesn't cost a thing. It only affected a couple of dozen of his political appointees at the top, who now had the right to visit their lovers at the hospital. At the same time, antidiscrimination language was on the table in contract negotiations with state-employee unions, and Weld refused it. Now the state workers are back at the table, and this time they will get antidiscrimination language.

Why will it be different this time?

Last time the state workers' alliance had voted to make this a strike issue, but the lesbians at the table withdrew it as a strike issue at the last minute because the workers had been without a contract for too long. It was the last unresolved issue at the table. But it will be a strike issue this time.

For gay union activists, what are the main workplace issues that are on the table? Obviously domestic partnership is one and nondiscrimination language is another. Are there others?

As far as contract language goes, that's all we need. Once antidiscrimination language is there, our rights fall into the grievance and arbitration procedures, and that covers everything. So it's an interesting question, because I can't think of anything else off the top of my head that's a contract issue. More, the issues are respect at work and equal treatment, not only by management but also by other workers. There are horrible issues of harassment that continue to go on—member on member harassment. And we want the union to stand up when that happens.

Can you talk about the degree to which you've made headway in that department?

Well, I believe very much that the existence of GALLAN and Pride at Work nationally and the visibility of the lesbian and gay movement serves to educate gay members that they should have rights. In the past, it did not even occur to union members who were harassed for being queer that they could go to the union. It wasn't defined as a right within the union movement; now it is. But there are people outside of the large cities who don't know this. What we're trying to do is create a broader and broader educational process about the right to go to the union in cases of harassment or discrimination.

The second part of the process is to get the unions to represent people. Unions have a legal obligation to fairly represent our members. If I'm your business agent and you come to me with a problem and you don't feel you are fairly represented, then you go to the labor board and file a DFR, a complaint on the duty of fair representation. When you do, there's a hearing process, and let me tell you, it is one of the swiftest administrative processes in this country. Now, there are still unions where you can get shot for doing this; it's not always an honest process. But in the main, the DFR keeps us fairly honest.

So today it's more widely known that lesbian and gay rights fall under DFR. If I'm harassed as a lesbian and I go to my business agent but I don't feel he or she is adequately representing me, then I can go right to the labor board and file a DFR and I will win.

What will be the outcome of that?

It depends on the nature of the grievance procedure in a particular contract. I handled the harassment of a gay male member in 1987 or 1988 and that man collected probably $100,000 from the company over a period of several years. This was after GAL-LAN was started; I never would have handled it this way had I not been in an organization and thinking of it in these terms.

Did the harassment stop?

Yes. There was another gay man who was being harassed, member to member harassment, in the United Auto Workers. It was a fairly well-known case: Ronald Woods. He brought action within his union. He was not represented. He had to escalate his complaints. He ended up with a transfer; he had to go someplace else to get away from these guys. But he was represented, and now he's on the civil-rights committee of the UAW.

Do you think gay activism has changed unions? How?

Yes. I like to quote Stanley Hill, who is the executive director of District Council 37 in New York. He's a straight African American man, and he gave the welcoming remarks at the first large lesbian and gay labor conference, held in New York. And what he said was that labor needs us, lesbian and gays, more than we need it. Because in the same period when labor has been losing, 1980 through 1995, lesbians and gays have been winning. In this era of ever-increasing oppression and repression, lesbians and gays have come out. We're coming out, we're discussing our issues, we're getting people to meetings. We're organizing people, and that has had a positive effect on the labor movement. We're not just talking diversity; we're actually doing it. We're sitting down, dinosaurs and queers, in the same room and hashing things out.

How do you think the perspective on the gay political agenda—not only workplace issues but the wider political agenda—that union people have is going to be different from the perspective that nonlabor people are going to have? In what ways do you think the lesbian and gay movement can benefit from more input from people within the labor movement?

For me it's a question of process. I think that the agenda-setting of at least large sectors of the mainstream gay and lesbian movement is defined by this "place at the table" strategy. It's very much about the individual advancement of lesbians and gays. It's a liberal strategy: if you get more people in advanced positions they'll take care of us. The political side of the strategy is getting our leaders to the table and the economic side is the development of lesbian and gay business. That leaves working-class people out in the same way that the capitalist strategies do.

The labor agenda is really to represent the interests of working-class people. It's about respect and dignity, and good jobs, and safe jobs—and in our case, safe for us to be at them and to be free to do our jobs without violence, harassment, and the other effects of homophobia. We see that the interests of lesbian and gay workers are united with the interests of workers. I think this is part of the problem that the mainstream has with us.

If tomorrow you were placed on an advisory board at the National Gay and Lesbian Task Force (NGLTF), what would you have to say that would be different from some of the other folks there? What do you want to do differently from what they're doing?

Let me give you a very simple example. We want them to use union labor. We want them to build their buildings with union labor. We want them to print their letterheads with union bugs. Some of them have two sets of letterheads; they have their union letterheads and they have their nonunion letterheads. We want labor representatives to be sitting on their boards and to be identified as such. We want them to risk alienating their rich, white male constituency by saying they're going to represent all lesbians and gays and let the chips fall. Human Rights Campaign Fund—we want them to give their money away fairly. To give it to the people who not only support lesbian and gay issues but also support lesbian and gay labor issues. We don't want them to contribute to conservative, antiworker, antilesbian and gay, but "gay sensitive" politicians.

NGLTF does a lot on workplace issues, and we'd like to see unions be more included. Regionally, there are all kinds of activities going on about lesbians and gays in the workplace that concentrate on issues ranging from benefits and domestic partnership to starting up e-mail clubs and coming out. Or actually about *not* being out at work—how to advance without a wife, that kind of stuff. We would like to see the issues of the majority of lesbians and gays who work getting addressed. That's blue collar and service jobs rather than just the progressive software companies and the gay ghetto economy, which is usually what's addressed.

In what way do you think the gay agenda would be different if gay labor were better represented? What particular issues would be addressed more or addressed less? For example, how would the take on gays in the military be different?

Well, the health care one is easier for me. I think we would have engaged in the national health care debate rather than keeping domestic partnership separate, as many of the national lesbian and gay organizations did. They represent disproportionately people who either have health care at work or can buy it. We are not that supportive of domestic partnership because we believe in universal health care. This is GAL-LAN's position; I can't speak for every part of Pride at Work, the national gay labor organization.

Had we been a stronger national organization when the health care debate was going on, or hopefully we will be the next time, we would like to engage that debate by saying that universal health care protects lesbians and gays too. Lesbians and gays are unfairly discriminated against in their access to health care, and we should be part of the movement for universal health care.

But many gay people in unions have fought for domestic partnership.

In the absence of universal health care; tactically. And for a lot of people, the struggle for domestic partnership provides a context for raising the issue of gay rights in the workplace and for showing people the fundamental unfairness lesbians and gay men face.

The military one is a little bit harder because we're a progressive organization. We don't support the military. As I see it, Clinton cut a deal that involved gay support in the election in return for the change in military policy. But when the deal went bad, there was no connection between the deal makers and the gay service members who actually needed the new policy, who needed the jobs. I think that were we able to undertake that struggle in a different context—say, if there were connections between the progressive movement and people in the military—then there might have been a basis for organizing and there might have been a different response when Clinton reneged on ending the ban. For instance, a massive coming out, or civil disobedience, or some other kind of action that might have been possible but wasn't, because this was just a deal cut at the top.

You said before that entrepreneurship is one facet of the "place at the table" strategy that, as a labor person, you oppose. But some people would view the creation of a gay-owned business sector as a plus for the gay community. Can you say more about this?

I think many gay entrepreneurs see the movement as a kind of fuel to accelerate their personal and financial advancement. It's a very seductive approach, this "place at the table" thing. Who wouldn't want some gay men as the press secretary to the president? It's great to see people up there. But it's not about who's up there; it's about who's down here.

There's some kind of gross dichotomy between this whole strategy that has grown up in the age of AIDS and the reality of AIDS. The AIDS industry has accelerated this advancement of the few. But there's no cure; more people continue to die. I think this is tragic. And it's tragic that this is how many people in America have been introduced to the gay movement.

You're saying that some gay people have capitalized on the AIDS crisis?

Yes. However, it's important to say that AIDS has had other results too. Since the early days of the gay/labor movement, the role of gay men has changed significantly, and I think that's the result of AIDS. In the beginning, this movement was all lesbians and a few gay men. Now, we have lots of gay men. When GALLAN first sat down with striking hotel workers in 1986 and 1987, and the impact of AIDS was not yet fully felt, a lot of gay men in working-class jobs were on the edge of the illusion that they would work themselves up. But it has become patently clear to the community that gay men are not working themselves up. Now, gay men are working for health care. In many cases, their identity has really changed from future manager to worker who needs benefits. So gay men now play a very important role in the national lesbian and gay labor movement. They have pushed these issues; they need benefits for themselves and for their partners.

So, to go back to the issue of gay entrepreneurship, you don't see any advantages in the development of the gay market in the business community?

I'm very biased on this. I'm not probusiness at any level, so I wouldn't view gay business positively either. I'm not saying I don't take advantage of them. I go to Provincetown. I know where to buy nice gifts—if I need a birthday gift, I know I can go to a lesbian birthday gift store. We live in capitalism and I have to live in it, too. Some small businesspeople just get by. Small businesses fail much more than they succeed, and if that's the way queers want to do it—hey, if you want to work seventy to eighty hours a week with only a 30-percent chance of succeeding, maybe a little better because your niche is already carved out, that's fine. I don't find it very interesting. I don't think it's political. But I think when people use it as leverage for political power—when they create gay business associations that begin to negotiate with municipal governments on advancing the cause of gay business associations, and that gets put forward as the gay movement—then it's potentially more destructive.

GALLAN has been involved with a number of political campaigns in Massachusetts: the governor's race, ballot initiatives, and so forth. How do you at GALLAN respond to figures like Governor Weld, who are viewed as progay but are so conservative in general?

It's our position that you're not progay if you're antiworker because where does that leave gay workers? There's just no such thing. You're not progay if you're anti-immigrant because where does that leave lesbian and gay immigrants? We can't separate ourselves out from the population that way.

In fact, I think that Weld's actions have really demonstrated this very clearly. His supposedly progay actions have benefited a very small group of mainly white men, but he has not been a friend to the majority of lesbians and gays. He's given jobs to a couple of dozen gay men and lesbians in his administration and at the same time, if we assume one in ten people are gay, he's cut the jobs of thousands of lesbian and gay state workers. I have a friend who worked at one of the state schools for over eighteen years, was laid off, and now is working for much less pay at a privatized state facility. He's a gay man in his middle forties who supports himself, has no other resources, and has an elderly mother. He's a fag and he's not going to just walk into a progressive software company and get himself a job. His employment opportunities are extremely limited and his gayness is a factor in those limitations.

This kind of politics not only leaves out lesbian and gay workers, it leaves out queers. It leaves out those of us who cannot pass. It's okay to be out, just don't look like it, don't talk about it, and don't offend. You don't see Weld hiring any drag queens. That's why when we say we're a lesbian, gay, bisexual, and transgender organization—GALLAN, and also the national organization Pride at Work—it's not just a theoretical inclusiveness. It's that transgender people who have a hard time working in this society need an organization that represents their interests. And transgender people who are in unions where they have antidiscrimination language can be transgender, can be pre-op, post-op, and change their identity, can be in drag if they have protection. Not to say that this is always easy or in ideal circumstances, but it is happening. And they have some limited protection.

Do you think the queerer side of the gay community in that sense is disproportionately working-class?

Yes. Some of it is just plain economics. Working-class people live in closer quarters, don't leave their families, and are not as transient as a lot of the middle-class lesbian and gay community is. If they're going to come out, they have to stay home and come out. So, my experience was that it's very common to have an uncle who was a drag queen or have a sister who was a dyke and lived with her girlfriend for twenty years.

I think that there is a certain kind of stereotype that if gay people are going to make headway in low-income communities, they have to do it by looking very nonqueer.

I don't think that's true at all. Walk through any working-class neighborhood, sit in front of a store, sit on a stoop, and you can spot the dykes. People aren't hiding.

One thing that we haven't touched on: unions are clearly going to bat at the bargaining table and in the local workplace setting for gay and lesbian issues. In what ways do you think unions can be asked to go to bat for gay issues in the wider political arena? Briggs was an example. Do you see unions putting their resources behind wider gay issues? If the federal civil-rights bill comes up again, will the AFL go to bat for it?

Unions have been involved in opposing all of the local and statewide antigay state ballot campaigns. Unions have been very active in Oregon; work has been done on dozens of municipal campaigns and the unions are very involved, not only in terms of endorsement and support but in terms of providing resources. We have offices; we have phones; we have staffs; we have mailing lists; we have faxes. And also unions were among the first to endorse ENDA, the federal Employment Non-Discrimination Act, which is a civil-rights bill for lesbians and gay men in the workplace. The unions have been instrumental in putting that together. And that's actually a place where the unions and the national gay rights organizations are working together. I don't think the act is going to go anywhere in the Newt Gingrich Congress, but there was a lot of agitation built nationally and locally through the unions. The unions are producing material and sending stuff out to support ENDA.

So you're saying that unions have resources that other progressive gay organizations don't have.

Yes. That's why we're in unions. I talked earlier about solidarity, but let's be practical. What we believe in is that we get together, we pool our resources, we pay our dues, and the product of that is resources to fight back against the boss. We own buildings. We have mortgages. We're the best organized progressive force in the country. Practically speaking it's a big mistake for progressives, lesbian and gay progressives, not to reach out to labor.

17

Class Action
Bringing Economic Diversity to the Gay and Lesbian Movement

Pat Hussain

Who directs and staffs gay-rights organizations? Who plans their activities and programs? And how do the answers to these questions shape both the agenda and the effectiveness of gay-rights organizing? In this essay, long-time gay-rights and social-justice activist Pat Hussain describes a lack of class diversity in the gay movement and demonstrates how this has limited the movement's success.

The meeting was called to decide whether, when and where our third national march should take place. The idea of getting in on the ground floor and being a part of the organizing was exciting enough for lots of people to buy plane tickets or fill up their cars for the trip to Washington, DC. That March 1991 weekend would be filled with political discussion and opportunities to make important decisions guiding the planning for the March as well as for gay participation in the 1992 presidential election.

Some of the people who attended the planning conference were paid staffers at various organizations and were selected to attend as part of their job. In all-volunteer groups with small budgets, though, the members who could afford to pay the expenses up front and be reimbursed later were the ones to go. This system left many of us in the same circumstance, figuring out how to pay our expenses in order to participate in the meetings. There was nothing resembling a uniform method or expectation of when you might be reimbursed. We knew it was probable that some of the money we spent would be repaid, but also possible that we would receive little or none. How much you could afford to spend up front, or how much you could afford to pay out with no definite expectation of reimbursement, determined your level of participation.

The expenses of participation are a clear example of the process of "self-selection" that silently guides the workings of the gay movement. Self-selection means that those who have time and money to spare become the organizers, the representatives, and the leaders of the gay-rights movement; it means that class and income are major barriers to many people's participation in gay politics. Self-selection has been used in the gay community for much of our organizing. Many of our organizations are small and run by volunteers. We presume that gay men and lesbians who are interested in working for equality will—in addition to putting out their own money to cover expenses—volunteer significant amounts of their time to the cause, possibly as an integral part or even the sole focus of their working lives.

But self-selection fails to acknowledge the reality of many people's economic circumstances. When you are working two jobs and still are not quite able to make ends meet, it doesn't matter how strongly you want to participate as an organizer, either locally or in the planning of a national march. If you can't get time off from work, if you can't live without the money you would have earned during that time, and if you can't provide your own travel, hotel, and food expenses, then your decision not to participate is framed by these concerns, not by how interested you may be in the issues. Since these kinds of concerns are often invisible to those whose participation is not similarly constrained, they may assume that you simply do not want to participate and, worse, that you have nothing to contribute. On that weekend in 1991, and in all of the planning sessions that followed, people who did not come or send a representative, or who did not send pages of faxes to support their positions on the matters under discussion, were considered by many to be apathetic or unconcerned.

I am not blaming the March on Washington organizers for the self-selection dynamic that tended to limit participation based on people's ability to donate time and money. In almost all of our organizing, we have allowed class to be an unspoken issue. In fact, March on Washington organizers took major steps to ensure that the group that planned the event was diverse and representative. These steps were very successful in creating race and gender equity but less successful in building class diversity. Nor am I suggesting that the straight community has done a better job of incorporating people of different classes into their organizations. However, I am saying that our lack of diversity along class lines has had deleterious effects on our work as a movement.

To begin with, the lack of diversity among the gay community's representatives has led this country to believe things about us that are not true. We have seen the surveys telling us how high our disposable incomes are. It would be more accurate to view those results as coming from a visible portion of our community, a portion that can afford to be visible and participate in surveys found in magazines that they can afford to buy. In reality, we go from being homeless to dwelling in mansions, from not knowing where our next meal will come from to dining on gourmet fare. Some of us dropped out in elementary school; some have Ph.D.'s. Just as we are everywhere, we are part of every class background and life style.

Our silence in the face of statistics saying that we all make lots of money, that we all have college degrees, that we vacation in Europe, and that we do not have children reflects either our lack of knowledge about who we really are or our reluctance to admit that we do not all fit into those statistics. What's more, some gay men and lesbians have not merely been silent on the reality of class diversity in our communities. We have all heard some of our gay and lesbian friends and colleagues quote survey results as an affirmation that gay men and lesbians are indeed solid citizens; we have all seen those same statistics used by gay businesspeople to sell us to corporations as a new consumer market.

Self-selection also presumes that those of us who are able to pay our own way to participate are the *best* people to represent the community. This is patently untrue. For one thing, when only a narrowly defined group of people is available to do most of the organizing, their needs will be in the forefront, while the needs of other constituencies are likely not to come up. So, having a more diverse group of organizers means they will be likely to see and plan for a wider array of needs. For example, if a member of your executive committee needs an interpreter, then you get one early on. It doesn't become an afterthought, one of those unmet promises—"Oh, we're really sorry we didn't do that."

A narrow leadership will also make different kinds of decisions about the gay political agenda than a more representative leadership would. For example, some people have theoretical objections to the idea of domestic partnership or marriage rights as an important goal for our movement. But if you can't afford to go to an attorney and have all kinds of documents executed, such as a special power of attorney so that you can make decisions when your partner is sick, then domestic partnership rights could be a matter of survival for you. The most impoverished heterosexual couple has these rights for the price of a marriage license. What class privilege gives some gay men and lesbians is the ability to buy what they want, including those attorney's fees, and they can be very cavalier about deciding what other lesbians and gay men *don't* need.

Similarly, the issue of gays in the military was the focus of one of the most class-driven discussions that took place at the time of the March in 1993. The reality for many young men and women who are poor is that the military is their prep school; it's the place where you can get a job that provides food, clothing, and a roof over your head *and* you can get an education. But many gay men and lesbians look at the issue from "above," where military service is beneath them and where the thought of entering the military is viewed as a statement about support for the military-industrial complex rather than as a stepping stone to financial independence and the acquisition of some class privilege. And their ambivalence about the issue has surely weakened the movement's attempts to get beyond "Don't ask/don't tell" and achieve real victory.

Apart from any particular item on the agenda, gay politics is weakened overall when our organizers and leaders do not include any low-income lesbians and gay men, because this allows the politics of division to be played out in our community. It is very easy for low-income communities and communities of color to be pitted against lesbians and gay men when the visible representatives of the gay community are almost all middle class and white. And a narrow leadership is likely to make decisions about our agenda that only make this worse. For example, I remember the elation in our community in 1993 when we had the support of the Southern Christian Leadership Conference, the NAACP, Mrs. King, and the King Center. We felt validated as a civil-rights movement. But now that the March is over and a few years have passed, I don't see that same desire to build our movement within a broad civil-rights coalition. I don't hear many voices in our community now that are quoting Dr. King, or that are responding to the attacks on affirmative action or welfare.

When the leadership of our movement is—thanks to self-selection—a fairly narrow group, then members of underrepresented groups are likely to feel alienated and avoid joining the movement at any level. This keeps the movement smaller and weaker than it could be. I heard these kinds of suspicions in my work on the March on Washington. People would call and say, "Why should we participate? It's all white people doing this thing." It was very important for us to be able to say, "No, that's not true. I'll let you speak with so-and-so." And the importance of this lay not in following some simplistic formula under which people are presumed to want to talk only with someone just like themselves, but rather in bringing people from all of the different lesbian, gay, bisexual, and transgender communities to understand that they were not being *invited* to this event—that they truly were its *hosts*.

Finally, when our organizing is not structured so as to address, at least partially, the economic needs of organizers who are not independently wealthy, one of the results is burnout. People get tired of starving because they're doing political work. Organizers have to pull out in order to keep themselves from crashing and burning; at some point everybody has to pay the rent. Unfortunately, this means a lot of turnover and the loss of experienced organizers attuned to class issues.

It will not be easy for the gay movement to get beyond the self-selection process. When our groups operate on a shoestring, as is often the case, there isn't much money to spread around. But there are steps that can be taken. An organization in Kentucky, the Louisville chapter of the Alliance Against Women's Oppression, decided to make providing transportation to meetings into an organizational objective. If you had a car, you knew that you were going to be asked to be the transportation coordinator for certain dates. That meant all the members would call and inform you whether they needed a ride to the meeting, and you would arrange transportation. This acknowledged the need for transportation to meetings—and that not everyone had access to it—and made it into an organizational responsibility. Another example is Project Open Hand in Atlanta, which provides home-delivered meals to people who are HIV-positive. The group drops off two meals at a time, one for lunch and one to be reheated for dinner. The first thing that they ask each new client is whether he or she has a microwave; if not, the first delivery includes two meals *and* a microwave. By paying attention to the situation of their low-income clients, this organization has eliminated the assumption that if you're too poor to afford a microwave, you'll just have to eat bacteria.

Computers also have the potential to lower the class barrier tremendously. If groups like Digital Queers can succeed in getting enough computers donated, handing them out, and getting every gay/lesbian organization online, that would have a significant impact. (One old computer donated by each gay man or lesbian working in Silicon Valley would probably be more than enough!) This would be a great leveler, but again, it will only happen if we incorporate it into organizational goals; right now, computers remain a class privilege.

To counteract the effects of self-selection, the organizers of the March on Washington tried to make sure that different voices were brought to the table. We placed requirements on the organizing structure for the March: the regional delegations, the executive committee, and the cochairs had to include a minimum of 50 percent people of color and 50 percent women. So, while we did not specify class as a category, these requirements focused on groups whose oppression has a significant economic dimension. In the loaded language used to describe affirmative action, some people viewed this as a "quota." Some saw it as a way to limit the participation of white men. I disagree. We *wanted* everyone who was interested to be able to participate. The racial and gender parity requirements were not designed to exclude, but to share power. All were welcome to come, discuss, and share opinions. But when consensus could not be reached and it was time to vote, it was critical that we speak with equal voices.

I think the difference between limiting participation and sharing power becomes clear if we look at the creative approach of six white men from one of the regions. All six wanted to participate on the steering committee. In order to stay within the parity requirements, they decided to take one seat as a group; on any issue that came to a vote under the modified consensus system we were using, they would each have one-sixth of a vote. My first response to their proposal was that this was just one more way of trying to circumvent the parity requirements. As I thought about it, though, I realized that they had come up with a good approach. Just because more of them could afford to come did not mean that they should have more power or more votes. But at the same time, this idea allowed everyone to participate.

Another important step that March organizers took to spread power and participation was to adopt a modified-consensus process in place of the traditional "Roberta's" Rules of Order. Achieving consensus meant hearing out differences of opinion and trying to craft solutions that would satisfy everyone—at least enough to enter into the consensus. This engendered a very different kind of communication from that traditionally found in governing bodies. Instead of working to form blocks that would give one side a simple majority, modified-consensus made us all really listen to each other and work together. It opened up the conversation to those who hadn't grown up familiar with parliamentary procedures, often those without class privilege.

One of the ugliest fights in the entire planning process for the March took place at that original planning meeting in the spring of 1991. Everyone was excited about duplicating the 1987 March on Washington on the same date in October, just before the 1992 election. The date had virtually been set when two people blocked consensus on it. The room disintegrated. The two Native American women explained that Native Americans were planning a full year of commemorative activities for 1992, the 500th anniversary of Columbus's arrival and the European invasion of America. Any other major political events, such as a massive gay-rights march in Washington, would draw attention away from their efforts, so they were asking that the March not be scheduled during 1992. Half of the room then joined them in blocking consensus; the other half offered lots of warm and supportive statements that were snapped in half by the word "but": "We stand in solidarity with Native Americans, *but* 1992 is an election year."

As it turned out, I don't know what would have happened if a million queers had descended on Washington a month before the 1992 election. I do know that if we had been using traditional parliamentary procedures, the two women's objections might never have been heard, and would certainly have had no impact on the outcome. I was accustomed to parliamentary procedure, and I had never thought of it as being exclusive or divisive. But this sequence of events made it clear to me that traditional rules of order silence people. If you don't know how the rules work, then you have to spend a long time just figuring out what's going on. The language is different, and the structure does not flow from normal conversation. In this case, a consensus that we were not going to march during 1992 was eventually achieved; the April 1993 date that we finally settled on turned out to be just right on a number of counts.

Even with this approach, it was impossible to represent lesbians and gay men of color adequately. Fifty percent of a four-person regional delegation was too small to include representatives of the Native American, African American, Asian and Pacific Islander, Latina and Latino, and Middle Eastern communities. The thought of being represented by someone who might be neither the same race, ethnicity, or gender was so uncomfortable for some organizers that they withdrew from the planning. Of course, representation by others has been the rule rather than the exception in my community. Just take a look at the number of black women elected as mayors, governors, presidents, and Congressional representatives or hired as executive directors of our organizations!

When you combine assumptions about race with silence about class, you get stereotypes lying just under the surface waiting to erupt into language. During the discussion of the requirement that 50 percent of the organizers be people of color, one white man questioned whether we were serious in insisting his delegation bring people of color with them. A black man leapt angrily to his feet to state that he had bought his own ticket. Nobody had brought him. Another white man insisted we "be honest with each other," that women and people of color were lazy and just didn't do the work. Some of the men sitting around him were nodding in agreement. I have heard uglier discussions, but not many. The only encouraging thing about this situation was that the discussion, usually reserved for rooms where only white people are presumed to be present, was taking place in a public forum.

To a significant degree, though, the parity requirement was carried out. Parity was not achieved at every meeting, but most regional delegations made a good-faith effort to comply with the requirement, and I believe that this did make a difference in the decisions that we made. For one thing, our outreach was much broader than the outreach for the national march in 1987 had been. As a member of the interim executive committee, I had volunteered to facilitate the organizing of the seventeen regional delegations across the country. This meant identifying where work had begun and who was doing it, providing information and sometimes acting as a referee in local disputes, and—where people had received no information—asking local organizers to take on this project. When the first national steering committee meeting took place, fifteen of the seventeen regions were present. I continued to do outreach as a member of the executive committee until the day of the March. My goals were to ensure that every lesbian, gay man, bisexual, and transgender in the United States knew about the March, to have at least one committee in every state, and to assist organizations and individuals in plugging into the organizing or participating during the March.

In order to reach the huge number of lesbians and gay men who do not lead "out" lives in large urban areas, we tried every tactic at hand. One was what we called the Outriders Program. Any contact we had, or anyone who was traveling to any destination in the United States, was asked to take a stack of March on Washington brochures along and leave them in laundromats, coffee shops, and bars. In some states, though, we could not find a single contact. For states like Wyoming and South Dakota, I would start what I called trolling for queers. I would ask everyone who called in on the March's 800 number, "Do you know anyone in South Dakota? In Wyoming? If you even know someone who knows someone, please ask them to call me." In South Dakota, I called a feminist bookstore from a national bookstore listing. When I said I was looking for some help with the March on Washington, she said, "What march?" I told her, and she replied, "Well, so-and-so does coffeehouses . . ." and we were off. We placed personal ads for the March in newspapers that wouldn't take a display ad for a gay event. We used the Internet. I called the Log Cabin Club—the gay Republicans. I knew their board had already voted not to come, but I asked them to reconsider because our community was gathering and I thought they really needed to be there.

Once the big week arrived, it was not hard to see the results of a more diverse organizing committee and of a broad, intensive outreach effort. It was not just the usual suspects who arrived in Washington. Out of about three hundred March-related events that took place that week, over sixty of them were given by and for people of color. This was absolutely unprecedented! As for the March itself, there was a sharp contrast between who was there in 1987 and who was there in 1993. In 1993, there was a beautiful sea of all different kinds of people. The participation of Puertoriqueños was tremendous. The number of gay American Indians at the March in 1987 was around ten; in 1993, over three hundred came. These are just a few examples; overall, the 1993 March was a hugely diverse event.

Ironically, some people gave the 1993 March unfavorable reviews, describing it as toned down and less political than the one in 1987. The March may have had a different feel to it in 1993, but that was because this time, tens of thousands of lesbians, gay men, and bisexuals attended who were *not* hooked into gay communities in large urban areas. For there are a lot of us who live somewhere, who go to work, who do not go to bars or subscribe to gay magazines. But once you have snuck out of your closet and come to Washington to march with a million other gay people, you can't just slip back in that closet when you go home. You may become one of the increasing number of people who are becoming empowered to live more openly where they are, people who are saying, "I live here. My job is here. I'm not moving off to some big city; I'm staying." And there has likewise been a bubbling up of activism in small and medium-sized towns around the United States—in 1995, Macon, Georgia, had its first gay-rights march.

There is an important reason for my going into some detail about the outreach work that I did. Many white gay men and lesbians who knew that I was doing outreach assumed that I was doing it solely for communities of color. It never occurred to them that I might be facilitating the creation of a national network to inform and bring people to Washington, or that my outreach efforts were extending from gay American Indians to the Log Cabin Club. The thought of a black woman directing outreach at a national level, not specifically to people of color, never entered their minds. In the same way, once the parity requirements had been established, I would get calls at the March office: "Why do we have to bring people of color with us? They're always trying to make us feel guilty. If those people can't afford to come, that's too bad." It never occurred to the people who called that the person at the other end of the phone might not be white. As I began to encounter people making these kinds of statements, I realized that something significant was happening in the process of planning this event. Some people walked away from the organizing, unable to accept the fact that the backroom deals were no longer being made. They said that the March wouldn't be successful, that we wouldn't be able to raise money because of the parity rules. They were wrong, but their very attitude is one example of how prejudice often limits the effectiveness of our work.

While the degree of race and gender equity in the planning process for the March was very high, self-selection was still at work, and the degree of class parity was probably much lower. The regional planning committees started with no resources, yet a lot of the outreach and other work they were trying to do cost money. Some regions were able to raise money to help their delegates travel to the national steering committee meetings, but that was the exception; most delegates had to cover the expenses themselves. Similarly, in volunteering to take on the outreach effort, I had to be able to pay the phone bill for all of those calls across the country. Yes, I knew I would be reimbursed, but Southern Bell would not wait until the March had some money. This was and continues to be true for organizers on all levels; whether for flyers, postage, or plane tickets, someone has to pay now. So, our organizing continues to be limited to those who can afford to participate rather than to those who can best represent us.

I want to see us move beyond that. The rainbow of people present in Washington for the 1993 March was a powerful testament to our ability to organize across race and culture lines. However, America still perceives our community as a small coterie of well-off white gay men. That will change when we consciously work to make our rainbow a reality. A community as creative as ours is capable of developing models of organizing that remove class as a barrier to participation. At the very least, it is critical for us not to limit our interactions by assuming that those who may not be able to afford to participate are apathetic. We have already spoken the unspeakable, our love for someone of the same sex. We have made a choice to be honest about who we are and who we love. We can create community and organize for equality across lines that traditionally divide. Some of us have already begun; it is time to broaden the circle.

18

Domestic Partner Benefits
A Primer for Gay and Lesbian Activists

Robert M. Anderson

How can you change the minds of employers and insurance companies reluctant to finance domestic partner benefits? Point by point, Robert M. Anderson explains exactly how. He answers each of their possible concerns, showing how a plan can be built that satisfies gay employees as well as firms and insurance companies.

In 1982, the San Francisco Board of Supervisors adopted an ordinance that allowed domestic partners to register their relationships. Under the ordinance, domestic partners of city employees could receive health insurance benefits through their partners' plans. Under pressure from the Roman Catholic Archbishop, then-Mayor Dianne Feinstein vetoed the proposal. The Archbishop did not object to the extension of health insurance *per se*; his concern was that a government-sponsored registration system for domestic partners would undermine the unique status accorded to marriage. Mayor Feinstein proposed a compromise to provide insurance while meeting the Archbishop's objections. She charged a task force to prepare a plan that would allow each city employee to enroll any one other person if s/he was unmarried or chose not to enroll his/her spouse. When the task force reported that Feinstein's proposal was not feasible, for reasons that will be explained here, the matter was dropped.

In 1994, San Francisco voters adopted a ballot measure equalizing the treatment of domestic partners and spouses in the City's pension plan. And on the national level, since 1982 a number of employers—governments, universities, private nonprofit organizations and private for-profit firms—have extended benefits to the domestic partners of their employees. Usually, these domestic partner benefits have included health insurance and certain other privileges, such as the right to use facilities like a gymnasium or library provided by the employer. The health insurance coverage is usually extended to children of the partner as well.[1] To date, a substantial percentage of the individuals added have been children, a fact that is helpful in convincing people to support these benefits.

Complex economic issues govern the provision of domestic partner benefits, and thus it is critical for activists working on this issue to be fluent in economics as well as politics. This paper identifies strategies to reassure employers and insurers who are sympathetic to the needs of employees with domestic partners but concerned about potential costs or disruptions to their existing programs.

Insurers' Concerns

The issue of domestic partner health insurance arises only because health care in the United States is financed primarily through private insurance offered as a benefit of employment. If the United States were to provide universal health care coverage, as every other major industrialized nation does, the issue would be moot. This paper addresses the issue of domestic partner coverage in the context of the current health care system, with all of its complexities, inefficiencies, and inequities.

In designing insurance plans, there are two central problems that must be controlled. These have come to be known as *adverse selection* and *moral hazard.* In working with insurers, it is important to recognize that these are real problems that *do* arise in practice unless steps are taken to prevent them. Experience has shown that domestic partner plans can be devised to control these problems.

Adverse Selection

Adverse selection arises if the pool of people who buy insurance is substantially different from the general population in a way that increases the dollar value of claims that the insurer will have to pay. The following simple (and somewhat simplistic) example illustrates the effects of adverse selection.

Suppose we have a group of 1,000 individuals.

Nine hundred of these people are at no risk of a heart attack in the next year, while each of the remaining 100 faces a 10 percent risk of having a heart attack in the next year. However, no individual knows to which group s/he belongs. Suppose the cost of treating a heart attack is $30,000, while the cost of providing all other medical care is $1,500 per person per year. The total expected annual cost of providing health care for these 1,000 people is thus 1,000 × $1,500 + 10% of 100 × $30,000 = $1,500,000 + 300,000 = $1,800,000. If each person were charged an identical premium, it would be $1,800,000 / 1,000 = $1,800 per year, or $150 per month.

Now suppose each individual knows to which group s/he belongs. The 900 individuals who are not at risk of a heart attack have a choice of buying insurance at a premium of $1,800 or of self-insuring, i.e., to drop the insurance coverage, save the premium, and pay the medical bills directly from their own pockets; this results in an expenditure of $1,500. All of them choose to self-insure. The 100 individuals at risk of a heart attack buy the insurance. The insurance company receives premiums of 100 × $1,800 = $180,000 per year, and has claims of 100 × $1,500 + 10% of 100 × $30,000 = $150,000 + 300,000 = $450,000 per year; it loses $270,000!

As a consequence, the insurer raises its premium to $4,500 per individual per annum; at this premium rate, 50 of the high-risk individuals drop their coverage, planning to seek care as indigents if they have heart attacks. Of the original 1,000 people, only 50 now have insurance coverage, and it is *very* expensive.

Of course, this example is simplistic, but adverse selection is a real phenomenon. The most visible example currently involves the rapid disappearance of traditional fee-for-service health insurance plans. Employers anxious to control health insurance costs have increasingly opted to pay for a relatively inexpensive insurance plan, such as a Health Maintenance Organization (HMO). Employees are permitted to opt for a more expensive fee-for-service plan, which allows unrestricted choice of doctors, provided they pay the difference between the two premiums. Many employees have chosen to enroll in the cheaper HMOs. The percentage of insured workers in the northeast United States enrolled in fee-for-service plans fell from 66 percent in 1993 to 37 percent in 1994, and was only 20 percent in the western United States.[2]

The people who have chosen HMOs are on average younger and healthier than those who have remained in the fee-for-service plans. Because the latter are older and sicker, they are more expensive to insure, so the difference in premiums between the HMOs and fee-for-service plans has risen, causing the enrollment in fee-for-service plans to fall further. The group remaining in the fee-for-service plans is *much* older and sicker than the general population. In large part, this is why fee-for-service plans are more expensive than HMOs, though some of the cost differences arise from the greater efficiency of HMOs.

Insurers fear that offering domestic partner coverage will lead to adverse selection if the definition of domestic partner is not narrowly drawn. Consider, for example, then–Mayor Feinstein's 1982 proposal to allow every employee to designate any one other person to receive insurance. Most people know one or more individuals facing unusually high health care expenses.

In particular, parents and grandparents are always older than the employee, while aunts and uncles are usually older. Since older people on average incur higher health care expenses, these older relatives are especially likely to want to be enrolled and especially likely to be expensive to cover. The cost of covering elderly relatives is further increased by a feature of the law governing Medicare. If a Medicare-eligible individual is covered as a retiree under the plan of a previous employer, Medicare provides the primary coverage, and the previous employer's plan provides secondary coverage; it pays only those expenses that Medicare does not cover. However, if a Medicare-eligible individual has coverage through the employer of an active employee, such as a son or daughter, the employer provides the primary coverage; Medicare covers only those expenses the employer's insurance does not cover. An employee who enrolls a Medicare-eligible dependent transfers a substantial burden from the federal government to her/his employer.

Under the Feinstein proposal, each employee would be free to sign up the friend or relative who was most in need of health insurance. Doing so would not be fraud;

the terms of the proposal explicitly allow individuals to choose in this way. It seems certain that the individuals who were enrolled under such a proposal would, on average, have substantially higher health care costs than would the spouses of employees. This would raise the premiums paid, probably substantially. Depending on how premium costs were shared between the employer and employee, it could also lead some employees to drop insurance coverage for themselves or their spouses. For this reason, insurers refused to offer coverage under the Feinstein proposal.

In 1991, the District of Columbia adopted a plan similar to the Feinstein proposal, in that it allowed District employees to enroll any other individual in the District's health insurance plan. Congress exercised its power to prevent this measure from taking effect. Ironically, Congress did the movement for domestic partnership benefits a favor. Its action prevented the adoption of an unworkable plan, whose very visible failure would have set back the domestic partnership benefits movement. Of course, I do not assert that this was what Congress intended to do.

Moral Hazard

The term "moral hazard" includes all actions taken by the insured party that increase the likelihood of claims. There are two basic types of moral hazard:

1. Fraud. A person who has insured a building against fire damage may commit arson to convert the building into cash, especially if the building is insured for more than the owner can obtain by selling it. The form of fraud most applicable to employer-provided health insurance is the enrollment of ineligible individuals.
2. Carelessness. An individual who has insured a building against fire damage may take less care to protect it from fire. For example, s/he may not take the trouble to ensure that smoke detectors are kept in working order, or may fail to remove flammable chemicals or vegetation from the property.

The analogous phenomenon in health insurance would be for insured individuals to engage in unhealthy habits such as smoking or consuming a large amount of fatty foods to a greater extent than uninsured individuals. Note, however, that the adverse consequences of unhealthy habits are borne to a substantial degree by the individual who indulges in them. While the insurer pays the *medical* costs associated with a heart attack, the individual suffers the consequences in terms of diminished quality of life or premature death.

Since it is unlikely that possessing health insurance makes individuals more willing to engage in unhealthy habits, this form of moral hazard is relatively unimportant in health insurance. Nonetheless, individuals who know that they are at risk of high health care bills as a consequence of their habits may be more likely to buy health insurance than individuals with healthier habits. Thus, well-insured individuals as a group may have less healthy habits than underinsured or uninsured individuals, but the main source of this difference is adverse selection, not moral hazard.

Controlling Adverse Selection and Moral Hazard

Any domestic partner health insurance plan must include measures to control adverse selection and moral hazard.

Controlling adverse selection entails ensuring that individuals are enrolled in the plan because of the nature of their relationship with the employee, rather than because of their health status. Allowing employees to enroll their spouses in employer health insurance plans has not resulted in serious adverse selection problems.[3] There are no anecdotes suggesting that people commonly marry just to obtain health insurance, in the absence of a bona fide relationship.[4] For this reason, domestic partner insurance plans have been designed with requirements similar to those imposed on married couples, as a way of controlling adverse selection.

Under California law, each spouse in a marriage is responsible for providing the other spouse with the "common necessaries" of life: basic food and shelter. Third parties who provide these basic survival items to one spouse can sue the other spouse to collect the costs of these services if the spouse who received them is unable to pay.

Individuals marrying may incur other obligations, such as the obligation to provide alimony or to divide property following community property guidelines in the event of divorce. However, these additional obligations are only the "default" arrangement; they can be waived or amended by a prenuptial agreement. The only obligations that cannot be waived are the obligations to provide basic food and shelter. Spouses in other states have similar obligations.

Employers who provide domestic partner health insurance typically define domestic partners as two people who have undertaken obligations similar to the obligations undertaken by married couples. For example, for the partner of a San Francisco City employee to qualify for benefits, the partners must satisfy the following qualifications:

- they have an intimate, committed relationship of mutual caring[5]
- they maintain the same principal place of residence[6]
- each is responsible to the other and to third parties for the other's basic living expenses, defined as basic food, shelter, and medical care[7]
- each is at least eighteen years of age
- neither is married currently, and neither has had another domestic partner in the previous six months;[8]
- neither partner is the parent, sibling, half-sibling, nephew, aunt, uncle, grandparent, or grandchild of the other.[9]

In order to control adverse selection, employers and insurers have sought to make the qualifications for domestic partnership as similar as possible to those for marriage. Of course, the requirements cannot be identical. Marriage has an important social significance that domestic partnership does not, at least currently. This explains, in part, the insistence of some insurers on stiffer requirements for domestic partners than on spouses, such as maintaining a common principal residence. With these requirements, employers and insurers have found that adverse selection has not been a problem within the domestic partner pool.

The principal moral hazard problem arising in domestic partner health insurance is the potential enrollment of ineligible individuals, i.e., individuals who do not meet the qualifications for domestic partnership. A parallel problem arises with coverage of spouses. Employers rarely ask employees to provide proof of marriage to enroll a spouse in employee benefit plans. Anecdotal information indicates that a small percentage of the individuals enrolled as the spouse of an employee are in fact not married to the employee.[10]

However, the problem is more complex with domestic partnerships. Marriage as an institution is comparatively well understood by most members of society. Virtually everyone knows whether s/he is married or not.[11] Domestic partnership, by contrast, is not very well understood. Many unmarried couples who have not signed a formal declaration of domestic partnership nonetheless consider themselves domestic partners. A substantial fraction of the general public probably has little or no understanding of what domestic partnership means.

Because no common understanding of domestic partnership exists, most employers require domestic partners seeking benefits to file an affidavit undertaking obligations similar to those entailed in marriage. Some people have argued that this is unfair, since married couples are typically not required to provide a marriage certificate to enroll. However, given the lack of understanding of the meaning of domestic partnership, the affidavit requirement is essential to protect partners against allegations of fraud. When an employee checks a box enrolling a person as her/his spouse, s/he knows whether or not the statement is true. If, as a result of a large medical claim, the employer or insurer investigates and finds that the statement was false, disciplinary proceedings, a civil suit, or even criminal charges are possible. If, however, an employer conducts an investigation of two domestic partners, it is possible that the partners could be charged with fraud for failing to meet all of the eligibility criteria even if they did not intentionally evade any of the requirements. Despite intentions to be responsible for each other's food, shelter and medical care, they may not have executed a legally binding agreement to that effect, thereby opening them up to a charge of fraud. The best way to protect people from this possibility is to include in the benefits enrollment form an affidavit that satisfies the criteria for domestic partnership imposed by the employer or insurer. Just as people become married by executing a specific legal document and publicly filing it, so people would become domestic partners for purposes of health insurance by executing a specific legal document provided by the employer and filing it with the employer or local government.

HIV Disease

Because gay men constitute a higher proportion of domestic partners than of the general population, and because gay men are more likely to be infected with HIV, the virus that causes AIDS, than the general population is, a pool of domestic partners is likely to incur higher expenses for HIV-related care than a pool of spouses. However, domestic partners as a group are younger than the group of spouses, and this tends to reduce their health care costs. Before adopting its domestic partner program, San

Francisco did a careful assessment of the likely number of HIV-infected partners that would be enrolled, and the likely costs.[12] The conclusion of the analysis, which has been borne out by experience, is that HIV costs are quite manageable. Since other regions in the country have a substantially lower incidence of HIV infection than San Francisco, there is every reason to expect that HIV-related costs will not prove to be a significant problem in domestic partner health insurance.

Pension Benefits

In discussions of domestic partner benefits, virtually all of the attention has been focused on health insurance. As noted above, a number of employers provide certain amenities such as library or gymnasium facilities to domestic partners of employees, but these benefits are small in monetary value.

But one very large benefit has received far too little attention: pensions. There are two main types of employer-provided pensions: defined benefit plans, and defined contribution plans. In a defined benefit plan, the pension is calculated as a percentage of the employee's final[13] salary, multiplied by the number of years of service. The employer and employee typically make contributions to the plan over the years. The pension benefit is not affected by the investment returns earned by the plan. If the assets of the plan prove inadequate to pay the pension, the employer must make additional contributions; if the assets prove more than adequate, the employer may suspend contributions or even withdraw assets from the plan. Thus, the employer bears the investment risk of the plan.

In a defined contribution plan, by contrast, the employee bears the investment risk of the plan. The employer and employee make contributions that earn interest, dividends, and capital gains over the years until retirement. At retirement, the employee typically uses the accumulated value to purchase an annuity, which provides regular payments for the rest of the employee's life. If the plan achieves high returns during the employee's working years, the annuity payments will be high; if the returns are low, the annuity payments will be low.

In both defined contribution plans and defined benefit plans, federal law guarantees the employee (at the time of retirement) the right to designate *any other person*[14] to receive a continuation benefit, which would provide continuing coverage in the event that the employee dies before the other person. A domestic partner could be designated in the same way as a spouse could. Federal law also requires that a married employee opt for a continuation benefit for the spouse equal to at least 50 percent of the employee's pension, unless the spouse consents in writing to waive the continuation benefit.

In defined contribution plans, the employee pays for the continuation benefit by accepting a reduced pension; the higher the continuation percentage, the lower the employee's annuity. Since the continuation benefit is more likely to be invoked if the designated beneficiary is younger than the employee, the level of this reduction (called an "actuarial reduction") also depends on the ages of the employee and the beneficiary.

In defined benefit plans, the provisions for continuation benefits often treat domestic partners less favorably than spouses. It is common to provide some continuation benefit to spouses *without any actuarial reduction.* However, an employee seeking a continuation benefit for a domestic partner must accept an actuarial reduction. Similarly, it is common to provide survivor benefits to the spouse and children, and pension benefits to the spouse, of an employee who dies before retirement. Yet domestic partners are typically ineligible for these benefits even if they are designated as the employee's beneficiary.[15] These differences are often hidden by the forms and the complexity of the plan descriptions. I know a number of people who have designated a domestic partner as the "beneficiary" of their pension plan and been told that this placed the partner on the same footing as a spouse. It does not.

To date, I am aware of only one employer, the City and County of San Francisco, that has amended a defined benefit plan to provide domestic partners the same benefits as spouses. Because the details of the San Francisco pension plans are specified in the City's charter, this required a vote of the people in November 1994 to approve a charter amendment.

Other Types of Families

As we have seen, the need to control adverse selection and moral hazard has led to a definition of domestic partnership that closely parallels the definition of marriage. As a consequence, certain family structures that are common within the lesbian and gay community are excluded. Many gay men with AIDS receive a substantial part of their care from a network of friends, some of whom are often former lovers; such a network is surely a family. If a gay man and a lesbian conceive a child and share responsibility for raising it, they surely are a family also, even if they live apart.[16] However, neither a network of friends nor a pair of coparents living apart qualifies as a domestic partnership as defined above.

Kath Weston argues compellingly:

> If legal recognition is achieved for some aspects of gay families at the expense of others, it could have the effect of privileging certain forms of family while delegitimating others by contrast. The most likely scenario would involve narrowing the definition of gay families to incorporate only couples and parents with children, abandoning attempts to achieve any corresponding recognition for families of friends. Legal recognition for friends, or at least measures that would eliminate any automatic elevation of blood ties over ties of friendship, must also assume its place on lesbian and gay political agendas.[17]

One cannot disagree. Unfortunately, the argument leads Weston to conclude that "an individual should be able to pick any one person as a partner—domestic or otherwise—and designate that person as the recipient of insurance or other employment benefits, even when that choice entails crossing household boundaries." But that is precisely the infeasible Feinstein plan. If a plan allows one to enroll any other person, without certifying some definable relationship, then adverse selection will doom the plan. It may be possible to loosen *somewhat* the definition of domestic partnership, particularly in the area of common residence, but it cannot be watered down very far if it is to serve as a basis for health insurance enrollment.

One should also recall the motivation behind the Feinstein plan. Feinstein wanted to allow employees to enroll any other individual because doing so avoided conveying societal recognition to unmarried relationships. This was intended to mollify the Roman Catholic Church, which did not object to the provision of health insurance but did object to the recognition of relationships outside of marriage. Curiously, then, Weston and the Church take the same position on the issue of domestic partner benefits.

This leaves the lesbian and gay movement with an unpleasant choice: seek employment benefits for domestic partners at the expense of leaving out other family arrangements; or seek recognition of a variety of family arrangements, but without the provision of employment benefits.

Including Opposite-Sex Partnerships

The vast majority of nonuniversity employers who provide domestic partner benefits provide them to both same- and opposite-sex couples. However, most universities have chosen to follow the lead of Stanford, which provided the benefits to same-sex couples only starting in 1992. The rationale appears to have been three-fold: (1) opposite-sex couples have the option of marrying, so that providing same-sex coverage is the more urgent need; (2) providing opposite-sex coverage might have the effect of discouraging marriage; and (3) covering same-sex couples only is much cheaper than covering both same- and opposite-sex couples.

The second part of the rationale rests on the premise that it is desirable for employers to set policies promoting marriage among their employees. This premise is unsound. In my view, employers should have no role in determining how employees choose to structure their personal lives. The employer's interest is best served by maintaining a productive work force, and this requires providing an attractive benefits package that is responsive to the needs of the employees. If an opposite-sex couple chooses, for whatever reason, not to marry, this does not in any way diminish their need for health insurance. Forcing an employee to marry or forego employment benefits, on the other hand, is likely to have a substantial adverse impact on the employee's morale and productivity.

The third part of the rationale is true, but misses the point. It would be even cheaper to provide coverage only to spouses, and cheaper still to eliminate coverage of all dependents. Employers provide a dependent-benefits package because it helps them to retain a productive work force. The needs of employees in opposite-sex domestic partnerships are no less significant than those of married employees or employees in same-sex domestic partnerships.

There is also a legal reason to offer coverage to opposite-sex as well as same-sex couples. Federal law prohibits employment discrimination based on sex. But if an employer offers coverage to same- but not opposite-sex partners, a female employee with a male partner is denied the coverage that is provided to a male employee with a male partner.[18] Arguably, the female employee is treated less favorably than an identically situated male employee, a violation of federal law. Whether it is legal to offer benefits only to same-sex couples will ultimately be determined by the courts.[19] It seems very likely that a challenge to same-sex-only plans will be brought within a few years.

Notes

1. The phrase "children of the partner" needs some elaboration. A significant number of lesbian couples, and a few gay male couples, have chosen to raise children jointly; the children consider the partners to be coequal parents. In some cases, both partners are able to obtain joint legal recognition as parents through the process of a second-parent adoption. Indeed, in May 1995, an Ontario court ruled that provincial law prohibiting adoption by two parents of the same sex violated the Canadian constitution. In most cases, however, the partner who is not a biological parent is regarded as being legally "unrelated" to the child, and typically does not qualify for health insurance from employers who do not provide domestic partner coverage.
2. Foster Higgins National Survey of Employer Sponsored Health Plans, as reported in "H.M.O.'s on Rise in New York State," *New York Times*, March 25, 1995.
3. Adverse selection does occur in the pool of enrolled spouses when employers require employees to pay a portion of the premium costs for spouses. In this situation, spouses who have adequate health insurance as a consequence of their own employment will not be enrolled; those who are enrolled are disproportionately individuals out of the labor force, and tend to be older and less healthy than the spouses who are not enrolled. From the employer's standpoint, this is a benign form of adverse selection. The cost per spouse enrolled may be fairly high, but the total cost is certainly lower than the cost would be if all the spouses were enrolled.
4. There may be instances in which unmarried heterosexual couples in a committed relationship choose to marry at a time when their insurance needs increase. If one partner became ill, the need for health insurance might override the reasons that had kept the couple from marrying previously. Or, the decision to have a child might increase the desirability of marriage for a variety of legal or social reasons.
5. This is not required of married couples, though it is part of the common understanding of the nature of a marital relationship.
6. This is not required of married couples. It was inserted at the insistence of the insurers, replacing a weaker requirement that partners share a place to live.
7. As noted above, the obligation to provide basic food and shelter are the minimum obligations of spouses that cannot be waived by a prenuptial agreement. The rationale for adding medical care is that health insurance is provided to people signing the affidavit.
8. In California, there is a six-month waiting period before a divorce becomes final, while San Francisco allows the termination of a domestic partnership without a waiting period. Thus, this provision treats previous marriages and previous domestic partnerships equally.
9. This requirement parallels the provisions of California law restricting marriage of close relatives. Note that this restriction plays an important role in controlling adverse selection.

An employee's parents and grandparents are, of course, older than the employee, and therefore likely to have higher health care expenses than the employee's spouse.

10. For example, a survey of San Francisco city employees conducted prior to the establishment of the domestic partner program indicated that 0.9 percent of employees had already enrolled a partner by indicating falsely that the partner was a spouse.

11. This is most true in states, such as California, that do not recognize common-law marriage. California residents become married if, and only if, they validly sign a set of legal documents and file them with their county clerk. They cease to be married if, and only if, one spouse dies or they are granted a divorce by a court. In states that recognize common-law marriage, it is possible (but uncommon) for parties to think they are single when they are legally married, and to think they are married when they are legally single.

12. City and County of San Francisco, Mayor's Task Force on Family Policy, Final Report, June 13, 1990. See also Robert M. Anderson, "Cost Estimates for Health Care Coverage of Domestic Partners of San Francisco City workers," April 2, 1991.

13. Actually, most plans specify the highest average salary over a certain consecutive period of time.

14. The reader may be puzzled to find that allowing the designation of any other person to receive a continuation benefit does not result in adverse selection, while allowing the designation of any other person to receive health benefits does. The situations are not parallel for a number of reasons.

The people who are costly from the point of view of health insurance are those who are currently ill or who, because of age or physical condition, are likely to become ill; these people often know who they are, and would differentially seek to be included in insurance plans. The people who are costly from the point of view of pensions are those who will live longest. For example, a twenty-year-old has a long life expectancy, and so might be thought to be the ideal person to designate to receive a continuation benefit. However, pension plans would impose a large actuarial reduction on an employee who designated a twenty-year-old, thereby compensating for the designee's long life expectancy.

In addition, the designation of the person to receive the continuation benefit is made only once, and is irrevocable; health insurance designations can be changed, usually annually. Thus, while the ability to give health insurance to any one individual at a time would allow someone to cover a number of different individuals with serious diseases over time, the employee cannot keep designating different people to receive the continuation until s/he finds one who outlives her/him.

15. For example, if a married employee of the University of California dies while eligible to retire, the spouse will receive the same benefit as if the employee had retired, elected a 100 percent continuation benefit, and then died. A nonspouse beneficiary receives only the return of the employee's contributions and earnings on those contributions, without receiving any benefit from the employer's contributions.

16. See "A 'Married, With Children' Bias?," *New York Times*, March 12, 1995. Jeffrey Lockman and Rebecca Mark are both professors at Tulane University in New Orleans. Ms. Mark and Mr. Lockman's partner are the biological parents of Benjamin. Tulane normally charges employees for dependent health insurance coverage. However, in the (unusual) case in which two spouses are both Tulane employees, the University provides them with dependent coverage for free. Ms. Mark and Mr. Lockman are seeking the analogous treatment, which would provide Benjamin with dependent coverage for free.

17. Kath Weston, *Families We Choose* (New York: Columbia University Press, 1991), p. 207.

18. Similarly, a male employee with a female partner is denied the coverage that is provided to a female employee with a female partner.

19. The General Counsel of the University of California has concluded that the University cannot legally offer benefits only to same-sex partners. Since his opinion has not been released, it is unclear to what extent this conclusion is based on the university's status as a state institution, and hence to what extent the reasoning would extend to private employers.

19

AIDS and the Moral
Economy of Insurance

Deborah A. Stone

This article, which appeared in *The American Prospect* in 1990, shows how what may seem to be an issue of narrow concern to the gay community alone can turn out to have far larger ramifications. Stone, a political scientist, looks at the controversy over insurance companies' use of the HIV-antibody test to screen applicants. Ultimately, she argues, this particular issue should raise serious questions about the use of predictive tests in general by insurers and even about the fundamental nature of insurance as a system for providing health care and financial security.

When a blood test to detect AIDS antibodies was first announced in 1985, the ensuing controversy over the use of the tests by insurance companies seemed to take a familiar shape. On one side were civil-rights advocates claiming discrimination if the insurers were permitted to use the tests to screen applicants for life and health insurance. On the other side was an industry insisting on its right to be free of government regulation. But despite the seemingly familiar pattern, the conflict over AIDS testing really concerned a novel problem with repercussions for many people who do not see themselves as having any stake in the issue.

The AIDS-antibody test is only one of a growing number of predictive diagnostic tests that can tell whether a person is highly susceptible to a disease or, very rarely, whether someone is certain to get sick. Other predictive tests include the recently identified genes and genetic markers for Alzheimer's disease, manic-depressive disorder, multiple sclerosis, muscular dystrophy, cystic fibrosis, and some forms of cancer, diabetes, and heart disease. Public health research has also identified numerous risk factors for chronic disease—such as high cholesterol, high blood pressure, obesity, and smoking—that are even easier than genetic abnormalities to detect in individuals.

Predictive diagnostic tests have created a new medical limbo between health and illness. Now it is possible to be labeled "at risk" without being ill or ever developing the disease in question. In fact, many predictive tests in clinical medicine are designed to be overinclusive to minimize the number of cases of illness missed by physicians, allowing them to treat or at least detect medical problems as early as possible. But when used by private insurers, predictive tests are turned to a contrary purpose: denying insurance coverage or charging more for it, thereby causing fewer people to receive the health care they need. The aim of preventive medicine is to extend the benefits of modern science, but, ironically, the more predictive tests there are available, and the more broadly risk categories are drawn by cautious clinicians and epidemiologists, the fewer people private insurance will serve.

In the United States, private insurance is the primary means to pay for health care and to provide for needs that are too big to meet through normal work income and savings. It is also the principal vehicle for fulfilling family financial obligations. Through health insurance, life insurance, disability insurance, pensions, and their related dependent benefits, Americans create their own networks of social aid within the larger society of strangers. Social insurance programs, such as Social Security pensions, disability insurance, and Medicaid, are designed only to be safety nets, not primary sources of support.

The private insurance industry, operating under rules set by law and public policy, controls access to the vital first line of defense against financial catastrophe. By determining who gets privately insured, for what misfortunes, and at what price, the insurance industry also affects the balance of responsibility—and costs—between the private sector and government. The more the industry uses predictive testing to limit access to private insurance, the more people and troubles fall to public programs. Furthermore, just as insurers want to limit their payouts, so employers want to limit their insurance premiums, and thus are increasingly likely to adopt predictive tests to screen job applicants.

The use of predictive testing thus raises major questions about the future of access to good jobs, health care, and financial security in America. The Unites States already has a patchwork system of health insurance that omits coverage of nearly one of every six citizens. If used to their full potential, predictive tests may relegate even more Americans to the ranks of the excluded. But the current framework of insurance, which concentrates costs on people with high health risks, is not the only possible design. We do have alternatives for creating a system that protects those at high risk— and all of us—from financial devastation and exclusion from health care.

Why Insurers Want to Test

The battle over AIDS testing initially seemed to go in favor of those opposed to it. Within a month of when scientists announced the test, gay advocates in California had obtained state legislation to prevent insurance companies from using it; in the next two years Wisconsin, New York, Florida, Massachusetts, and the District of Columbia adopted similar restrictions. The commercial insurance industry, however, mounted an all-out effort to repeal the regulations, and by the end of 1989 only California's ban on testing health insurance applicants remained in place.

The money at stake for insurers because of AIDS was not their chief concern. Insurance companies mobilized their political influence because they feared losing their overall ability to screen applicants and set rates according to the health risks that the applicants appeared to represent. The companies consider control of those decisions crucial to their competitive strategies, even their financial survival.

In the jargon of the insurance business, the process of selecting risks is called "underwriting." Underwriting involves determining whether any particular applicant's likely loss experience (accident, illness, fire, etc.) is similar to that assumed by an insurance company in setting its standard rates. If the applicant represents a greater risk, the company may offer a "substandard" (that is, higher) rate or deny coverage altogether. By accurately predicting losses and setting premiums accordingly, insurers seek to maintain their solvency and profitability. They also use underwriting to design policies with specialized features for carefully selected groups of people. Indeed, life insurers compete not so much on price or service as by marketing special policies to target groups.

In health, disability, and life insurance, insurers use medical information and other factors such as age, gender, and occupation to determine coverage and rates. Besides asking applicants (and sometimes their physicians) to fill out questionnaires about their health, they may also require a physical exam, including laboratory and clinical tests, such as urinalyses or electrocardiograms. Tests are used in part to find out whether applicants are concealing important facts. For example, insurers sometimes screen blood for prescription drugs to determine whether applicants are being treated for a disease they did not disclose.

This information is not kept privately by the individual insurance firm checking out an applicant. The industry maintains a central laboratory, the Home Office Reference Laboratory (HORL), to perform most medical tests. The HORL shares its results with a central data bank, the Medical Information Bureau, which is a membership organization of about 700 companies. An applicant for health, life, or disability insurance to any of these companies must sign a consent form allowing the company to report its findings to the bureau. Once an applicant has filled out a questionnaire, had medical records sent to the company, or had blood sent to the HORL, the results are available to other insurers. So despite the appearance of a highly competitive industry, the prospective purchaser of an individual policy effectively faces only one supplier.

Before the advent of the AIDS-antibody test, insurers were already using supposed indicators of homosexuality as underwriting criteria. Single men between the ages of twenty-five and forty-five, particularly if employed in occupations deemed stereotypically gay, were being denied individual policies for life and health insurance. So, in one sense, the development of the blood test was a blessing to both insurers and gay men. It enabled insurers to rely on objective medical evidence and took the focus off sexual orientation. But gay men still perceived a threat, because the blood test was likely to be imposed selectively on the basis of presumed sexual orientation. Moreover, those who tested positive were still discriminated against, since the test does not disclose who actually has the disease, only the presence of antibodies in the blood to the human immunodeficiency virus (HIV) which causes AIDS. Development of the disease can take a decade or longer, and we cannot predict how soon the disease will develop in any HIV-positive individual.

Once gay activists defined the issue as discrimination, the industry's strategy was clear. This was not the first time that insurers had to defend their use of classifications that public sensitivities no longer readily accepted. In the late-nineteenth century, several states banned the use of race in setting insurance rates. More recently, the use of gender in pension, disability, and automobile insurance has faced attack. The industry's case for AIDS testing reflected its arguments over the last century in defense of its underwriting practices.

HIV testing, the industry maintains, has nothing to do with attitudes toward homosexuals. For insurers, discrimination is the essence of the business, not a dirty word. It means differentiating among policy holders according to their risk of incurring the loss for which the policy will pay out. HIV tests are just one more means of determining risk status, and they are no more discriminatory than blood pressure readings. According to the industry, it would be unfair *not* to use the HIV tests.

Insurers distinguish between "fair" and "unfair" discrimination. As Spencer Kimball, a leading professor of insurance law, puts it, fair discrimination means measuring as accurately as possible "the burden shifted to the insurance fund by the policy holder and charging exactly for it." Fairness, in this view, means ideally that no one pays for anyone else. That, however, is not the only definition of equity.

By its very nature, insurance is redistributive. We could theoretically squirrel away our individual savings to provide financial security for any of the contingencies we commonly insure against. Through insurance, however, we join with others to "pool" our risks and our savings. Only some people in the pool will experience the insured harm (say, fire, theft, or illness). Since only those who experience the harm will receive a payout, the others necessarily pay to help them.

Some advocates for the industry call the redistribution that is built into insurance a "cross-subsidy" and deem it anathema to fairness when it can be foreseen. In a 1987 *Harvard Law Review* article, Karen Clifford and Russell Iuculano, who at the time worked for the American Council of Life Insurers, argued that insurers have a legal duty to separate policy holders with serious, identifiable health risks from those without such risks. "Failure to do so represents a forced subsidy from the healthy to the less healthy."

The argument makes sense only if we understand the purpose of insurance as allocating costs to the people who generate them, rather than spreading the costs of misfortune and thereby making them more manageable. All insurance entails cross-subsidy; that is what makes it insurance instead of personal savings. Insurers typically put the adjective "forced" in front of "subsidy" when defending an underwriting criterion against regulatory challenge, but there is no reason why any *particular* cross-subsidy is more coercive than all the other cross-subsidies that insurance entails.

The debate about HIV testing in insurance, then, comes down to a fundamental disagreement about the purpose of insurance, regardless of whether an insurance fund is operated as a commercial enterprise, a social program, or some hybrid. Ultimately, the disagreement concerns whether to distribute the benefits of insurance according to prior contributions or according to need. Medical testing of any kind is valid only to the degree that we want our insurance system to minimize redistribution from the healthy to the (potentially) sick. With enough predictive tests of sufficient accuracy, insurers could virtually eliminate risk-sharing and redistribution. We would each pay strictly for our-selves. The industry argument about fair discrimination assumes a vision of insurance as a personal savings plan operated by insurance companies instead of banks.

Fairness in Insurance

What kinds of differentiation are fair? The industry answer is not helpful: Fair dis-crimination is what each state's Unfair Trade Practices Act allows, and unfair dis-crimination is what it forbids. The state laws were all adopted at the behest of the industry between 1947 and 1960. They typically define unfair practices as "making unfair discrimination between individuals of the same class," "discrimination between similarly situated individuals," or—one of my personal favorites for its tautological brilliance—"discrimination between insureds having like insuring characteristics."

How does one know whether people belong to the same class, are similarly situated, or have like insuring characteristics? *Sesame Street*, that universal mentor of the preschool set, has something to say on the matter. In one segment, the kids are shown three cardboard stars of different sizes and colors and a cardboard moon and asked, "Which of these things is different?" The lesson is not that the moon is different, but that several equally valid answers depend on which criterion a person uses to differenti-ate—say, color, shape, or size. The moon is different only if the children select by shape.

In health and life insurance, many different factors could be used to answer the question, "Which people are most likely to get sick?" The industry most commonly uses age, gender, medical history, and occupation, but it could avail itself of other cri-teria. Why not use race? Blacks have higher rates of heart disease and kidney disease and lower life expectancy than do whites. Insurers could also use residence. Cancer rates vary by state, and people living near major medical centers are at greater risk of expensive surgery than others living farther away. The industry could use veteran sta-tus: Vietnam veterans have higher rates of accidents and premature death than do nonveterans. The industry could use marital status: illness is much greater among the widowed and divorced than among the married or single. On what basis, then, do we say that an insurer's classifications are fair?

There are many predictive criteria insurers could use to predict disease and estab-lish costs—race, occupation, medical history, veteran status, residence, age, and who-knows-what-else. Their choice among criteria is not dictated by the predictive validity of the criteria so much as by political constraints. The industry cannot use race be-cause it is legally forbidden to do so as a result of a political choice made outside the industry. It does not use veteran status because it does not dare to penalize political heroes. Medical criteria, by comparison, have been less controversial.

Insurers have decided that certain diseases render people ineligible for life insur-ance. These generally include diabetes, leukemia, schizophrenia, emphysema, coro-nary artery disease, and now AIDS. People with these diseases are deemed "medically uninsurable." Risk factors, such as uncontrolled high blood pressure, are also a basis for exclusion. The rationale is that people with these diseases and risk factors have a very high probability of early death. If they die prematurely, they will not pay enough money in premiums to cover the losses that they will generate unless the insurer charges them such high rates as to make the insurance unaffordable.

According to the industry view, admitting people at high risk to a general insurance pool would be unfair to the other, lower-risk policy holders, whose premiums would go up. Industry representatives portray any effort to ban the use of HIV tests by insurance companies as granting "favored status" to carriers of one disease. Since the industry already screens applicants for heart disease, cancer, stroke, and other diseases, why should AIDS be privileged?

One can see how policy holders would not want to be burdened with the costs of people likely to be very sick or to die prematurely. Indeed, the industry tries to foster this lifeboat mentality by running advertisements explaining why we should not want to pay for people who run high risks. "If you don't take risks, why should you pay for someone else's?" asks one such advertisement, showing a man high up on a steel scaffolding. Never mind that the man is building an office tower that presumably contributes to our economy. (He's wearing a hard hat and a tool belt, so he's probably not climbing for the thrill of it.) In the insurance industry's view, fairness means concentrating the costs of accidents and illnesses on the individuals who bear the risks.

What if we step outside the privileged circle of people protected by private insurance policies? From that vantage point, equity might seem to require that those who are ill or at risk for illness and injury ought to have greater access to insurance, not less. If they face high medical expenses, they need health insurance coverage all the more. If they have dependents, they need life insurance all the more to protect their family's well-being. From a societal perspective, the people who require protecting the most are precisely those whom commercial insurance companies find it economically necessary and "fair" to exclude.

Outside the privileged circle, people with diabetes or high blood pressure might feel that they have been singled out only because they have a condition that scientists and insurers now recognize as leading to early death or disease. But in reality, each of us is a living bundle of risk factors. We all have a multitude of characteristics—socioeconomic status, heredity, race, gender, education, residence, family status, occupation, degree of happiness, eating habits, driving habits, work habits, and who knows what else—that are or could be associated with illness and premature death. Scientists have investigated only some of these factors, and insurers have chosen to use only a few in setting rates. Therefore, people with recognized medical risk factors are disadvantaged by our scientific knowledge. Given medical progress in identifying the precursors of disease, the number of people facing these new penalties of predictive knowledge can only grow. Groups of policy holders and the companies that insure them have every incentive to determine who is likely to be sick, disabled, and prematurely dead, and to exclude these people from their risk-sharing plans or to set higher insurance prices for them.

Many would argue that insurance companies are justified in charging more to high-risk people to encourage them to lead safe and healthy lives. When a person can reasonably be expected to understand the dangers of an action and refrain from it—say, speeding, hang gliding, or smoking—then using that behavior as a basis for setting insurance premiums might serve the goals of education and prevention.

While creating incentives for healthy behavior is sometimes a reasonable consideration in designing insurance classifications, we ought to be wary of using incentive effects to set health insurance prices. Few health risks are truly voluntary. Even smoking, the favorite candidate, is doubtful. Nicotine is addictive, and the decision to start smoking, usually made when people are quite young, is heavily influenced by societal pressures, such as commercial advertising. Most known risk factors, including smoking, are heavily concentrated among the poor and less well educated. Many reasons for this disparity have their origins outside the sphere of individual choice: for example, alternative sources of satisfaction and stress reduction are less available to the poor, and the poor tend to have more dangerous jobs. Even though we don't understand all the causal mechanisms, virtually every risk factor for disease has a high correlation with poverty. To increase health insurance prices for people already disadvantaged by poverty and poor health is to penalize them triply.

There is nothing wrong with creating incentives for healthy behavior, but health insurance is simply the wrong place for society to conduct its education of good habits. Health insurance should guarantee access to health care. Health is essential to life, happiness, and productivity. No matter whether people may have inflicted illness or injury upon themselves, we ought not to withhold compassion or medical care once they are sick. And denying health insurance on the basis of disease risk factors—even the most controllable actions—effectively denies care to the sick.

Here another tension of insurance becomes evident. Insurance is about sharing risks within a community. Underwriting is about exclusion. The industry term "uninsurable," applied to people deemed to be at very high risk, suggests that insurability is a quality of individuals. In fact, insurability is the set of criteria and internal policy decisions made by insurers about whom to include and exclude from its redistributive system. It is not a trait, but a concept of *membership*. Treated as a scientific fact about individuals, the notion of insurability disguises fundamentally political decisions about membership in a community of mutual responsibility.

A system of competitive insurers based on medical underwriting guarantees that, as insurers scramble for customers and seek to control their risks, society will be divided into more homogeneous risk classes, and more people will be left out of insurance pools altogether. From a commercial insurer's perspective, that may be good business practice. But from a social perspective, the splitting up of insurance pools means the erosion of mutual aid.

How Predictive Testing May Affect Health Insurance

The insurance industry's use of HIV tests and other new predictive tests will significantly affect access to health care. In the United States, eligibility for health coverage depends on work, age, or disability. Employee group plans, the most common form of protection, cover approximately 60 percent of the population. Through Medicare, Medicaid, the Veterans Administration, the Indian Health Service, and various other federal and state programs, government provides coverage for an additional 20 percent. Of the remaining population, some 5 percent obtain individual insurance policies, and 15 percent have no coverage at all.

Many of those lacking insurance either have no way to obtain it or face much higher insurance premiums than do the typical members of large employee groups. About two-thirds of the uninsured are employees or their dependents, but the smaller firms where they tend to work can purchase group insurance only at high rates. Individual policies are often prohibitively expensive. Moreover, of applicants for individual health insurance, around 8 percent are rejected outright as medically uninsurable. Commercial insurers designate another 9 percent as substandard risks and charge them even higher premiums than are normal in the individual market; Blue Cross–Blue Shield plans rate about 20 percent of applicants as substandard. Of course, anticipating rejection or higher rates, many of the uninsured who are sick or disabled do not bother to apply for individual policies.

Until recently, only applicants for individual policies and groups of fewer than twenty-five or so employees were subject to medical underwriting. But a survey by the Office of Technology Assessment recently found that more health insurers are beginning to screen *group* applicants for high-risk status. Three of every four commercial and Blue Cross companies were either screening or planning to screen for high-risk applicants in small group plans. For large groups, 58 percent of commercial insurers and 7 percent of Blue Cross–Blue Shield plans were using or moving toward screening. Medical underwriting in the group market will raise greater obstacles to employers who wish to provide all their employees with health insurance.

As a result, employers themselves may increasingly take health risks into account when deciding whether to hire a prospective employee. In recent years firms of all sizes have faced staggering increases in health insurance costs; one way to keep those costs down is to avoid employing people with high risks of illness. In countries with national health insurance, employers have less incentive to exclude the potentially sick from jobs, but employers in the United States pay directly for the health costs generated by their own workers. The group plans sold by insurance companies are typically "experience" rated; that is, the premiums charged by the insurer are based on each employee group's profile. Moreover, a growing number of employers operate their own health insurance plans, chiefly to take advantage of a provision in the 1974 Employee Retirement Income Security Act (ERISA). Under that law, if a firm "self-insures," its health plan is exempt from state insurance regulations as well as state taxes on insurance premiums. Today more than half of all workers are covered by employer self-insurance arrangements. As a result, employers today *are* insurers, and all the difficulties surrounding the use of testing by insurers come up with employers, too, without the minimal protections provided by state insurance regulations.

Rising costs and self-insurance give employers strong incentives to use predictive testing to screen out high-risk applicants for jobs. State and federal handicap discrimination laws have begun to protect employees from being fired simply because they have some potentially costly health risk that does not affect their current job performance. But these laws do not necessarily bar employers from refusing to hire an applicant who appears to be a health risk according to one of the new tests. Thus people deemed "uninsurable" may also become "unemployable," at least at firms with good jobs that carry health insurance as a fringe benefit.

As screening and underwriting exclude more people from private health insurance, the costs of their care fall primarily to Medicaid and public hospitals. Recent studies have estimated that of all people with AIDS, Medicaid covers 40 to 50 percent nationwide, while private insurance pays for only about 17 percent (and that share is probably declining). Taking all sources into account, hospitals are being paid only around 80 percent of their costs for AIDS cases in the Northeast, Midwest, and West, and a mere 45 percent in the South. Public hospitals face the greatest burden. In cities hard hit by AIDS, such as New York, San Francisco, Newark, and Miami, municipal hospitals are having to shift resources from other services to AIDS care—a pattern symptomatic of the wider problem. As private employers and insurers avoid the sick and high-risk individuals among us, they displace the costs onto the public sector, which simply lacks the resources to meet those demands on top of the others it already faces.

One possible response, advocated by many people in the insurance industry, is to create state high-risk pools to cover people whom insurance companies turn down. Such pools already exist in some fifteen states. Since people relegated to the pools are by definition (or at least assumption) at high risk for disease, they pay up to twice the usual rate for health insurance and face very high deductibles. These costs put high-risk pools out of the financial reach of most people. Even so, the pools run at a loss. Insurance companies are then assessed to subsidize the pools, based usually on their *pro rata* share of business in the state. Some states also subsidize the pools out of state revenues.

High-risk pools permit insurance companies to continue skimming off the people who are least likely to become expensively sick and to shunt the others into public programs. Those people lucky enough to gain regular insurance protection pay cheaper premiums because they share their expense with others who also are unlikely to get sick or die early. True, they may face higher taxes to help pay for those who depend on public programs and public hospitals. But precisely because they enjoy the privilege of cheaper and better private insurance, they are not likely to be strong advocates for improved public services. The political effects of segmented insurance pools thus reinforce the economic forces at work when insurers are able to take the best risks and exclude the bad ones.

Life Insurance and the Bottom Line

Most medical testing by insurance companies occurs in the sale of life insurance, where the monetary stakes are much greater for the insurance industry. Insurers are particularly worried about people buying insurance policies when they know themselves to be at high risk for early death, while the insurer does not. (This is known as "moral hazard" in insurance jargon.) Such purchases produce the phenomenon that insurers dread more than any other: adverse selection, that is, a skewing of policy holders toward those with heavier-than-expected losses. Insurers raise the specter of legions of people exposed to HIV taking out large life insurance policies. Without HIV testing, these policies would be priced at standard rates, but the policy holders would likely die in a few years after having paid only a fraction of the premiums on which the companies were counting. Thus, without testing, the companies say their solvency is in jeopardy.

The little information currently available about life insurance payouts to AIDS victims suggests that the industry has not yet suffered major losses. The most likely reason is that few people at high risk of AIDS have had life insurance policies in the first place. Historically, life insurance has been sold primarily to married people with children, and then only to those with enough regular disposable income to make monthly payments. That set of people does not include large numbers of gay men and needle-sharing drug users—the two largest risk groups for AIDS. Nonetheless, insurers worry that if they were now to be denied the ability to require tests, carriers of the AIDS virus—and other people identified as high-risk by predictive testing—would sign up for policies and produce big losses.

The adverse selection argument serves an important rhetorical function in the debate. It casts moral doubt on people with high risk for AIDS or any other life-threatening disease. The unspoken message is that people who buy insurance knowing they are high risk are social parasites. Adverse selection, Clifford and Iuculano say, "unfairly burdens other policy holders who must support the increased claims through higher premiums." Thus the insurers' representatives subtly turn sick people into moral outcasts to justify excluding them from risk-sharing arrangements.

However, many healthy people simply have no opportunity to contribute to an affordable health insurance plan. When and if the uninsured later face extraordinary medical expenses, the only way they might be able to repay their friends and families is to make them beneficiaries of life insurance policies. Of course, some people who discover they have a fatal disease might try to buy as much life insurance as they could afford, not only as a hedge against their own catastrophic expenses but also to enrich their family or partner, or even to borrow against the policy and enhance their own current consumption. Insurance companies and other policy holders should be protected from such knowing exploitation of the risk-pooling mechanism. But predictive medical testing by insurers has so many bad consequences that we ought to find other ways to prevent life insurance abuses.

Other mechanisms besides medical testing could ameliorate the problem. Insurance regulators could redesign "incontestability clauses" in life insurance policies. In most states, these clauses allow an insurer to refuse to pay if the policy holder dies within two years of the policy's issue and has misrepresented information on the application. After two years, the insurer may no longer contest the validity of the policy. Since the latency period for AIDS is considerably longer, we could extend these clauses for AIDS to some reasonable length, perhaps five years.

If we remember that life insurance is primarily a mechanism to strengthen family income security, we could first ensure that basic levels of insurance are available to everyone. In addition to providing a guarantee of basic health insurance, we might expand the survivorship component of Social Security (broadening the concept of survivors to allow benefits to be paid to people regardless of marriage, blood ties, or sexual orientation). With universal health insurance in place, the need to take out life insurance at the onset of illness would diminish, thereby lessening concern about insurers' access to predictive medical information. With such strengthened arrangements for financial security, we could then permit private life insurers to test applicants for policies with large face values.

Some Political Lessons

If ever there were an issue that ought to have propelled us to national health insurance, the AIDS epidemic should have been it. No recent experience so graphically demonstrates the limitations of private health insurance as a method of paying for sickness.

The insurance industry has made clear its concern to escape as much of the cost as possible. Nonetheless, efforts to stop insurers from testing for AIDS and excluding the victims have failed. What can we learn for the next round?

Perhaps the biggest mistake in the HIV-testing controversy was the failure to grasp the full import of medical underwriting and predictive testing. Representatives of public hospitals, Medicaid agencies, and state health and welfare departments were nowhere to be seen in the legislative and regulatory hearing rooms as HIV testing was debated. Nor did any of the disease-based groups, such as the American Heart Association and American Cancer Society, see their stake in the testing issue. Gay rights and AIDS advocacy organizations were left to do battle alone.

As a result, HIV testing was treated solely as an issue of discrimination and privacy, not as the profound structural issue it also is. Because gay men and lesbians do face substantial discrimination, and because prejudice against people who test positive was running rampant, the advocacy groups focused their arguments on the injustice of burdening a minority, the insurers' use of crude stereotypes, and the lack of counseling and confidentiality for people tested by insurance companies.

The charge of discrimination is often a powerful political resource in American politics, but it backfired here. Insurers were able to trump the charge with their own wild card: they threatened not to write business in states that restricted testing. Moreover, because opponents of testing framed the issue as discrimination against gay people, they lost the opportunity for alliances with other groups whose members stand to lose from increased medical underwriting but who do not see themselves as victims of discrimination.

The underwriting issue is bound to come up again, given the rapid pace of discovery of genetic markers for disease and the near-weekly announcements of environmental, dietary, and behavioral hazards to health. If we understand the broad values at stake, we should be better prepared to frame these emerging issues and mobilize alliances to defend a wider vision of social protection.

In the struggle over AIDS testing, the insurance industry adopted the argument used by all industries seeking to resist public regulation: we cannot operate efficiently, perhaps not even at all, if we are burdened with social objectives. This argument might be persuasive if there were a wall between the public and private sectors. But that is not our world. Private and public forms of social aid are intimately entwined, since the people and troubles that commercial policies do not cover get pushed into the public sector. Either public insurance programs fill the gaps in private insurance, or the victims wind up on the streets, the welfare rolls, the doorsteps of voluntary agencies, and in the beds of public hospitals.

Private insurance companies might point out that their policy holders still pay taxes to care for the "uninsurables," but that argument misses an important point. Why should medical underwriting be used at all for health insurance? Why should certain diseases, such as AIDS, be socially financed, while others are privately financed? And why should insurers be the ones to decide, through their underwriting policies, which diseases taxpayers will have to finance and which ones private insurers will cover?

The political debate is likely to focus on which risk factors and tests insurers ought to be permitted to use in selecting applicants. The choice of permissible underwriting factors is not neutral, for it defines a set of people likely to be excluded from the better coverage of most private programs. In addition, medical underwriting on the basis of diagnoses has a particularly cruel and perverse result. After determining that a person is sick or at high risk, insurers turn around and deny aid for exactly that need. True, if insurers were to accept an applicant knowing he or she was already sick, they would no longer be insuring but simply providing a payment mechanism. But that point merely illustrates the limits of private insurance as a method for financing care of the sick. Private insurers do not hide their interest in denying coverage to the high risk; they insist it is their obligation to their low-risk clients to turn their backs on people once it is clear that they are or will become expensively sick.

The problems in health insurance are so severe that many major insurance companies are beginning to realize they must reform their practices or have their business either taken over or regulated by government. Small business associations and even some insurance trade associations are actively pressing for state and federal laws that would stop some of the cream-skimming. As Robert Laszewski, executive vice president of Liberty Mutual, recently told the *New York Times,* "The notion that an insurance company should be making a profit by figuring out which Americans not to cover is no longer viable."

When used to exclude people from such basic services as health insurance, predictive testing divides our society in dangerous and undesirable ways. The debate should focus not on which tests insurers use but on how medical testing undermines our institutions of social protection.

To tackle the insurance conundrum, we need to take community as our starting point. From there, it is clear that the purpose of health, disability, and life insurance, at least at levels providing security against devastating losses, is precisely to distribute according to need. An effective campaign for broader risk sharing has to demonstrate that insurance practices are issues of membership, and that the predictable result of medical underwriting is to exclude those people who need help the most. Such a perspective should help build coalitions among all the disease and disability groups who are similarly affected by insurance underwriting. Finally, we must reveal the distinctions between private and public social-aid systems as being wholly artifice. The selection of people and troubles to be covered by each sector ought to be a matter of conscious public policy, not the result of efforts by the insurance industry to skim off the good risks. That process inevitably puts the high risk and the poor into a public sector, where they lack both adequate resources and majority political support.

Note

This article originally appeared in *The American Prospect*, Fall 1990. For a related article with references, see Deborah Stone, "The Rhetoric of Insurance Law: The Debate Over AIDS Testing," *Law and Social Inquiry*, 15:2 (Spring 1990), pp. 385–407.

Contributors

Robert M. Anderson is Professor of Economics and Mathematics at the University of California, Berkeley, where he has taught since 1983; he chaired the Department of Economics from 1989 to 1992. He served on the San Francisco Mayor's Task Force on Family Policy, which recommended the city's domestic partner benefits policy, in 1989–90, and on the Academic Senate committee which recommended that the University of California provide domestic partner benefits in 1992–93. He currently chairs the Berkeley Academic Senate Committee on University Welfare.

M. V. Lee Badgett is a labor economist and Assistant Professor of Public Affairs at the University of Maryland, College Park. She is the Executive Director of the Institute for Gay and Lesbian Strategic Studies. Her ongoing research topics consider the labor market effects of race, gender, and sexual orientation. Her work on workplace discrimination against lesbians and gay men and on the economics of coming out appear in academic journals, book chapters, and magazine articles. More recently, she has been studying domestic partner policies and other economic issues related to lesbian and gay families.

Dan Baker is the coauthor (along with Sean Strub and Bill Henning) of *Cracking the Corporate Closet* (Harper Collins, 1995), which surveys America's largest corporations on workplace issues affecting gay men and lesbians. He is president of Quotient Research, Inc., which publishes *Quotient: The Newsletter of Marketing to Gay Men and Lesbians*. He has been involved in gay and AIDS activist organizations since 1972 and helped organize the first Gay Pride Parade in Honolulu when he was a graduate student at the University of Hawaii. He has served as treasurer of ACT UP/New York and was Deputy Executive Director of Gay Games IV, held in New York in June 1994.

Richard Cornwall, born on the western coast of puritanical America (Middlebury, Vermont, 1940) and educated in bourgeois respectability, as well as economics and mathematics, at Princeton University (A.B. 1962), Oxford University and the University of California at Berkeley (Ph.D. 1968), studies the use of economic theory to understand human interaction. Starting with publications in mathematical economics (e.g., *Introduction to the Use of General Equilibrium Theory*), he has modeled "transactions" among humans that promote or diminish socioeconomic inequality. He has taught courses on queer studies and socioeconomic inequality for the last five years at Middlebury.

Jeffrey Escoffier is an editor and writer living in New York City. He is the author of *John Maynard Keynes,* a biography in the series of lives of notable lesbians and gay men published by Chelsea House. Escoffier taught economics at Rutgers University, the University of San Francisco, and San Francisco State University, and lesbian and gay studies at the University of California at Berkeley and Davis. From 1980 to 1987, he was the executive editor of *Socialist Review.* In the late 1980s, he became one of the founders and the publisher of *OUT/LOOK: National Lesbian and Gay Quarterly,* an award-winning magazine of culture and opinion. His writing has appeared in *The Nation,* the *New York Times Book Review, OUT/LOOK, Utne Reader,* the *San Francisco Chronicle Book Review,* and *Socialist Review.* He is currently on the editorial collective of *Radical History Review* and the board of the Center for Lesbian and Gay Studies of the City University of New York.

Amy Gluckman teaches social studies and mathematics in an alternative high school in Lowell, Massachusetts. She is a member of the editorial collective that produces the progressive economics magazine *Dollars and Sense.* She lives in Salem, Massachusetts.

Jean Hardisty is a political scientist with a Ph.D. from Northwestern University. After eight years' experience teaching and researching conservative political thought, she left academia and opened Political Research Associates, a Cambridge, Massachusetts-based research center that analyzes right-wing authoritarian and antidemocratic trends and publishes public education material on the Right. She has been the executive director there for fourteen years.

Pat Hussain, a native Atlantan, is codirector of SONG, Southerners On New Ground, an alliance-building project working to help shift translesbigay equality organizing into an antiracist justice-seeking context and to integrate work against homophobia into freedom struggles in the South. She is a founding trustee of the Atlanta Lambda Center, a board officer of the National Gay and Lesbian Task Force, cochair of Olympics Out of Cobb Coalition, member of the Black Gay and Lesbian Leadership Forum, and former board member of First Metropolitan Community Church. She cofounded GLAAD/Atlanta. Pat was a member of the 1993 March on Washington Executive Committee, serving as Director of Outreach. She has also worked in community television, producing *In God's Image* and *Cracker*

Barrel: Menu of Shame. She lives with Cherry, her partner of eight years, and Spencer, their son.

Michael P. Jacobs is a financial and economic analyst for the City Council of New York, Finance Division. He is the coauthor of *Financial Services, Financial Centers* (Westview Press, 1990) and currently serves on the editorial board of the *Review of Radical Political Economics*. He has taught at a number of New York–area colleges, including the New School for Social Research, where he received a Ph.D. in economics.

Mary C. King is Assistant Professor in the Economics Department at Portland State University.

Lawrence Knopp is Associate Professor of Geography and Director of the Center for Community and Regional Research at the University of Minnesota, Duluth; and Adjunct Associate Professor of Geography at the University of Minnesota, Twin Cities. He has written articles on social movements, urbanization, gentrification, and sexuality, and is currently working on a book-length manuscript concerning geography and gay male cultural identities, communities, and politics in the United States, United Kingdom, and Australia.

Tony Kushner, author of *Angels in America*, is a playwright.

Julie Matthaei is Professor of Economics at Wellesley College. She is the author of two books, *An Economic History of Women in America: Women's Work, the Sexual Division of Labor, and the Development of Capitalism* (Schocken, 1982), and, with Teresa Amott, *Race, Gender and Work: A Multicultural Economic History of Women in the United States* (South End, 1991).

Donna Minkowitz, a former writer for the *Village Voice*, is working on a book about the religious right and the gay movement.

Duncan T. Osborne is a contributor at the *Advocate*, a national gay and lesbian biweekly news magazine, *Plan Sponsor*, a monthly magazine for pension fund managers and pension plan sponsors and participants in the United States and Canada; and *LGNY*, a biweekly newspaper serving New York City's lesbian and gay community. He has also published in the *Village Voice*, the *Daily News*, and *New York Newsday*. He lives in Brooklyn, New York.

Betsy Reed, formerly an editor at *Dollars and Sense* and *Boston Review*, is managing editor of *The American Benefactor*, a magazine about philanthropy. She lives in Brooklyn, New York.

Lisa Rofel is Assistant Professor of Anthropology at the University of California–Santa Cruz. She is finishing a book on modernity in post-Mao China, and is working on a project on gender, sexuality, and public culture in China.

Deborah Stone is a professor of political science at the Heller Graduate School, Brandeis University.

Before **Kath Weston** became a member of the National Writers Union and Associate Professor of Anthropology at Arizona State University West in Phoenix, she flirted with the prospect of becoming a mechanic. With the money from a day job (mechanics) or a night-and-day job (academics), she wanted to write about the ways that sexuality is intertwined with race and class. She is the author of *Families We Choose: Lesbians, Gays, Kinship*; and a coeditor of *The Lesbian Issue: Essays from SIGNS*. Her recent essays include "Requiem for a Street Fighter," "The Virtual Anthropologist," "Do Clothes Make the Woman?" and "Lesbian/Gay Studies in the House of Anthropology." Her latest book is titled, *Render Me, Gender Me: Lesbians Talk Sex, Class, Color, Nation, Studmuffins and Such* (forthcoming from Columbia University Press).

Index